# THE PRICE OF HEALTH

# Studies in Australian History

Series editors: Alan Gilbert and Peter Spearritt

# THE PRICE OF HEALTH

## Australian Governments and Medical Politics 1910-1960

### JAMES A. GILLESPIE

School of History, Philosophy and Politics
Macquarie University

The right of the
University of Cambridge
to print and sell
all manner of books
was granted by
Henry VIII in 1534.
The University has printed
and published continuously
since 1584.

CAMBRIDGE UNIVERSITY PRESS

Cambridge
New York  Port Chester  Melbourne  Sydney

Published by the Press Syndicate of the University of Cambridge

The Pitt Building, Trumpington Street, Cambridge CB2 1RP, UK
40 West 20th Street, New York, NY 10011, USA
10 Stamford Road, Oakleigh, Melbourne 3166, Australia

Printed in Hong Kong by Colorcraft

*National Library of Australia cataloguing-in-publication data*

Gillespie, J.A. (James Andrew).
   The Price of Health : Australian Governments and Medical Politics.

   Bibliography.
   Includes index.
   ISBN 0 521 38183 5.

   1. Medical policy – Australia – History. 2. Insurance, Health – Australia – History.
   (Series : Studies in Australian History (Cambridge, England)).

362.10994

*British Library cataloguing-in-publication data*

Gillespie, J.A. (James Andrew).
   The Price of Health : Australian Governments and Medical Politics.

   Bibliography.
   Includes index.
   ISBN 0 521 38183 5.

   1. Medical policy — Australia — History. 2. Insurance, Health — Australia —
   History. (Series : Studies in Australian History (Cambridge, England)).

362.10994

*Library of Congress cataloguing-in-publication data*
Gillespie, James A.
   The Price of Health : Australian Governments and Medical Politics.
   James A. Gillespie.

   p. cm. — (Studies in Australian history)

   Includes bibliographical references.
   Includes index.
   ISBN 0–521–38183–5.

   1. Medical policy — Australia — History — 20th century. 2. Social medicine —
   Australia — History — 20th century. I. Title. II. Series. (DNLM: 1. Health Policy
   — history — Australia. 2. Politics — Australia. 3. State Medicine — history —
   Australia. WA 11 KA8 G47p)

RA395.A8G55 1990
362.1'0994—dc20

# Contents

# Tables

# Preface

Of all the areas of public policy commonly lumped under the rubric of 'the welfare state' none has been as hotly contested as health policy. The extent, and very legitimacy, of state intervention in the provision and subsidization of medical and other health services has fuelled clashes involving most of the major interest groups and political parties, and the institutions of the state themselves, as each level of government has vied for control of the direction of the system. Along the way, Australia has been the only liberal democracy to legislate to establish a popular national health insurance system, only to see it promptly dismantled.

The bitterness of this political history calls for some perspective to be placed upon contemporary events. In tracing the course of these battles my aim has been to explain some of the structural causes which have made a lasting settlement so intractable. This understanding can only be achieved by moving away from a view of conflict as a simple clash between medical professional independence on one side and state intervention on the other. The hostility of organized medicine towards state intervention was neither automatic nor consistent. Similarly, this history was by no means unique to Australia. Some of the ingredients of Australian medical politics have been common to the medical profession – or to the sociology of the professions – in general. In carving out and defending a privileged labour market the Australian medical profession was acting much as their colleagues elsewhere in the world. Similarly, government intervention, to affect both the pattern of services and access to medical care and its cost, has hardly been unique to Australia. What does demand exploration is the specific direction events took in this country. The forms taken by government policy and the interests and political coalitions which determined their outcome cannot be reduced to mere local variations of a standard international pattern.

This account stresses the importance of politics in forming our present health system. It identifies the structural interests at play. As advocates of the free market have long lamented, the market for medical care has ever been one of the most restricted and regulated areas of the economy. Whatever defences may be made for restrictive practices, it remains that the balance of strength between doctors, patients and the state has been set by these restrictive market conditions.[1]

Most accounts of the rise of the organized medical profession attribute its strength, 'the most powerful trade union in the British Empire', to this market position. Controlling the major institutions as well as access to the health system, able to use professional licensure and a privileged relationship with the state to regulate or exclude competitors, the medical profession in most industrialized capitalist societies has provided the model of professional autonomy. The political and social power of the medical profession has been seen as a function of independence from lay control and especially from state regulation of the relationships, both therapeutic and financial, between doctors and patients.

In the Australian context critics and apologists alike have seen two influences as central to this autonomy. The first of these was the dominance of registered medical practitioners over rivals within the market for health services. Medical dominance in Australia has been seen as predicated upon the successful subordination of potential competitors (such as midwives and optometrists) with the reduction of their status to 'ancillary' services under medical direction and the marginalization or outright persecution of more direct rivals such as chiropractic and homoeopathy.

The intervention of the state is central to this analysis. By handing over control of registration to the medical profession and giving it a privileged position in advice of policy questions it provided doctors with a means of isolating and destroying their rivals at a time when standard medical practices were not demonstrably superior to those of their rivals.[2]

At the same time, forms of remuneration have taken on great significance in medical politics as the embodiment of particular relationships between practitioners, their clients, and third parties.

The dominance of an expanding and increasingly homogeneous market for medical services underpinned the shift from relative poverty and low public esteem in the late nineteenth century to the improved economic and exalted social status of medical practitioners by the 1930s, a progress underpinned by the establishment of fee-for-service as the major form of remuneration for personal medical services. Fee-for-service embodied the central features of medical autonomy – the freedom from contractual arrangements to outside bodies, the ability of the individual doctor to vary charges according to the means of the patient, and the assumption of individual responsibility for the costs of illness. Consequently, the dominance of fee-for-service has been seen by both its critics and advocates as a prior condition for the autonomy and political power of the medical profession.[3]

An adequate account of the relationship of the state to the provision of health care must start from premises other than the stark opposition of 'intervention' and 'autonomy'. The British sociologist Terence Johnson's concept of 'professionalization' as a 'process towards partial autonomy, being limited to specific areas of independent action which are defined by an occupation's relationship to the state; areas of autonomy which arise from time to time and place to place', provides the basis for an analysis which can explore the contradictory record of the political practice of the medical profession in the face of state involvement in the provision and regulation of medical services. 'Medicalization', the transformation of western notions of the body, health and illness through the dominance of scientific medicine, should not be reduced to a question of social control, of the dominance annexed by one social/professional group, but should recognize the important differences in which knowledges are taken up, the contradictions within the profession and the strength of lay knowledges.[4]

The argument presented here is that a particular model of the relationship between public health and private practice underlay Australian medical politics from 1920 to 1950. The advocates of a national health policy attempted to subordinate the general practitioner and 'curative' medicine within a broader framework of preventive public health, with national co-ordination, or even direct control by the Commonwealth Department of Health. The turning point in Australian health policy during the 1940s was not the defeat of schemes of 'socialized' medicine, but the defeat of this wider vision of public health and its replacement by policies which concentrated on access to the existing pattern of private health services. While the approach to the incidence of costs and the provision of benefits differed sharply – as it does today – between the main political parties, this was within a wider consensus. From the end of the Second World War, both the major forces in Australian politics agreed that the central problem was the subsidization of existing services. Within this consensus, conservative and Labor governments differed on how health care should be financed and the extent to which benefits should be the target. Federal and state Labor administrations were hostile to the demeaning conditions of the means-tested public wards and did not share the social assumptions of the conservative parties – the fear that older traditions of charitable giving would crumble in the face of massive state subsidies. But these conflicts were fought within a common set of assumptions. Government had a duty to provide access to medical care for those citizens unable to afford the fees of private practice. The extended boundaries of public intervention were not to challenge the profession's control over how those services were supplied.[5]

The first section of this study analyses the structure of interwar medical practice and the limits on state intervention. The limits imposed on the market for medical services and the threat to general practice posed by the growing importance of the hospital and medical specialism set the context for conflict. Chapter 2 examines the failure of the project of national hygiene, the attempt to use the state to impose a new conception of public health, making medical reform the centrepoint of a progressive recasting of social relationships. Chapter 3 develops this account of medical institutions, and conflict over their control, moving to the level of the states – where most direct administrative responsibility was exercised – and looking at the very different relationships between the medical profession and governments which emerged. The attempt to introduce national health insurance in 1938–9 was the first serious move towards a national health policy based on subsidization of medical expenses. Chapter 4 takes the analysis of the power relationships in Australian health policy further by examining the failure of this campaign.

The second section examines the attempt at medical reconstruction during the 1940s. The wartime governments of Menzies and Curtin and the postwar Labor government of Chifley all commissioned schemes for a major alteration in medical practice. Although they have been seen as the principal attempt to socialize medicine, or at least introduce a comprehensive national health service on the British model, a closer examination of these projects shows quite different aims. The plans of the National Health and Medical Re-search Council and the Joint Parliamentary Committee on Social Security were vehicles for reviving the projects of interwar health administrators, the national hygienists, and for averting the danger of medical planning falling into the hands of politicians. Organized medicine remained seriously divided over the attractions of a fully salaried medical service. The effective, and ultimately successful opposition to these radical schemes came from the Commonwealth Treasury and the planners of postwar reconstruction who successfully subordinated health policy within their social security programme. Any notion of direct service or attempt to restructure medical practice was lost, and the national health scheme was reduced to a series of cash benefit programmes. It was on this narrow scheme that the major conflicts between organized medicine and the Common-wealth were fought.

The final section examines the creation of the Page–Menzies health scheme of the 1950s. Far from an unalloyed victory for organized medicine, Page's initial project continued many of the obsessions with cost-control which had circumscribed Labor's approach. His heavily means-tested scheme was widened in the face of medical resistance, and especially the BMA's successful destruction of the only administrative agencies which could have implemented the Page scheme. Chapter 12 develops the implications of this political history for later attempts at reform of the health system. The institutional structures formed during the conflicts of the 1940s have set the limits of subsequent reform.

# Acknowledgements

This book would not have been written but for the personal interest taken by Dr Neal Blewett, then Commonwealth Minister for Health. Most of the research and writing was carried out in the Social Justice Project in the Research School of Social Sciences at the Australian National University, funded with a grant from the Commonwealth Department of Community Services and Health. My greatest debt is to Pat Troy, the initiator and co-ordinator of the Project, who provided such a congenial setting and unstinting encouragement. George Morgan and Sue McGrath gave research assistance at the Project with help and ideas which contributed significantly to the final result.

The following libraries and archives provided materials and other assistance: the John Oxley Library, the Fryer Library, the National Library of Australia, the libraries of the Australian National University, the Brownless Library at the University of Melbourne, the Mortlock Library, the State Library of Victoria, the La Trobe Library, the Mitchell Library, the University of Melbourne Archives, the Archives of Business and Labour at the Australian National University, the Archives of the Australian Broadcasting Corporation, and the Rockefeller Archives Center. Any historical study of public policy must rely heavily on the help of sympathetic archivists to negotiate the maze of official records: a great debt is owed to the staff of the Australian Archives in Canberra, Sydney and Brisbane, the Victorian Public Record Office, and the New South Wales and Queensland State Archives. The presiding officers of the House of

Representatives and the Senate allowed me access to the papers of the Joint Parliamentary Committee on Social Security.

Both the New South Wales and Victorian branches of the Australian Medical Association provided me with generous access to their unpublished records, as did the British Medical Association in London.

Particular thanks are due to Deena Shiff. In addition, I have benefited from comments or other assistance from Richard Gillespie, Milton Lewis, Dr John Matthews of the AMA Victorian branch, Dr John Powles, F.B. Smith, Peter Spearritt, Dr Margaret Spencer, Geoffrey Sherington, Charles Webster and numerous others. Shirley Purchase, Cambridge University Press's copy-editor, ironed out many of the more obscure passages in the writing and Trish Holt prepared the index. Many of those thanked above may disagree with the views expressed here, so I must emphasize that I alone am responsible for the interpretations advanced.

# Abbreviations

| | |
|---|---|
| AA | Australian Archives |
| ABL | Archives of Business and Labour, Australian National University |
| ACTU | Australian Council of Trade Unions |
| ALP | Australian Labor Party |
| AMA | Australian Medical Association |
| AWU | Australian Workers Union |
| BMA | British Medical Association |
| CMCC | Central Medical Co-ordination Committee |
| CPP | *Commonwealth Parliamentary Papers* |
| DHA | Drug Houses of Australia |
| DSS | Department of Social Services |
| EMS | Emergency Medical Service |
| FPSG | Federated Pharmaceutical Services Guild of Australia |
| FSDPA | Friendly Societies Dispensaries and Pharmacists Association |
| HCF | Hospitals Contribution Fund |
| JPCSS | Joint Parliamentary Committee on Social Security |
| MBF | Medical Benefits Fund |
| MECC | Medical Equipment Co-ordination Committee |
| MHSC | Medical and Hospital Survey Committee |
| MPA | Medical Policy Association |
| NHI | National Health Insurance |
| NIC | National Insurance Commission |
| NHS | National Health Service |

| NHMRC | National Health and Medical Research Council |
| NHS | National Health Service |
| NLA | National Library of Australia |
| *NSWPP* | *New South Wales Parliamentary Papers* |
| NSWSA | New South Wales State Archives |
| PMS | Pensioners' Medical Service |
| *QPP* | *Queensland Parliamentary Papers* |
| QSA | Queensland State Archives |
| RACP | Royal Australasian College of Physicians |
| RAC | Rockefeller Archives Center |
| RACS | Royal Australasian College of Surgeons |
| RPAH | Royal Prince Alfred Hospital |
| *SAPP* | *South Australian Parliamentary Papers* |
| SCMO | Senior Commonwealth Medical Officer |
| SEC | State Electricity Commission |
| SMCC | State Medical Co-ordination Committee |
| *Tas.PP* | *Tasmanian Parliamentary Journals and Papers* |
| UAP | United Australia Party |
| VPRO | Victorian Public Record Office |
| VTHC | Victorian Trades Hall Council |

# PART I

# Medicine and the State: 1900 to 1939

# CHAPTER 1

# 'A Game of Animal Grab': Medical Practice, 1920 – 1939

By the 1920s the Australian medical profession had achieved a nearly unchallenged dominance over the supply of personal health services. Its rivals in homoeopathy and other irregular medical traditions had been driven out or marginalized and in each state medical boards, dominated by the profession, ensured that this dominance would remain unchallenged. The costs of medical education were enough to restrict new entrants to the profession. Practitioners, the public and governments agreed that shortages of practitioners rather than excessive competition was the major problem. Paradoxically, these professional advances were accompanied by growing economic insecurity. Private medical practice on a fee-for-service basis faced the insuperable obstacle of a lack of capacity to pay from all but an affluent minority of the population. The politics of organized medicine increasingly centred on finding a means to guarantee medical incomes, and extend services to wider sections of the population without compromising professional autonomy.

At the same time the plight of the 'middle classes' entered the language of medical politics. Conflict over the future of medical practice revolved around growing demands to widen access to the public hospital system to sections of the population previously excluded from charitable institutions. The growing sophistication and expense of hospital-based technologies made the small private hospital and home-based care increasingly inferior for all but simple ailments and operations. In all states organized medicine, represented by the state branches of the British Medical Association (BMA), fought a losing battle to exclude potential paying patients from the public system. By the early 1930s the profession realized the futility of obstructing these encroachments on private general practice, and investigated ways to widen the market for medical services to embrace those presently excluded. These class boundaries remained hazy, ranging from those 'just above the basic wage' to 'just barely comfortable in life people' who pay their way, and who make so large a proportion of a doctor's paying patients, comprising those Macintyre has recently described as the 'anxious class', earning somewhere between £200 and £500 a year and struggling to maintain their status above the mass of the manual working class.[1]

Far from asserting their independence of the state, by the end of the decade each of the Australian branches of the BMA was calling for greater government or other collective intervention in the provision of medical services, and influential sections of the medical profession were entertaining plans for radical changes in the remuneration of medical practitioners. At the same time, the financial pressures on the public hospital system forced state, and then Commonwealth governments to move health services from the margins of politics.

## General practitioners and the medical market

Medical practice during the interwar years was a small-scale cottage industry dominated by general practitioners in sole practice. In 1921 over two-thirds of those describing themselves as 'medical practitioners' were in sole practice (Table 1.1). Only a very small proportion listed any employees. In keeping with this small business ethos most medical graduates starting in practice could expect a long battle before they achieved any economic security and overcame their heavy burden of debt. The pressing issues were not questions of therapeutics but the day-to-day struggle to build up or keep a viable practice. The competitive suspicion that often raged between rival general practitioners was portrayed by Herbert Moran, a Sydney surgeon, as 'like a game of animal grab, but you've got to grab according to the rules, otherwise they'll be reporting you to the Ethics Committee of the BMA' – rather than the idyllic image of professional co-operation presented in medical school.[2]

Unlike medical practitioners in the more free market atmosphere of the United States, where the struggle between regular 'allopathic' medicine and its rivals, homoeopathy, chiropractic and osteopathy, raged bitterly up to the First World War, the Australian doctor had less difficulty in maintaining professional prestige. Despite regular complaints about competition from 'quacks' and a widespread preference for patent medicines over the expensive and uncertain results of medical advice, the prestige of the imperial connection – the 'British' in the title of the BMA was not dropped until 1962 – and state registration controlled by BMA-dominated medical boards helped to assure the status of regular medicine in Australia. In all states but Queensland the medical acts required that all board members be qualified medical practitioners. Intense conflicts could occur over the subordination of 'ancillary' professions, such as midwifery and optometry, but by the 1920s this rarely took the form of open conflict. The slow strangulation of homoeopathic medicine in Victoria – limited to one new registration a year – was more typical. Starved of new doctors, Melbourne's Homoeopathic Hospital gradually opened its doors to more orthodox members of the BMA. These exclusionary tactics were also used successfully against refugees from Nazi anti-semitism in the 1930s. After intense pressure from the BMA from 1937 to 1939 the medical acts in Victoria, New South Wales, Tasmania and Queensland were amended to refuse recognition of medical qualifications, unless from a country already agreeing to reciprocal recognition. In effect this barred German and Austrian doctors from practice if they were not prepared (or able) to undergo lengthy and expensive retraining.[3]

Table 1.1 Employment Status of Australian Medical Practitioners, 1921

|                | No.   | %    |
|----------------|-------|------|
| Employer       | 483   | 14.7 |
| On Own Account | 2,247 | 68.5 |
| Employee       | 549   | 16.7 |

Source: *1921 census.*

These firm barriers to entry meant that overcrowding of the medical profession was not a major problem for most of this period. The ratio of doctors to population, admittedly a very rough means of estimating the supply of services but the only one available, remained relatively high. In 1920 the average population served by each doctor in the United States was 746 and in Canada 1,008. In contrast, Australia had a marked shortage of medical practitioners throughout the interwar years. In 1920 each Australian medical practitioner served an average population of 1,351. Although this number fell slowly over the following two decades – by 1940 the Australian population per doctor was 1,061 – it remained high by international standards.

These aggregate statistics must be qualified in the light of regional differences in the market for medical services (see Appendix Table 1.7). In 1920 Queensland – lacking its own medical school and with a relatively poor and scattered population – had one doctor for each 1,826 people. This contrasted sharply with Victoria's more favourable – but still high – ratio of one doctor for just over 1,000 inhabitants.

If legal and regulatory restrictions were not enough to impede entry, these barriers to competition were augmented by financial obstacles. The costs of entering medical practice were heavy. Burdened with the debts of education and the establishment or purchase of a practice, newly registered general practitioners were faced with a professional life of long hours and hard work in return for relatively low remuneration for at least the first decades of their careers.

The first of these costs was the acquisition of a medical degree. Medical education was a long and expensive process. An American visitor noted in 1924 that medical fees at the University of Melbourne amounted to £25 per annum and that only 20 (out of 619) medical students received free places at a time when the basic wage stood at well under £4 a week. The lengthening of the medical course, first to five years (in 1922) and then to six (1934), extended the clinical components of the degree, but at the cost of even more prohibitive financial barriers. In 1930 the full cost of a medical degree at the University of Sydney, excluding living expenses, was £350 and a decade later the potential general practitioner required £400 alone in fees for six years of university and hospital training. These costs were sufficient to exclude most students without substantial financial means from medical courses. During the intercensal years 1921 to 1933 there was an absolute decline in the numbers of women doctors in private practice; their proportion of the profession fell from just under 10 per cent to 5.7 per cent.[5]

The newly registered doctor was then faced with the costs of establishing a practice. Those with sufficient private means or family support could buy an established practice; for their less wealthy colleagues the choice was either working as an ill-paid assistant or 'squatting' – setting up in a likely neighbourhood and surviving the enmity of local doctors until a practice was built up. Neither offered a secure or lucrative living in the early years and eliminated the chances of all but a wealthy few to pursue post-graduate studies abroad, still the principal route to specialization. Purchase of a practice, usually with finance provided by a medical agency, saddled the future general practitioner with a debt amounting to one year's gross takings, averaged out from the receipts of the previous three years. To this encumbrance was added the price of the house and surgery which went with the practice. The value of the practice to the new incumbent depended almost entirely upon its transferable goodwill, its 'appointments' – the size of the previous doctor's friendly society panel of patients, appointment as a part-time medical officer of health to the local council, access to hospital paybeds and the chances of appointment as a local medical officer for the Repatriation Department (effectively restricted to doctors with a service record themselves). Financial survival during the first years of practice depended on these guaranteed sources of income and the new doctor's ability to attract fee-paying patients, 'cultivated sedulously around the lodge, the local church and a chemist shop'.[6]

Private practice on a fee-for-service basis, while the most lucrative area of work, was difficult to establish as the mainstay of a practice in all but the more affluent middle class suburbs. The attractions of this work meant that these areas of the large cities were relatively over-supplied with services, leading in turn to greater competition between doctors and lower incomes than could be earned in many of the less salubrious lodge practices in industrial suburbs. Consequently 'the doctors in residential suburbs do not earn as much as those in the industrial suburbs...[but] they live more pleasantly. Many of them are men who have come from country practices to the city and have earned enough to keep them in retirement'.[7]

## 'The crux of present medical practice': the friendly societies

Nowhere were the limits to the free market for medical services more apparent than in the continued strength of the friendly societies. These mutual benefit societies, organized in local lodges, provided their members with general practitioner services in return for a weekly contribution. General practitioners contracted with a society to provide a limited range of services to a panel of lodge members and their dependants. Particularly during the difficult first years of practice, doctors could expect to earn the bulk of their living from the capitation fees of lodge patients, fee-for-service practice remaining only a supplement to this basic income. Remuneration for lodge work remained entirely by capitation fee, a fixed annual payment for each patient on the lodge doctor's panel. No further charges were made to the patient for a limited range of medical services. Although the size of this fee and the range of services remained a point of conflict between the societies and each state branch of the BMA, there was never any suggestion by the profession that fee-for-service could ever become the basis for medical practice in working class areas. For members of the urban working class with sufficiently regular incomes to keep up with contributions this represented the most effective way to ensure cheap health care for themselves and their families. By the same token, lodge practice provided the principal source of income for doctors in industrial suburbs.

By the third decade of the twentieth century the societies had changed greatly from the mutual benefit social clubs of the late nineteenth century. As ceremonial and self-help activities declined, friendly societies such as the Oddfellows, the Manchester Unity and the sectarian-based Hibernians and Protestant Alliance became more exclusively concerned with financial services to members, providing insurance for sickness, unemployment, old age, funerals and, above all, medical benefits. Constrained by state legislation which enforced relatively stringent regulation of assets and contributions to benefits, membership requirements and the use of surplus funds, friendly societies remained non-profit associations of their contributors. Despite the gradual decline of a vigorous internal life, their constitutions still included government by representatives of the individual members, and policies were established at meetings of the membership, such as the annual 'Courts' of the Manchester Unity.[8]

The lay control of the societies, their financial power and dominance of the funding of health care for the better-off members of the working class, meant that they were always a target of hatred amongst doctors. Responsible for the solvency of contributors' funds, the friendly societies kept a jealous scrutiny of the cost of medical services, leading to persistent complaints of 'sweating' by medical practitioners contracted to the lodges.[9]

It has been a common view that by 1920 the lodges were effectively vanquished. In a series of extended conflicts in all states (and mirroring earlier disputes in Britain), the Australian branches of the BMA weakened the control of the lodges over the conditions of medical practice. By the early 1920s each state branch of the BMA had secured a Common Form of Agreement with its friendly societies, establishing the Association's control over the terms and conditions of access to lodge practice. The strict income limits imposed by the BMA excluded from lodge lists all who could afford private fee-paying treatment. Similarly, restrictions on the range of services offered to lodge members forced patients to pay fees for most minor operations. By 1920, Willis has claimed, 'The medical profession had achieved its aim of the right to control the conditions of medical practice, and established fee-for-service as the mode of medical treatment henceforth'.[10]

The 'battle of the clubs' before the First World War ended with major setbacks for the friendly societies. BMA members in each state refused to renew lodge contracts until restrictive conditions were imposed on eligibility, and the range and control of medical services. The Common Form of Agreement imposed by the BMA effectively restricted the societies to a working class clientele – although in the late 1930s, when the income limit was set at £365 in New South Wales, only 80,709 Commonwealth income tax-payers were assessed on incomes greater than £300 a year. The most fundamental victory for the BMA was the abolition of the Medical Institutes set up by friendly societies which had directly employed salaried doctors. Henceforth lodges were restricted to a concessional service mainly catering to the needs of working class families. In Victoria, where the dispute had been most bitter, the Wasley Royal Commission accepted the BMA's claim for a capitation fee of twenty shillings (20s.) in urban areas with twenty-five shillings (25s.) in non-metropolitan districts.[11]

Despite the new constraints on the friendly societies, the lodge system of contract practice and remuneration by capitation fee was grudgingly accepted by the BMA as the only means of integrating the working class patient into paid medical services. As a Queensland doctor told the Royal Commission on National Insurance in 1924, it 'means a regular income, and when attached to other work is good enough'. Nor was any attempt made to exclude the dependants of members from lodge medical services, as the BMA had achieved in England. Income limits were left to the individual lodges for enforcement, and these usually adopted a very generous approach to existing members. In 1938 an official of the New South Wales Friendly Societies' Association agreed that 'in ordinary practice, if a member exceeds [the income limit of] £365 in some degree nothing happens. No inquiry is made by the friendly society'.[12]

The limitation of services, the main area in the control of the lodge doctor, enabled a slow erosion rather than a destruction of lodge services as panel patients were forced to pay for an increasing range of basic services. In New South Wales the Common Form of Agreement excluded all operations, treatment for fractures and dislocations, anaesthetics and, most significantly, midwifery. The main effect of this restriction of services was to reinforce class distinctions in medical provision. Despite denials by the BMA, most observers conceded that lodge patients were often treated in a peremptory and grudging manner. The high administrative costs of the societies, in 1929 estimated at 19 per cent of the revenue from contributors in Victoria, created further pressures for restrictive services and complaints that 'If any economy has to be effected by lodges it frequently is done first at the expense of medical benefit'. While these limitations did not lead to a displacement of the friendly societies they may have encouraged the stigma attached to lodge practice by many of its recipients as well as the medical profession. [13]

Table 1.2 Membership of Friendly Societies, 1910–1949 (10,000s)

|       | 1910 | 1915 | 1920 | 1925 | 1930 | 1935 | 1938 | 1945 | 1949 |
|-------|------|------|------|------|------|------|------|------|------|
| NSW   | 12.2 | 16.1 | 17.6 | 20.9 | 25.0 | 20.5 | 21.2 | 23.0[a] | 18.9 |
| Vic.  | 13.9 | 15.9 | 14.4 | 15.5 | 16.5 | 16.4 | 18.9 | 20.6 | 20.2 |
| Qld   | 4.1  | 5.2  | 5.5  | 6.2[b] | 6.8 | 6.7 | 7.2 | 7.4[c] | 6.8 |
| SA    | 5.1  | 6.5  | 6.9  | 7.4  | 7.7  | 7.1  | 7.5  | 8.0  | 7.6  |
| WA    | 1.6  | 2.0  | 1.8  | 2.1  | 2.5  | 2.3  | 2.7  | 3.0  | 2.9  |
| Tas.  | 2.1  | 2.3  | 2.3  | 2.4  | 2.7  | 2.4  | 2.5  | 2.4[d] | 2.1 |
| C'wlth | 39.0 | 48.0 | 49.0 | 54.6 | 61.1 | 55.4 | 60.0 | n.a. | 58.6 |

[a] 1947      [b] 1924      [c] 1944      [d] 1946

Note: D. Green and L. Cromwell, *Mutual Aid or Welfare State?: Australia's Friendly Societies*, Sydney 1984, Appendix 4, have suggested that to estimate the total population covered, including dependants, these numbers should be multiplied by a factor of 4.34 up to 1930 and 3.2 from the mid 1930s. Although it gives a better representation of long-term trends their procedure has not been followed here as the sudden decrease in size of the multiplier gives an exaggerated view of the decline of the societies' coverage in the late 1930s.

Source: *Commonwealth Yearbooks*.

'Industrial practice' based on the lodge panels remained the main source of income for medical practitioners in working class areas of the cities. Table 1.2 shows the slow growth of the societies in all states during the 1920s. The depression, rather than medical opposition, provided the greatest check to expansion and after 1935 membership recovered. In 1925 the Royal Commission on National Insurance had found that 40 per cent of medical practitioners had friendly society contracts. Two decades later the societies still occupied a pivotal position; 900 out of the 1,950 members of the Victorian branch of the BMA had lodge practices, in Queensland up to one-third of medical incomes were earned from capitation fees, and nationally over one-quarter of the population was covered by friendly society medical benefits. The importance of the friendly societies to the economics of medical practice was even greater than these numbers suggest. The Royal Commission found that during the earlier stages of their careers most metropolitan doctors were dependent on lodge work. A national survey revealed that in 1943 one-third of the prescriptions dispensed by private chemists were on lodge prescriptions and this did not include those supplied through friendly society dispensaries.[14]

The financial strength of the friendly societies cushioned medical practitioners from the worst effects of the depression and assisted the societies to recover some of their lost ground. Expenditure on medical services by the friendly societies increased in real terms throughout the interwar years, even when membership was falling, as the societies drew on reserve funds to subsidize the contributions of unemployed members (Tables 1.3 and 1.4).

This was recognized by the BMA lodge doctors in Western Australia who agreed to donate 10 per cent of their capitation fees to keep all unemployed lodge members who were married or with dependants on the medical lists. In 1928 the Victorian branch had reopened its efforts to obtain a revision of the Wasley Award. With

**Table 1.3** Expenditure of Friendly Societies, 1920–1949:
Medical Attendance and Medicine (£'000)

|  | 1920 | 1925 | 1930 | 1935 | 1938 | 1945 | 1949 |
|---|---|---|---|---|---|---|---|
| New South Wales | 317 | 307 | 331 | 278 | 306 | 419[a] | 456 |
| Victoria | 186 | 210 | 230 | 247 | 293 | 381 | 549 |
| Queensland | 73 | 87[b] | 106 | 96 | 105 | 105[c] | 131 |
| South Australia | 39 | 80 | 101 | 91 | 100 | 109 | 170 |
| Western Australia | 20 | 25 | 34 | 32 | 41 | 48 | 82 |
| Tasmania | 22 | 23 | 30 | 28 | 31 | 36[d] | 46 |
| Commonwealth | 658 | 736 | 831 | 772 | 876 | n.a. | 1433 |

[a] 1947     [b] 1924     [c] 1944     [d] 1946

Source: *Commonwealth Yearbooks*.

**Table 1.4** Expenditure of Friendly Societies, 1920–1949:
Medical Attendance and Medicine at 1925–7 Prices (£'000)

|                    | 1920 | 1925 | 1930 | 1935 | 1938 | 1945  | 1949 |
|--------------------|------|------|------|------|------|-------|------|
| New South Wales    | 264  | 308  | 339  | 325  | 338  | 340[a]| 267  |
| Victoria           | 155  | 211  | 235  | 289  | 323  | 333   | 322  |
| Queensland         | 61   | 88[b]| 109  | 112  | 116  | 92[c] | 76   |
| South Australia    | 33   | 80   | 104  | 106  | 110  | 95    | 100  |
| Western Australia  | 17   | 25   | 35   | 37   | 45   | 42    | 48   |
| Tasmania           | 18   | 27   | 31   | 33   | 34   | 31[d] | 27   |
| Commonwealth       | 549  | 738  | 852  | 902  | 966  | n.a.  | 838  |

[a] 1947    [b] 1924    [c] 1944    [d] 1946
Source: *Commonwealth Yearbooks*.

the onset of depression this campaign was all but abandoned; in late
1932 the branch president noted: 'In the profession there is a great
divergence of opinion, but I know that at present there are many
medical men who, if it were not for their lodge payments, would be
in a very invidious position, and they feel that they would be
unwilling to have any misunderstandings with lodges'.[15] It was not
until 1940 that another attempt was made to raise Victorian capitation rates to the levels enjoyed by lodge doctors in other states.

Even more significantly, the hitherto successful campaign to
restrict specialist services under lodge contracts was increasingly
flouted. During the 1930s several friendly societies were able to
establish specialist panels, despite BMA warnings to its members that
concessional specialist services were only to be available on a fee-for-
service basis and open to all recognized members of a specialty, not
through an exclusive contract with a lodge. Specialists who participated were assigned panels of up to 10,000 patients, each paying an
annual fee of one shilling. A (possibly exaggerated) estimate in 1941
was that most lodge specialists would see, on average, one per cent of
these patients in a year, drawing in return a handsome supplement of
around £500 a year to their earnings from fee-for-service practice.[16]

Neither the BMA nor the lodges accepted that the political issue
of control of conditions of lodge medical practice had been settled
once and for all. While the friendly societies in New South Wales,
Queensland, South Australia and Western Australia soon re-
established more or less amicable relations, conflict continued in
Victoria and Tasmania. Facing the strongest and most aggressive of
the societies, in particular the Australian Natives Association, the
Victorian branch of the BMA saw many of its achievements under-

mined. Capitation fees remained lower than in any other state and the fight for the more stringent enforcement of income restrictions was unsuccessful. After a seven-year struggle to achieve a Federal Common Form of Agreement with the friendly societies, which would have brought capitation fees and conditions in all states up to the New South Wales standard, by 1947 the BMA had to admit its lack of success, accepting state by state agreements which left Victorian and Tasmanian lodge doctors considerably worse off than their interstate colleagues.[17]

Capacity to pay remained the main barrier to alternatives to prepaid panel practice in working class communities. In areas where the BMA had succeeded in eliminating friendly society medical services lodge practice was replaced by a remarkably similar substitute, although decisively under medical control. In Newcastle, where a dispute with the lodges led to the resignation of all BMA members from lodge practice, successful 'doctors' clubs' were established by the former lodge doctors on the same basis as the friendly societies, contracting to provide a limited range of services for a fixed annual charge. Again, as with lodge practice, a fee was charged for each additional service. The clubs operated on a small scale, doctors' wives carried out the administrative work, and weekly contributions were deducted from wages by agreement with the trade unions and employers. Similar contract personal health services were provided for occupational groups such as timber workers in Victoria and miners on the West Australian goldfields through their trade unions. These doctors' clubs showed the attraction of contract service to general practitioners in working class areas, as they involved minimal bookkeeping and a reduction in bad debts while providing a service to all family members. Moves by state and federal governments to establish limited contract services for particular social groups proved equally acceptable to organized medicine. The Commonwealth Repatriation Department provided medical services for war widows and their children by subsidizing friendly society contributions. In 1937 the New South Wales government established a medical service for the unemployed on a similar basis with no dissent from the medical profession.[18]

As a result, the line between capitation-based contract practice and fee-for-service was often hazy. While most specialist services and general practitioners in middle class and rural areas, where the friendly societies were weak or non-existent, were exclusively fee-for-service, those with working class practices usually depended on a mixture of fee-for-service and lodge practice. The contract practice committees of each state branch of the BMA worked assiduously to extend the range of services excluded from the lodge contract. The societies fought equally hard, but with decreasing success, to develop a complete capitation-based service.

There is little hard evidence on the size of the market for private medicine. Thame has suggested that one-half the population depended on fee-paying medical care, a figure which appears to have been reached by elimination – identifying the proportion of the population ineligible for concessional or charitable services. However, exclusion from free or concessional services did not always mean ability to pay for private practice: the cost of a visit to a general practitioner's surgery – between 10 shillings and 2 guineas – meant that for much of the 'middle classes' medical services were an emergency resort. In less serious cases many relied on the unpaid advice of pharmacists or on fringe practitioners such as the Chinese herbalists still prominent in most country towns.[19]

Given the complicated mixture of pre-paid and fee-for-service practice, fee structures varied considerably. In New South Wales local or regional associations of practitioners issued confidential recommended fee schedules to their members, with little central co-ordination or interference and no binding power. In Victoria the BMA's state council played a more active role. A British investigator found that, unlike the English practice of income-related sliding fees, Australian doctors tended to charge a flat minimum fee for each service, restricting the scope for cross-subsidy between wealthy and poorer patients. The evidence on this point is contradictory. A manual of advice for general practitioners noted that the use of sliding scales was one of the more difficult skills of private practice. Years of experience were required to instantly assess a patient's true income. Its author concluded, however, that, despite this challenge, most general practitioners ended up using some form of sliding scale.[20]

Far from achieving dominance, fee-for-service co-existed in uneasy association with capitation systems of remuneration through the interwar years and few lodge doctors or leaders of the medical profession seriously visualized a system based on different principles. The most that could be hoped was that the middle classes would continue to be excluded from lodge practice and that the range of services outside the lodge contract would continue to grow. Charles Byrne, a medical critic of the lodge system, noted that, despite his colleagues' hostility, the friendly societies remained 'the crux of present medical practice. The lodge patient was welcomed by the doctor with open arms when he came as a private patient [to receive services outside the restricted lodge list] but the same could not be said of the lodge patient as such'.[21]

## General practitioners, specialists and the 'closed' hospital

The Australian medical system was a complicated hierarchy based on a limitation of access by suppliers of services and by patients. Panel doctors and outpatients' clinics catered for those who were unable to afford entry to the market for private medical services. This professional pyramid has been conventionally depicted as the result of technological imperatives. The advance of scientific knowledge led to a fragmentation of medical practice and a proliferation of specialties. Rising costs and other restrictions to access to medical services were a consequence of the failure of administrative and financial institutions to adapt to the pace of scientific and technological change. In this view, the problem of access to modern medical care, and the political conflicts around attempts to widen this access, were not the result of the restrictive practices or outright greed of the medical profession but of a cultural lag in institutional adaptation.

In recent years this technological determinism has come under increasing attack from sociologists (largely from the left) as well as economists supporting an extension of the free market to health care. Although they draw quite different political conclusions, both groups of critics have argued that, far from being the mere reflux of technological change, the advance of specialization has resulted from struggles by professional groups to establish restrictive monopolies on market entry. In Australia specialists have usually relied on the power of the state to exclude their rivals, a social closure grounded in politics. Advocates of the free market have castigated this state intervention to establish monopoly power, but have provided little explanation outside abstract models of the rent-seeking propensities of economic man. Leftist critics have suggested a natural affinity between the dominant ideology of the capitalist state and the individualism of curative medicine. However, neither of these approaches has been particularly fruitful. The bases of medical autonomy have been confused between the professional dominance established over the immediate execution of work – medical control of hierarchies in the division of labour within the health system – and the institutional regulation of relationships between clients and experts. In the latter the power of the profession has been far more contingent on wider political considerations.[22]

In contrast, this account stresses the politics of access and control of medical services. General practitioners and specialists, hospital administrators and the lay boards to whom they were responsible, state governments, trade unions and political parties, and the patients all were allegedly serving had different interests and (often intermittently) expressed distinctive views of desirable forms of access and control of the health system. The power of the medical profession was not simply a question of a privileged access to the state (which was frequently absent), nor of a homologous relationship between curative medicine and capitalist ideology, nor merely of the strength of the British Medical Association.

The crucial question of medical politics has always been in the manner in which the 'interests' of patient and doctor are formulated. Health economists have long argued that the unique characteristic of medical services is the extent to which monopoly of knowledge enables the service provider to construct the demand for his or her services. Put simply, patients depend on their doctor to define their malady and propose the alternative treatments available. This monopoly of therapeutic knowledge has been the key to the political strength of the medical profession. The distinctiveness of the medical discourse has been the basis, not the result, of the political power of the medical profession.[23]

In interwar Australia the public hospital was the main site of this conflict. As hospital practice was the main route to professional advancement, through the acquisition of specialist knowledge and qualifications, the exclusion of general practitioners from access to public hospital patients underpinned the hierarchy of highly paid honorary consultants and marginalized general practitioners. Specialization represented the application of scientific advances and the creation of barriers to exclude less favoured colleagues from lucrative areas of work. This interaction of market and political pressures, therapeutic and technical change provided the major theme in the consolidation of specialties, and the successive attempts by general practitioners to reverse their exclusion from significant sections of the market for medical care.[24]

The interwar crisis in medical services centred on the finance, organization and access to the public hospital system by both patients and doctors. Here the effects of social class and income on access to health services were most starkly posed. If much of the urban working class depended on friendly society contract medical cover, the poor and unemployed relied upon free outpatients' clinics of the public hospitals. Similarly, in several states country hospital boards, dominated by local trade union or producer groups, removed means-tested restrictions on access to hospital treatment by establishing insurance schemes. This development spread to the large metropolitan hospitals in the 1930s, helping them to meet financial pressures while enabling middle class subscribers to have access to beds in the new private and intermediate wards of what were previously charity hospitals. As general practitioners found their rights to attend – and charge – hospital patients increasingly restricted, the dominance of the hospital in the system of medical care became a central issue. As with contract practice, the economic problem of integrating those outside the market into a position of paying (or being paid for) became the *leitmotiv* of medical politics.

Therapeutic, technological and social changes combined to reinforce the public hospital as the centre of the health system. The vast improvement of diagnostic and surgical techniques during the First World War required levels of investment which private hospitals were rarely able to match. In the capital cities the public hospitals and larger denominational private hospitals attracted middle class rather than purely charity patients. Particularly after 1926 when the New South Wales and Victorian state governments sponsored a visit by Dr Malcolm MacEachern, the Director of Hospital Activities of the American College of Surgeons, the American model of the 'community hospital' dominated debate on hospital finance in those states. Instead of relying on charity and state subsidy the community hospital erected separate private and intermediate wards for paying patients, thus opening access to the resources of the public hospitals to the middle classes. Despite considerable resistance from the defenders of voluntarism, state hospital authorities saw fee-paying patients as a means of relieving the rising costs of public hospital services, and during the 1930s the major public hospitals in both states introduced paybeds. These developments marked the culmination of the long development of the public hospitals from their nineteenth-century origins as charitable institutions, supported by voluntary subscriptions, with access limited to the sick poor and enforced with stringent means tests. By 1939 governments in all states recognized that the public hospitals were no longer 'homes for the sick poor' but had now become 'the training ground of the whole medical profession, the foundation of modern medical practice and the source of most of the advancement and progress in medical knowledge'.[25]

In the early 1920s specialist practice in Australia existed on a restricted scale compared to Germany, Britain or the United States – a socially exclusive elite to which few could aspire without family connections or money. As the *Medical Journal of Australia* noted in 1924, 'only a few can emancipate themselves from general practice'. This truncated development of specialization resulted from problems of both demand and supply. Specialist practice suffered from the same market limitations afflicting other forms of fee-for-service, only a minority could afford to pay. At the same time, the tight and intensely hierarchical circles of specialists blocked the development of contract or other concessional services which could widen the market only by devaluing the practices of the elite.[26]

The cost of education and the limited scope for postgraduate work in Australia restricted the supply of highly qualified surgeons and physicians. Medical graduates with means travelled to Britain or (less frequently) Europe for post-graduate study. Each of the larger state capitals had its small circles of these consultants who were able to confine their practice to a specialty and provide clinical teaching, on an honorary basis, in the public hospitals. The specialist's income depended on private patients treated in consulting rooms or private hospitals. Former students and the social contacts gathered through family, school, university college and hospital provided referrals of private patients. Sir Henry Newland, a founding member of the Royal Australasian College of Surgeons, formed a successful practice during the 1920s based on his status as an honorary surgeon at the Adelaide Hospital. His private patients were attended at Ru Rua Private Hospital in North Adelaide, which he owned with five of his colleagues. Similarly, an 'Ormond College network' provided the starting point for the careers of many Melbourne specialists. Consequently, few outsiders broke into the inner circle. Women only achieved a minimal representation in the specialties after the formation of the Queen Victoria Hospital in Melbourne (1896) and the Rachel Forster Hospital in Sydney (1922). Both these hospitals appointed predominantly female honorary staffs, weakening some of the barriers to a specialist career.[27]

The major impetus to the development of specialization was provided by advances in surgical and anaesthetic technique during the First World War which vastly extended the scope for medical treatment of wounds and fractures and increased the supply of experienced specialists. Many of the AIF medical corps remained in Britain after demobilization and completed further hospital training, especially in surgery, the area in which wartime advances had been most marked. Techniques of blood transfusion, orthopaedic surgery and the extensive use of radiology were developed or received their first widespread use in the military hospitals of the Western Front. These technical advances in surgery were consolidated in the conditions of peace. The widespread ownership of the motor car provided the second great stimulant to these new forms of surgical practice. Orthopaedic surgery provided one of the fastest growing areas of hospital practice during the 1920s as casualty wards filled with the victims of car accidents. At the great public hospitals, such as Melbourne's Alfred Hospital, almost all new beds added during the 1920s were for surgical patients. These technical changes and the greater supply of experienced surgeons, helped by the expanded post-graduate facilities of the Australian medical schools, created pressures to widen access to the more advanced facilities of the public hospitals, such as radiology. A symbol of these changes was the establishment of the Melbourne University Permanent Post-Graduate Committee in 1920.[28]

These changes in the hospital-based division of labour were formalized as professional organizations covering specialist areas of practice were established on a national scale and Australian medical schools developed post-graduate education. Again, this took the form of a catching-up with overseas models. The initial stimulus, as with the MacEachern Report and the introduction of paybeds, came from America, with attempts to set up a local version of the American Association of Surgeons. The result conformed to the anglo-centrism of the Australian medical profession, with closer ties to the British Royal Colleges. The Royal Australasian College of Surgeons was founded in 1926, and began to publish the *Australian and New Zealand Journal of Surgery* in 1930. By 1938 the College claimed 491 Fellows in Australia, admitted by passing the examination of the (British) Royal College of Surgeons. Over 70 per cent of these Fellows practised in Victoria and New South Wales. The example of the surgeons was followed seven years later by the Australasian Association of Physicians (Royal Australasian College of Physicians from 1938) with 231 foundation Fellows in the two countries. As with the RACS the criterion for membership was not exclusive practice in the specialty but qualification by examination. Similar independent associations of specialists or Australian regional councils of the appropriate British College were formed for gynaecologists (1929), anaesthetists (1934), radiologists (1935), orthopaedic specialists and urologists (1937) and ophthalmologists (1938).[29]

Despite these moves, by the end of the 1930s a medical system based on a hierarchy of full-time specialization and general practice was still only an aspiration. Neither of the Royal Colleges demanded that its members confine their practice to their specialty. Most remained general practitioners, developing a particular interest and treating patients referred by their colleagues. Full-time specialization remained confined to 'more or less isolated groups in the various capital cities'. In 1935 the New South Wales branch of the BMA warned recent medical graduates that most should expect to enter general practice. For those contemplating a future as a consultant:

> the lean years are many, and except in the case of a few, it is doubtful if the total earnings of a long life thus spent would exceed by much, if at all, those of a good general practitioner.
>
> [Consequently]…In Australia there are but few true consultants; these are chiefly radiologists, pathologists and biochemists, who do not undertake the care of patients. For although introductions from other doctors form a variable proportion of the specialist's work, his practice is swelled by his own personal clientele, and the smaller the centre is the more is this the case. But none the less, all aspirants to consulting rank should endeavour to avoid the lure of dabbling in practice outside their professed ambit, for their work should be distinguished by its type and standard, not by the fees it commands. [30]

Many succumbed to the lure. The ethical rules published by the BMA for the guidance of its members remained undecided on where the dividing line was to fall. While fee-splitting between referring general practitioners and full-time specialists was a recurrent problem – although emphatically banned by the BMA – new problems were posed by the emergence of doctors who combined general practice with specialist sidelines. In 1922 the Federal Committee ruled that general practitioners were only to list specialties on their nameplates if they saw these patients in a separate consulting room. In 1928 this judgement was supplemented by a warning that specialists should see patients 'as far as possible' only after a written referral from their regular doctor and confine their services to the particular illness or complaint for which the referral was made. Beyond this, the committee argued, 'the time is not quite ripe for definite pronouncements on the subject'.[31]

This mixture of honorary hospital work and general practice existed at all levels of the profession. In the late 1930s Sir James Barrett estimated that up to 60 per cent of practitioners in Melbourne did some form of honorary work. For David Browne, a successful general practitioner in the Victorian regional centre of Wangaratta, election to the Royal Australasian College of Surgeons encouraged his colleagues to refer their more complicated cases to him. While this added to the intellectual stimulation and financial returns of his practice, general practice still provided most of his income. Cecil Colville, chairman of the Victorian branch of the BMA from 1939 to 1966, combined a large general practice in Hawthorn with an honorary appointment as a paediatric surgeon at the Alfred Hospital. Even the full-time specialists usually started with mixed general practices. After his return to Adelaide from postgraduate training in England before the First World War, Sir Henry Newland went into general practice for several years before he could afford to develop an exclusively specialist surgical practice.[32]

A survey of medical practice in Tasmania in 1951, carried out by the Commonwealth Department of Health, found that little had changed, at least in the smaller states: 'The specialist rating is self-awarded and doctors listed under this heading also do some general practitioner work'. By the late 1960s this underdevelopment of full specialization was still a major feature of Australian medical practice. The only attempt to enforce formal registration of specialists came in Queensland in 1939, a development resisted strongly by all sections of the medical profession and owing more to an ambitious programme of centralized control of medical services and the abolition of honorary hospital practice than a radically changed division of labour within the profession.[33]

The threat posed by specialization stemmed from attempts to restrict access to certain classes of medical work, a 'growing tendency . . .for the belittling of the work of men in general practice and. . .a whittling away from them of certain spheres of activity to which they should have a certain claim'. The minor surgical operations which made up the excluded services of lodge practice were a jealously guarded supplement to capitation fees, as well as the main means to develop competence as a specialist. As paying patients moved to the larger urban hospitals, general practitioners complained that their livelihoods were being threatened and that the family doctor was being steadily reduced to 'little more than a clerk'. The medical journals of the 1930s have frequent predictions of the imminent demise of the family doctor and the fragmentation of medical practice among a myriad discrete specialties, which were losing all sight of the patient as an individual.[34]

These developments were most marked in obstetrics where the development of a new type of specialist general practitioner seemed to threaten one of the economic mainstays of most ordinary general practices. Ever since the subordination of female midwives to the overwhelmingly male medical profession (completed by the 1930s), attendance at childbirth had been of crucial importance in the economics of medical practice. Obstetric services were excluded from friendly society contracts and were a major source of fee-for-service income in working class lodge practices. This lucrative area of practice had been underwritten since 1912 by Commonwealth maternity allowances which provided mothers with a £5 cash grant on the birth of each child, the 'baby bonus'. Although there were no restrictions on how the allowance was to be spent, most recipients appear to have used it to pay for medical attendance at childbirth. In 1925 almost 80 per cent of recipients of maternity allowances had a doctor at the birth, an increase from 63 per cent in 1913. Even more importantly, conventional wisdom ruled that the doctor who attended the birth could expect mother and child to become his regular patients, an important step in building a new practice. The campaign for the hospitalization of childbirth provoked deep hostility amongst general practitioners who saw the fruits of the medical control of childbirth purloined by the specialists, sharpening the dividing line between those with access to public hospital beds and those excluded. The testimony of Dr Thomas Small, a general practitioner with a thriving suburban practice in Manly, New South Wales and separate Macquarie Street consulting rooms for his obstetric patients, displayed this growing contradiction:

> Until the last few years and until I got on the honorary staff of the Women's Hospital at Paddington I had the greatest difficulty [in getting patients admitted to hospital]. I would ring hospital after hospital and be told that no bed was available, and would finally ring the Board of Health and leave the matter to them. But I have since become wise. I found that if I rang the Sydney Hospital and asked for certain Residents with whom I was acquainted, particularly the Superintendent, I was rarely turned down . . .and I always get cases into the Women's Hospital at Paddington, even at the greatest inconvenience to the hospital, because I am on the honorary staff there. They took one for me last night. It was the last bed, and to make it they had to take a woman out of it and put her upstairs in another ward where she did not belong. I have no difficulty because I have been able to use personal influence. Possibly it is unfair to other medical practitioners, but I can get away with it. Years ago I, too, suffered.[35]

The 'closed hospital' blocked general practitioners from access to their patients, placing them under the exclusive care of honorary consultants or salaried medical officers. In the larger Victorian public hospitals paybeds in private or intermediate wards, introduced during the early 1930s, were 'practically reserved for the patients of the honoraries of that hospital'. The development of hospital insurance schemes expanded the demand for this private accommodation in most urban centres; the expansion of the Hospitals Contribution Fund in Newcastle led to 'fairly bitter competition between outside doctors and the hospital and its honoraries'. This was not a purely financial question. Hospital work provided the general practitioner with intellectual stimulation and exposure to new developments in medical knowledge and technologies and, not least, remained the principal route for developing a specialist practice. A Sydney general practitioner noted with bitterness the appearance of:

> a relatively large group of general practitioners serving mostly as clinical assistants, who devote hours of each week to honorary hospital work without hope of commensurate monetary reward. From choice, and because of competition, because they have not been able to get overseas and acquire higher degrees, and because of the necessity of appointing the extra brilliant young graduates, few of these men can hope to obtain appointment to the full staff of a hospital and so reach the stage of full consultant with its higher monetary rewards.[36]

One response to this exclusion was direct financial involvement in private hospitals. As the right to practise was not limited to honoraries but open to any practitioner with paying patients, the cottage hospital was an attractive option to the general practitioner wishing to develop surgical skills and to keep the more lucrative areas of medical practice to himself. As one advocate of a greater general practitioner involvement in private hospitals argued, 'A doctor's time is uneconomically used if he has to waste it in travelling to visit and treat in their own homes a number of patients who would be better attended in a single hospital'. The size of this for-profit sector is not clear. Statistics on the numbers of beds and the operations performed were not collected; private hospitals remained outside the purview of regulatory bodies as long as they observed public health sanitary regulations. Such small suburban and country town hospitals frequently took the form of a few rooms added to the doctor's residence, lacking specialized resources. Outside the cities this could exacerbate problems of access to modern diagnostic aids and lead to conflicts of interest: 'in some places private hospitals, often with relatively poor equipment, are used by patients in preference to better equipped public hospitals; it is alleged that on occasions this has been due to the advice of medical practitioners who are themselves interested in the private hospitals'.[37]

## The dissolution of charity: outpatients and insurance

If changes in hospital practice shifted the balance between the public and private sectors and between general practitioners and specialists, a major shift in access to hospital services further narrowed the base of private practice. For working class patients outside the friendly societies the outpatients' clinics of the public hospitals provided a free, means-tested service. At the same time, financial crises encouraged the public hospitals to widen access to their paybeds with insurance schemes. In several areas, particularly in Queensland, this led to a political struggle between the medical profession, the state government and trade unions over access.

Despite a lengthy history of warnings on the demoralizing effects of liberalized access to public wards, in the past this charity sector of medical care had not constituted a serious challenge to the dominance of private practice. It provided a safety net, relieving political pressure for a reorganization of the whole system of medical care to provide adequate care for all, regardless of income or occupation. The honorary services of surgeons and physicians to public ward patients also stemmed from strong traditions of altruistic service. At the same time, its resilience owed much to discriminatory pricing and the needs of teaching hospitals for compliant and interesting cases for instructional purposes.

**Table 1.5** Public Hospital Outpatients, 1920–1950  (per '000 of population)

|  | New South Wales (whole state) | Victoria (metropolitan area) |
|---|---|---|
| 1920 | 113 | 104 |
| 1925 | 141 | 159 |
| 1930 | 165 | 154 |
| 1935 | 190 | 207 |
| 1940 | 217 | 219 |
| 1945 | 217 | 184 |
| 1950 | 283 | 246 |

Note: These statistics refer to total distinct cases treated, hence they undoubtedly include a large but unknown amount of double counting.

Source: NSW and Victorian *Statistical Registers*.

Again, the depression years proved to be a watershed. Mass unemployment set further limits on the market for personal medical services, forcing large sections of the urban working class to rely on the charity of free hospital services, either in outpatient clinics or public wards. These free, means-tested public hospital outpatient services provided the most rapidly growing sector of health care between the wars. Table 1.5 shows this expansion in Victoria and New South Wales, the only states for which comparable statistics are available over the whole period. The growth of outpatient and free hospital services was seen as a major threat by many BMA members. The public hospitals provided major competition to private practice, and ominous warnings appeared about the long-term erosion of the private market as patients discovered the attractions of the free public hospital: 'many of our sick, during the depression, who would otherwise have been in private hospitals were, through lack of finance, forced into public institutions, and, realizing how efficient these institutions are, continued in better times to patronize them, frequently paying much less than they could really afford for the treatment'.[38] While the medical profession had argued strongly in the past that public hospitals 'are charitable institutions. . .for the purpose of providing the indigent sick with the best medical care and treatment available', and that honoraries 'are prepared to give their best services to the poor and refuse to accept fees from any patient', discussions of the 'hospital problem' warned that:

> Whilst providing for expert treatment and advice for the less fortunate of our community, we must not lose sight of the fact that a poor person in a big public hospital has more facilities at his command than the wealthy man in a less well-developed private hospital. Attempts to overcome this anomaly are shown by the introduction of private and intermediate wards to the bigger hospitals.[39]

This was not simply a question of lost income. In cases of acute sickness charity patients often received better care in the public hospitals than private institutions could offer. Unable to obtain home visits for minor ailments, poorer patients were forced to queue in the overcrowded outpatients' clinics. Medical critics observed that the unemployed and low-paid workers tended to postpone medical treatment until their condition was severe.[40] The remnants of charitable provision of hospital services were dissolved as the public hospitals failed in their attempts to restrict admission to the public wards by more thorough screening of patients. Official reports on the hospital question increasingly conceded that the introduction of private or intermediate wards and paybeds offered no solution for the majority of the population, merely providing temporary relief for hospital finances.[41]

In all states the hospitals responded by experimenting with hospital benefit insurance schemes aimed at the middle classes and the more financially stable sections of the working class. At the same time, pressures mounted to improve the standards of care and comfort for those forced to use outpatients' clinics. As the Hurstville Old Age and Invalid Pensioners' Association protested to the New South Wales government, those thrown on to medical charity were no longer prepared to 'wait shivering for hours to see their Doctor'.[42] In Victoria F. Oswald Barnett and the slum clearance campaign of the late 1930s argued that the abolition of inner city slums must be accompanied by measures to make medical care more accessible, in both financial and physical terms. Private fee-paying medical care was beyond the resources of those earning the basic wage and the alternatives were little better; it was 'often difficult to journey to public hospitals, difficult to give up long hours to sitting in rows in the Out-Patients' Department, difficult to arrange for the children in their absence. Thus only in the later stages is medical help sought. Some belong to the lodges, but regular contributions require regular incomes'.[43]

Most attention has been given to the great urban hospitals, particularly in Melbourne, which lost much of their autonomy in the face of a greater reliance on state funding during the interwar years.[44] On a national level, the pattern was more differentiated. In other states, and in the Victorian rural and provincial areas, hospital boards remained in lay hands. As the (lay) secretary of the Mildura District Hospital replied to calls by the Charities Board to tighten means testing of patients at the height of the depression:

> To demand from every patient the average bed cost and leave the onus upon him to prove his inability to pay it, will, in the opinion of the [Hospital] Committee ultimately alienate the sympathy of a large section of the community. . .it is impossible to have it both ways; i.e. from patients and the public, and as the chief object of a hospital is to help people in times of sickness, it is far better to have them satisfied as patients and rely upon their generosity as citizens.[45]

The most determined moves towards greater lay and political control over access to the health system took place in Queensland where, by 1917, the charity system had collapsed and state governments were forced, often reluctantly, to fill the gap. During the 1920s and 1930s hospitals developed contributory systems, with free treatment for all members. Many of these were based on occupational, trade union or producer groups and were particularly strong in the sugar producing areas. In many smaller communities, as medical services shifted from the doctor's office to the hospital, general practice became increasingly unprofitable and was displaced by salaried hospital doctors.[46]

Access to hospital medical services became easier for those not content with public ward treatment. By the late 1930s hospital contribution funds paying benefits for private or intermediate ward treatment were seen as the answer to the financial problems of the large metropolitan hospitals. The funds epitomized the two major tendencies of the organization of interwar medical practice – the move towards collective responsibility for the costs of health care and the hegemony of the hospital. The funds were based either on individual insurance subscriptions or through group schemes enrolling members of producer or trade union bodies.

The funds found their most secure base in New South Wales. The newly formed New South Wales Hospitals Commission saw voluntary insurance as the most practicable way of easing the crisis of hospital finances and launched the Metropolitan Hospitals Contribution Fund of New South Wales (HCF) in 1931. Controlled by nominees of all participating hospitals and the Commission, the HCF offered benefits of 6s. or 7s. per day towards the cost of accommodation in private or intermediate wards and provided for free outpatient treatment for one month after discharge. This met with resistance from the BMA, dominated by the financial constraints of the large public hospitals. It objected to the exclusion of medical fees from the benefit and found the provision for outpatient treatment without means test 'not acceptable'. After five years of operation the profession remained critical of the failure to include medical benefits but, in testimony to the collapse of the charitable principle, BMA arguments now centred on the best way to ensure medical control of benefit funds. By 1939 the Sydney metropolitan funds had achieved considerable success, at least from the hospitals' point of view. In that year more than 10 per cent of hospital current funding was derived from the MHCF. Herbert Schlink, the chairman of Sydney's Royal Prince Alfred Hospital, called for a state-controlled compulsory hospital insurance scheme modelled on 'that conducted by the hospitals themselves, the Metropolitan Hospitals Contribution Fund, the reason being that the money is not paid to the patient but directly to the hospital. Most friendly and other similar societies' schemes, and insurance companies which underwrite hospital and sickness insurance, pay direct to the patient, who nearly always fails to pass on his benefit payments to the hospital'.[47]

Contribution schemes based on single industries or occupational organizations provided the major early successes of the hospital insurance movement. They played an important part in a limited welfare capitalism associated with some of the largest and most progressive industries of the 1920s and 1930s. Their most forceful advocate was the industrialist Sir Gerald Mussen, who worked first at Broken Hill Associated Smelters at Port Pirie in the early 1920s, then as managing director of Australian Pulp and Paper Mills at Burnie in Tasmania. Mussen saw industrial medical funds as part of a wider vision in which mutual interest and co-operation would supplant trade unionism and class conflict. In more remote areas, such as Mt Isa, the company provided its own hospital for employees. In larger centres employers such as BHP at Newcastle, Mt Lyell Mines and Electrolytic Zinc Industries, both in Tasmania, preferred to subsidize their workers' contributions to gain full free hospital care. Schlink argued:

> I am of the opinion that modern people want some return for their money, and I feel that there is more hope in encouraging big firms and corporations to give large donations and in return to allow them the privilege of free hospitalization for their employees. As an example, I persuaded one big employer to give the RPAH a £2,000 donation, and I promised him as much free hospitalization for his employees as the 4% interest on the donation would provide. Employees recommended by him now occupy a bed free of charge for a total of twenty-four weeks in one year. [48]

The individual subscriber funds, aimed more at the middle classes, met with greater initial problems. Early failures led the Victorian branch of the BMA to express grave doubts about the viability of this form of hospital insurance. It argued that a state-run compulsory scheme, administered by a statutory corporation to avoid the danger of political interference, would have greater chances of financial success. This was despite a real 'risk that a statutory body might do something not in the interests of the profession at a later date, [but that] is one that will have to be taken'.[49] Only when the state government refused to oblige did the BMA reluctantly move to set up its own scheme. The Melbourne Hospital Benefits Association (HBA) was established as a limited liability company in 1934 and had a shaky financial start, in spite of initial subsidies from the BMA and the Lord Mayor's Fund. In mid 1935 the Association had only enrolled 3,725 contributors and its finances were causing anxiety and requiring additional injections of funds from its BMA supporters. A similar experiment in Adelaide also had disappointing results.[50] The weaknesses of voluntary hospital insurance schemes in Victoria led to increasing support for compulsory insurance and new forms of state subsidy as the solution to the growing 'hospital problem'.

By the eve of the Second World War fee-for-service occupied a limited space in the market for medical services. Attempts to extend the sphere of paid medical services through hospital-based insurance schemes had deepened the divisions within the medical profession between those who had access to hospital patients and those who faced a bleak future as mere referral agents. Debates on the future of medical practice in the *Medical Journal of Australia* and within the state councils of the BMA were dominated by the inability to extend the structures of the private market to a growing proportion of the middle classes and the expansion of non-market forms of medical provision for the working class. Consequently, political conflicts over state intervention were rarely posed in terms of outright rejection. Instead, debate concentrated on the terms under which the state should intervene. Dr William Upjohn, of the Victorian branch of the BMA, giving his qualified support for a salaried national health service, summed up prevailing doubts on the future of the profession without an even greater level of state intervention:

> the best days of the profession so far as earnings are concerned have gone. Since the last war, general practitioners have had little opportunity to make provision against the years when they are beyond the age at which they can practise hard. That is the point about the salaried service that will attract a lot of men.[51]

# Appendix

**Table 1.6** Numbers of Registered Medical Practitioners by State, 1920–1945

|      | NSW     | Vic   | Qld | SA  | WA  | Tas | Total |
|------|---------|-------|-----|-----|-----|-----|-------|
| 1920 | 1,377   | 1,530 | 411 | 349 | 207 | 148 | 4,022 |
| 1925 | 1,904   | 1,730 | 560 | 434 | 260 | 158 | 5,046 |
| 1930 | 2,152   | 1,975 | 579 | 445 | 314 | 184 | 5,649 |
| 1935 | 2,158   | 1,985 | 640 | 480 | 345 | 181 | 5,789 |
| 1940 | 2,516   | 2,367 | 632 | 527 | 372 | 254 | 6,668 |
| 1945 | 3,000[a]| 2,749 | 803 | 883 | 430 | 317 | 8,182 |

[a]    Estimate of numbers resident in NSW.

An attempt has been made to exclude those doctors registered in more than one state, however these statistics remain very approximate. Most states automatically reregistered medical practitioners each year; little attempt was made to check whether they were still in active practice. Only Queensland and South Australia required an annual fee for reregistration. In 1951 a Commonwealth survey found that only 269 doctors were in active practice in Tasmania, although 465 were registered. On the inaccuracy of figures see *Medical Journal of Australia*, 27 March 1920 and 25 October 1930; 'The Capacity of a Region to Employ Doctors', 31 Aug. 1951, AA CRS A1658 611/1/13.

**Table 1.7** Population per Registered Medical Practitioner by State, 1920–1945

|      | NSW   | Vic   | Qld   | SA    | WA    | Tas   | Total |
|------|-------|-------|-------|-------|-------|-------|-------|
| 1920 | 1,519 | 1,001 | 1,826 | 1,407 | 1,621 | 1,438 | 1,345 |
| 1925 | 1,208 | 966   | 1,538 | 1,271 | 1,280 | 1,374 | 1,188 |
| 1930 | 1,152 | 904   | 1,583 | 1,308 | 1,340 | 1,199 | 1,151 |
| 1935 | 1,232 | 931   | 1,518 | 1,223 | 1,290 | 1,287 | 1,145 |
| 1940 | 1,109 | 810   | 1,632 | 1,135 | 1,259 | 957   | 1,061 |
| 1945 | 978   | 749   | 1,351 | 716   | 1,144 | 787   | 926   |

Source: *Government Gazettes*.

Note: Calculated on estimated population of each state, divided by the number of registered medical practitioners.

# CHAPTER 2

# National Hygiene and Nationalization: the Failure of a Federal Health Policy, 1918–1939

I well remember that, after the last war, my medical colleagues returned to Australia filled with a desire to apply to the civil community the great lessons of successful medical control and prevention of disease which had been applied in the army. I remember, too, the progressive sense of depression and disillusion with which they came to realize that there was no place for such measures in the civil social system.

Dr J.H.L.Cumpston, Commonwealth Director-General of Health, 1921-45.[1]

The interwar years saw the emergence of health care as a national political issue in Australia. While debate within the medical profession remained dominated by the immediate economic questions of markets, incomes and demarcation disputes between specialists and general practitioners, the upheavals of the First World War placed new intellectual and administrative problems at the centre of debate. Medical and population policy as the means to national renewal dominated thinking amongst public health doctors and a wide section of the medical profession. Stimulated by wartime experiments in medical control, this new public health lobby urged that the power of the state be harnessed to the wider project of health education and preventive medicine.

'National hygiene' was to be attained by the medical regulation of all stages of family life, from pregnancy through child rearing and nutrition, in order to build a superior Australian race. Drawing on earlier British concerns for building national efficiency through health reform, the national hygienists developed a vision of national destiny which linked a multitude of population and developmental questions – from the settlement of the tropics and remote areas to the physique and military potential of slum dwellers – to medical control. Although major differences existed between state health officials and the private profession over how far the state should impinge on private practice and the relative powers of local, state and federal governments, there was wide support for a permeation of national policy objectives by medical considerations. A 'nationalization' of health would not abolish private practice but instead place public health, population policy and preventive health care at the centre of national policy. At the same time, 'nationalization' implied major changes in administrative structures, the assumption of greater responsibilities by the federal government, co-ordinating the activities of the states and forging the subordination of 'curative' private practice to 'preventive' state medicine.[2]

The term 'preventive medicine' only gained general currency during and after the war, displacing the older term 'public hygiene' and its connotations of municipal nuisance inspections, with a notion of public health claiming a central place in the medical curriculum and directly challenging the dominant mode of medical practice.[3] Although this implied major changes to the conduct of private medical practice – its subordination to national policy objectives – it did not mean the abolition of the market nor radical reform of access to hospital and other institutional care. Instead, the new public health concentrated on using administrative means to re-place the emphasis on curative medical care within the whole health system. Public health policy was to shift from the policing functions of sanitary reform towards modifying the behaviour of individuals through education and other forms of social control.

## Progressives, liberals and national hygiene

During the interwar years this realignment of the boundaries of public and private medicine became a major administrative and political project for a key group of public health doctors in Commonwealth and state employ. The most influential figures were men who entered public health administration before the First World War. J.H.L. Cumpston was director of the Western Australian department of health before becoming head of the Commonwealth's Quarantine Service in 1911. Similarly, J.S.C. Elkington had been the Queensland Commissioner for Public Health but, despairing of a consistent and resolute public health policy at state level, he also joined the service of the Commonwealth as Queensland's Chief Quarantine

Officer. Harvey Sutton, who had been in the same year as Cumpston at the University of Melbourne medical school, directed school medical services in Victoria from 1909 to 1915 and then became chief medical officer of the New South Wales Education Department during the 1920s, retaining strong links with his Commonwealth colleagues to become the first director of the Commonwealth School of Public Health and Tropical Medicine in 1930. During the war years and the 1920s these men worked closely with leaders of the private profession, such as Dr Frank Hone of Adelaide and Sir George Syme in Melbourne, to persuade the federal government to establish institutions capable of developing health policies at national level. When the Commonwealth Department of Health was formed in 1921 it seemed the first instalment of this dream.[4]

Michael Roe has recently argued that these leading lights of public health policy took their lead from the wider politics of 'progressivism'. Linking Cumpston and Elkington to exponents of liberal reform in other areas of national life such as A.F. Piddington and R.F. Irvine, he has suggested that they constitute a coherent non-socialist tradition advocating social progress through enlightened state intervention. As with American progressivism and the British movement for 'national efficiency', these men shared a concern for the preservation of racial vitality and the strengthening of the nation. Roe suggests an affinity between the modernism of his progressives – united by a philosophical vitalism drawn from Nietzsche, Bergson and James – and the irrationalist deification of race and nation of interwar fascism. Hence, in his lectures to students at the School of Tropical Medicine and Public Health at Sydney University Harvey Sutton argued for the compulsory sterilization of the 'unfit' so as to improve progressively the 'inherited worth' of human beings and guard 'against degeneration of the race by great numbers and proportion of "duds"' and thus encourage the breeding of a superior 'national type'.[5]

This notion of 'progressivism' remains rather vague and all-embracing. Such attempts to subsume non-socialist political thought between the wars into a single general category such as 'liberalism' obscure real distinctions between individuals and social groups. As will be seen, there were major differences between medical reformers and laymen over the correct scope of state action in achieving a national health policy: where the national hygienists saw the development of centralized state co-ordinated public health services as the only viable path to national health, liberals such as Piddington placed their faith in national insurance schemes, increasing access to the existing framework of services. While most liberals shared, in some form, a belief in the need for eugenic reform, a closer examination again shows deep divisions. The language of eugenics was a pervasive discourse which structured most interwar debate on the relationship between the health of individuals and the national welfare, and could accommodate radically different mixtures of environmental and genetic determinism.[6]

In a suggestive study of the political and philosophical ideas of interwar public health administrators John Powles has pointed to some of the distinctive features of the 'national hygienists'. 'National hygiene' was based on a philosophical 'naturalism', a strong belief in fixed laws of nature which governed the rival destinies of races. Naturalism placed a special responsibility on physicians as the guardians of the racial health of the nation, an attitude which easily incorporated support for the doctrines of scientific racism prevalent in most western countries. In its more conservative forms this eugenism and racism had been used to justify social inequality and racial domination. Powles follows Roe in suggesting a natural affinity between national hygiene and fascism — again, a position which relies heavily on some rather abstract parallels. He accepts, however, that the sympathies of most of the Australian national hygienists lay more with British scientific racialism than with the mysticism of Nazism. This captures much of the distinctive flavour of the political thought of the public health movement, and helps to explain the sharp divergences which developed between mainstream liberalism and the advocates of a medically-controlled national health policy during the 1930s and 1940s. It recognizes that, above all else, Cumpston and his colleagues had an almost religious sense of calling to their medical work. All these senior state officials had sacrificed potentially lucrative careers in private practice for an often soul-destroying life of never-ending battles with an indifferent public and short-sighted recalcitrant politicians. Their political and professional judgements must be understood primarily within this closed medical discourse.[7]

The national hygienists were distinguished from other currents of liberal collectivism and from the individualism and anti-statist attitudes of most medical practitioners by a medical materialism, which saw political and economic phenomena as the social manifestations of more fundamental medical causes. Only positive action by the state, under the control of medical experts, could remedy these problems.[8] In this view, the relative success of the white settlement of the tropics of north Queensland was not primarily a question of the economics of land settlement, migration and the development of viable export industries but the result of '(1) The successful institution of adequate measures of preventive medicine; (2) the exclusion of races with lower standards of life and higher rates of disease and reproduction; and (3) the continual increase in locally born inhabitants'.[9] The settlement of the north was seen as a medical question, to be resolved by research and propaganda on the endemic diseases of north Australia and the diet and sanitary habits of settlers.

Similarly, the fall in the birth rate and Australia's impending 'race suicide' could only be averted by strengthening the medical direction of reproduction and child rearing. Like the eugenism which dominated interwar debates on population questions, medical materialism provided a linguistic terrain which was traversed to different political ends. At the one time it informed the mild reformism of the social medicine of the 1930s, calling for slum clearance, improved nutrition and programmes of national fitness as well as the racialist theories of national regeneration associated with Elkington, Harvey Sutton and Raphael Cilento.[10]

Concern for national regeneration led to support for a stronger state. 'Strategic demography', the search for medical solutions for population decline, in turn identified with national vitality, dominated public health debates of the interwar years. As an immediate defence priority, Sutton argued for the compulsory medical examination of every male child at the ages of six and thirteen. In its most articulate form, in the work and writings of Sir Raphael Cilento, it spilled over into anti-democratic politics. Cilento's sympathies with fascist Italy and Nazi Germany were more open and extreme than those of most of his colleagues. Unlike other fellow travellers of the right, he did not draw back from calling for Australia to follow their example: 'Italy shews what a new "Augustan age" it might be with leadership and inspiration...It makes life seem real to have such an objective'. Increased state control was seen as 'the natural expression of the fact that the health of each individual is an asset to the State as well as to the individual'.[11]

Indeed, this sympathy for the 'strong state' and an identification of race and nation was shared by a wider range of medical and social leaders. Sir Herbert Schlink, of the Royal Prince Alfred Hospital in Sydney, combined antipathy to state intervention in Australian medical practice with admiration for the 'honest leadership' and discipline of Hitler's Germany and Mussolini's Italy. Much of this apparent sympathy for European authoritarianism must be seen in the context of a general ignorance of the exact content of fascist

policies, and comparison of the vacillations of Australian governments unwilling or unable to assert a national vision of public health
against resistance from sectional interests. Hence many, including
Cilento, were prepared to draw on examples from the Soviet Union
when it suited their purposes: illustrating the need for firm government guided by experts. At the same time, support for a strong
Australian state did not necessarily imply anti-democratic sentiments. Cumpston's long advocacy of an enhanced state role in public
health did not extend to advocacy of more authoritarian government
in other aspects of national life. He managed to offend the more
zealous advocates of state control by arguing that, even if desirable,
eugenic programmes were administratively and politically unrealistic
in the Australian political system.[12]

The programmes of national hygiene were formed in a context in
which the development and co-ordination of the machinery of public
health administration in the states was minimal and, at a national
level, non-existent. Public health, except for quarantine, remained a
state responsibility, suffering from financial neglect, tempered by an
occasional surge of activity during the panic of a severe epidemic.
The danger past, it quickly reverted to lethargy. In most states
administration of public health, reporting of infectious disease and
the enforcement of sanitary regulations lay in the reluctant hands of
weak local authorities. Dependent on a narrow revenue base of
property rates and subsidies from parsimonious state governments,
most local councils did only the minimum to enforce the law. Despite
repeated calls for more centralized public health administration from
their own professional leaders in the BMA, general practitioners
resisted carrying out their statutory duties to report notifiable diseases
to the state health authorities. To compound the problem, the
medical profession, whatever its public avowals, regarded public
health work as a markedly inferior area of activity, its administrators
poorly paid servants of state governments determined to undermine
professional autonomy.[13]

## The Commonwealth Department of Health and a national health policy

The formation of the Commonwealth Department of Health in 1921
was a crucial event in the development of the new politics of public
health. It set the problem of co-ordination, the formation of a new
relationship between state medicine and private practice, at the heart
of its programme and recruited many of the most forceful advocates

of a greater state role in health. The new department was permeated by a deep sense of Australian nationalism, reinforcing a conviction that the political fragmentation imposed by federalism was a barrier to effective health policies. As Cumpston recalled in a speech made just after his retirement in 1945:

> Whatever action has been taken by the Commonwealth Department of Health, and criticized in some quarters as being 'outside the Constitution', has been directed to some aspect of national needs and has been no more than an intelligent anticipation of that time when the disjointed Australian communities will honestly admit the truth that they have a joint as well as a several liability.[14]

The origins of the department lay in the deep political changes of the war years: the new powers taken on by the federal government and a wide popular support for an active national policy in broader areas of social life. Although the project of a national department of health had been shared by many public health administrators it required the crisis of war, and an offer of funding from the International Health Board of the Rockefeller Foundation to achieve action from governments. The medical problems of war, and the fears of the diseases returning servicemen might bring home with them from the Middle East and New Guinea added urgency to calls for a stronger central government role. In 1916, faced with a crisis in drug supplies, the Commonwealth government established the Commonwealth Serum Laboratories in Melbourne to manufacture and distribute sera not otherwise available. The ground for a wider federal part in postwar health policy was strengthened by the work of the Committee Concerning the Causes of Death and Invalidity in the Commonwealth, which completed a comprehensive series of reports covering such issues as infantile mortality, venereal disease, 'the risks of middle age' and tuberculosis. At the same time, wartime experiences had encouraged a new interest in planning to solve social problems and many shared the faith of C.E.W. Bean, the war correspondent and historian, who called on Australians to construct a more just postwar social order, declaring that 'The lesson of the war was that by organization you can do anything'.[15]

The fiasco occasioned by attempts to use existing administrative agencies to control the spread of the 1919 Spanish influenza epidemic showed the limits of Bean's dictum in the absence of national co-ordination. Rival state governments withheld vital information on the spread of the disease and closed their borders in a vain attempt to keep out infection. The national scandal – and Cumpston's judicious use of the crisis to support his claims for a strong co-ordinating role – cleared the way to complete Commonwealth control under the Quarantine Act of 1920 and the quarantine service became the administrative backbone of the department.[16]

The new faith in planning and state intervention was especially strong in the ranks of the former army medical officers from whom a new generation of public health officials was recruited. Having received their first experiences of medical practice in army sanitary administration, many remained in state employment in the face of the oversupply of repatriated medical officers after the war. They brought with them a strong faith in the efficacy of central state regulation which long outlived the enthusiasm for planning in other areas of society. Advocates of the more centralized approach used military metaphors to emphasize the need for a strong authority and a strict hierarchy and to draw parallels between the achievements of military sanitary administration and the problems of civilian life. In 1920 the Australasian Medical Congress in Brisbane resolved that, 'the real principles which underlay the success of Military Public Health Administration during the Great War can be readily adapted to civil life', conditional on sufficiently powerful 'control by a Central (Commonwealth) Authority, directing public health activities through an expert medical staff and co-ordinating action and legislation between States'. These views were echoed by some private practitioners, such as Dr J. Corbin of Adelaide who argued that a national medical service, financed by compulsory health insurance, should be based on the model of the army medical corps as:

> the full possibilities of the scientific medical world is made available for the treatment of every individual in the whole army, regardless of social rank, army rank or financial status. And each and every item in this great service is by means of an excellent administration made available for the sick and wounded at the earliest possible moment.[17]

Hence the Commonwealth Department of Health nurtured aims far more ambitious than its limited administrative base would suggest. Its leading lights, such as Cumpston, Elkington and Raphael Cilento, shared the vision of a widened public health policy as the basis for national regeneration, adopting three main priorities: initiating research and treatment of the medical problems of tropical Australia; establishing a national chain of public health laboratories based in provincial and rural centres to provide diagnostic facilities to local doctors and to educate them in the latest techniques. Finally, the department was to carry out surveys on problems of industrial disease and hygiene. Its administrative divisions embodied the main elements of the project of a new national public health. While the divisions of marine hygiene and plant quarantine developed the established powers and interests of the Commonwealth government, plans for divisions of epidemiology, tuberculosis and venereal disease, public health engineering, industrial hygiene, maternal and infant welfare and tropical hygiene indicate the range of public health areas within its ambit.

Each of these projects was grounded in a new conception of the relationship between public health and the private practice of medicine. 'Nationalization' (a word for which Cumpston professed some disdain) was identified not with the abolition of the private market for medical care, but with the subordination of the general practitioner to the requirements of a centrally-directed public health policy. The existing structure of private practice was criticized for its excessive individualism; administrative reform would achieve a new relationship between the medical practitioner and the state. Consistent reporting of disease, research into its causes and supervision of the official response were to be achieved by new hierarchical forms of supervision of health authorities and general practitioners. This did not imply direct state control over the content of private practice. The acceptance of the independence of the private practitioner came in part from the conservatism of the public medical officers; however, it also came from a confidence that the widening of the sphere of state and preventive medicine would eventually reduce the demand for curative services by eliminating the roots of much disease. While there would always be a place for private medical practice, this would 'naturally diminish in proportion as the efforts of the doctor to prevent disease were successful'. The state would pay a growing proportion of medical incomes as the importance of preventive medicine increased.[18]

In 1920 Cumpston summarized the national hygienists' programme in an address to the public health section of the Australasian Medical Congress, arguing that the first line of defence in any improved system of preventive public health must be:

> the general practitioner, who must, under the direction and supervision of the trained district and central staffs, accept the responsibility for all those measures of preventive medicine which can be applied in the home and must be prepared to accept the responsibility for failure to require or carry out prescribed or obvious measures of prevention. This means a greatly increased range of duties performed for the State and may involve

possibly a readjustment of financial values of professional sources in many directions.

Briefly, the health department must say what should be done and the local government authorities and the medical profession, each in their sphere, must do it. The central health authority should have power to see that they do their duty and, clearly, the association between the preventive and curative branches of the profession must be intimate.[19]

The general practitioner was to play a central part in Cumpston's schemes of national health policy. He described 'my favourite ambition – to see every medical practitioner saddled with a definite responsibility for many functions in public health, and an orderly scheme of devolutionized local administration with paternal central supervision'.[20]

Prewar medical practice had been marked by a cultural lag between the advances of medical science and their application in therapeutic practice. For Cumpston, the major task before the department was to bridge this gap. In the view of the federal government's health administrators the sphere of public and preventive health should embrace previously sacrosanct areas of private practice. The inability of general practitioners to remain abreast of the growing complexity of diagnostic equipment and the barriers of cost and knowledge inhibiting the application of advances in medical research meant that a collective solution was necessary. Hence, while the financial relationship between doctor and patient would remain undisturbed, the content of practice, its relationship to public health administration and the doctor's access to and use of laboratory medicine were to be profoundly redirected. In the large cities this responsibility was already fulfilled by the state-subsidized public hospitals, but rural and provincial areas were falling behind. Few practitioners outside the big cities had access to x-rays, and climatic problems made it very difficult to send cultures or specimens for pathological examination. In addition, many practitioners resisted the new diagnostic technologies, which were seen as the entering wedge of specialization that would destroy the basis of general practice. In 1930 the Melbourne Permanent Committee for Post-Graduate Work was warning its mainly general practitioner audience that 'the use of the chemical laboratory as an aid to diagnosis is very limited, and only in a few conditions are the results of any real value'.[21]

To remedy these deficiencies, Cumpston argued, 'the idea of laboratory work...[is] the most important thing to be undertaken in Australia in connection with public health at the present time'. The energies of doctors would be harnessed to the cause of public health by establishing a chain of public health laboratories in rural areas, providing decentralized pathology services and a distribution network for the products of the Commonwealth Serum Laboratories (CSL). The laboratories were to form the 'first line' in the longer-term project of the subordination of medical practice to preventive medicine and the introduction of more advanced scientific methods to a sceptical profession. Referring to the British Dawson Report of 1919, he suggested that in this way 'the English system of Primary Health Centres would be commenced, and a beginning made in the application of scientific knowledge to the practice of medicine for the prevention and cure of disease'.[22]

Given the Commonwealth government's lack of formal constitutional powers over health policy, the laboratories were constructed and officially justified as part of the nation's quarantine defences. Commonwealth health laboratories, however, were soon playing an active part in research in industrial hygiene (at the Bendigo, Port Pirie and Kalgoorlie laboratories) and in the Australian Hookworm Campaign initiated by the International Health Board of the Rockefeller Foundation (at Lismore, Townsville, Rockhampton and Rabaul). In Bendigo, the assistance of local medical practitioners was enlisted to carry out mass swabs of school children for the early identification of diphtheria and a test of immunization with CSL produced toxin anti-toxin on a mass scale.[23]

The second major national project of the department was the investigation and encouragement of white settlement in the tropics. In 1920 Cumpston had argued that 'at this stage in the national development [few things are of] more importance to Australia than the maintenance of White Australia. As the Medical Congress pointed out, this policy is bound to fail unless a properly organized scheme of control of disease is brought into operation without delay'. A tropical medical service could, he argued, reverse the precipitate decline of the populations of Melanesia, opening the field for the economic development of Australian interests in Papua and New Guinea. The medical knowledge gained could be used to encourage white settlement of tropical Australia, to prepare for the inevitable clash between the white and yellow races in the Pacific. The Division of Tropical Hygiene and the Australian Hookworm Campaign based on their connection with the International Health Board of the Rockefeller Foundation were justified by the conviction that the promotion of health in the Australian tropics was the precondition for national vitality.[24]

These views had had a wide currency since Federation and an institutional embodiment since 1909 when the Commonwealth government established the Australian Institute of Tropical Medicine in Townsville. Elkington's support for the project of a Common-wealth Department of Health rested on the need for a stronger authority for the North; he became the first director of the division of tropical hygiene and Raphael Cilento, his protege and successor, carried the concentration on tropical hygiene even further. The division's project involved research into tropical disease, but from the start it asserted a more ambitious goal of altering the attitudes of all Australians on the development of the tropical North, arguing that 'The whole problem of civilization in any region consists in the degree to which endemic disease can be controlled, modified by the ease by which the human organism can adapt itself to the situation'.[25]

Despite having some suspicions concerning the ultimate aims of the Commonwealth, the new department won the wary support of the British Medical Association for these early projects. The Federal Committee of the BMA declared in 1920 that a strong Common-wealth Department of Health could co-ordinate the extension of uniform public health services throughout Australia and:

> In many other directions, e.g., in connection with Infant Welfare work, prevention of puerperal mortalities, treatment of ascertained defects in school children, the practising profession as a whole could be included in a comprehensive scheme under the general direction of the Health Department for the improvement of the standard of community health.
>
> By means such as the above a great advance could be made in the direction of making preventive medicine an organic part of the practice of medicine generally, without affecting the independence of the practitioner, an advance which would give effect to the desires of those who wish to see the medical profession more actively concerned with the prevention of disease than is the case at present.
>
> For all such services payments should be made according to an approved scale. There should be corresponding responsibilities both on the Profession and on the State. The Profession would need to be prepared for the imposition of penalties for failure to observe prescribed methods, and the State would have to supply a Health Organization which would command the confidence of the profession in its own domain, and would have to provide the necessary laboratories, wholetime advisory health officers, and similar accessories.[26]

This did not mean that the BMA saw any legitimate scope for the direct involvement of the Commonwealth in private practice. The Federal Committee insisted that any national scheme must recognize that 'there is an essential difference between curative medicine and preventive medicine and that they should be kept distinct in any scheme which may be devised to meet present-day needs'.[27]

## National hygiene or social welfare?

The programmes of national hygiene were developed within a con-sensus shared by the department and much of the medical profession. Questions of the finances and access to medical care were outside the proper sphere of public health policy. The federal government's medical officers accepted the medical profession's aversion to state intervention in medical matters based on cash benefits rather than 'institutional supervision' by medical practitioners. Instead, govern-ment benefit schemes should bind recipients to specific medically-controlled courses of treatment. Child endowment, maternity allowances and invalid pensions were attacked as achieving far less than similar expenditure on the direct provision of services. Cump-ston criticized the invalid pension as 'unbusinesslike'. Although many of its beneficiaries suffered from preventable diseases, little was spent on prevention or rehabilitation. The pension gave victims of tuberculosis the means to remain active in the community, avoiding medical treatment and strict segregation, as pension payments to the sufferer were drastically reduced on admission to hospital or a sana-torium. Similarly, when the department reluctantly conceded that a child endowment cash benefit was inevitable, its officials warned that the scheme should be calculated according to the costs of meeting the nutritional needs of the child. They warned against creating a nexus between child endowment and the basic wage which would tie it to the vagaries of the industrial relations system.[28]

Given this hostility to cash benefits, proposals for a national health insurance system along British lines met with opposition from both the British Medical Association and the Commonwealth Department. From 1925 to 1927 the Royal Commission on National Insurance examined the possibilities of introducing a scheme of con-tributory unemployment, health and sickness insurance at a national level. The Commissioners' *First Interim Report* into sickness, invalid-ity and maternity benefits bowed to this resistance, accepting the profession's arguments that any system of national health insurance should be strictly separated from social welfare or national insurance to ensure a strong medical voice in its control and that it was not eroded by pensions or sickness benefits drawing on the same funds.[29]

In response to the moves for national health insurance, Cumpston worked closely with sympathizers in the BMA to change the terms of public debate. With the support of his Minister, Sir Neville Howse (the former Director-General of Army Medical Services) and Dr Earle Page (the medically-trained Federal Treasurer), a Royal Commission on Health was established in 1925. Although two lay commissioners were appointed, the membership was dominated by medical practitioners. Sir George Syme, the chairman, was a leading Melbourne surgeon, Dr R.H. Todd, the Federal Secretary of the BMA and Dr Frank Hone, who combined his post as Commonwealth Quarantine Officer for South Australia with private practice, played the leading role in drafting the recommendations of the report. The unity between the department's priorities and those of the leading circles of the BMA were underlined when Hone was nominated to the Commission by both the Department and by the South Australian and Queensland branches of the BMA.[30]

Dominated by the BMA, the work of the Royal Commission has been seen as an essentially conservative project, restricting state intervention in public health to those areas which were unprofitable to the private profession, forging a new charter rigidly demarcating the public and private sectors. This view underestimates the independence of men such as Hone and Syme. The former had played an active role in the formation of the Commonwealth Department, served as a part-time quarantine officer in Adelaide in the early 1920s and remained personally and intellectually close to Cumpston throughout the interwar years and in no way a mere puppet of the BMA. The Commission's implicit rejection of state-sponsored health insurance as the best route to national health, while congruent with the prejudices of the BMA, did not mean a repudiation of state intervention. Instead of identifying the problem of public health as a question of financial access to curative medicine, the Commission concentrated on the relationship between curative and preventive medicine. Confirming the tendency of national hygiene to seek administrative solutions to all public health questions, this balance was to be redressed by state action. National health could best be advanced by setting public health at the centre of medical practice, not by introducing cash benefit schemes which merely confirmed the existing pattern of medical services.

To achieve this centralized co-ordination the main objective of the Commission, and the seed of its ultimate failure, lay in its attempt to erode the states' control of public health. The report called for the national co-ordination of health services with a hierarchy extending from the Commonwealth Department of Health. Following the model which Cumpston had been advocating, the federal level would set general policy objectives to be implemented by state health councils and regional district administrations. Public and private practice would be integrated through publicly-financed pathology laboratories, radiology clinics, baby and child welfare centres. These regional centres would provide the focus for co-ordinating the work of general practitioners and medical officers of health to bridge the sharp line between curative medicine and preventive health.

Recognizing state hostility to this enhanced administrative role for the Commonwealth (the New South Wales government had already refused to release Harvey Sutton for service as a commissioner), the Royal Commission avoided many of the more difficult questions. The relationship between the national administration of public health and the state-run public hospitals was not broached. Although the report did not deal directly with national health insurance, it expressed opposition to cash benefit programmes outside medical control and hostility to any state encroachment on the finance of personal medical services, outside an enhanced public health function. Despite the attempt to redefine the relationship between state intervention in public health and private medical services the findings of the Royal Commission went largely unnoticed. A Federal Health Council was established to provide a forum for consultations between the Commonwealth and state health departments. With this exception, little resulted from the Commission's labours.[31]

In the wake of the Royal Commission much of the direction departed from the department. The grand scheme of national co-ordination had resulted in the toothless Federal Health Council while the state governments resisted Commonwealth projects as encroachments on their prerogatives. James Stopford, the Queensland Home Secretary, argued that they represented 'nothing more than an attempt on the part of Dr Cumpston to carry into effect what he had for a long while intended, namely, the control of the health services of Queensland'. In 1929 Dr M.J. Holmes, the director of the Department's Division of Tuberculosis, prepared an ambitious and farsighted scheme for the control of tuberculosis for presentation by the Federal Health Council. Following the Royal Commission's hierarchical model, the scheme required the federal department to co-ordinate state and local government services to achieve earlier notification and isolation of sufferers. General practitioners would be required to report cases in return for payments from the Commonwealth for their tuberculosis work for the indigent. Again, the scheme came up against the brick wall of non-co-operation by the states. Holmes' plans were abandoned for two decades, only to be revived after another world war as the basis of a national scheme which enlisted state and local governments in a comprehensive programme of screening and notification of infection.[32]

The failure of the department to realize its more ambitious projects stemmed directly from its dependence on co-operation from the states. In the absence of a constitutional federal health power, other than quarantine, the department was left in an anomalous position, marginalized within the federal bureaucracy. Even during the confident years of the 1920s the politics of federalism had set firm limits on the success of the department's initiatives. The bait of Rockefeller funds lured New South Wales and Queensland into co-operation with the joint Australian Hookworm Campaign and several of the public health laboratories conducted epidemiological studies on a small scale, but both these schemes were faced with continual suspicion and obstruction from state and local officials. The laboratory programme brought out some of the differences between the aims of the national hygienists and the views of an older generation of health administrators. In 1928 Ramsay Smith, the Director of Public Health in South Australia since 1898, told the Royal Commission on the Constitution that the construction of Commonwealth laboratories was a clear infringement of state rights – although under questioning he admitted that he had no idea of the functions performed by the Port Pirie laboratory in his own state. More adventurous state and local government medical officers, such as John Dale, Melbourne's medical officer of health, objected to the laboratory scheme on the grounds that the resources could be used more effectively under local control.[33]

Of the other major divisions of the department, industrial hygiene received considerable resources during the 1920s, but state obstruction again meant that it was restricted to research in a few statutory corporations and within the public service. In 1930 a Division of Maternal and Infant Welfare was approved after a report by Dame Janet Campbell, of the British Ministry of Health, stressed the need for the 'effective supervision of maternity'. An early victim of the great depression, this division was never staffed. Outside these limited activities the Commonwealth's health officers were restricted to campaigns of education and exhortation.[34]

This institutional weakness was apparent in the cavalier manner in which the Commonwealth Treasury excluded the Department of Health from active participation in discussions of the national health insurance scheme. Cumpston responded to this snub with a plaintive and unheeded plea that the federal government use the department as its main technical adviser on specialized health questions, with an authority in medical matters comparable with that of the Treasury in financial matters:

> no matter of finance can be dealt with by any Department except under Treasury direction and approval; no matter of works construction can be carried out except by the Department of Works and Railways but every Department is at present presumed to be competent to deal with all medical questions. This is quite wrong.
>
> The system should be such that every medical question dealt with by any Department should come under review for approval by the Health Department just as the Treasury now controls finance.
>
> Especially it should be clearly laid down in connection with the Insurance scheme that no new medical service should be created but that the medical work under the Insurance scheme should be entrusted to the Health Department and that the Act should be so drafted as to make this definite.[35]

The atrophy of the programme of national hygiene was even more apparent in the exclusion of the department from the one area in which the Commonwealth became a major direct provider of health services. From its establishment in April 1918 the Repatriation Commission controlled a large medical service. The work of its medical section was initially confined to treatment of discharged nurses, sailors and soldiers for disabilities due to or aggravated by war service. At the end of the war the Commission inherited former military hospitals in most capital cities, and although most of these were rather basic hutments, they provided inpatient and outpatient services for an increasing number of ex-service personnel without the means testing of the public hospital system. During the 1930s, the numbers of ex-servicemen and women eligible for treatment grew, with a widening of the definition of 'war related disability' to those suffering from tuberculosis. The repatriation medical services, however, remained strictly separate from the formulation and administration of other aspects of Commonwealth health policy. Even in his most ambitious moments, Cumpston does not appear to have contemplated bringing these medical services under the control of his department, and in the discussion of potential control of hospital services by the Commonwealth during the 1940s there was no suggestion of using the model or experience of the Repatriation Commission.[36]

The attempt to develop state intervention in health on a Commonwealth level had stalled by the end of the 1920s. Elkington resigned in despair in 1925 and the department spent the next decade fighting for survival. As one of the weakest federal departments it weathered the depression retrenchments of 1932 only at the cost of most of its administrative programmes outside quarantine and the supervision of medical examinations of Commonwealth public servants and invalid pensioners. The divisional structure of the department, which embodied its commitment to areas such as tropical and industrial hygiene, was abolished. Although the public health laboratories survived, financial constraints and a scandal in 1928 which followed the death of twelve children in Bundaberg who had been immunized with contaminated diphtheria toxin-antitoxin supplied by CSL, helped to block the further expansion of the laboratories. Meanwhile, the vision of the laboratories as the nuclei of a national network of health centres, integrating general practice and public health, had foundered in the combination of lack of interest from the medical profession and inadequate leadership from the department's local officers. A report by Cilento on the future of the Australian Institute of Tropical Medicine in Townsville, once the linchpin of Commonwealth activities in the far north, argued that the 'propaganda' role of the Institute had been allowed to slide so badly that it no longer provided authoritative leadership to the local medical profession. To his disgust, a local branch of the BMA had been formed and was allowed to meet in the Institute's offices. Cilento followed his mentor out of the department in 1934, taking service with the Queensland government. The vision of the Commonwealth forging a new relationship between public health and medical practice appeared moribund. By the late 1920s Frank Anstey, one of the more able Commonwealth ministers of health, remarked that his department required of its minister 'neither brains nor energy'.[37]

## The National Health and Medical Research Council and the new social medicine

When restrictions on government activities eased in the mid 1930s the department returned to some of its earlier projects, but with a less confident air. The emphasis shifted to co-operation with the states, developing more elaborate machinery for co-ordination to encourage state activities in public health, rather than developing a direct Commonwealth role. The Commonwealth Department of Health maintained its disinterest in policy questions of health finance and was completely excluded from the intense debate over the Lyons government's ill-fated national health insurance scheme. The planning and politicking for the scheme were left firmly in the hands of the members of Treasury and the National Insurance Commission.

If the chances of presiding over a realignment of medical practice seemed more remote, this did not mean that Cumpston or his department had abandoned the main elements of the national hygienists' programme. The emphasis on the integration of the general practitioner within public health administration remained central. Harvey Sutton, now the director of the University of Sydney's School of Public Health and Tropical Medicine (financed and controlled by the Commonwealth department from 1930), took this as his major theme in lectures for the diploma of public health: 'the chief unit in future health work is the general practitioner. He is the front line for attack and defence'.[38]

The projects of the early 1920s seemed vindicated by the social and intellectual climate of the late 1930s. Public debate on the future direction of Australian society was dominated by a more confident middle class liberalism. Calls for the application of education, rationality and 'thought' to political processes and for disinterested rule by experts revived the themes of the national hygienists. The rediscovery of inner-urban slums, the need for planning of cities and other areas of social life intersected with the priorities of medical men and women concerned about the effects of economic hardship on public health.[39]

The legitimacy of a socially concerned health policy received a new underpinning as a new 'social medicine' penetrated Australian medical circles. If advances of bacteriology had inspired the new public health of the early twentieth century, physiology was the major source of influence in the 1920s and 1930s. Etheridge has shown the manner in which the identification of pellagra in the United States as a disease of nutritional deficiency helped to touch off a wave of research into other deficiency diseases. By the 1930s this had become the major theme of public health research and debate in Britain and the United States. The world-wide depression added an additional political dimension: the adequacy of relief policies for meeting the minimum nutritional requirements of the unemployed and their dependants.[40]

This shift in medical thought had two important consequences for the practice of public health in Australia. First, it confirmed the move of public health away from a narrow concentration on problems of infectious and epidemic disease to a concern with wider questions of diet and lifestyle. The regulation of foodstuffs shifted from merely policing adulteration and mislabelling to a recognition that nutrition could provide a unifying key to the prevention of disease. Second, this implied that the scope of public health must be widened beyond the narrow ambit of the laboratory. The focus of preventive health moved from sanitation and bacteriology to take in wider environmental questions. Although many public health authorities resisted the notion of a connection between unemployment, low family incomes and nutritional deficiencies, the warnings of two pioneering British investigators were increasingly heeded. 'As each fresh vista of investigation is scanned there looms up, dominating the problem, the question of the economic sufficiency of the group of individuals under consideration. Ignorance of the laws of health can be dissipated by education but economic stringency may negative the possibility of applying the newly acquired knowledge'.[41]

In Australia, social medicine was taken up enthusiastically by the national hygienists, an identification which was assisted by the ease with which it was assimilated to the existing model of preventive state medicine. The transition was thus summed up by Cilento as a progression from 'being plain "plague-scared", and then "drain conscious" and "pauper provident" in a superior sort of way, we have at last realised the possibilities inherent in being "health minded" in the social sense'.[42] Questions of nutrition had loomed large in the tropical medicine of the early 1920s, so its new place at the centre of public health debate confirmed the value of the now disbanded division of tropical hygiene. In Cilento's Livingstone Lectures of 1936 (delivered after he had left the Commonwealth Department to become Director-General of Health in Queensland) he provided a survey of the importance of nutrition in world history. Cilento employed an eclectic mixture of Malthus, Spengler and recent physiology to argue that only resolute action by the state could restore the balance between population numbers and nutrition. Lingering in the best medical materialist manner on the dietary causes of the collapse of the Roman Empire, he ascribed the 'hysteria and spasmophilic disorders', so frequent in cities, to calcium deficiencies:[43]

> food is so closely bound up with vitality, fertility, morbidity, and mortality, that it may be regarded as the most important of all the factors in the great parabola of the human life course...
>
> Every country, save Italy, Germany and Russia, shows a gradual fall in the birth rate. In these authoritarian States with their 250,000,000 white people, an effort is again being made to lead whole nations back into a balance between nutrition and numbers by the application of every aid that science can provide towards that objective...They have not overlooked the fact either, that man is something more than the series of tables provided by his chemical, physical, and physiological analyses. The 'Youth' movements, the 'Land-year', and all other actual and psycho-

logical aids, are being co-ordinated with the new necessities of the country, and the eyes of their rising youth are being deliberately deflected from the defeatism and decline associated with every ageing civilization to a new future of hope and advancement.[44]

Social medicine remained a rather vaguely linked set of doctrines, sharing the common stress on the complexity of the causation of disease and the importance of the environment. Most of the doctrines were imported from Britain, the United States and the Soviet Union. Although the original sources of inspiration were often based on detailed empirical epidemiological studies, Australian social medicine remained derivative. Much of its polemics were mere summaries or glosses on overseas research, with lessons drawn to suit the political preconceptions of the commentator. For Cilento, social medicine provided new material to feed his apocalyptical warnings of coming racial struggles for world power, but its influence was considerable across the political spectrum. On the more conservative side stood the rather vague environmentalist 'social pathology' of John Ryle, Professor of Social Medicine at Oxford and a regular correspondent of Cumpston.[45] On the left, Eric Dark, a socialist strongly influenced by the British social critics, M'Gonigle and other campaigning medical officers of health, produced several studies linking ill-health to unemployment and a capitalist social order. Again, his work relied heavily on British research, drawing little from Australian investigations and using the assumed superior record of the Soviet Union as a 'control'. More mainstream work treated unemployment, poor housing and low rates of unemployment relief as essential elements in the aetiology of diseases such as tuberculosis.[46]

The Commonwealth department responded to these new challenges by reviving its administrative schemes for the national co-ordination of public health. The key event in this new phase was the replacement of the ineffectual Federal Health Council with a stronger and more independent National Health and Medical Research Council (NHMRC). The NHMRC was an uneasy compromise between the demands of the medical profession for increased Commonwealth research funding and moves from within the health bureaucracy to revive the projects of the 1920s. The BMA and the universities had long campaigned for an independent organization modelled on the British Medical Research Committee (founded in 1912) to channel government grants for medical research. These proposals took shape in discussions at the 1935 BMA Congress in Melbourne and the Council's establishment was announced at the

7th Australian Cancer Conference the following year. Its initial funding was drawn from the Commonwealth's Jubilee Appeal for Maternal Welfare and Lord Nuffield's Gift for Crippled Children. This made it a measure 'which gave an impression of concern but cost little'. Consequently, W.M. Hughes, as Minister for Health, had little trouble winning Cabinet approval. The Commonwealth government established a fund of £15,000 for medical research. By 1938 this allocation had increased to the (still miserly) sum of £30,000.[47]

In contrast to its British equivalent, the NHMRC did not confine its activities to the support of research. From its inception the administrative problems of public health held a central place in the Council's activities. The importance of public health in the NHMRC's programme was underlined by its membership. Chaired by the Commonwealth Director-General of Health, the Council was dominated by the heads of the state public health departments, with minority representation from the two Royal Colleges, the BMA and the university medical schools. In addition, there were two lay members, including one woman. The organized medical profession showed some disquiet at this preponderance of state officials. While welcoming the new body, the BMA objected to the addition of the word 'Health' to its title and the broader interests that this implied beyond the funding of medical research. Even the Council's allocation of medical research funds was directed by public health officials. Academic researchers were a minority on the Reference Sub-Committee which allocated research funds.[48]

The programme of the NHMRC showed the strong influence of the new social medicine over Cumpston and the national hygienists. At the Council's first session, in Hobart in February 1937, Cumpston argued, 'We cannot say today that the governmental machine must stop at the "individual" barrier at any point, for the public has been educated to a stage at which it will not recognize close preserves for the Government and the private doctor respectively'. Preventive health, he argued, was to be the centre of the NHMRC's programme, leading to a 'widespread national campaign which will ensure complete and adequate supervision of an intelligent kind over the bodily health of infants, pre-school children and school children, over the physical culture of the school child and over the diet of the community'. The emphasis of public health shifted from disease control – still central in the national hygienists' programmes of the early 1920s – to 'the care and culture of the body of the infant and the school child, and his education and the care of his body'. The NHMRC was to be responsible for the 'control of medical practice' to ensure that general practitioners discharged their responsibilities in this task of supervision. Although the NHMRC programme of grants to individual researchers encouraged the development of academic medical research within the tight constraints of its budget, its main impact was in giving a new leadership in public health policy, providing state and Commonwealth health officials with a new and relatively independent platform.[49]

'Supervision of an intelligent kind' was extended in the direct activities of the department. Hughes, the Minister for Health for most of the period from 1934 to 1937, actively promoted the message that 'Australia must... populate or perish'. As a result, maternal and infant welfare ranked high in its priorities. Despite its lack of financial resources and constitutional powers, the department intervened in these areas by setting up demonstration schemes and encouraging state and voluntary activities. Reviving Dame Janet Campbell's scheme for Commonwealth involvement in the 'supervision of maternity', experimental Lady Gowrie infant welfare centres were established to train mothers in the care and instruction of the pre-school child. The centres also provided a focus for research on child health, providing the location for a major survey of the nutrition and growth of children sponsored by the Australian Institute of Anatomy during the war years.[50]

The most important initiative taken by the department was a study of nutritional problems. Established in February 1936 and integrated as a sub-committee of the NHMRC the following year, the Advisory Committee on Nutrition examined the effects of diet on national well-being. This initiative was informed by an intelligent opportunism on Cumpston's behalf. As with most public health officials, he had long learned the lesson that appeals to fear or cupidity were the best means to achieve action from politicians in an area where few votes were to be won. Many Australian politicians and economists had long lent their enthusiastic support to international calls for an expansion in world trade in foodstuffs to overcome malnutrition and the aftermath of years of world depression. Representing Australia at the League of Nations, in 1936 Stanley Bruce and Sir Frederick Stewart had been prominent in moves for a world campaign against malnutrition. Given Australia's position as producer of agricultural goods the political benefits of this attempt at 'marrying Agriculture and Health' were obvious. As an immediate response to the world campaign, at Cumpston's initiative the Advisory Committee on Nutrition was modelled on a British body with the same title. The Committee included Sir David Rivett and George Julius of the CSIR, and leading academic physiologists and biochemists: W.A. Osborne and S.M. Wadham (from the University of Melbourne), Sir C. Stanton Hicks (from Adelaide), D.H.K. Lee and Cilento (from Queensland) and C.G. Lambie and Henry Priestly (from Sydney – the latter as the nominee of the BMA). The Commonwealth Department of Health was represented by Cumpston and Harvey Sutton. The NHMRC took over the advisory committee's national survey of nutrition as its first major project.[51]

The revival of the programme of national hygiene was always present in the early work of the NHMRC, resisting attempts to restrict its activities to the sponsorship of pure scientific research. Cumpston worked in close but uneasy alliance with Sir Raphael Cilento, his former subordinate and current rival who represented Queensland as well as sponsoring similar work with the Queensland Nutrition Council. Cilento warned early in the project of the dangers in allowing research to become dominated by the academic interests of the physiologists on the committee. An emphasis on the quality of nutritional intake rather than on cruder measures based on quantity of intake could shift attention from 'the sort of thing the government would appreciate...indications upon which it might work towards the development of that association between public health and agriculture which Mr Bruce and subsequently Mr Hughes made so much of recently'.[52]

The committee confidently launched a nation-wide survey of nutritional intake, based on sketchy statistics drawn from a small and hastily assembled sample of households. An attempt at a household survey of diets ended in confusion as newspaper advertising and recruitment of volunteers through infant welfare centres resulted in a sample hopelessly biased towards more economically secure households. Its first report, in July 1936, revealed to the distress of its political sponsors that: 'no evidence is available to your Council of any general or gross under-nourishment of the population. All the evidence points to the conclusion that, speaking generally, the people of Australia are, by contrast with the older and more densely populated countries, well nourished and well-developed'. It qualified this optimistic picture by noting the prevalence of rickets in urban slums and goitre in rural areas, especially in Tasmania, as well as the rapid deterioration of the health of Aboriginal people in contact with whites. None of these problems, however, had been revealed in the Council's own survey.[53]

Given the short time frame of research and the lack of any local expertise in survey work, mistakes were inevitable. However, political demands that it should produce definite statements and policy recommendations led the committee to ignore the advice of its researchers and draw hasty conclusions which in turn provoked hostile responses to its work. Under attack from the trade union movement, which saw its results as 'a disguised attack on the basic wage', Colin Clark, the director of the Queensland Bureau of Industry, lambasted the committee's initial report for its statistical inadequacies and failure to use the methodologies of the British surveys of Boyd Orr to link household income and nutrition. A major blow was struck when Hughes, still the Minister of Health, publicly criticized the Council for complacency.[54]

The other main activities of the NHMRC were also dominated by the political programme of national hygiene.

As the threat of war deepened, the NHMRC launched a national fitness campaign. As with nutrition, 'fitness' provided a unifying concept of health which brought together the social and physiological, with strong overtones of social Darwinism. Based on state committees which were co-ordinated at Commonwealth level by an NHMRC sub-committee, it aimed to encourage physical education in schools, further developing the medical supervision of all stages of the life cycle and with the aim of producing:

> a race of strong, virile, stalwart individuals who would provide an invincible bulwark for defence at times of crisis or emergency...[while accepting that physical fitness is] primarily an individual responsibility but since it is an essential quality of soundly efficient citizenship, it is obviously a matter of direct concern to the State.[55]

National fitness was soon overtaking nutrition at the centre of public health policy. By 1939 Frank Hone was complaining that despite considerable advances in public awareness of the need for preventive health care, 'at the moment "physical fitness" is emphasized to the obscuring of other [aspects of preventive health care]'.[56]

The major programmes of the NHMRC – nutrition and national fitness – relied on exhortation to change public attitudes towards the care of the body. Neither envisaged a major change in medical practice. The only attempt to return to the more radical themes of the 1920s remained tentative and undeveloped. From 1939 to 1944 the NHMRC funded Dr Clifford Jungfer, a general practitioner in the Adelaide Hills, to survey health standards amongst school children, and access to and the quality of local medical services in this rural backwater. Jungfer produced a powerful indictment of the normal methods of general practice, arguing that malnutrition amongst school age children in the Adelaide Hills was an unfortunate by-product of the medicalization of childbirth and the destruction of older informal networks of learning as 'when the old "gamp" style of nurse passed out of existence, there also went much of the confidence and competence of mothers in their dealing with problems of child welfare'.[57] Jungfer's findings were published after the outbreak of war, their radical implications unheeded for the moment in the face of more urgent concerns.

The experience of national hygiene at a Commonwealth level illustrated the limits imposed by the federal system as well as more general failings of interwar social policy. Starting with a coherent vision of an integrated national health policy founded on the subordination of curative private medicine to preventive public health and with promising administrative experiments such as the national network of public health laboratories, the attempt to substitute expertise for party politics foundered on the limited administrative powers possessed by the federal government. Blocked from direct influence on the state public hospitals and the regulation of private practice, the Commonwealth could only make a major contribution in areas where the states were indifferent or absent, such as the medical problems of tropical Australia. The most lasting achievements of the department started from a recognition of these limitations: through the use of Commonwealth grants-in-aid to encourage states to develop specific programmes and through the work of the NHMRC, co-ordinating national health and research policies. The national hygienists' antagonism to the substitution of cash benefits for direct state services meant that the Commonwealth department of health remained a passive bystander during the most serious attempt to assert national control over the health system – the Lyons government's national insurance scheme of 1938.

**Table 2.1** Employees of the Commonwealth Department of Health, 1922–1940

|                                          | 1922 | 1925 | 1930 | 1935 | 1940 |
|------------------------------------------|------|------|------|------|------|
| Permanent                                | 166  | 203  | 273  | 270  | 316  |
| Medical officers [a]                     | n.a. | n.a. | n.a. | 37   | 49   |
| Total (including temporary and exempt)   | n.a. | n.a. | 452  | 463  | 675  |

[a] Excluding medical officers at Institute of Anatomy, Commonwealth Serum Laboratories and Canberra Hospital.

Source: Commonwealth Public Service Board, *Annual Reports; Knox's Medical Directories.*

# CHAPTER 3

# Doctors, the States and Interwar Medical Politics

The programme of national hygiene fell victim to the absence of federal constitutional powers over health and the financial constraints – and lack of political will – of Commonwealth governments. While the primary level of health policy-making lay at state level, the Commonwealth could do little more than exhort or provide the inducements of tied funding to persuade the states to expand their public health activities. Responsibility for the support of university medical schools, medical registration, and, above all, the public hospitals lay in the hands of the state governments and each of the states experienced disputes over hospital finance, access to free beds in public wards and intervention to provide medical services in remote districts. The co-ordination of public and private medicine – the integration of curative and preventive services which lay at the heart of Cumpston's vision – remained elusive as long as his department had no mandatory powers.

This fragmented institutional structure helped to stunt the development of a national framework of health politics. The prime focus of organized medicine remained on the state governments, which were responsible for the regulatory structure which governed the hospital systems, professional licensure and the friendly societies. Hence, although each state faced similar problems of financing its hospitals and political pressures to enable access to adequate health care, institutional and political differences ensured that conflicts often took radically different forms, and were resolved by opposing methods. Policy differences followed from contrasting traditions of state intervention in the local economy, the relative political strengths and make-up of the labour movement and its opponents, and variations in regional political cultures. In the 1920s and 1930s Tasmanian and Queensland governments responded to crises in their public hospital systems with aggressive intervention to exclude organized medicine from any active participation in health policy-making and open public beds to patients from all social classes. At the other extreme, Victorian governments of all political affiliations kept a considerable distance from the administrative and political problems of their financially stressed public hospitals, which remained independent 'voluntary' institutions, despite an increasing dependence on assistance from the state.

This chapter explores the main directions taken by state governments to intervene in the provision of health care. Despite being ad hoc, grudging and unplanned, the changes in finance and control of the public hospitals during the interwar years provided the political framework for any scheme for a national health service. At the same time, experiments in public subsidy – or outright salaried payment – of doctors' incomes reinforced the tendency of the Australian public and the medical profession to rely on state assistance.

## The states and medical practice

State intervention centred on the most expensive – and politically charged – health services: the increasingly shaky public hospitals. Policies were developed as panic reactions: the more costly, the more their sponsors tried to avoid any long-term commitment to public intervention. At the same time, this meant little thought was given to the more lasting effects on medical practice. In most states, government involvement in general practice was reluctant, and unconnected to any larger scheme of state medicine but a series of incremental adjustments to temporary crises and market failures.

Much of this state intervention took indirect forms: the establishment of regulatory frameworks – as with the Medical Boards which controlled the registration of doctors – or by imposing obligations on private institutions. By the late 1920s workers' compensation was a significant part of the industrial relations framework in each state, establishing legal obligations on employers to insure against work-related injuries, an approach which did not strain the capacities of state administration as management and finance remained in private hands (except in Labor-ruled Queensland, where the State Government Insurance Office was the sole insurer). In industrial areas a significant part of the incomes of many doctors was derived from

workers' compensation practice. Employees establishing a compensation claim were treated as private patients, and received medical
benefits directly from the insurer. The medical attendant, whether
hospital or practitioner, had to recover the fee in the normal way –
through the courts in cases of default. Under the Workers' Compensation Act 1926 New South Wales introduced payment of the
medical fees of successful claimants and, with the encouragement of
the newly established Workers' Compensation Commission, the
BMA and the insurers agreed to the direct payment of medical fees
and charges in return for doctors agreeing to adhere to a schedule of
fees, an arrangement which helped restrain the costs of medical treatment while guaranteeing the doctor's fee.[1]

Most workers' compensation practice was carried out by lodge
doctors, demonstrating again the complexity of the financial
relationship normally classified under the simple rubric of 'private
practice'. As workers' compensation practice became financially
more important, the BMA moved to ensure that all general
practitioners who wished to participate could share in the bounty,
opposing the development of a specialized system of industrial
medicine. While this was justified as ensuring continuous care of
patients, rather than adding yet another specialized service it also
represented a claim by general practitioners for a monopoly over this
lucrative area of medical practice. In 1940 the Footscray and District
Outpatients Clinic and Welfare Centre felt the wrath of the BMA
when it canvassed local employers in Melbourne's industrial west to
fund one or two salaried medical officers to attend industrial emer-
gencies and accidents. The state executive of the BMA issued a
'Notice to Members' forbidding their participation. In the face of this
boycott the clinic backed down, agreeing instead to employ a roster
of local doctors drawn up by the BMA's Western Suburbs sub-
division.[2]

Fully salaried medical services were a growing but limited sector of
health care. Most were confined to regions poorly served by private
practitioners and ranged from the comprehensive health care system
offered by the State Electricity Commission of Victoria to its
employees at Yallourn to the state government salaried medical practitioners' services in outback New South Wales, Western Australia
and the remoter parts of Tasmania. Communities could also subsidize
the local practitioner's income. Dr K. Welch, working for the flying
doctor service in Queensland in the late 1920s, noted that:

> It is unlikely that the amount of private practice available in the smaller
> towns would attract a Doctor, hence the policy of paying a salary of
> £500–700 a year to attend the hospital, and giving the right of private

practice. Many of the little hospitals are empty for long periods, and others average two or three patients a day. It is an expensive system, but commends itself to many communities.[3]

Responses to the failure of the market to provide even minimal standards of practice, these interventions were tolerated by the mainstream of the profession. More important were the rising state subsidies and even direct payment of salaries to many general practitioners. In remote areas and in poorer industrial districts a significant structural interest favouring further state intervention was created.

The depression of the 1930s provided a spur to these ad hoc interventions into general practice. The collapse of rural incomes during the depression of the early 1930s led to intense pressure for state financial help. Faced with the imminent demise of many rural and remote area health services most states introduced measures for the support of medical incomes and the maintenance of access for the unemployed and farmers to personal health services such as the New South Wales government's subvention of the friendly society contributions of the unemployed. Similar public subsidies of private practice were introduced as temporary expedients in other states at the height of the depression. The Farmers' Relief Act, covering the hard-hit wheat areas of South Australia, gave medical practitioners a 'second preferential claim' for the recovery of fees for medical attendance from relief funds provided to farmers. In Victoria the Farmers' Relief Board administered a similar system for the payment of medical accounts while in suburban Melbourne the BMA came to an informal arrangement with local public assistance committees for treatment of sustenance workers at two shillings a case, on the condition that they were brought in groups of ten, twenty or thirty to suit the convenience of the practitioner.[4]

Unplanned and incremental, by the end of the 1930s financial intervention by state governments had established substantial inroads into the dominance of private practice: 'what began as a gradual process, one of infiltration, is now assuming the proportions of a veritable landslide'.[5]

## The hospital question

Health policy in the states was dominated by the hospital question. The direction of hospital politics was shaped by three conflicting interests. The first was at the level of state fiscal policy. As public hospital budgets collapsed from the financial strain of the growth of demand for their services, the search for new sources of revenue became a central priority for state governments of all political persuasions. All states experimented with systems of cost-recovery from patients, encouraging the paybed and contributory schemes outlined in the first chapter, or diverting to hospitals the proceeds of lotteries such as Queensland's Golden Casket. Financial problems were exacerbated by political pressure for more equal access to hospital services. The labour movement had long campaigned for an end to the demeaning conditions of public wards and for the abandonment of means testing. The depression years, as we have seen, added to this pressure of rising demand for public hospitals. Finally, the longstanding conflicts within the medical profession over access to hospital beds, and for the exclusion of potential fee-paying patients from public wards, inspired fierce resistance to the pressures for universal access.

Interwar hospital administration was marked by experimentation with new forms of revenue-raising. Two rival models were available. In Victoria and New South Wales, where the voluntary system had been strongest, state support followed an indirect path of subsidization with autonomous boards allocating government subsidies amongst the public hospitals and other charitable institutions but few powers to direct hospital policy outside narrow questions of financial management and the co-ordination of public fund-raising activities. At the other extreme stood 'the stark departmentalism of Western Australia' and the smaller, less wealthy states. By the 1920s the public hospital systems of Tasmania, Queensland, Western Australia and South Australia depended directly on state and local governments for most of their budgets. These hospitals paid a price, as governments asserted their right to involvement in the intimate details of appointments, administration and financial management, with the potential for regular and debilitating conflicts between hospital committees, managers and the medical profession.[6]

The appointment of independent administrative boards, free from any direct ministerial direction, had become the characteristic Victorian means for de-fusing potentially dangerous political problems. Caught between rising costs, and public demands for wider and cheaper access to their services, the public hospitals were a perfect case for this devolution of authority. The establishment of the Charities Board in 1923 set a pattern for state intervention in Victoria and New South Wales. These more populous states, with their well developed systems of voluntary contributions to charities supported by an affluent middle class not found elsewhere in Australia, required less direct state financial support. By keeping government subsidies at arm's length, the large public hospitals preserved the legal fiction of remaining voluntary charitable institutions, while ruling parties of all persuasions could point to the massive administrative and constitutional obstacles in the way of nationalization of the hospital system.

The Victorian Charities Board consisted of fourteen members, appointed by the state government but nominated by the major interest groups in hospital administration: eight were from the Metropolitan and Country Hospitals Associations, four from the non-hospital charities subsidized by the board, and there were two independent members. The board allocated government funds to subsidized institutions for current purposes and co-ordinated their fund raising activities. The board's control over charitable institutions was indirect: it could audit the accounts of subsidized institutions and direct changes in financial administration, or allocate grants to encourage new activities. This autonomy from the government of the day, which only decided the global amount to be distributed, gave the board's senior administrators enormous potential power. Cecil McVilly, the state's chief inspector of charities from 1923 to 1948, ran his empire with little outside interference, even from ministers of health, so that Victoria often appeared to have two parallel health administrations. At the same time, the board was lay-dominated. Only two of its members were medical practitioners – both nominated as hospital representatives.[7]

In New South Wales hospital politics had a more explosive history, largely because of the greater political strength of that state's labour movement. Fred Flowers, as minister for public health in the prewar McGowen and Holman Labor governments, had attempted to bring in a free hospital service, but was defeated by medical obstruction and the outbreak of war. The main legacies of this venture were a greater degree of direct state intervention than in Victoria and a stronger public demand for free access to public hospitals. Consequently, the Hospitals Commission of New South Wales was given a wider set of regulatory powers than its Victorian equivalent, a less cumbersome and representative membership of five (including one representative of the medical profession), and was far more open to political interference. Its brief was also more sweeping: to provide 'a complete hospital system in the State whereunder every person requiring treatment will have ready and convenient access to a properly equipped and managed institution capable of giving the requisite attention'.[8]

Financial constraints kept this rejection of the charitable principle a pious aspiration. But the great growth in use of hospital clinics and public wards during the depression increased the political pressures for a more interventionist approach. As the public became more 'hospital minded', pressures for the expansion of services caused hospital boards to sink heavily into debt, threatening resignation if the state government failed to honour its guarantees of their borrowings. A New South Wales parliamentary committee reported in 1940 that there was a 'definite drift' towards a crisis which could only end with full state control unless new forms of finance were quickly adopted. Hospitals were:

> tending to become public utilities rather than charitable institutions ... many of our citizens are inclined to look upon them as something they should receive free of cost in the same way that they receive free education. This must eventually result in a very heavy burden being imposed upon the taxpayer. If it continues, your Committee fears that those now interested in the humanitarian side of hospitals – they are many – will shed their responsibility and lose interest in their hospitals.[9]

By 1940 these fears had been realized. Government control of the New South Wales public hospitals grew along with state responsibility for funding. As conservative opponents feared, charitable donations fell as public support increased. State involvement grew irrespective of the political party in power.

Hence, despite the attempt to set up an independent authority, in New South Wales the hospital question was more politicized than in Victoria. As a token of New South Wales' intention to follow the Victorian model of statutory independence R.J. Love, McVilly's deputy at the Victorian Board, had been appointed chairman of the Hospitals Commission. His attempts to assert administrative independence aroused such hostility from his political masters that he was dismissed after only three years. Reginald Weaver, the Minister for Health (and deputy UAP leader) in the conservative Stevens–Bruxner government took this several stages further. He moved to centralize control over the state's hospitals by increasing departmental administrative powers over hospital boards and outraged the BMA by proposing the Queensland system of exclusion of medical practitioners from the boards. In 1934 he capped these hospital reforms with an amendment to the Public Hospitals Act to make the minister of health ex officio chairman of the Hospitals Commission. Weaver's confrontational style appears to have alienated his leader – he was dropped from the Cabinet in February 1935 – but these moves from an impeccably reactionary government showed how far New South Wales had strayed from the Victorian path of administrative autonomy.[10]

## Tasmania: the BMA defeated

Lacking the south-eastern states' vigorous tradition of voluntary action, from the first days of colonial settlement the smaller states had relied on government finance for their hospitals. Calls for the 'nationalization of health' were also more common, if vaguely defined, in their labour movements. Labor Party programmes supported universal access to medical institutions and state control of hospitals. This did not imply free health care – beds would continue to be reserved for the indigent while those who could afford it would be made to contribute according to their means. In practice, state Labor governments limited their initiatives to widening access to public hospital beds. Despite a vigorous programme of state control of industry and transport, the Western Australian Scadden government, in power from 1911 to 1916, ignored calls from its rank and file for a thoroughgoing nationalization of health care. The relative poverty of the smaller states – in comparison with the private and public resources of Victoria and New South Wales – made demands for sweeping public intervention more compelling. At the same time it set firm limits on the ability of state governments to meet the demands of their supporters. Despite the failure of these earlier experiments, the same questions of access to public beds and the control of hospital boards and their admission policies lay at the heart of two more systematic projects undertaken by reformist Labor governments in Tasmania and Queensland.[11]

State control of public and private medical services proceeded further in Tasmania. The inability of the market for private medical care to meet basic needs outside the most settled districts combined with a financial crisis of the public hospital system to give state governments little choice but to intervene. An open clash with the BMA saw conservative and Labor parties join in successful opposition to the degree of medical autonomy considered normal in New South Wales and Victoria.

The Tasmanian conflict centred on the Hobart Public Hospital. Before the First World War the Labor government of John Earle had established a royal commission to examine complaints about nepotism in hospital appointments and the exclusion of general practitioners from access to patients. This began a ten-year struggle in which the Tasmanian branch of the British Medical Association fought unsuccessfully to exclude all but the most indigent patients from the public hospital system, while most of Tasmania's political establishment, both Labor and conservative, resisted moves for restriction of the entry to hospitals. Founded as recently as 1911, the BMA's Tasmanian branch was a weak organization, no match for the political forces ranged against it. In 1917 the Liberal–Nationalist Lee government completed the takeover of hospital services. Paying patients were now admitted to public hospitals previously set aside for the indigent and salaried medical officers were employed.[12] Its denunciation of state control and the admission of non-paupers to public hospitals unheeded, the BMA attempted more drastic action. Amid dire warnings from the *Medical Journal of Australia* of the imminent destruction of private medical practice, in 1917 all Tasmanian honoraries withdrew their services. The BMA feared, with some justice, that in small cities such as Hobart and Launceston the salaried medical superintendents would gain such a reputation from hospital practice that fee-paying patients would be unwilling to consult other surgeons.[13]

An even more bitter and protracted struggle followed. The state government circumvented the boycott of hospital appointments by recruiting doctors overseas, and appointed Victor Ratten as superintendent surgeon of the Hobart Hospital. Ratten was already a controversial figure in BMA circles. A graduate of a small (and short-lived) proprietary medical college in Chicago, he had been admitted to practice in Tasmania in 1907 despite the opposition of British and Australian trained doctors who queried the validity of his degree. Although the BMA had reluctantly accepted his right to practise, his appointment to the Hobart Hospital, breaking the honoraries' boycott, led to open war. The Tasmanian Medical Board, dominated by the BMA, immediately moved to disqualify him from practice. With the firm support of the Labor opposition, the state government moved to protect the popular surgeon by amending the Medical Act to extend formal recognition to non-British qualifications. To reinforce this attack on medical control over entry to practice, the Tasmanian Supreme Court was empowered to force the state's Medical Council to register, or restore to the register, the name of any person 'unreasonably refused' a licence. In late 1918 a new Hospital Act further protected Ratten's position as surgeon superintendent and opened the public hospitals to all patients – not only the indigent. Patients were to be charged fees for treatment and accommodation according to means, but no distinction was created between pay and public wards.[14]

Defeated over Ratten and the control of hospital admissions, BMA members remained outside the public hospital system until the election of the Lyons state ALP government in 1923 opened the way to conciliatory moves. In Launceston a full honorary service was quickly restored on government terms. However, although Hobart Hospital's services continued to function without the boycotters, the BMA refused to admit its defeat until 1930. Under the final settle-ment Ratten's position was protected and those seeking appointment had to accept far more onerous regulation of their conditions of practice than did their colleagues in the other southern states.[15]

The Tasmanian doctors' strike was defeated by a unique alliance of political parties and public opinion. Although Labor was in opposi-tion until 1923 and then from 1928 to 1934, both Joseph Lyons and Albert Ogilvie, its two most prominent leaders, were outspoken in defence of Victor Ratten and the state government's firm action against the BMA. This bipartisan agreement on an interventionist health policy continued after Labor began its long period of power in 1934. Both sides of politics agreed on the need for an expanded state public health service, including the hospitals, and central co-ordination of other medical services. Neither advocated 'free' health care, accepting the need for means testing, but parted company on the best means to finance the system. Where the Nationalists demanded private beds, segregated from public wards and funded by a contributory scheme, Labor called for common wards with a more redistributive funding from general revenue. In the financial and political crises of the depression years, however, both sides of politics dropped any plans for reform of the health services.[16]

In 1934 the election of the Ogilvie ALP government initiated a more radical phase in Tasmanian health policy, extending state control from the hospitals to the direct provision of personal medical services. Dr John Francis Gaha, a Labor member of the Legislative Council, was appointed as minister for health. Born and educated in Ireland, Gaha had been an honorary surgeon at Hobart Hospital under the Ratten regime, following this with service as the state's chief medical officer. His attitudes towards medical reform were shaped by these experiences of private and public medicine and deeply coloured by his contempt for the BMA, a detestation which was heartily reciprocated. In 1935, shortly after his appointment as minister for health, he made an extensive overseas tour to look at hospital and medical administration in Britain, Europe, the United States and South America. His report was deeply critical of honorary practice and the other traditions of charitable service which under-pinned the voluntary hospitals, arguing that overseas experience had demonstrated that 'the shift of public opinion will be from the voluntary system to the state or municipal one and thus more and more towards nationalized medicine'. This pace should not be forced, but 'must be a gradual one and will meet with only dire consequences if any attempt is made to rush the situation'.[17]

In 1937 a small salaried medical practitioner service was established under the direct control of the public health department. In government circles the scheme was seen primarily as a pragmatic response to the failure of private practice in marginal areas. The first beneficiaries were remote rural areas unable to attract a doctor in private practice. Ogilvie justified the increased state involvement in the control of medical services in terms of improved access to existing services. No criticism of the content of medical practice was offered. Instead, he argued that:

> with the rapid passing of class and the wider distribution of wealth, the people are daily becoming more appreciative of medicine and medical achievements. If their desire is to participate, and if the only thing frustrating that wish is the fact that they do not have the means, then the state must step in and offer it. In practice this is what is happening. It was in this spirit that the Tasmanian Government entered upon an expansive hospital programme in the several departments of medical service, which are available to all classes, and because they are largely maintained from consolidated revenue, no suitable person is debarred.[18]

More radical politicians, such as Gaha, shared the BMA's view that this was a move towards a completely state-controlled salaried health service. In late 1937 Dr John Hunter, the General Secretary of the Federal Council of the BMA, led a worried delegation to meet with Ogilvie and express strong opposition to the development of a free health service. Little reassurance was offered:

> The Premier stated that was, in effect, what he desired, and his Government hoped that by the end of their term of office (another four years) the medical services of the State would be nationalized and administered by the Public Health Department. . .[Hunter's report concluded] The position in Tasmania is a very serious one not only from the point of view of the local practitioners, but from the point of view of the profession in Australia, as there is no doubt that what is happening in Tasmania will be watched with a great deal of interest by the Governments in the other States. In discussing the matter with the Council of the [Tasmanian] Branch I said that I thought that no good purpose would be served by adopting an attitude of open hostility to the Government's policy. I reminded them that the Association had not yet recovered from the effects of the injudicious action of members of the staff of the Hospital who resigned their appointments in 1917.[19]

Hunter warned the Tasmanian branch to accept the inevitable, while ensuring that state doctors received an adequate level of remuneration and limited their encroachment on private practice in more economically viable regions. To drive the lesson home, Ogilvie threatened to by-pass BMA obstruction by recruiting refugee Jewish doctors. By 1939 thirteen municipal districts were involved in the Country Medical Officers' Scheme with the reluctant acquiescence of the BMA and the enthusiastic support of the powerful Australian Workers Union. As state finances improved with economic recovery a hospital building programme was launched and by early 1938 Tasmania was moving towards a centralized hospital service, co-ordinated with a growing network of salaried medical officers.[20]

The extension of the Tasmanian scheme was constrained by the limits of state finances and the outbreak of war, rather than any effective resistance provided by the BMA. With only a limited amount of hyperbole, Gaha complained to the Federal Joint Parliamentary Committee on Social Security in August 1941 that:

> All Tasmania could be nationalized tomorrow, but for the fact that we are a mendicant state. Social service is one of the bases on which we obtain our grants from the Commonwealth. The cost of social services is now at a point which if exceeded will result in this state being penalized. For that reason I have had to stop at the position we have now reached.[21]

Even given these limitations, the Tasmanian experiment left the BMA demoralized, its local leaders convinced that they were witnessing the gradual eclipse of private medicine with hospitals incorporated into the civil service and the family practitioner 'one of a dying race'.[22]

## Queensland and nationalization: the first phase

In 1917 the financial stress of the war led to the collapse of private funding for Queensland's voluntary hospital system. The Ryan Labor government was forced to assume full financial responsibility for the Brisbane Hospital. Although this implemented  longstanding party policy there was little political calculation in the move, which was made in an unplanned and panic-stricken reaction to an immediate crisis by a reluctant and financially embarrassed government. The lack of ideological content became even more evident as a procession of other impecunious hospital boards pleaded unsuccessfully with the state government to nationalize them. Labor's abolition of the conservative-dominated upper house in 1922 removed one major obstacle to change, but the government postponed any thorough-going reform of the state's hospitals until five years after the war. The only major action was to apply the proceeds of the Golden Casket lottery to hospital funds.[23]

The nationalization of the Brisbane Hospital had been a pragmatic response to a sudden crisis, not the implementation of a more
far-reaching political programme. Unable to pass its new financial
responsibilities back into private hands, and facing increasing
demands from other hard-pressed voluntary hospitals, the postwar
Labor governments postponed a major overhaul of the system of
funding and control. The Brisbane Hospital continued to be funded
from general revenue and the pleas of other institutions went
unheeded.

The early 1920s saw a move towards more radical reform. The
Australian Workers Union (AWU), the cradle and main power base
of the Labor Party in Queensland, had always had a commitment to
improving access to health care for its isolated rural workers. Dem-
ocratizing control of the hospitals and opening the doors of the
public wards to any worker had been persistent demands since the
1890s.[24] In 1923 James Stopford, the Home Secretary, introduced a
new Hospitals Act which established this new approach. Borrowing
from a New Zealand model of funding which combined local government rates and state government subsidies – with hospital boards
controlled by nominees of both levels of government – Stopford
proclaimed that state control had spelled the end of the charity
hospital:

> The nationalization of the Hospital system, as advocated by the Labour
> movement at its inception, had its origin in a different set of circum-
> stances. In those days hospitals were what are termed 'voluntary hospitals'
> – that is, they were wholly dependent upon charitable contributions in
> the first instance for their existence. Many humiliating conditions were
> connected with the hospital system in those days. For instance, a poor
> person desiring admittance had first to seek the patronage of a contribu-
> tor. If unable to pay anything for the service of the Hospital he was
> labelled a 'pauper', and the Hospital walls were strewn with notices
> telling the sick they were recipients of charity. It was these humiliating
> conditions which brought about the insistent demand for nationalization.
> And at that time there was no local representative organization as there is
> now under the local franchise. But these conditions are of the past, and
> now nationalization merely means...State control.[25]

While Stopford's claims about the demise of pauperism were far
too sanguine, he captured an element common to the Labor-
controlled states. Since the late nineteenth century the labour movement had called for the 'nationalization' of the public hospital
systems, the replacement of fund-raising from charities and voluntary
subscriptions by direct government support and the abolition of the

demeaning pauper status of means-tested public wards. The Queensland Labor governments of the 1920s developed a wide programme of state intervention in health services, with radical tones absent in the medical politics of the southern states.

The policies of Queensland Labor followed two main directions: redistribution, both in class and regional terms, and developmentalism. The development of medical services in non-metropolitan regions lay at the centre of the programme. With a small urban working class, Labor electoral support was based on an alliance between rural workers and smallholders. The management and control of health services were gradually devolved to local hospital and ambulance boards, incidentally giving Labor another instrument of patronage by appointing supporters. This redistributional theme was strengthened by Labor's commitment to rural-based developmentalism: economic advance through population increase, the pronatalist sentiments common to interwar progressive opinion. Health and the hospital question were used prominently in Labor's political appeals to women, which promised improved maternal health and infant welfare.[26]

The second main feature of Labor's programme was its heavily institutional bias, centred on the expansion and decentralization of the hospital system. Personal health care and the relationship between the doctor and patient were left to individuals and the friendly societies. Most government policy was directed to the financial status and expansion of the hospitals. Labor governments continued their predecessors' parsimonious attitude towards preventive public health services. J.S.C. Elkington complained in disgust that the Ryan government 'would let the people rot before they would lift a hand to improve the [public] health [services]'.[27]

The aims of the reforms of the early 1920s were mainly financial. The 1923 Hospital Act came at the end of the most vigorous era of reform in Queensland, as British financial institutions blocked the Theodore government from raising further finance for its more ambitious schemes of state control. Consequently, the 1923 reforms were calculated to improve hospital finances but kept responsibility from the state government, shifting at least a third of the financial burden on to local ratepayers – including the landowners in rural areas. The Hospital Act established a decentralized system in which most power rested at the local level in the hands of the hospital boards, subject to final veto by the Home Secretary. His control of hospitals remained distant and concentrated on levels of expenditure rather than admission policies and the planning of services.[28]

The Act made participation optional, so its coverage was gradual, opening fierce political conflicts for the control of the hospital boards. Because members were nominated by the state and local governments which provided the funding, board membership became a major area of political patronage. Local branches of the ALP or the AWU (in much of rural Queensland these were identical) sent lists of nominees who were usually confirmed by the minister. The appoint-ment of honoraries and hospital policies on access to public wards would then be decided on political lines.[29]

This local control was accompanied by a marginalization of medi-cal influence over hospital administration. Charles Chuter, the under-secretary in the Home Department with prime responsibility for hospitals during the 1920s and 1930s, saw the strength of the honorary system as the main barrier to progress. He staunchly opposed the appointment of medically qualified hospital superintend-ents, insisting that questions of administration, finance and access to hospitals must remain in lay hands. Doctors should stick to purely medical matters:

> The whole position may be summed in the question whether the Honor-ary Medical system (which is representative of the private interests) or the Hospital Board (which is representative of the community which has to maintain the Hospital) is to control the Hospital and direct the policy of the Hospital. The Hospital Board's duty is to provide an efficient and economic service for the community. It cannot do so if the control of the Hospital is placed under private medical interests.[30]

In line with this encouragement of local control came attempts to devolve financial responsibilities. In Queensland, unlike the south-ern states, contributions through group insurance schemes were treated as donations and met a matching government subsidy and the right to vote for the hospital board. Trade union based occupational group schemes flourished under the Labor governments of the 1920s. The state government adopted a far more restrictive attitude towards producer-and employer-based groups, denying them the matching grant – and more importantly, the voting rights which went with private donations. Consequently, the BMA was highly suspicious of contributory schemes, warning that their weak enforcement of income limits: 'means medical men who are fortunate enough to hold the hospital appointment, would obtain all the medical work of that district'. Even worse were anti-Labor fears that 'an industrial group could easily [use its voting strength to] get control of a public hospital'.[31]

The election of the conservative Moore government in 1929 was followed by a swift purge of Labor appointees. Fulfilling an electoral pledge to its rural landowning supporters and the BMA, the new government set up a Royal Commission on Hospitals to investigate the finances and control of the public hospital system. It was chaired by W. Harris, a police magistrate, while the other commissioners were E. Sandford Jackson – effectively the BMA nominee – and the deputy auditor-general, S.A. Glassey.

The venom of the government and BMA fell on Charles Chuter, the principal architect of Labor's financial and managerial reforms. Chuter was a crucial figure in Queensland's interwar hospital politics. After entering the Queensland public service in 1898, he had risen by 1922 to become assistant under-secretary in the Department of Home Affairs with particular responsibility for hospital finance and local government and had established strong links within the ALP. In the same year he became the first chairman of the Brisbane and South Coast Hospitals Board.[32]

Chuter's anomalous position as chairman of the Brisbane board and in charge of the government department charged with regulating public hospitals soon became a target of regular complaints from the BMA. The hostility of organized medicine to this concentration of power in lay hands was exacerbated by his close connections with Labor politicians. The public hearings of the Royal Commission turned into a hostile scrutiny of his administration. While the Commission was predictably scathing of Chuter's dual allegiances, its report offered only tepid support for medical control. The majority (with the BMA nominee dissenting) called for a greater use of advisory committees, but recommended that doctors practising in public hospitals should continue to be excluded from board membership. On an even more contentious note, the Royal Commission recommended that Queensland adopt a hospital tax, following a Western Australian precedent. While this would please the pastoral interests, shifting the financial burden from property rates to wage earners, Chuter noted with wry pleasure that it would create precisely the demands for free access to hospitals which the BMA most feared. Finally, the BMA had hoped that the outcome of the Commission would be an autonomous hospitals commission on the Victorian model, ending the domination by lay-controlled hospital boards, but even here it was disappointed. Although the Commission recommended a Central Hospital Commission with three members to co-ordinate hospital finances, again Harris recorded his formal dissent, while Sandford Jackson felt compelled to write his own minority opinion calling for a much stronger body.[33]

The Moore government was soon overwhelmed by the impact of the great depression, and its plans for administrative reform and new taxes were buried. The conservative parties were decisively defeated in the 1932 election and remained in opposition for the next quarter of a century. The BMA achieved nothing by declaring its political sympathies but to confirm Labor's suspicions: Chuter's arguments for the exclusion of doctors from positions of administrative power were affirmed as Labor restored control of hospital boards to its supporters. A plea from the Nambour branch of the ALP shows local reactions towards the change of regime. The branch secretary requested that the source of nominations remain secret, that they should be repre-sented as a whim of Brisbane rather than a local initiative as:

> Pat Carrol and myself will be victimized we are working under the Treasurer of the Hospital Committee S.Baildon who is very anxious to get back but he is unfit for more than political reasons as also W. Whally a director of the Sugar Mills on the committee for political reasons these two men have bothered Carrol to nominate them he has told them the unions have decided to leave the matter entirely to the Home Sec-retary.[sic][34]

The conservatives had been unable to remove Chuter from all of his positions within the bureaucracy, and much of his influence was restored under the new regime, although he did not regain his position as chairman of the Brisbane and South Coast Hospitals Board. Queensland's brief flirtation with the Victorian model had ended in disaster for the BMA. The Labor governments of the 1930s were to turn to a more radically interventionist and centralizing approach.

## Cilento and the Queensland model

> It was thought that there was an essential and natural difference between the treatment that should be provided to the indigent, to the middle classes, and to the well-to-do. And this must always be the case when people think in terms of social classes and not in terms of the nation as a whole.
>
> It was obvious to a few that the real problem was to provide a service which should be available to every person in a  community, and should be equal in every respect to the best service that money could buy. This meant, of course that there must be a unification of all medical provision – preventive, medical and convalescent – and that to provide it on a basis that was economically sound, the standards of medical practice and hospital efficiency must be continually perfected.[35]
>
> Whatever system of medical practice eventually prevails, it will of necessity be largely controlled by the Government, and to make it a

success it is essential that it should have behind it the best elements in the profession.[36]

After the brief interregnum of the Moore government, Labor returned to dominate state politics for the next quarter of a century. During the 1930s the government of William Forgan Smith was marked by its authoritarianism and rural conservatism, which placed a brake on any return to the social experimentation of the early 1920s. The management of the state's health system provided the one great exception to this lacklustre record. With the able E.M. (Ned) Hanlon as Home Secretary and Sir Raphael Cilento as state director-general of health, Queensland launched an experiment which, for a short time, appeared to unite the programmes of national hygiene and the labour movement's concern for equal access to health care. Directed by a unified Department of Health and Home Affairs, Queensland attempted a radical reshaping of the relations between the state and the medical profession.[37]

At first this seemed merely a return to the policies of the 1920s. Medical influence on admissions and administration was restricted while political appointments to hospital boards were renewed. Again, trade union group contributory schemes were encouraged while producer and general hospital contribution schemes were tolerated but received no matching subsidy.[38]

In other important respects, the new government's approach broke with that of its predecessors. Under Hanlon, Queensland's hospitals moved into a period of even more vigorous state intervention in which the concerns of traditional labourism were increasingly meshed with the ambitious projects of national hygiene.

The move of Raphael Cilento from the service of the Commonwealth to become Queensland's director-general of health in 1934 signalled a radical change. Over the next six years he attempted to apply the policies that had been thwarted at national level within the boundaries of one state. His plans relied on the support of Hanlon and Chuter, who was still vested with administrative and financial powers over the state's hospitals. As long as Cilento's programme coincided with their more traditionally Labor emphasis on widening access to the health system, he achieved more than his colleagues at federal and state levels. The authoritarian and centralist political style of the Queensland Labor governments gave an enormous amount of influence to the individuals in charge of policy-making. In the 1920s this had given Charles Chuter an unparalleled power over the state's hospital system. Although restored from the disgrace of the Royal Commission's attacks, in the 1930s Chuter faced competition from two rivals, Hanlon and Raphael Cilento. By the end of the decade, however, the more ambitious goals had been frustrated by departmental and party politics. Despite these obstacles, for the next decade the Queensland experiments provided a model and framework for debates over the future direction of state intervention in health care.

Cilento's move to Queensland was precipitated by the troubles faced by the Commonwealth Department of Health. The department had barely survived the financial cuts of 1932, Cilento's Division of Tropical Hygiene being one of the early victims. Transferred to Canberra and chafing at the indignity of serving as Cumpston's second-in-command, Cilento cultivated an old acquaintance with Chuter, hoping for an early return to Brisbane. Chuter appears to have introduced Cilento to the new Labor Home Secretary. In 1932 Hanlon borrowed Cilento's services for a major survey of Aboriginal health and the following year, again at Chuter's initiative, Cilento was seconded to report on the controversial poliomyelitis therapy developed by Sister Elizabeth Kenny in Townsville. Kenny had won Chuter's warm support but was already arousing the intense hostility of sections of the medical profession to her unorthodox use of muscle manipulation therapy. Cilento's report was guarded but favourable. To Chuter's satisfaction he recommended that the state government fund a Kenny clinic for an experimental period.[39]

Having attracted the attention of Hanlon, Premier Forgan Smith and Chuter, Cilento was a natural choice to work on a major reorganization of the state's health services. In October 1934 he accepted appointment as director-general of health in Queensland and was knighted, much to the chagrin of Cumpston. Cilento set out to accomplish for Queensland what the Commonwealth Department of Health had failed to achieve at national level. Reviving the programme of national hygiene, he saw a unified Department of Health as the focal point of a medicalization of state administration. He saw the problem in essentially administrative terms. The department would be transformed from a sleepy backwater concerned with the enforcement of sanitary regulations into a modern organization centralizing control over all health services in the state. Medical practice was to be reorganized in a hierarchy extending from the state director-general's office through the large public hospitals to a decentralized system of district general hospitals and group clinics staffed by general practitioners and visiting specialists. Every state activity which touched on health, nutrition, occupational health and safety as well as public and private medical services would be brought under central supervision. This vision was based on a strong organic view of political and social obligations shared by the state, the citizen and the doctor, in turn based on a sense of racial and national solidarity. Hence, conflict with the individualism of the medical profession was inevitable, not merely on questions of finance but on fundamental medical ethics. When Cilento attempted to compel doctors to report all cases and suspected cases of illegal abortion to the police, the resistance from the BMA was so intense that the project, dear to the hearts of the national hygienists, had to be abandoned.[40]

Although consistent with the projects of national hygiene of the 1920s, Cilento's early plans were also closely attuned to Labor's established attitudes to health policy, widening access to hospitals and clinics as well as centralizing control of the hospital system. He won Hanlon's strong support. In a speech bearing the marks of Cilento's influence the minister argued that 'Today is the day of specialization, and gradually the medical profession is breaking into specialized groups. The ordinary medical practitioner will soon be only a glorified commissionaire, directing his patients to the best services available'.[41]

In a detailed blueprint sent to Hanlon in 1936, Cilento called for a radically centralized, hospital-based medical service for the state. All state health services would fall under the authority of the director-general of health: school medical services would be transferred from the Department of Public Instruction, industrial hygiene from the Department of Labour. In contrast to the temporary and ad hoc quality of health planning by other state governments, the Cilento scheme tackled the central problems of medical practice: the poor cousin status of public and preventive medicine, the divorce of general from hospital practice and the access of the middle classes and non-metropolitan residents to sophisticated public hospital services. It also made the regulation of the family a central objective: from pre-natal and mothercraft educational programmes through school medical and dental services and nutritional advice to mothers.[42]

Group practice was the key to this co-ordination of private and state medical services. This had been a persistent theme in medical politics since the  British Dawson Report of 1920. Faced with demands for a more thoroughgoing reorganization of medical services under state control, the committee chaired by Lord Dawson of Penn, the King's surgeon, had recommended a system of primary health care centres to integrate outpatient and domiciliary services and shift responsibility for maternal and infant welfare and other aspects of public health and preventive medicine from state doctors to private

practitioners so as to integrate the health care system. The immediate political context of the Dawson scheme was conservative,
framed to block the alternative of a salaried national medical service,
and it received a reasonably warm reception from organized
medicine. In December 1920 the *Medical Journal of Australia* accepted
that 'the application of team work to the civil community is prevented by its excessive cost. Some method must be devised to bring its
advantages to the large middle class which is handicapped at the
present time'.[43]

The group practice model exercised a fascination over all sections
of the medical profession. If radicals and the national hygienists
looked to the state-sponsored clinics of the British, Soviet and European models, their more conservative colleagues turned to the
United States for inspiration. The Mayo Clinic at Rochester, near
Minneapolis, and other large co-operative clinics in the United
States, offered a means to co-ordinate specialist services without state
involvement. The work of numerous specialized physicians was
organized under one roof, linking research, specialization, general
practice and, not least, commercial success. This form of private
enterprise group practice was seen by its American adherents as an
alternative to direct state control. In the United States the group
practice model was recommended by the Committee for the Control
of Medical Costs, an influential advocate of preventive health care
and health insurance. The Mayo Clinic achieved a near legendary
reputation amongst its admirers. When William Mayo visited
Australia in 1924 he was feted by the leaders of the local medical
profession. At a BMA banquet held in his honour in Melbourne the
surgeon, Sir George Syme, described 'Rochester as a surgical Mecca,
regarding which pilgrims in surgery the whole world over cried:
"there is only one clinic and Mayo is its prophet"'. The American
group clinic became both a popular destination for Australian public
health and medical leaders on study trips and the focus of discussion
as a model for Australian medical practice.[44]

By the end of the 1930s, group practice was becoming strongly
identified with those desiring a radical reorganization of medical
practice and the inspiration for interwar medical reformers seeking to
overcome the fragmentation of specialism. In 1937 the influential
Political and Economic Planning (PEP) *Report on British Health
Services* carried this further, arguing that the clinic should become
the focus of the system of medical care.[45]

The one Australian attempt to develop a fully-integrated group
practice drew an ambivalent reaction from the medical establishment. The Brisbane Clinic pioneered a model of group practice,

incorporating general medicine, surgery and psychiatry under one roof. Founded in 1930 by Dr L.J. Jarvis Nye, a young physician with a formidable research and clinical reputation (and an early pilgrim to Rochester) and Dr John Bostock, a psychiatrist, the Brisbane Clinic was a response to the threat posed to general practice by increased specialization and hospital-centred medicine on the one hand, and the vastly increased use of outpatient clinics by those who could not afford medical services on the other. With specialist and diagnostic services under one roof, patients' financial arrangements were with the group, not the individual doctor. By the early 1940s the Clinic's staff consisted of three surgeons, five physicians, an eye, ear, nose and throat specialist, and two physiotherapists, with a support staff of technicians and nurses who carried out routine preliminary examinations of patients, pathology tests and x-rays. Many of Nye's colleagues saw the Clinic as a threat. During its first few years the Brisbane Clinic met strong opposition from sections of the Queensland branch of the BMA, an antagonism which cost Nye his seat on the branch council in 1930. By the end of the decade an accommodation had been reached. Thomas Price, the BMA branch president in 1936, was even proclaiming that 'teamwork' on the Nye model should provide the basis for a thorough reform of general practice.[46]

The work of Nye and the Brisbane Clinic influenced Cilento's stress on group practice as the basic cell of the health service. Despite entering private practice rather than the service of the state, Nye was sympathetic to the more radical schemes of the national hygienists. In a series of books and educational pamphlets written with his colleague John Bostock, Nye warned of the coming clash with the awakening racial threat from Asia. Cilento and Nye shared a conviction that the reform of the health system must provide the first step towards a reversal of the weakening of Australia's racial stock, and had a common horror of the 'orientalization' of Australian youth. They advocated the need for a strong state, pointed out the dangers of the 'rule of the unfit' , and attacked the failure of party politicians to learn from the 'new spirit of optimism and hope' engendered by Mussolini and Hitler in the face of the menace of the awakening East.[47]

The reorganization of the health system was to play a major part in the work of national rejuvenation: the direction of practice by experts would prevent the service degenerating into a pauperizing system of free medicine, while state financial control would ensure that the longer-term interests of the race and nation were served. Cilento set out these preoccupations in a letter to Nye:

Everyone has been forced to agree that the profession should be organized on the group plan, and note the word 'organized'. I am strongly of the opinion that, while as much as possible, group control should rest within the clinic, there must be an external administrative thread linking all aspects of the problem as a whole, and that this shall be to a degree accepted by the public, representative of and protective of the public's (i.e. the patient's) interest. In other words, I agree thoroughly with internal control in professional matters, compulsory staff conferences monthly, – the building-up so to speak of an ever-improving *vertical* excellence, on the one hand. There must be, on the other hand, a linkage *laterally* by planned distribution, restriction, and enlargement as and when such services are needed, in order that they may be spread over the whole community in the interests of the whole community. . .

The only organization that is big enough and *impersonal enough* to do justice in this matter is the STATE. By this I do not mean the political State but the organic State, delegating its powers to informed bodies of medical men and representatives of the people as a central co-ordinating committee – decentralizing its powers through various subsidiary advisory bodies...

Such bodies will make mistakes, but they will be the mistakes of over-eager enthusiasm and not of carking conservatism. They will require the constant pruning of their exuberance by the considered opinion of wise medical men but it is not so difficult a task as it would be to emulate the biblical prophet who threw down his withered staff and saw it bloom with roses.[48]

Reform would start with the public hospitals. With the University of Queensland Medical School due to produce its first graduates in 1940, the state would no longer be dependent on the graduates and educational practices of the older state universities. The foundation of the Medical School owed a great deal to Cilento's initiative. In the context of reorganizing the state's medical services he seems to have convinced Forgan Smith that a local medical school would be a useful tool towards overcoming shortages, at the same time tackling the political embarrassments posed by outbreaks of unidentified tropical diseases. The industrial disruption caused by outbreaks of Weil's disease on the canefields in the Premier's own electorate helped to secure his support for the project. Cilento was able to use his influence to set the direction of the new school. Queensland was to break with the ad hoc system by which those with personal or family connections gained appointments in the teaching hospitals, while their less favoured colleagues were forced to turn to provincial towns or the struggle of establishing a private practice. Instead, all Queensland graduates were required to serve a full year in a hospital before graduating. The abolition of the honorary system would open the way for a fully salaried system of hospital specialists, appointed directly by the state director-general of health.[49] This permanent salaried service, Cilento predicted, would give:

> good men an incentive to take up hospital work as a life job, and will give the Government the opportunity to build up a service of nationalized medical men, the best of whom can aspire to becoming full-time specialists. . .
>
> In twenty years every medical man will have had a part-time relationship with the Department of Health and an actual experience of nationalized and social services. Queensland itself will have by that time an unequalled body of trained hospital superintendents and specialists in every branch.[50]

Rejecting Chuter's support for a relatively decentralized system with lay-controlled boards and strong representation from local trade unions, Cilento called for power to be concentrated in the hands of the (medically trained) director-general of health in Brisbane. He urged Hanlon: 'the Government should have a controlling voice and must indeed have it if there is to be any continuity of policy throughout the country. The Central Executive, i.e. the Minister of Health and his Department, must control policy rather than submit it to any local "rank and file".'[51]

Queensland's new health policies were developed in a very restricted circle of officials dominated by Hanlon, Chuter and Cilento. While enthusiastic in initiating reform, even by his own account Cilento was a difficult man to work with or under. In his unpublished autobiography he recalled that 'Pride and poverty combined, made me solitary and wrapped me in a protective cloak of disregard for any opinion but my own'. He admitted that he had little taste for team work and found delegation of tasks to subordinates difficult. These faults of character undermined his achievements as an administrator when projects became embroiled in clashes with colleagues who saw his behaviour as 'ruthless and disloyal'. Such a major breach in the personal relationship between Cilento and Chuter had serious repercussions for the success of the reform programme in Queensland. Although Cilento successfully challenged the exclusion of doctors from administrative influence, he was never able to gain the control over Queensland's hospitals which his grandiose vision required.[52]

In mid-1934 relations between the two men, already irritated at the slowness of the state government to act on his proposal for a new ministry, broke down over Cilento's apparent about-face on support for Kenny. A second report on the Kenny clinic, delivered by Cilento at the height of the state election campaign in May 1934, gave a much more guarded assessment of her techniques. Cilento suggested that her apparent high success rate owed more to psychological suggestion – and her dominant character – than to any new methods which could be used elsewhere. More immediately, his report contained vague hints of improper behaviour and involvement in sectarian conflicts in Townsville, apparently a reference to her naive but imprudent use of assistance from a local Presbyterian church. Chuter later claimed that this created prejudice in the mind of Hanlon, a strong Catholic in a Cabinet dominated by his co-religionists, and led to the immediate withdrawal of funds from the clinic. After the election Chuter was able to repair some of the damage done to Kenny, but the rift between the two men deepened. Funding for the clinic was restored and Hanlon ordered Cilento to cease his involvement in the Kenny controversy.[53]

The conflict over the Kenny clinic reinforced the suspicions that Cilento's ambitions aroused in many Labor politicians. In January 1935 Chuter was appointed as under-secretary (permanent head) of the Department of Home Affairs and until his retirement in December 1941 he was able to use this powerful base to frustrate many of Cilento's schemes. Relations between the state's two most senior health bureaucrats had permanently soured. Chuter now referred to Cilento as an 'idol of clay', a 'wolf in sheep's clothing' and accused him of 'treachery', holding secret meetings with the BMA to discuss government plans for hospital policy. In return, Cilento's invective against Chuter's support for local lay influence on hospital boards became more heated. During discussions of the new hospital act he denounced demands from local boards for the appointment of members '"more sympathetic" to the worker, presumably under Mr Chuter's leadership'.[54]

Only direct intervention by Hanlon resolved this bitter infighting. In December 1935 Cilento's Health Bill was finally shelved. Hanlon established a division of authority to ensure that neither of his powerful officials could dominate the state's health services. The director-general of health was confined to purely medical matters while finance and administration were left in Chuter's hands. A Hospitals Sub-Division within the Home Department kept control of the administration and admissions policies of the public hospitals outside medical control. Similarly, Cilento's attempt to eliminate local government from the administration of public health was blocked. Instead of 'a national health policy', in Queensland control was to remain in local government hands.[55]

Cilento saw the defeat of his wider plans as only a temporary setback. Although largely drafted under Chuter's supervision, the 1936 Hospital Bill contained elements of centralization which the latter found anathema. Cilento prevailed on Hanlon to remove the power of boards to appoint and dismiss medical officers, despite Chuter's denunciation of this as a fundamental attack on 'local control and responsibility' as 'the authority of the Board will be seriously undermined as it will no longer control the medical organization'.[56]

Cilento's ambitions had always gone well beyond those of his employers: the Queensland reforms were merely the proving ground for a national health service, providing 'a ready-made system onto which future Commonwealth proposals might be tacked, not as new and revolutionary advantages provided to the people of the State by the Commonwealth, but as a normal extension of a State service already introduced'.[57] In an 'Open Letter' published in the Brisbane *Telegraph* in 1937 he warned his colleagues of the inevitability of increased state control:

> Whatever the path we take, the health service of tomorrow inevitably will conform to whatever is the governmental framework, regardless of how earnestly, as doctors, we may fight for it or against it...
>
> Society has left to the physician all the decisions as to what the art and practice of medicine should include. There is to be no interference with medicine as a science, but what the public does demand is the right to say not HOW medicine shall be practised, but how it shall be purchased and PAID FOR and who has a better right to say this than those who do the paying? After all, those who have to find the money must control the economics of the situation...
>
> It is becoming evident that without some regulated relation with the State, a large proportion of medical practitioners cannot be adequately remunerated; while a large proportion of the public cannot receive adequate medical treatment.[58]

The 1936 Hospitals Act achieved the primary objective of controlling appointments in hospitals, and Cilento moved to tighten regulation of private hospitals and increase his control over the private practice of medicine. In 1938 this 'regulated relation with the State' led to the end of the honorary system at the public hospitals of the Brisbane and South Coast Hospital Board and payment of sessional fees to consultants. The hospital consultants now conceded that 'medical charity', such as the honorary system, had become:

> unnecessary and an anachronism. In Queensland the Government has taken over the responsibility of caring for the sick poor, and redeemed it

from any charitable motive. It has also opened the hospitals to classes of the community, which at other times would not have been regarded as fit subjects for medical benevolence. The retention of free service by doctors is tolerated by the Government only because it saves money. But if the doctors finally decide such service should cease, there should be no criticisms levelled at them for an action which is long overdue.[59]

Much to Chuter's disgust, the honorary system ended by mutual agreement and with generous concessions to the consultants. They continued to staff the hospitals, on a sessional salaried basis, rather than being displaced by a full-time salaried service. However, the Act established an unprecedented state control over hospital appointments, over the clinical years of medical training – as noted earlier a compulsory year of hospital work had been added to the medical curriculum – and the distribution of services throughout the state.

When Cilento's attention turned to private medical practice he met with more intractable resistance. The Queensland branch of the BMA had initially welcomed him as its liberator from state government oppression. The state branch had adopted a 'Policy for a General Medical Service' in 1935 which had started from the admission that 'the present system of private practice does not bring the necessary medical attention within the reach of the great proportion of the people in a manner which is satisfactory'. This honeymoon proved short-lived. From the start of his employment in Queensland Cilento had assumed the inevitability of conflict with the medical profession, between 'the individualistic ideal of both the patient and the professional man, and the communal ideal of the state'. However, unlike the earlier clashes between Labor administrations and the BMA, Cilento never questioned the need for professional control of the hospital and health services. His attack on medical autonomy was in the name of efficiency, of rationalization of the health system and the application of the principles of public health under state control to prepare for the struggle for national and racial survival – themes strongly identified with national hygiene. Unlike Chuter, Cilento saw little reason for lay intervention within medical institutions. His project for a full-time hospital service included medically trained administrators, a prospect previously regarded as anathema.[60]

By the late 1930s the displacement of general practitioners by hospital salaried doctors was well advanced in country areas. The appointment of full-time salaried medical officers was compounded by state government encouragement of contributory hospital benefit schemes and the construction of regional outpatient clinics. Consequently, when the remnants of honorary practice were replaced by part-time salaried service, the medical profession embraced the charge with some enthusiasm.[61]

This acquiescence did not mean support for further reform. The Medical Act of 1938 carried centralization of control even further and marked the full breach between Cilento and the medical profession. In future, medical registration was directly in the hands of the Director-General of Health, rather than a BMA-dominated Medical Board. A judicial tribunal was established to hear complaints of malpractice and excessive fees brought before it. Finally, for the first time in Australia, a register of specialists was established, again bitterly opposed by the BMA, fired by general practitioners who saw the dominance of full-time salaried medical officers in the hospitals squeezing them out of surgical and other specialized practice.[62]

BMA concerns at the national implications of the Queensland moves led to a visit by John Hunter, the federal secretary, in June 1937. He reported that the reorganization of medical services around the hospital was so well advanced that, as in Tasmania, the medical profession must move to accommodate itself, drawing on the support of the equally threatened friendly societies to prevent a total displacement of private practice by salaried hospital staff. Hunter pointed to Maryborough, a town of around 11,500 inhabitants with a general hospital of 100 beds, as a sign of things to come. There the local hospital board had appointed a superintendent, described as 'a very good type of general practitioner', at a salary of £1,250, with free housing and the assistance of two medical officers earning considerably lower salaries. The services of the hospital were available to all members of the community with a means-tested sliding scale of fees, assisted by a contributory insurance scheme for wage-earners. The friendly societies in the town were already suffering from this competition and Hunter warned that 'with an efficient staff, the Hospital must be a very serious competitor with private practitioners'.[63]

By the outbreak of war the new system was well-entrenched and increasingly influenced debate in states such as New South Wales, where the Thomas Committee, inquiring into the future of clinical medical education gave a favourable hearing to Cilento's evidence on the effects of the reform of Queensland's hospital training system. However, although the reorganization of the hospitals was well advanced, other areas of reform had stalled. Public health, despite its integration in the same portfolio as the more politically important curative services, was still starved of resources and left to the vagaries of local government. Equally, little progress had been made in controlling general practice and in organizing group clinics. Sections of the medical profession had always been sceptical of the feasibility of the Mayo model in Australian conditions. In 1939 Professor J.C. Windeyer, the dean of the University of Sydney Medical School, admitted that standards of medical education would be raised if students could serve an apprenticeship at a group clinic. He added, however, that 'I doubt very much whether a Mayo Clinic would pay here yet. You have to have a terrifically big population'.[64]

A report to Cabinet in 1941, unsigned but bearing evidence of Cilento's hand, looked critically at the future direction of national-ization in the state. After a lengthy discussion of the meaning of the word 'nationalization' in the party platform, it concluded that the new hospital system was a complete success as it:

> was a definite step in Nationalization and has produced results. It has, in fact, brought a big expansion and development in hospital and ancillary services. It has also broadened the outlook of the community generally, indeed, so far as public acceptance of the principle of Nationalization is concerned, it is indicated by the fact that 55 per cent of the babies born in the State in the years 1939–40 were born in the public hospitals. One in ten of the population was treated in the public hospital last year and one in four received outpatient (clinic) treatment in the out-patient and clinical departments of the public hospitals. Perhaps, most important of all, is the change in the attitude and outlook of the medical profession. It is not long since the medical profession fought for the retention of the honorary system as something that was sacrosanct. Today, the honorary medical service as a principle is as dead as the dodo, and medical men are seeking payment for services. A further indication in the change in med-ical outlook is the development of full-time medical services in the public hospital system. Out of all this is the development of a type of medical men, who prefer to work in hospitals only in preference to private practice with its meanness and petty and narrowed outlooks, for it is now borne in upon them that it is in the public hospital where the construc-tive work of medicine is undertaken, and that it will be in the National-ized Hospital where the constructive work of medicine can be undertaken to its fullest degree in the common good. [65]

However, any further attempt to bring personal medical services under state government control would fail, given the likelihood of resistance from the medical profession, and the administrative complexities and expense. Cilento's sweeping plans for Queensland were frustrated first by the breach with Chuter, then by an increasing lack of sympathy from the minister. In the late 1930s Hanlon under-took a massive programme of hospital construction. Services were centralized in the heart of Brisbane rather than the local group clinics of Cilento's vision. While Chuter's defeat over honorary prac-tice weakened his power, other lay advisers ensured that Cilento never obtained the unrestricted access to the minister his plans required. Recognizing that the state government would never give him the free hand or complete control over medical services that he craved, Cilento accepted a part-time appointment as Professor of Tropical and Social Medicine. However, within Queensland's borders the achievement proved lasting. The final seal was placed on this phase of reform with the Hospitals Act of 1944 which ended all means testing and fees for public patients. The hospital policies of the non-Labor parties and the BMA recognized that the days of charity hospitals were over.[66]

By the end of the 1930s there was a wide consensus that major changes in the organization of medical services were inevitable. As Herbert Moran, a prominent Sydney surgeon, warned his colleagues in 1939:

> the Government is occupying itself more and more with the health of citizens – with the rise or fall in infantile mortality, with the incidence of tuberculosis, with the ante-natal care of women. Can we deny its right? We private doctors have failed. We have made collective medicine in some form or other not only inevitable but necessary...our motives are constantly being questioned. In the presence of this increasing distrust we must offer a nobler example of personal integrity and of public devotion. We have given our attention too much as single doctors to individual patients. If the patient has a right to health, the community as a whole has also a right to protective measures. The State has intervened because we forgot the people as a whole.[67]

The grand projects of the national hygienists had failed in the face of weak federal powers and a reluctance to challenge the institutions of private medicine. But the limited successes of Labor governments in Tasmania and Queensland showed that however strong the political will, individual states were unlikely to carry through a thoroughgoing programme of reform. Whether they viewed this development with reluctance or enthusiasm, critics of medical practice still saw a thoroughgoing extension of intervention at Commonwealth level as the only route to real reform.

# CHAPTER 4

# The Defeat of National Health Insurance

In 1919, Dr J. Corbin, an Adelaide lodge doctor, published a vehement attack on the effects of private medicine on Australian health care. He contrasted the manner in which:

> the lodge patient consults his medical attendant before he is gravely ill. The private patient either consults no-one or takes some quack medicine or a prescription from a chemist and it is not until he is seriously ill that he seeks medical advice.
>
> This does not apply to the really well-to-do, but to the intermediate class, to whom economy is essential, and this class forms the largest part of any community, and is the class which is most likely to be benefited by a scheme of national insurance. The very poor and destitute are well provided for; the very rich can pay for any skill or advice; it is the intermediate class that is always sure to suffer.[1]

Support for national insurance spanned the conservative parties, academic economists and participants in the forums of the Australian Institute of Political Science as well as sections of the labour movement. Contributory insurance schemes were at the heart of a programme to bolster social solidarity as well as individual financial security. Faced with the threat of class conflict, yet hostile to the social inequities of uncontrolled capitalism, liberals embraced schemes which appealed to a higher notion of community. Social insurance, along with industrial arbitration, was to provide the basis of a new social order founded on ties of mutual obligation between social classes and the state. Regular, compulsory contributions by both employers and workers would establish funds from which benefits could be paid, as a matter of right, to tide insured workers over periods of sickness and unemployment. It offered both a limited redistribution of income between social classes – the employers' contribution was in effect a tax on employment – while the employees' contribution transformed the social relationship of the individual and the state. Contributory insurance would provide a sharp break from the charitable overtones of the existing Australian pensions system, which was funded from general revenue and paid on a strictly means-tested basis, and further hedged with an intimidating array of deterrent and intrusive conditions.

The intellectual and political origins of National Health Insurance (NHI) lay in this liberal tradition. In sharp contrast to the national hygienists' schemes of medically-based state tutelage, NHI extended the existing friendly society approach to health care, relieving the economic strains of illness and increasing the access of the sick to personal medical services. The content of those services was not in question.[2]

For exponents of insurance such as R.G. Casey and Sir Frederick Stewart, both cabinet ministers in the Lyons government, NHI was one more application of this universal panacea. Although proposals for national insurance had been advanced before the First World War, it only became a real political possibility during the 1920s. In 1911 Britain had successfully introduced national health insurance, using the friendly societies and other 'approved societies' to administer it, under strict Treasury supervision. As with other areas of Australian social policy, this British precedent set a seal of legitimacy around NHI. Even many of its sternest critics within the BMA appeared to accept that Australia would inevitably follow Britain's path, arguing for resistance only in order to enhance the profession's bargaining power rather than in expectation of an effective veto.[3]

The push for national health insurance did not last long in the relatively prosperous 1920s. When the conservative Bruce government established a Royal Commission into National Insurance in 1924 to look at the whole issue of unemployment, sickness, old age and health insurance the medical profession reacted with indifference. While the *Medical Journal of Australia* accepted that national insurance was inevitable, given Australia's pattern of adopting British models, it warned that NHI had very little to do with a rational health policy. The BMA presented a shopping list of demands for expenditure on vaguely defined areas of public health and prevention, but contributed little to the public debate: admitting that schemes based on fee-for-service, the profession's preference, would be too expensive and administratively complex.[4] BMA witnesses at Royal Commission hearings argued that national health insurance might be useful in Britain but expressed scepticism at the value of greater public funding for personal medical care and hostility to the British style of contract service, in particular the power it would vest in the friendly societies. This was not simply a matter of obstruction from the more conservative elements of organized medicine. The doubts expressed by the BMA were shared by the advocates of national hygiene, who still advocated a more directive role for state intervention. Frank Hone, for example, argued that increased expenditure on hospitals and preventive medicine would provide swifter returns in improved public health.[5] In the face of this hostility from all sections of medical opinion, the commissioners recommended that NHI should be excluded from the general scheme of national insurance. The project died with the defeat of the Bruce government in 1929.[6]

Medical hostility to insurance did not survive the great depression. As we have seen, general practitioners in working class districts were hit hard financially, many were thrown into greater dependence on the friendly society lodges while losing their poorer patients to the free outpatients' clinics of the public hospitals. In these circumstances national health insurance, with its guarantee of remuneration, began to look more attractive to many doctors, patients and governments. Several state branches of the BMA developed their own schemes culminating in a national policy which was adopted in 1936. Based on an extension of contract service, on the friendly society model, it offered a strictly means-tested and restricted range of services. To avoid the participation of friendly societies the scheme would be administered directly by the Commonwealth government, with majority medical representation on all administrative bodies. Patients were to preserve their freedom of choice of doctor and doctors the right to remain outside the scheme. Remuneration would be by capitation fee, with the excluded services paid on a fee-for-service basis. This new support for national health insurance was confirmed when John Hunter, the general secretary of the BMA, was sent to Britain to study the workings of contract practice under national insurance. Hunter came back declaring that 'national insurance is necessary for the health of the community'. It would solve the problems of the restricted medical market, bridging the financial gulf that restricted access for non-charity patients to public hospitals and private medical care and freeing practitioners from dependence on the restricted fee-for-service market and the oppressive conditions of lodge practice.[7]

Hence, when the Lyons government began to talk of extending its national insurance proposals to personal medical services the immediate reaction from the medical profession was favourable. Many saw NHI as the only way to break the barriers blocking the middle classes from expensive health care. The market had failed these groups and charity had proved an inadequate and increasingly dangerous answer, opening threats of more radical demands for completely free care. Insurance, especially if it was administered outside friendly society control, could solve the economic problems faced by patients and doctors without threatening medical autonomy. Lindsey Dey, a general practitioner and president of the New South Wales branch of the BMA in 1937, warned that medical care was moving beyond the financial reach of much of the population. Confining themselves to better risks, the friendly societies and other forms of voluntary insurance were unable to bridge this gap. Only compulsory national health insurance could offer a solution to the main problems facing general practice:

> and still preserve to the public the personal service that characterizes the general practitioner type of practice. This should check the drift to the public hospitals, which must end in a form of nationalization of the medical services, such as is foreshadowed in the recent legislation in Queensland.[8]

## Bacon and eggs for breakfast: the Kinnear scheme

> The Englishman abroad demanding his bacon and eggs for breakfast, and in other respects expecting other countries to conform to English customs, has long been an international figure of fun. The two distinguished English experts whom the Commonwealth Government called in to prepare reports on Unemployment Insurance and Health and Pensions Insurance respectively, have the same bland assurance that things as they are done in England must be as nearly perfect as is likely to be found anywhere in this sinful world.[9]

As BMA policy at national and state level favoured national health insurance and the medical press had expressed sympathy, it appeared that agreement with the national insurance scheme would be swift. While some bargaining over rates of remuneration and administrative controls was inevitable, these problems did not appear insuperable. Hence the defiance with which organized medicine met the Lyons government's scheme seems paradoxical. This conflict has often been seen as one of the high points of the assertion of the autonomy of the medical profession, a rejection of state intervention which set the pattern for the conflicts of the 1940s.

During the 1937 election campaign the United Australia Party had promised a scheme of national insurance to cover pensions and health care. The promise served to harness a spirit of progressive reform to a UAP increasingly devoid of new ideas after two terms of office. At the same time it aimed to serve the long-term goals of reduction of direct government expenditure. As Watts has recently pointed out, the national health insurance scheme was merely an afterthought in a wider project to shift the fiscal load of old age pensions from general revenue to a contributory basis. By the mid 1930s projections by the Auditor-General suggested that the cost of pensions would become insupportable in future years as the population aged. Richard Casey, the Treasurer since 1934, had been an advocate of contributory insurance as a means of avoiding such a fiscal crisis and received strong support from the maverick UAP minister, Sir Frederick Stewart, a public advocate of national insurance. Lyons himself appears to have been lukewarm and from the beginning it faced hostility from many Country Party MPs sceptical about any new impost on employers.[10]

There were to be two main parts to the new national insurance system: unemployment insurance, and pensions and health insurance. Both schemes were closely modelled on their British equivalents. The unemployment insurance scheme was drafted by G.H. Ince, who was seconded from the British Ministry of Labour, while the pensions and health insurance schemes were produced by Sir Walter Kinnear and Thomas Lindsay, officials loaned by the British Ministry of Health. Kinnear, 'a hard-hearted insurance man devoted to contributory principles', visited Australia in 1936 and held some private talks with BMA representatives in Sydney. However, he carried out little research in Australia and his report gave no consideration to the future direction of health services, the relationship between general practice and the hospital and the development of specialist services.[11]

The Kinnear scheme transferred British national health insurance practices: means-tested panel practice which excluded hospital and specialist benefits. As well as limiting the range of benefits, Kinnear ignored a major contrast between British and Australian lodge practice – the inclusion of dependants in Australian friendly society medical benefits. While the actuaries could only welcome this move to exclude the greatest users of medical services, this only underlined the mean-spirited fiscal calculations which had inspired government action. These lacunae were compounded by an even more serious political error: the exclusion of the self-employed, including those earning below the means test (a group previously eligible for lodge practice), old age and invalid pensioners, the unemployed, and farmers. The only major concession to Australian conditions was the vesting of administrative control directly in the hands of the Commonwealth government's National Insurance Commission – in contrast to the British state's indirect control through the friendly societies. In Britain this had provided the Treasury with a painless means of restricting the costs of insurance through regulation of the fiduciary standards of the approved societies, while taking no direct responsibility for the level of benefits each society offered. Direct government control went very much against Kinnear's preferences, but recognized the different political realities, given the unlikelihood of the Australian branches of the BMA (especially in Victoria) conceding such power to their old foes in the societies.[12]

With its origins in fiscal policy the insurance scheme was dominated from the start by actuarial considerations. It was required to become self-financing as soon as possible by establishing a pool of contributors large enough to meet all expected claims. This link between pensions and health insurance raised the ire of the advocates of social and preventive medicine, long critical of cash benefit and insurance schemes for merely providing inadequate finance for the existing pattern of sickness. As we have seen, a major part of the programme of interwar national hygiene and the liberal case for state intervention was based on the regulation of the health and child-rearing practices of women. Given this context, it appeared even more astonishing to contemporary critics that NHI should omit most married women and children. Cumpston later recalled that:

> The whole attitude of this type of approach was condensed in one remark made to me by Sir Walter Kinnear when he was brought to Australia to advise on the Insurance system. When I called on him to offer any assistance I could give, his reply to me was that the only concern a Health Insurance scheme had with doctors was to police them. He declined my assistance and did not again discuss Health Insurance with me.[13]

The British model accepted so lightly by the government was already under heavy attack in its own country by the medical profession because of the workload panel practice imposed, and from the trade unions and other critics on the left for its restrictions and the second class treatment of panel patients. The economist Colin Clark, the director of the Queensland Bureau of Industry, argued that this controversy had set strict limits on what the two British civil servants were prepared to countenance in Australia. Charging Kinnear and Ince with 'extreme complacency', he argued that their loyalty to their employers had undermined their independence and rendered them unwilling to make the criticism of the British system that a more generous Australian scheme would imply.[14]

From the beginning the federal government recognized that the co-operation of the medical profession would be essential for the success of the scheme, so in the last half of 1937 informal talks were held with Kinnear. These initial discussions between the BMA and the Commonwealth government were amicable: in August the Federal Council declared itself 'unanimous that it was the duty of the medical profession to provide a willing and efficient service'. While expressing reservations about details of the proposals, such as the size of panels, and the effective enforcement of the means test – both points of grievance in the British scheme – these objections were seen as matters for negotiation, not insuperable obstacles. The Council warned that 'a medical practitioner should be allowed to undertake the treatment of only such numbers of persons as he could treat in an efficient and adequate way'. Panels must be limited to a maximum of 1,500 patients. A means test of £365 would keep a large section of the population outside the scheme as private patients – possibly as many as 15 per cent. The capitation fee should be set at £1 for individual patients, or £2 if families were to be included. In addition, Commonwealth maternity benefits should be introduced, increasing doctors' incomes from obstetric fees. In October this scheme was endorsed by the annual meeting of the New South Wales branch, with strong representation from the suburban and country general practitioners most affected, although, in an ominous foretaste of what was to come, the meeting called for the capitation rate to be raised from £1 to £1 6s. for single patients, doubling this for families.[15]

Although the Kinnear scheme would only affect general practice, the BMA negotiating committee was limited to leading specialists from four states: Sir Henry Newland, the federal president, Drs John Newman Morris and Francis L. Davies from Victoria, George Bell from New South Wales, Thomas Price from Queensland, and John Hunter, the federal secretary. While each man had a long record of activity in medical politics, none had recent direct experience of lodge and general practice. Compounding this problem, the Commonwealth required that the content of the discussions must remain secret, so little was done to prepare the state branches for the terms of the agreement.

Under these conditions swift progress was made. Meeting in early March 1938, the Federal Council's negotiating committee extracted what both sides believed were large concessions. Requiring a standard capitation fee to cover the entire country, the Treasury had calcu- lated a weighted average of 27s., based on existing friendly society rates in all states. These rates included the treatment of dependants. Using Victorian statistics, the Commonwealth assumed that each contributor had 3.2 dependants. As NHI would not cover dependants this reduced the capitation fee to around 8s. 6d. per annum. The BMA replied with a demand for a minimum rate of 14s. After much argument, the Commonwealth raised its offer to 9s. (the British rate) and finally to 11s., although protesting that the younger average age of national insurance contributors would mean that panel patients would demand fewer medical services than their friendly society equivalents. In March 1938 the Federal Council ratified this rate, to be renegotiated after five years, as well as the general principles of the scheme. During April and May the *Medical Journal of Australia* published articles supporting the Council's stand affirming that 'on existing data it would be extremely difficult to justify claims for better conditions'.[16]

This co-operation proved short-lived. When details of the agree- ment were released to the state branches loud protests followed from general practitioners over the coverage of the scheme and the size of capitation rates. Country practitioners were particularly incensed at the restrictive conditions which, unlike existing lodge practice, did not offer differential rates in recognition of the greater problems of rural practice, nor mileage rates for the long distances covered by many rural doctors – usually between 3s. 6d. and 5s. a mile.[17]

While the size of the capitation fee remained the central public objection expressed by general practitioners this touched other, more inchoate fears. Increasing panel practice and further limits on excluded services could only weaken the position of the general practitioner in the medical division of labour. Thomas Price was a Queensland representative on the original negotiating committee who quickly changed his views, leading his state into repudiation. He warned of the danger that under NHI 'general practice should be looked upon merely as a clearing house to separate minor ailments from more serious complaints', referring the latter to specialists in base hospitals. In a paper prepared in June for the Queensland branch of the BMA he calculated that NHI would greatly increase the workload of the average general practitioner. Assuming that unin-sured pensioners and the unemployed would remain a burden on practices, Price calculated that to earn a gross income of £1,182 under the Kinnear scheme general practitioners would have to build up panel lists of at least 1,744 patients. Based on current friendly society rates of five visits to the doctor per year, general practitioners would have to provide an average of 31 services a day (in a 278-day working year). In contrast, the Federal Council's limit of 1,500 to a panel meant closer to 20 services a day. Without extra allowances for holiday or night work and lacking long service or study leave, he argued that standards of service and the net incomes of general practitioners could only fall.[18]

In the face of this hostility, the Federal Council was forced into an ignominious withdrawal, repudiating the agreement and returning to the original demand for a capitation fee of 14s., with a 25 per cent loading for country doctors, increases in the mileage allowance and the addition of penalty rates for night calls. Facing bitter attacks from federal ministers for its sudden change of heart, it opened a long and bitter confrontation.[19]

The early stages of the conflict over NHI provided the BMA with its first serious test as a national institution able to represent and defend the interests of the medical profession. It failed miserably. Critics of the Federal Council from within the profession focused on its dominance by specialists. Cut off from the realities of panel practice, they argued, councillors were easily gulled by the Common-wealth's professions of good intention, and prepared to sign away the rights of general practitioners. This split between leaders and ordinary members, paralleling the growing conflict between specialists and general practitioners, owed much to the cumbersome federal structure of the BMA. The Federal Council, its highest decision-making body, was formed in 1933 to replace an earlier and even less effectual Federal Committee. The council was not based on a formal federation of the state branches but inherited an uncertain constitutional position, as each of the state branches remained independent branches of the parent organization in London to which they paid affiliation fees. All changes to the rules and articles of association of the Federal Council and state branches had to be approved by London, a measure which was as much the result of interstate rivalries and suspicions as of imperial sentiment. The Federal Council co-ordinated the limited national activities of the BMA, but could not commit the branches without their consent. Despite regular pleas for a stronger national organization to prepare the Association for the coming struggle over NHI, the state branches were unprepared to make the necessary sacrifices of power.[20]

Consequently, the states gave their Federal Council few resources. It shared a part-time secretariat with the New South Wales branch, and from 1933 to 1936 survived on annual subsidies of £1,000 from London. The Federal Council's dilemma was compounded by its narrow membership. Given the difficulties of assembling members from all over Australia at its half-yearly meetings, the two representatives from each state tended to be senior consultants with the time and money to devote attention to national questions. Until the NHI conflict, federal issues concerning the BMA had been limited – the largest matter had been co-ordinating evidence to the Royal Commission on Health and other questions of public health policy – issues distant from the day-to-day concerns of general practice. The trade union issues which were the bread and butter of the BMA – the hospital question and conditions of workers' compensation and lodge practice – remained the exclusive province of the state branches.

The image of an implacably united rank and file turning on their aristocratic leaders has proved lasting, but explanations based on the isolation of councillors from the rank and file of the profession are seriously flawed. The BMA in London kept the Federal Council well informed of Kinnear's movements and the inevitability of a clash over the size of the capitation fee. When the Commonwealth government brought Kinnear back to Australia in February 1938 to assist in detailed negotiations, G.C. Anderson, Hunter's British equivalent, passed on information concerning Kinnear's background, views and itinerary. In that month Hunter informed his colleague that:

> it looks as if we are in for more trouble as Kinnear has apparently come to Australia with a fixed idea that a nine shillings capitation rate is more than enough – in fact he believes that eight shillings is adequate payment. Any such offer, of course, would be strongly resisted by the profession. Nothing less than fifteen shillings would even be considered.[21]

Confirming these forebodings, Anderson reminded his colleague:

> I think I warned you some time ago to be wary of Kinnear. I know that he has always felt that the doctors in this country are overpaid and he would gladly have reduced the present capitation fee of 9/- had it been possible for him to do so. He is not a bad chap in many ways but he is a typical Irishman in others. Watch him very carefully. I am perfectly certain that you will probably have a fight with the Government if he is to advise them on the pay question.[22]

The Federal Council also had ample indications that the branches were unlikely to accept a low capitation rate. In early January the New South Wales Council approved a rate of 52s. including dependants – 16s. 3d. if calculated by Kinnear's formula – and two months later a meeting of the local associations from throughout the state raised this to £1 for the metropolitan area and £1 6s. 8d. for the country.[23]

Why then did the Federal Council accede to the government's terms? Amy McGrath has suggested that the council was afraid that a Labor government would impose an even more onerous scheme: NHI was then the lesser of two evils. This explains the council's sense of urgency and willingness to ignore deficiencies in the scheme for the sake of rapid implementation. Joseph Lyons' coalition United Australia/Country Party government had won a federal election in 1937 but held only a narrow majority in the Senate. Many commentators noted a weary atmosphere in the conservative ranks as the policy and personality clashes which were to destroy the coalition emerged into the open. However, this threat from the ALP is easily exaggerated. Although Labor was formally committed to a policy of national insurance, previous Labor governments had shown little interest.[24]

It seems more likely that the BMA leadership accepted that some form of NHI was inevitable, whatever the party in power, so attempted to entrench the principles of its own 1935 policy – a policy which had already been accepted by the state branches. Anxious to reach a quick agreement on essentials, it acceded to the federal government's insistence on secrecy, excluding the state branches from early discussions. The BMA negotiators recognized that Anderson's warnings on the capitation rate were being realized, accepting this as a regrettable but temporary problem.

From the start the Federal Council recognized that winning the profession's support for NHI would be no easy task. Its agreement with the Kinnear proposals was surrounded by heavy qualifications, conceding that the scheme had been launched in 'a primitive form', but holding forth the hope that once the principle was established it could develop into a 'complete organization, worthy of the Commonwealth and its people', the best method to block a more drastic form of nationalization. The BMA negotiators complained that NHI failed to take recent advances in social and preventive medicine seriously. They objected to its incompleteness – merely providing an extension of lodge practice – and, finally, to the low rate of remuneration.[25]

Given this grudging endorsement of the Kinnear scheme, the Council's subsequent repudiation of support became all the easier as opposition flared. Even the main opponents of NHI shared this initial ambivalence. *The General Practitioner*, soon to lead the denunciation of the Federal Council's treason, gave the scheme a very low-keyed reception, noting that it would create major obstacles to Labor moves to nationalize medicine in Queensland and Tasmania and warning that as national health insurance was official BMA policy doctors should be cautious in making public criticisms.[26]

The next months saw a conflict between two interest group strategies. The Federal Council attempted to influence outcomes by becoming directly involved in government decision-making processes, hoping to win hegemony over key areas of policy: the confident tactics of a group of men used to ruling. This corporatism, the partial devolution of public policy-making and enforcement to a private organized interest, was well established at state level in Victoria. The next step, for many BMA leaders, with Victorians prominent, was to extend this model to the nation. By repudiating this approach and refusing to propose a better alternative, the other state branches shifted BMA tactics to those of a veto group, providing a prickly deterrent to state control by making intervention as costly and painful as possible. Over the next half century this bitter internal conflict over strategy became a regular element of most BMA negotiations with the federal government.[27]

## The campaign against NHI

On 4 May 1938 the National Health and Pensions Insurance Bill went to Parliament. Its main provisions now included contributory benefit schemes for sickness and disability, old age, widows' and orphans' pensions, supplemented by child allowances. Employee contributions to the scheme were to be collected by the friendly societies. However, medical benefits and pensions would be directly administered by the National Insurance Commission, advised by a Medical Benefits Council and District Medical Benefit Committees.

The bill faced a torrid passage. In the 1937 federal elections the ALP had increased its Senate representation from five to sixteen, and the new senators were due to take their seats on 1 July. If Labor could delay the Senate vote until after this date the deep divisions within the coalition parties might enable major amendments to the scheme. So the ALP, aided by a small group of dissident Country Party members led by H.L. Anthony and Arthur Fadden, bogged the bill down in parliamentary opposition. The Country Party group demanded the inclusion of small farmers in the scheme (and on a somewhat contradictory note, their exemption from employer contributions, effectively excluding their employees). Publicly embarrassed by two backbench revolts – one of which had reduced its majority in the House to only three – the government offered concessions to its Country Party critics. A new insurance section would be created for the self-employed with a firm income limit and double the level of contributions. This ensured Country Party support for the bill through the House (aided by frantic radio-telephone conferences with Sir Earle Page, the party leader, who was in London), although it still required a guillotine motion on 16 June to suppress further parliamentary debate. Even after the principal bill had passed, Fadden and Anthony led a final attempt to exempt small employers from contribution when two supplementary appropriation bills came before the House, but parliamentary opposition had been effectively thwarted. The National Insurance Bill was passed by the Senate with three days to spare before the new Labor senators were seated.[28]

Other foes proved more intractable. The BMA state branches had stepped up their campaign, a plebiscite of members in New South Wales voted almost unanimously to reject the 11s. capitation fee and the branch warned that the exclusion of dependants would have a catastrophic effect on doctors' incomes: 'We know quite well that the average man on the basic wage will not be able to pay any more for the medical treatment of his dependants. In other words, remuneration for the treatment of these dependants will be lost forever by the medical profession'.[29]

While Casey recognized that the scheme was unworkable without medical co-operation, his concessions attempted to avoid compromising the basic principles of national insurance, especially central control of benefits. He offered a wider list of excluded services – to be charged separately by fee-for-service: anaesthesia, pathology, x-rays, the treatment of venereal diseases, abortions, miscarriages and stillbirths were all removed from general cover. If these retreats pleased the BMA, the government quickly destroyed this goodwill with a concession to the friendly societies and trade unions, by offering to subsidize the subscriptions of dependants in approved society medical schemes. Medical opponents of NHI saw this as a move to hand over administration to the societies.[30]

While the bill remained mired in parliamentary filibustering, the initial disquiet of the state branches of the BMA had changed into open repudiation. Under this pressure, the Federal Council of the BMA began to fire criticisms at the scheme, concentrating on the low level of capitation rates and claiming that the NHI scheme had been based on the relatively unfavourable conditions of Victorian lodge practice. The National Insurance Commission retorted that they were based on the high rates in New South Wales. These claims of bad faith helped to create an atmosphere of mutual distrust which made further negotiations impossible.[31]

The Federal Council's attempt to reopen negotiations on the capitation fee came too late to re-establish the shattered national unity of the BMA. Each branch waged its own campaign, and while all were hostile to NHI, their responses, and forms of leadership and action, varied greatly according to local conditions – a direct consequence of the diversity of forms of state intervention, the strength of lodge practice and the depth of hostility between specialists and general practitioners.

Victoria and New South Wales were at the forefront of the struggle, with the initiative in both states taken by younger general practitioners. Most of these had previously been at the margins of BMA leadership; the integration of these dissidents within existing branch power structures became a major preoccupation of BMA leaders – avoiding the threat of an open schism. This process of incorporation was relatively smooth in New South Wales. Branch unity was rebuilt in a campaign which refrained from total rejection of NHI, but demanded that the new scheme adopt standards of remuneration equivalent to those of lodge practice under the New South Wales Common Form of Agreement. A publicity committee was appointed to co-ordinate the branch campaign, including seven sitting councillors as well as nine metropolitan and country general practitioners. Although this included more established leaders of the profession, such as the surgeon George Bell and W.F. Simmons, the committee was dominated by the more militant opponents of the scheme, such as A.J. Collins and H. Ronald Grieve. Grieve, the leader of New South Wales militancy for the following two decades, had strong connections in conservative politics. He had been active in the formation of the United Australia Party and served as a member of the New South Wales Legislative Council.[32]

Medical opposition in New South Wales focused on the terms and conditions of the scheme, rather than the principle of national insurance and contract medical service. Instead, the principal fear – shared with South Australia and Queensland, with similar records of favourable agreements with the friendly societies – was that the Kinnear scheme would reduce capitation fees to the parlous position of Victoria and Tasmania. A major attraction of NHI for general practitioners had been the promise of finally ending the power of the

friendly societies. Consequently, the most vehement opposition to
the scheme was not directed against Commonwealth involvement,
but towards similarities with lodge practice. By covering more wage-
earners and including a wider range of medical services NHI would
narrow the supplementary area of private practice enjoyed by general
practitioners.[33]

In June the state council recommended a complete boycott of the
scheme and began to enlist the support of the membership in a
pledge of non-cooperation.[34] The branch's alternative to the
government's proposals allowed for a scheme controlled by the
friendly societies, generalizing the favourable conditions which New
South Wales lodge doctors had won to the rest of the Commonwealth. Opposition stemmed more from fear of government involvement – a legacy of earlier clashes with state Labor governments. The
most intransigent challenge to NHI was initiated by the branch's
Southern Medical Association when the doctors of Goulburn
pledged to refuse co-operation in any bureaucratic scheme. The
Goulburn Pledge immediately became central to the BMA campaign
in New South Wales, affirming the unity of the profession. Whatever
the value of the threatened boycott as propaganda, many BMA
leaders were less than convinced of the prospects of success.
Anything less than 75 per cent of the members signing would be seen
as a reverse, a dangerous gamble.[35]

Despite the hot words which accompanied the rejection of the
Federal Council's agreement, a similar coalescence of the old elite of
specialists and the rank-and-file general practitioners took place in
the smaller states. In South Australia, Rupert Magarey, from one of
Adelaide's oldest medical dynasties, initiated the repudiation of the
Council's agreement. BMA branches in the less-populated states had
more trouble in mobilizing opposition. In a plebiscite of Queensland
doctors only 61 per cent voted to oppose national insurance, while in
Tasmania less than half the membership responded to a call for emergency funds to fight the scheme.[36]

In Victoria, where passions had always run hot on the subject of
contract practice, the existing branch leadership did not have such
an easy ride. C.H. Dickson, the branch secretary, had welcomed NHI
as an acceptable 'instalment'. Critics of the scheme saw this as yet
another example of the pusillanimous conduct of the patrician-
dominated Victorian branch council, which 'strove manfully to rally
around the old school tie and put the general practitioners in what
many councillors felt was their proper place'. Led by younger general
practitioners, such as Charles Byrne and John H. Gowland, few of

the opponents of NHI had been previously active in branch affairs. To publicize their case they moved outside the existing organs of BMA publicity. William H. Fitchett used his editorial control of *The General Practitioner* – once the journal of the state branch's general practitioners' section but now independent in both control and politics – to pursue a radically anti-statist line, drawing heavily on American opponents of national health insurance as the first step on the slippery slope towards socialism. At the height of this campaign there were even moves towards a breakaway, general practitioner-led organization.[37]

With a greater history of hostility to the lodges, the Victorian opposition was unwilling to compromise with any scheme based on lodge practice. This control by outsiders formed the core of their hostility to NHI: some were even prepared to countenance greater Commonwealth involvement if this would destroy the medical activities of the lodges once and for all. This led to the paradox that although the split within the BMA was more bitter in Victoria than elsewhere, opposition to NHI appears to have been narrower. Fitchett complained that 'there is a distinct possibility that the Government plan will fail in New South Wales and be accepted in Victoria. Do the Victorians wish to be looked on as the "scabs" of the profession?'[38]

This combination of militancy and isolation meant that to a greater extent than in other states the campaign in Victoria was dominated by rank-and-file general practitioners. Excluded from leading positions within the state branch, they were forced to form alliances with some curious political partners. Watts has found evidence of strong Communist participation in the campaign, leading to the denunciation of national health insurance as 'fascism' at meetings of State Electricity Commission workers. As president of the United Electors of Australia (Non-Party), John Dale, the Medical Officer of Health of the City of Melbourne, claimed to have issued 20,000 protest letters to politicians in Canberra. At the same time local Citizens Anti-Insurance Action Committees organized public meetings with support from the mainstream of the labour movement. The Mayor of Williamstown chaired a mass meeting in the town hall addressed by the veteran trade union leader, E.J. Holloway (who was soon to be at the receiving end of BMA wrath as Minister for Health in the Curtin government). Similar committees were active in the working class suburbs of Port Melbourne, Altona and Coburg. Maurice Blackburn, the left-wing Labor lawyer and civil libertarian, took an even more active stand, using Fitchett's *National*

*Insurance Newsletter* and *The General Practitioner* to offer his free legal advice to medical opponents of NHI.[39]

In July 1938 the Commonwealth government conceded the strength of medical opposition and established a Royal Commission into the Remuneration of Doctors, chaired by Judge Detheridge from the Arbitration Court. One of the concessions to dissident back-benchers to get the bills through Parliament, the commission succeeded in diverting discontent, as well as providing an excuse for the Federal Council and the *Medical Journal of Australia* to suppress further public discussion – and criticism of their role – by declaring the matter sub judice. Starting on 8 August in Sydney, the commission held extensive public hearings in all capital cities and Kalgoorlie. Closed sessions heard evidence about incomes from medical practices and the BMA presented carefully arranged figures to support its case. However, from the start the Federal Council had admitted the strength of the Commonwealth's arguments for 11s., so the chances of winning on this single issue may have been remote. The commission having served its function of removing the heat from opposition, its proceedings were halted on 25 October when the BMA's legal counsel were killed in the Kyeema aeroplane disaster. The commission came to a desultory end with Justice Detheridge's death in December. No report was completed and the issue disappeared in the war crisis.[40]

In the meantime, the Commonwealth proceeded with the establishment of the scheme. In the second week of July the National Insurance Commission was gazetted with the economist J.B. Brigden as chairman, and on 11 and 12 July Kinnear addressed a meeting of approved society representatives in Canberra and gave a final frosty warning to 'see that your politicians do not debauch the National Insurance Scheme, and give a lot of benefits that it cannot afford'. At this stage his warnings still seemed unnecessary. Although the government was prepared to offer discussions and further inquiries to quiet opponents, it made only slight, and inexpensive, changes to appease some critics, but at the risk of arousing hostility from other quarters. Although medical benefits would still be controlled by a national Medical Benefits Council, the approved societies would play a larger part in local administration. This aroused the fears of the Victorian critics. Charles Byrne focused on this point, noting that the capitation fee had dwindled into insignificance by comparison, attacking the administrative expense and waste of a multitude of competing private funds and the danger that: 'such a potentially powerful organization could easily get a stranglehold on the profession'. He called for an independent statutory authority on the lines of the State Electricity Commission of Victoria, controlled by the medical profession.[41]

In a rueful survey of the fragmentation of the BMA campaign, *The General Practitioner* noted in mid-1939 that in response to the greater strength of its friendly societies, Victoria had now become the main seat of opposition to the scheme. The New South Wales doctors, while maintaining their pledge of non-cooperation for the moment, were prepared to participate if the conditions of their Common Form of Agreement with the friendly societies were observed. In Queensland, where the medical profession was in a new phase of a long struggle with Labor governments for control over health policy-making, renewed conflict with the state government:

> has brought doctors and Friendly Societies together as companions in trouble. A mutual assistance pact is understandable there. And both in New South Wales and Queensland the AWU formed a very strong Approved Society under the National Health Insurance Act, so that in this respect also there is a certain common interest between doctors and Friendly Societies there.[42]

The narrow base of the medical profession's opposition was underlined in December when Casey made some major concessions which met many of the objections of the critics. Under the new proposals the dependants of the insured would be included as beneficiaries and, resolving another major anomaly, women leaving the workforce upon marriage would receive a lump sum 'dowry' consisting of their past contributions, instead of forfeiting all entitlements.[43] In a last effort to save the collapsing scheme, in March 1939 he abandoned the pension scheme, reintroduced unemployment insurance (although with few details) and accepted the major demands of the BMA on capitation rates, raising the basic rate to £1. Two months later, after a tour of New South Wales country districts, the BMA's state president reported that members were unanimous in their approval of the government's new proposals. Combined with the subsidy for dependants in friendly societies this would increase the cost of the scheme by more than one-third over Kinnear's estimates.[44]

The BMA's repudiation of NHI, while generating much strident rhetoric condemning government interference in the sanctity of the doctor–patient relationship, demonstrated weaknesses in organized medicine as a political force. State jealousies remained a hindrance to strong federal organization. These hostilities were firmly based in the different power relationships between the profession, friendly societies and governments in each state. Furthermore, the structural interests which divided the profession internally – particularly the conflict between general practitioners and specialists for access to patients – provided another line of fissure. The Federal Council had proved unable to provide unified leadership; instead the BMA campaign had rapidly fragmented at state level, with each branch working for different goals.

## Employers, trade unionists and the death of national insurance

If the BMA remained an ambivalent and internally divided opponent to the principle of national insurance, the failure of the scheme still requires explanation. This can be found in the array of other political forces hostile to contributory insurance. Faced with the inability of the BMA to agree on the terms of medical participation in the scheme, the government also had to contend with the hostility of the trade union movement the friendly societies and, most importantly, from within the ranks of its own supporters. It was this broad spectrum of opposition which made the government's task in reaching a compromise almost impossible. Any concession to please one sectional group was almost certain to raise the ire of another.

A deeper problem lay at the heart of the scheme. Inspired by narrow fiscal motives, the Kinnear scheme had little to inspire enthusiastic support. Its supporters were unable to project the sense of national destiny which drove the national hygienists, nor the feelings of social obligation which underpinned similar advances in social legislation in Europe. In the absence of these links to a wider national purpose, the future of national insurance was tenuous. It offered little to meet the objections of a working class movement highly suspicious of any state intervention outside the arbitration system and wary of the regressive effects of a contributory scheme – from women who were required to contribute while in the workforce but faced the loss of all entitlements upon marriage, from employers reluctant to carry the burden of their contributions, from state governments fearing that contributions of 1s. 6d. a week to the Commonwealth scheme would lead many workers to withdraw from contributory hospital funds, from the friendly societies which resented their exclusion from the administration of medical benefits, and from politically powerful rural interests which saw threats but few advantages in national insurance. The Lyons government failed woefully in the task of forging acceptable compromises between these rival groups.[45]

The attitude of the labour movement to NHI was ambivalent and inextricably mixed up with policies towards the pension and (absent) unemployment provisions of the scheme. John Curtin, the federal leader of the ALP, encapsulated Labor's objections in an attack on three aspects of the bill. Curtin's first target was the regressive effects of the contributory principle: 'purporting to deal with a national problem, the bill contemplates an anomalous system of class taxation. Its benefits are not equally shared, and its burdens are not equally distributed'. If the support of the aged, disabled and the sick were social obligations – as the scheme implied – then the cost should fall on the entire community, not merely employers and workers. He extended this attack to the notion of citizenship assumed by the scheme. The link between past contributions and benefits established a connection between participation in the workforce and entitlements, assuming society had lesser obligations to those outside the wage economy. Finally this entrenched the principle of sex discrimination at the heart of the scheme. Working women were restricted to inferior benefits as their wages and contributions were lower. Women outside the paid workforce, he argued, were subjected to an even more offensive insult, being excluded from any benefits at all. Not only was this: 'a new heresy in the relationship of man and wife as we understand it in Australia, but [it] also strikes unnecessarily and unjustifiably a blow at the very civic status of the wife'.[46]

The trade union attack followed similar lines, but with a crucial ambiguity about participation if the scheme was enacted. Charles Crofts, secretary of the Australian Council of Trade Unions (ACTU), circulated a detailed and very critical account of the workings of the British model provided by the British Trades Union Congress. The ACTU case focused again on the inadequate coverage that the scheme offered and its regressive financial principles. At a time when few wage-earners paid income tax, the consistent theme of the union movement was that national insurance should be funded by the government and the employers, not from a new tax on workers.[47]

Recent critiques of the limitations of the Australian welfare state have set great store on the labour movement's rejection of social insurance. By relying on the wages system for income security and redistribution, Australian workers entrenched a 'wage-earner's welfare state' which permanently marginalized those not in the workforce. The rejection of the contributory principle in favour of funding from general taxation revenues paved the way for a selective and narrow approach to welfare expenditures, with extensive use of means testing to restrict eligibility. Leaving aside the excessive influence this view ascribes to the labour movement during a period of conservative political dominance, it also ignores the contemporary context of conflicts over the finance of health and pensions. The union movement had recently been through these arguments about contributory insurance when state workers' accident compensation schemes were extended a decade or two earlier. As with the Lyons scheme there had been considerable discussion about the extension of existing friendly society schemes or a national scheme based on contributions from both employers and workers, an approach favoured by the conservative parties. As Cass has shown, the success of schemes based on contributions by employers alone was a major victory for the trade union movement: it was not surprising that labour leaders hoped to replicate this achievement in other areas of the social wage.[48]

Union opposition, then, had a strong tactical element, a hostility to the financial basis of national insurance and its coverage, not to the general principle of state provision. This presented major, but not insuperable obstacles to winning trade union acquiescence. Consequently, when the scheme appeared to be proceeding the union movement was quick to organize its own approved societies to gain the maximum advantages.

These contradictions were present in the campaigns organized by each of the state trades and labour councils. The Hobart Trades and Labour Council called for a High Court challenge to the legislation, while in August 1937 their colleagues in Melbourne issued a rather contradictory statement declaring that national insurance was an 'essential' reform, but only if the full cost was placed on the capitalist class. Restrictive contributory schemes on the British model were vehemently opposed. In their place, the more articulate critics of national insurance from opposite political wings of the labour movement such as Tom Wright, the Communist secretary of the Sheet Metal Workers Union, and Henry Boote of the AWU, advocated a model on similar lines to workers' compensation, funded by taxing employers and the rich. A pamphlet prepared for the Labour Council of New South Wales summed up the trade union case, asserting that 'the Government is desirous of unloading a large portion of social service expenditure on the backs of the workers'. Similarly, the *Catholic Worker* attacked national health insurance as calculated to drive the artisan, the small farmer and the shopkeeper out of business. Even if they employed but one person and made less than £7 a week they would have to provide an employer contribution to a scheme from which they could gain no benefit. From the workers' point of view, means-tested benefits could only lead to a poor law system, an 'abominable scheme' in which workers were forced to pay for their own pensions. Instead, wages should be sufficiently high so that workers could afford to pay for their own medical care. Pending this happy outcome, health services and pensions should be universal and funded out of general revenue, not contributory national insurance. Only Ben Chifley, out of Parliament since 1931, but fresh from the financial education of sitting on the Royal Commission on Banking, offered the government his support to sell the scheme to the trade unions.[49]

While in public the ACTU continued to castigate the limitations of the scheme, in private its leaders held discussions with Brigden and Casey to prepare the way for the union-based societies: 'so that the trade union movement could control its own members'. Crofts argued that this did not mean endorsement, as union approved societies could become a formidable pressure group to improve the system. Brigden spoke at a meeting of the Victorian Trades Hall Council in July 1938 to explain the mechanisms of approval and by October the Council's energies were directed against provisions of the Act which would give unfair advantage to the friendly societies. The Queensland Trades and Labour Council followed the same course of action. By July 1938 its opposition was mainly verbal; it had abandoned a public campaign against the Act and moved to recruit members to its own approved society. The ACTU Congress of March 1939 went further, dropping the demand for a repeal of the Act and merely calling for it to be remodelled.[50]

This new union acquiescence remained half-hearted. Maurice Blackburn, the Melbourne Federal Labor MP and solicitor, warned ACTU affiliates against hasty involvement in approved societies. The unions' limited financial reserves and competition from more established institutions would give most of their members little incentive to transfer to union-based approved societies. Instead, the latter were more likely to attract 'friendly society rejects'. He added, 'the harshness of the scheme's conditions...will, in my belief, make the scheme unpopular. The workers' resentment will not be visited on the government only, a substantial part of it will be diverted to the trade unions who have undertaken the administration of the scheme'.[51]

As with the BMA, union opposition to national insurance only goes part way to explaining the failure of the scheme. At most, the propaganda campaign of the labour movement press and speeches by the federal opposition, led by Curtin, helped to create the political climate in which national insurance drew the active support of no major interest group. In this it was helped by the parallel campaign by women's organizations to liberalize pension conditions which discriminated against women in the workforce. Even women within the UAP added their public protests against these aspects of NHI.[52]

## The rural revolt

An older view of the failure of NHI has placed much emphasis on the machinations of shadowy financial cabals. The BMA has been seen as a minor player in a vaster conspiracy in which Melbourne financial interests, the 'Temple Court' group which had been instrumental in persuading Lyons to defect from the Labor Party in 1931, destroyed national insurance for its own economic benefit. As no direct evidence has been uncovered to support assertions that business interests were able to use their direct links with the Lyons government to kill the scheme, the argument has rested heavily on vague assertions. In practice, the strongest opposition did not come from big business or financial interests. The most vocal opposition came from small business, which had little to gain from national insurance, while facing increased costs, and from the rural export sector. In the economic climate of 1938, with the fear that the world was about to sink into another depression, business interests agreed with the warnings of the prominent economist, Douglas Copland, that the contributory element of national insurance could become a dangerously deflationary measure.[53]

Strong political pressures were exerted from within the rural sector, and here there is no need to rely on unsubstantiated rumours of big business conspiracies. Cost pressures, the ravages of drought and the exclusion of farmers from benefits were major grievances. The campaign against national insurance was most intense within the pastoral industry. Unions and larger employers agreed in their opposition to the scheme, while manoeuvring to obtain the maximum benefits if the government was successful. From the start, the participation of seasonal workers had been a major problem for the scheme. Should they receive reduced benefits in recognition of their lower annual contributions, a solution which would introduce administrative complexities and expenses to a scheme which was calculated on the basis of standard benefits for all contributors? The main alternative, canvassed by Brigden in October 1938, was for higher rates of contribution by seasonal workers and their employers in the pastoral industries. In the face of this threat, even the AWU and the Graziers' Association in New South Wales, in all other respects implacable enemies, made temporary common cause, while in Queensland both the Council of Agriculture and the Cane Growers Council joined the protests.[54]

This opposition revealed the difficulties that national insurance created for employers. The hostility of the graziers' associations went well beyond the immediate economic issue of employers' contributions. Fearing the industrial might of a powerful AWU approved society the Graziers' Co-operative Shearing Company (Grazcos) explored the possibility of establishing its own society. Conceding that the administrative problems were too great, it recommended that employers sponsor friendly society recruiting campaigns to 'prevent, if possible, station hands in particular from coming under the influence of the Union'. In August 1938 the pastoralists' worst fears were realized. The AWU National Insurance Approved Society was registered and by October it was enrolling members.[55]

This hostility of the rural employers continued to spill over into the parliamentary Country Party, exacerbating the existing tensions between the coalition partners. Fearing a temporary alliance between Country Party dissidents and Labor to force an early election, the government postponed the start of the scheme. It was at this political level that the scheme died. When this delay was added to the Royal Commission set up to appease the BMA, it reinforced perceptions of government indecision and drift, a lack of resolution which provided the occasion for Menzies' dramatic resignation from the government in March 1939. Although he had not played a leading part in defending the national insurance schemes, he took Lyons' prevarication and capitulation to a sectional rural interest as symptomatic of a more general malaise.[56]

The health insurance scheme ended as it began, subordinated to wider political forces. The resignation of Menzies, the death of Lyons and the departure of the Country Party from the coalition helped to seal its fate. Although Casey and Stewart remained in Cabinet and regarded the failure of the scheme as a mere temporary setback, by early June the BMA had accepted that further government action was very unlikely. The outbreak of war confirmed this indefinite postponement of the proclamation of the Act.[57]

The BMA drew several major lessons from the dispute. It taught the Federal Council to be wary of negotiations with the Commonwealth. At the same time, the state branches acquired a suspicion of their federal leaders which was to haunt national negotiations up to the present day. At the same time, it demonstrated some of the potential strengths of the BMA, particularly its flexibility in dealing with dissidents within its own ranks. Within a year most of the general practitioner leaders were active on the federal or state councils and provided the leadership core during the conflicts of the next decade. Others were less self-critical. The disarray in Victoria was more serious. The branch elections in 1939 saw a turnout of 750 members (compared to the usual 300). Five new members were elected on a general practitioners' ticket, explicitly repudiating the old leadership. The established leaders of the branch responded in kind. J.P. Major, the retiring president of the Victorian branch, launched a stinging attack on the critics, arguing that throughout the dispute the Federal Council had honestly attempted to carry out BMA policy. It was the apathy of the ordinary members, their failure to take an interest in the day-to-day affairs of medical politics which had led to the debacle. Admitting the justice of the government's claims of bad faith on the part of the BMA, Major warned that, whatever the fate of national health insurance, the profession must prepare itself for sweeping changes in the conduct and finance of medical practice. It must abandon its resistance to reform if it was to ensure medical control.[58]

Those who refused to become reconciled, such as Fitchett, were left out in the cold. Both the *Medical Journal of Australia* and *The General Practitioner* ceased to campaign, and the *National Insurance Newsletter* was absorbed in Fitchett's new journal, *Medical Topics*. From May 1939 the BMA effectively 'gagged' the critics of NHI, using the specious argument that the matter was sub judice until the Royal Commission reported.[59]

Perhaps the best obituary for NHI came from Frank Hone, the Adelaide doctor closely associated with Cumpston and the national hygienists' programme. Surveying the halting progress of preventive medicine since the First World War he noted that:

> medicine, besides being scientific, must become more and more social in its outlook. Theoretically, we all agree with this, yet the distressing part of the discussion on the proposed national insurance scheme last year was the realization of how individualistic still is the outlook of the medical profession. More distressing still was the fact that this insurance scheme only insured treatment for sick people and made no attempt at the prevention of sickness. Equally distressing was the revelation that the leaders of the profession, at any rate at first, failed to see this and were prepared to acquiesce in the scheme.[60]

# PART II

# The Reconstruction of Medicine? Planning and Politics, 1940 to 1949

# CHAPTER 5

# The BMA Wins the War

Although it was some time before distant battles in Europe and North Africa affected civilian life in Australia, the outbreak of the Second World War marked a decisive stage in relationships between the state and private medical services. For the first time, the organization of medical and hospital services became a national question with a federal government armed with war powers which enabled it to enter areas normally barred by states' rights.

The medical profession, and the state and Commonwealth governments, were forced to make hard choices between providing adequate supplies of medical officers for the armed forces or maintaining civilian services. During the First World War a free-for-all had left many regions bereft of services, while elsewhere doctors who had volunteered to join the armed forces returned to find their practices taken over by competitors who had remained at home. This dual problem, maintaining a minimum level of services while protecting the interests and incomes of absent doctors, provided the central theme of medical policy-making during the war years.

The solution adopted for the medical profession was unique amongst occupations essential to the war effort. Instead of central control – the 'manpowering' applied to other essential industries and occupations – the medical profession was given its own administrative structure, effectively controlled by doctors. In sharp contrast, dentists, nurses and other 'manpowered' health employees fell under the same regulatory controls as coalminers and munition workers and their professional associations were excluded from participation in

policy and administrative decisions. The early war years saw a
conflict between the military medical authorities, the BMA and state
public health administrators. As with prewar attempts at medical
reform this ended in disappointment for those, like Cumpston, who
saw central co-ordination as an opportunity to revive the programme
of national hygiene. Although technically under the control of a
Department of Defence committee, from the start the BMA was
accorded a major influence over civilian practice. After three years of
war the system was effectively one of self-regulation, with minimal
disturbance of prewar conditions. Instead of the first step towards a
radical reshaping of the control of and access to medical services,
wartime regulation effectively extended the power and prestige of
organized medicine. The mechanisms of wartime control were not to
be available for postwar planning.

## The politics of medical mobilization: the Central Medical Co-ordination Committee

Australia entered the war with an elaborately planned system of
control, on paper at least, of medical personnel and supplies. At a
government level, planning for a war emergency had begun as early
as 1927 when new War Book regulations were drafted to cover the
co-ordination of civilian and military medical services.[1]

One of the legacies of the First World War was a close connection
between the upper echelons of the civilian profession and the armed
forces medical services. The experience and contacts gained during
service in the army medical corps had proved vital in the careers of
many medical officers of the first AIF. In peacetime the medical
services of the armed forces remained closely integrated in the
hierarchy and professional culture of civilian medicine. Former medical officers remained active in the militia, in ex-service organizations,
and worked as part-time medical officers for the repatriation services.
Demobilization had left the armed services dependent on these part-
time officers – in 1939 the Australian Army Medical Corps possessed
only three full-time officers. Major General Rupert Downes, the
Director-General since 1934, was a leading member of the
Melbourne medical establishment and used his civilian and military
connections to ensure that recruitment and  allocation of civilian
resources would be based on the consent and active co-operation of
the profession. Later BMA protests at excessive military control

always struck a strange note given the high ranks held by former leaders of the civilian profession.[2]

The Central Medical Co-ordination Committee (CMCC) was at the apex of a system of tripartite control. Formed early in 1938 as a standing committee within the Department of Defence, the CMCC was chaired by the Director-General of Medical Services (Army) and based at army headquarters in Melbourne with representatives from the military medical services, the Commonwealth Department of Health, the Royal Colleges and the BMA. It provided a forum in which the intense political arguments over the regulation of medical practice could be settled in private amongst members of the profession. A powerful Medical Equipment Co-ordination Sub-committee surveyed and managed essential drug and equipment supplies.[3]

Although its titular powers of control over recruitment and the distribution of medical services were extensive, in practice the CMCC had a difficult task in asserting its independence of the military. Cumpston complained that 'The committee was in the curious situation that it was presumed to be an executive body, but was actually a body whose decisions were often ignored'. As the sole representative of the public health services on the CMCC, he had the lonely job of securing a place for the existing health administrative machinery. He used the opportunity to argue for the models of administrative co-ordination which he had persistently but unsuccessfully advanced since the establishment of the Commonwealth Department of Health: the central co-ordinating body should devise the general lines of policy while implementation was devolved to state level. This central co-ordination could provide a valuable testing ground for the foundation of a peacetime national medical service.[4]

Cumpston achieved partial success in his campaign for decentralization of administration when State Medical Co-ordination Committees (SMCCs), with representatives from the BMA, the military and the state health departments, were given executive powers to implement the policies decided in Melbourne. However, his views on civilian influence and devolution of executive power faced continual military obstruction. Even on one occasion when Cumpston managed to win the CMCC's formal agreement to give greater influence to state governments, Downes later ordered the erasure of this decision from the minutes of the meeting. Cumpston found his indignant protests brushed aside with a bland statement that confidential 'military necessities' had intervened. The Commonwealth Director-General could only lament that 'When I get up against military secrets, of course, I just flap my hands and cry, because I do not know what I am talking about. That was all the satisfaction I got'.[5]

Military dominance meant that decisions with radical effects on civilian medical care were made without even a gesture of consultation. In July 1941, Downes, acting as chairman of the CMCC but without informing his colleagues, persuaded the Minister of Defence to conscript all medical practitioners up to the age of sixty to serve as medical officers in the Citizen Forces or to make themselves available to fill shortages in civilian practice. Cumpston could only complain yet again to a hastily summoned CMCC meeting that 'the most important matter that the Committee had yet dealt with...should be discussed by a full meeting of the Committee and not be dealt with in an arbitrary military attitude'.[6]

Military dominance meant that all was subordinated to the need for military recruits, although this meant major gaps in civilian services. Shortages quickly became apparent in rural areas, in the 'one-man towns' where recruits had been eager and alternative medical services few and far between. The CMCC only interfered directly in the most politically sensitive cases, when the war effort was threatened. When the militant Wonthaggi coalminers complained that their local doctor had been conscripted into the army the decision was swiftly reversed. However, when in late 1940 the *Medical Journal of Australia* criticized the voracity of the military machine and queried whether army medical officers were being effectively deployed, the Standing Committee of Services Medical Directors blandly affirmed 'the inability of the Services to aid our civilian colleagues in any greater measure than that which at present is being done'.[7]

Although the CMCC had accepted the need for state committees, the military continued to resist any moves to vest them with real power. The authority of the SMCCs was undermined by the arbitrary nature of much military planning, its disregard for inconvenient decisions by the CMCC, and the hostility of the state authorities. Lacking financial independence or a clear policy function, at best the SMCCs, confining their tasks to recruitment, watched civilian health administration develop outside their ambit. In New South Wales the SMCC's blood transfusion sub-committee:

> showed a definite inclination to cut adrift altogether from the Co-ordinating Committee and to throw its lot in completely with the Red Cross. This is quite understandable because the State Co-ordinating

Committee is widely regarded as ineffectual, and is known to have no authority and no funds at its disposal, whereas the Red Cross has come forward with considerable sums not only for material but also for salaries.[8]

If the military proved reluctant to devolve real power, the state health departments provided further formidable barriers to central co-ordination. Not only did most of the departments of public health have the history of direct involvement in medical service provision lacking at Commonwealth level, but Queensland and Tasmania were only too eager to use the war emergency as a vehicle to achieve ends unattainable in peacetime. Even the less interventionist states faced the political opprobrium which would follow shortfalls in hospital services – especially if the war with Japan resulted in mass civilian casualties – and were reluctant to surrender powers to the SMCCs. E. Sydney Morris, the New South Wales Director-General of Public Health, responded with some asperity to Cumpston's call for a transfer of state powers, stressing 'the impossibility of the SMCC, composed of outside people, many of them in active medical practice and unable to devote the time necessary to the meeting of these problems and the difficulty of obtaining approvals and decisions which would no doubt have to be obtained through the Central Medical Co-ordination Committee in Melbourne'.[9]

Instead, the states introduced their own emergency plans for hospitals and state emergency services. The New South Wales Hospitals Commission provided an advisory committee to the state's National Emergency Services Department to survey existing resources. As the war entered a more serious stage a strengthened Hospitals Directorate, consisting of the government architect, a lay member of the Hospitals Commission and the medical superintendent of the Royal Alexandra Hospital for Children, was given power over the hospitalization and treatment of civilian war casualties. In early 1942 a more powerful Committee on the Hospitalization and Treatment of Civilian War Casualties was established under Morris's direct control to plan the evacuation of key regions, such as the Wollongong area, and to provide more adequate emergency accommodation in the event of enemy aerial attack or invasion of Australian soil.[10]

Despite reluctant agreement by the more recalcitrant states to follow some CMCC recommendations, such as shortening the university medical course by one year, by early 1941 the state committees were still weak and in some cases refused to carry out their duties of planning civilian services. In both Victoria and Queensland all planning of medical resources remained in the hands of the State Emergency Services. The Victorian SMCC only moved to draw up plans after strong pressure from the CMCC and the BMA. In Western Australia the state government kept control of the admission and accommodation of civilian casualties in public hospitals in its own hands, with the aim of avoiding any 'discrimination in the admission of cases to hospital'. The situation in Queensland remained intractable until well into 1942, with a three-way conflict between the military, the state government and the medical profession.[11]

## War and the BMA

After nearly three years of war Dr William G.D. Upjohn, the Executive Officer of the Victorian SMCC, observed that:

> The younger medical men have been taken in very large proportions for the services...Medical practitioners of a higher average age and decreased physical capacity for work are now engaged in giving essential civil medical service. Nowhere has medical service broken down, but the strain on practitioners is increasing, and it is becoming more difficult to fill the gaps caused by sickness and death in the profession.[12]

War landed the BMA in a dilemma. With their victory over national health insurance and the apostasy of the Federal Council still fresh memories, the state branches were deeply suspicious of any increase in federal powers. Opponents of national health insurance argued that acceding to state regulation, even in wartime, would open the way to greater control of medical practice in peace. A persistent fear was that men serving in the armed forces would become used to salaried conditions of work and be loath to return to the uncertainties of private practice.[13]

The BMA was equally vexed at the scant attention the early meetings of the CMCC paid to the needs of the civilian population and to the strains imposed on the general practitioners who remained in civilian life. John Hunter, who was secretary of both the New South Wales and federal councils of the BMA, attacked the excessive influence of military considerations in the control of the profession. He argued that the refusal to use the BMA as an instrument of control had deprived the government of a ready source of information on medical resources and allowed a singleminded emphasis on recruitment, resulting in dangerous shortfalls in civilian services. Concern about the physical and mental demands on its overstretched civilian members was also influenced by the need to defend the practices of absent members. The attitudes of organized medicine were deeply coloured by memories of the lack of co-ordination during the previous war. In the absence of protection for the practices of doctors in the services, many returned medical officers found that they had lost patients to rivals. This bitterness deepened as before discharge returned medical officers were required to work in military hospitals at low army rates of pay while, as the official war historian noted, 'his competitors, who had not enlisted, dug themselves in'.[14]

In the early months of war advocates of complete resistance to state regulation were in a minority. Rejecting calls for complete self-regulation, the Victorian branch council agreed that 'For the BMA to set up such a Committee to enquire into the private lives, incomes and circumstances of members was tantamount to an assumption of the powers of the State. Members or the State had given the council of the BMA no such warrant.' An attempt to strengthen the BMA's negotiating position by carrying out its own survey of medical resources also failed when too few replies were received to justify analysis of the results.[15]

Even limited attempts by state branches to regulate the practices of absent members failed. In late 1939 F. Kingsley Norris, the honorary secretary of the Victorian Branch of the BMA, drafted an insurance scheme to compensate practitioners for financial losses incurred by entering the services, while a group scheme, controlled by the BMA regional sub-divisions, would protect the practices of absentee members.[16] Only 10 per cent of Victorian members responded to branch pleas that members pledge a proportion of their earnings to a central fund. A report on the local groups found that it was soon 'fairly obvious that the scheme for the protection of practices would prove a failure'. A BMA councillor from Melbourne's southern suburban sub-division complained that his colleagues displayed 'almost an entire ignorance of the group part of the scheme and an inclination to rely upon the [Commonwealth government's] Medical Co-ordination Committee, about whose powers and functions there appeared to be some misapprehension'. Only in the most affluent areas of the cities were schemes successful. From 1941 to 1945 the Protection of Practices Fund of the Eastern Suburbs Medical Association in Sydney raised contributions of £19,450 from sixty-two local doctors for the security of the twenty-one local doctors who had left their practices. Greater success was achieved with the friendly societies which agreed that the interests of lodge doctors in the services would be protected if the BMA would work to guarantee a full lodge service for the duration of the war. Others worked out local individual solutions. In Victoria and New South Wales departing general practitioners employed locums, came to individual agreements with local doctors or, as in the previous war, abandoned their practices.[17]

The inability of the BMA to implement self-regulation became even clearer when New South Wales, its best organized branch, proved unable to stem moves towards contract, pre-paid practice in war industries. The high incomes of war workers combined with shortages of doctors to encourage the extension of the contract and group services anathema to the profession before the war. These pressures were exacerbated in industrial areas, as the influx of munitions workers combined with the recruitment of doctors to create extraordinary pressures on already inadequate services. In the Illawarra, for example, the pre-war ratio of doctors to population stood at 1 to 1,500: by 1943 this had deteriorated to 1 to 5,000. The ratio in Bankstown, in Sydney's western suburbs, was 1 to 8,000. This wartime crisis led to new pressures for the collective provision and centralization of services.[18]

The outbreak of war opened the way for a great expansion of contract and salaried medical services organized on regional and industrial lines as labour-starved munitions factories included hospital contribution and pre-paid medical schemes in award rates. The initial response of the BMA was to counsel resistance. When munitions workers in Bathurst won a provision for a complete medical service provided on contract and funded on a contributory basis with no income restrictions, joint action by the friendly societies and the BMA was not sufficient to prevent local doctors from participation. Similar schemes were launched successfully at munitions establishments at Lithgow and Orange and an agreement between the South Eastern Medical Association and the Australian Coal and Shale Employees Federation included members of the Mineworkers Pension Scheme. Other industrial schemes grew rapidly. Sir Gerald Mussen's Burnie Medical Fund had enrolled 750 employees by the end of 1940. Typical of these wartime schemes was an agreement between Goulburn branches of the railway trade unions and local doctors. One thousand railway workers contributed 2s. 6d. a week in return for a complete medical service, including all forms of diagnosis and treatment available locally. This scheme was a union initiative, but met the full approval of the BMA, despite the lack of income restrictions.[19]

A memorandum prepared for the executive of the BMA's New South Wales branch stressed the difficulties of holding the line of private practice and income limits on contract practice in the face of these new pressures, noting that wartime conditions encouraged:

> medical services being rendered on an organized mass basis. If there is added to this change in the social organization – temporary though it may be – the demand on the part of many persons for a nationalized medical

service, it is obvious that the profession must be prepared to meet the position.

The memorandum concluded by advocating a system of contract practice with relaxed income limits, in effect bowing to the inevitable as rising wartime wages had led to the effective collapse of any attempt to enforce income restrictions and argued for an extension of contract services as:

> If an efficient Contract Service can be provided to a moderately large section of the community, it may well be the means of preventing the establishment of a nationalized service.[20]

The failure of self-regulation and the growth of new forms of group practice encouraged fears that these developments and wartime regulations could provide the basis for a salaried nationalized medical service after the war. As a letter in the *Medical Journal of Australia* warned, the '"bound apprentices" of subsidized students [put through university with Commonwealth scholarships] loom like a shadow over the future'. Recognizing the futility of its usual approaches to regulation of professional behaviour, the BMA moved to extend its powers within the new network of government regulatory bodies. The state branches of the BMA worked to strengthen the powers of the SMCCs and extend medical representation. As D.M. Embleton of the Victorian Branch Council argued:

> in England the profession controlled the Medical Services on behalf of the Government and he failed to see why a similar arrangement was not possible in Australia. It was just a matter of time when the medical services of the country would have to be controlled, otherwise there would be chaos. The powers of the Co-ordination Committees should be extended to enable them to really co-ordinate. The time for long-distance planning had passed. Immediate action was a pressing necessity, otherwise there would be a breakdown in the nation's medical services.[21]

These moves to exert greater control over regulation were concentrated at state level. Rather than challenge the military dominance of national co-ordination, the state branches took the less direct route of demanding a formal distinction between recruitment – which would be left in military hands – and the allocation of the remaining resources for the civilian population, which would be placed under professional control through stronger and more autonomous SMCCs. The military majority on the CMCC saw this as a small price for continued support for recruitment from the profession – particularly as it accorded with the preferences of former BMA leaders in the higher military ranks.

This goal was achieved swiftly in the two largest states. Dr W.G.D. Upjohn, a long-standing member of the BMA's Victorian state executive, was appointed as executive officer of the SMCC:

> Until May 1941 their concern was primarily to secure medical officers for the services and little heed was paid to the needs of the civil community. Hospitals were depleted and practitioners in the cities, suburbs and the country who felt the urge left their practices and joined the services. The result was dislocation in civil medical services. But early in 1941 the State Committees were re-organized and since then a little more emphasis was paid to the needs of the civil community. It is true that most of the re-organized state committees regarded themselves as being accessory recruiting bodies. An exception was the Victorian Committee which from its inception took a very different view. It refused to go out into highways and byeways and gather in recruits for the services. It concentrated its efforts to persuading the younger graduates to volunteer. The Committee invariably recommended against the enlistment of men who volunteered from one-man-towns and from their positions in civilian medical services, and the recommendations of the Committee were never flouted by the Services Medical Directors.[22]

Similar successes were achieved in New South Wales. By early 1941 the SMCC was housed at BMA House and relied primarily on BMA records, while John Hunter was seconded from the BMA to become the full-time secretary of the SMCC for the next two years.

The BMA's painless victories in New South Wales and Victoria reflected the considerable power which the profession already possessed over medical policy in both those states. Organized medicine faced greater obstacles in the smaller states. Part of the energies of the two senior branches were directed towards stifling the protests of less advantaged colleagues lest this result in a review, and possible reduction, of overall BMA influence. A call from the Western Australian Branch of the BMA for the Federal Council to oppose the appointment of a lay member to each of the SMCCs met with a reproof from the Victorian branch, which warned that 'no action be taken to draw the Federal government's attention to the position the profession now enjoyed'. The Federal Council was advised to 'lie low and leave well alone'. Similarly, protests against specific policies, such as National Security Regulation 330, which allowed conscription of medical practitioners up to the age of sixty-five for the government's new Emergency Medical Service, were rejected by New South Wales and Victoria. Instead, they argued that the BMA should push to increase the powers of the SMCCs, to ensure that administration was in BMA hands.[23]

As in peacetime, the BMA faced its most bitter opposition in Queensland where Hanlon and Cilento were determined to concede nothing. The conflict was embittered as sections of the military medical establishment, closely linked to Cilento's old foes in the BMA, used allegations about his prewar fascist sympathies to prevent him gaining a military commission. Despite this personal setback, Cilento saw the war as an opportunity to reopen the administrative reforms which had proved too difficult in peacetime. From the start the Queensland government affirmed its direction of civil defence planning, allowing that the CMCC and SMCC had a legitimate role in co-ordinating recruitment of medical personnel to the armed forces, but controlling the medical side of civil defence planning through the existing hospital and ambulance authorities. Cilento was appointed to draw up plans for meeting an enemy attack (presumed to be from the air) on the Brisbane area. Working with him were two representatives of the SMCC, Dr J.G. Wagner (the president of the Queensland branch of the BMA) and Colonel Talbot, the Deputy Director of Medical Services, Northern Command, along with the medical officer of health for Brisbane City Council and a consulting surgeon. The technical aspects of the committee's work included plans for first aid posts, emergency equipment, blood transfusion services, ambulance services and gas decontamination squads.

The committee's proposals represented the high point of attempts to use the emergency to increase state control of medical practice, arguing that war organization must be based on a system of group clinics, with a centralized dispensary system conducted by the Brisbane Hospital. In short, this was an attempt to further the reorganization of services that Cilento had been attempting for the previous five years. As he warned Hanlon:

> I find the medical representatives, however, particularly the BMA representatives, very suspicious that the organization might mean a step towards nationalization. Personally, I think that the war has made nationalization in some form inevitable, no matter what happens, but I submit that fears on this score cannot be permitted to stand in the way of the efficient organization of central and suburban medical services for the civilian population.[24]

Unable to win control of co-ordination at state level, the BMA in Queensland had to turn to its colleagues in other states, and the CMCC. BMA branches in the southern states made regular complaints to the CMCC that the Queensland SMCC was being used to 'coerce' doctors, 'a policy which might be very dangerous in the postwar era'. Intervention from the CMCC soon limited these activities.

In May 1942 Wagner was appointed as full-time executive officer in Queensland. By 1944 the BMA had asserted enough control of the Queensland SMCC, so that, instead of denouncing its dictatorial powers, Wagner was protesting over military actions which by-passed its authority.[25]

## The BMA and the control of planning: the Emergency Medical Service

From the outbreak of war the attitude of the medical profession contrasted sharply with that of most of the Australian population. At a time when general public support for the war was decidedly unenthusiastic, the recruitment of medical practitioners was an outstanding success. In late 1938, the newly established CMCC arranged for the Department of Defence to send a questionnaire to each registered medical practitioner in Australia which asked for information to be provided for a central register of medical practitioners. With 70 per cent of the forms returned, 83 per cent of the respondents declared themselves 'both willing and able to give their services'. Many senior members of the profession, including a large proportion of the teaching staffs of the teaching hospitals, joined the services. By June 1941, 390 doctors had joined the armed services – over 20 per cent of those not in essential services. Nationally, by the following February, 26 per cent of those eligible had joined the armed services. The entry of Japan into the war in December 1941 and its rapid and stunning military victories increased the demands of the armed forces for more medical personnel. At the height of the war against Japan over 2,500 medical practitioners were serving in the Australian Army Medical Corps, more than one-third of those registered to practise in 1939.[26]

To the great irritation of civilian doctors and administrators, the army soon had more medical officers than it could profitably employ – at least before massive casualties were suffered by Australian troops – while the civilian population faced increasing shortages. Management of this growing crisis provided the major test of the new administrative arrangements. The CMCC and its state committees had proved they could provide the armed forces with the medical expertise required. They were more sorely stretched when it came to rationing civilian care. Initially concerned only with the volume of recruitment, the CMCC took little interest in the effects of this exodus on civilian services and the education of medical students. It confined its attention to locating new sources of medical officers and campaigned for measures to stimulate enlistment, such as shortening university medical courses.

The new danger of bombing or invasion of Australia strengthened the hands of those advocating greater planning of civilian services. Although conscription of all medical practitioners up to the age of sixty had been gazetted under National Security Regulations on 14 August, little practical action had followed. In the dark days of February 1942 a national survey of medical personnel found that, of 5,610 registered doctors, 1,100 were ineligible for recruitment on grounds of age, sex or infirmity. As 1,200 were already in the services, the survey calculated that another 1,000 doctors could still be recruited. After allowing for those unable to practise, this left a total of 2,810 for the entire civilian population. As this shortage began to bite into civilian services, the use of compulsory powers became more attractive.[27]

The only full-blown attempt to use directive powers to relieve civilian shortages showed the ease with which regulatory bodies established to meet civilian needs became mere defenders of the position of the medical profession. The Civil Emergency Medical Service (EMS) was established in March 1942, borrowing its name from the successful British hospital organization of the London blitz. The EMS regulations gave the CMCC the power to order the hours and area to be covered by each practitioner, enforcing a severe limitation on home visits. Detailed administration was left to the state committees with the Commonwealth Department of Health confined to the strictly financial side, providing for accommodation and administrative expenses. The SMCCs were given the power to order any practitioner to proceed to any place within the state or another state and conduct practice there as directed. This met with immediate resistance from the BMA. Sir Henry Newland warned that any measures of compulsion would be deeply resented, hinting darkly that the EMS was 'an attempt at the nationalization of the medical profession'.[28]

The EMS provided the first testing ground for a BMA attempt to wrest control of civilian planning from the military and (more importantly) to block its rivals from the state health departments. Arguing that 'whatever form of national [medical] service emerges in the future will be determined by the attitude [BMA] Council takes towards the State Medical Co-ordination Committee', the BMA fought hard for exclusive control by:

a medical committee composed of medical officers who have recently
been in active medical practice.

...to secure that the control of medical affairs in regard to conscripted
personnel should not pass out of the hands of the medical profession into
the hands of a lay authority...It was not a question of dealing with the
exigencies of the moment but of laying down a permanent council policy
or rather the endorsement of a principle.[29]

Over-riding Cumpston's objections, the military authorities soon
acquiesced. Professional control of the EMS was a small price to pay
for active assistance with recruiting. Control of the EMS was placed
in the hands of the SMCCs, with their full-time administrators
nominated by the BMA. They quickly redefined the principal
function of the scheme as the protection of the medical profession,
particularly those away on military service, from inroads by refugee
alien doctors. In deference to BMA resistance, few attempts were
made to order practitioners to move between towns, and existing
services in rural areas were maintained by subsidizing the incomes of
practitioners, making up the difference between military pay and the
receipts of private practice. In Laverton, Western Australia, the local
practitioner's pay was brought up to the level of an army major to
encourage him to remain in the town. Despite constant declarations
about the need for compulsion, the central and state committees
followed a line of gentle persuasion, although over 3,388 doctors
were enrolled (121 of these over the age of sixty), the EMS remained
a paper organization. By mid-1942 a total of only eighteen refugee
doctors had been directed to country areas while Tasmania and
Western Australia, with severe shortfalls in remote area services, had
not joined the scheme. At the end of the war there were only fifteen
EMS practices in the whole country.[30]

The SMCCs were only prepared to use their full powers in
response to cases of real or imagined threats from refugee doctors.
The first threat of legal action against a practitioner in South
Australia occurred in late 1942 when an alien doctor who had
qualified for full registration through a shortened medical course at
Adelaide University set up practice in a suburban area vacated by a
doctor on active service. The SMCC ordered him to leave Adelaide
and move to a one-man practice in a remote area of the state. Unlike
its British namesake, the EMS was hardly the precursor of nationalized health, more a protective device to preserve the practices of
absent doctors and ensure that the crisis did not provide governments
with the opportunity to weaken organized medicine's control of entry
to the profession.[31] As Dr H. Boyd Graham, the Victorian branch

president noted, the administration of the Emergency Medical Service:

> coincided almost completely with the desires of the profession... – it gave practically complete control to the British Medical Association through its members composing the [State Medical] Co-ordination Committees. It was very desirable that the present close contact between the Association and the State Co-ordination Committee by the present arrangement of housing the Committee in the Association's building should continue.[32]

The wartime struggle over control of medical services had many longer term repercussions. In other areas of economic and social life the war had seen a massive increase in the influence and legitimacy of state control. The allocative planning and rationing of scarce resources and manpower planning set the models around which postwar reconstruction was discussed. Civilian medical services remained an exception. Where planning and control were necessary these were devolved to BMA-controlled bodies. The Commonwealth Department of Health, already weakened by loss of its own officers to the armed forces, gained little experience of medical administration. In its constant conflicts with the military authorities to ensure a minimal coverage of civilian services the department increasingly relied on the support of the BMA. The devolution of control to the state committees completed the process. By the end of the war the BMA felt so effectively in control that its leaders happily urged the Commonwealth government to use the State Medical Co-ordination Committees to control the education schemes established with Commonwealth funding to assist returning medical officers back into civilian practice.[33]

# CHAPTER 6

# From 'Sales and Service' to 'Cash and Carry': the Planning of Postwar Reconstruction

Accounts of the development of national social welfare policies in Australia have taken the Second World War as a key political moment. The federal Labor governments of Curtin and Chifley have been seen as the catalyst of a first serious – and for many years the only – attempt to accept state responsibility for social provision on the model of British and European social democracy, a 'radical liberal (or even mildly socialist) experimentation in social welfare'. Much of the medical profession has shared this view of the 1940s as a sustained attempt to introduce socialized medicine to Australia, abolishing the free market, destroying the direct relationship of patient and doctor and making both subservient to the wishes of the state.[1]

While the views of organized medicine have not softened on this score over the last four decades – the mild reforms of Medibank and Medicare were opposed in similarly apocalyptic tones – more leftist analysts of the origins of the welfare state have become increasingly sceptical of the socialist pretensions of the Labor governments of the 1940s, pointing out both their unquestioning acceptance of the capitalist organization of the economy and the extent to which social reforms owed more to the exigencies of war finance than to the 'Light on the Hill'.[2]

Health policy has played little part in this critique. The very vehemence of medical opposition has appeared to place it in a separate category to other reforms; the needs of fiscal management, the labour market or a vaguely defined 'capitalism' will clearly not suffice. Much of this difference can be explained by peculiarities in the planning of health policy. With the advocates of NHI temporarily discredited, during the early years of the war the supporters of a more radically reformed health scheme were able to take control of the direction of policy, using the NHMRC as their main platform. From 1940 until the end of 1943, planning was dominated by the ideas identified with the national hygienists, embodied in major reports prepared by the NHMRC and the Joint Parliamentary Committee on Social Security. However, during 1943 and 1944 the victories of these paper schemes were swiftly reversed. Plans for a national health service based on salaried service and the integration of public and curative health services were discarded as the federal Labor government reduced its health scheme to a minor part of a wider programme of social security cash benefits.

In no sense was this a capitulation to pressure from organized medicine – nor was it a retreat from 'socialism' – but a repetition of the conflicts between Cilento and Hanlon, between national hygiene and labourism, of the previous decade. The cash benefit-based health policies of the Curtin and Chifley governments were squarely in a long Labor tradition of concern for the material well-being of the sick by establishing equality of access to medical care, destroying the stigma of charity, and providing income support for those temporarily incapacitated through illness. The radical critique of medical practice – the recognition that equality of access involved more than the destruction of financial barriers – was abandoned while, in the words of C.E.W. Bean, federal government policy accepted the objective of 'literally equal attention' for all.[3]

## Wartime planning: the NHMRC from Menzies to Curtin

The basic lines of debate on postwar health policy were set well before Labor came to office. The failure of national insurance had eclipsed, at least temporarily, the influence of those who wished to subordinate health policy to wider objectives of fiscal policy, leaving the Commonwealth government wary of further conflict with the medical profession. At the same time, it provided an opening for the medical critics of NHI to push for an approach owing more to the programmes of national hygiene, the Cilento scheme in Queensland and the work of the Commonwealth Department of Health.

During the early years of the war Cumpston and his colleagues moved to shift the initiative in health policy-making back into the hands of public health officials in state and Commonwealth employ. They had three immediate objectives. In the first place, it was vital to block any attempt to base a postwar national health scheme on national health insurance. A postwar national health policy had to be built on the more positive foundations of national hygiene, not the mere subsidy of illness. Second, planning must be vested in medical hands, averting the danger that it would be subsumed as a minor item in wider welfare schemes. Finally, they wished to gain the co-operation of state and BMA colleagues for a revival of the projects of the early 1920s – the central co-ordination of public health and preventive services with private medical practice – to set the agenda for discussions of postwar health services.

In November 1940 Cumpston proposed to Sir Frederick Stewart that the National Health and Medical Research Council should be given the task of planning a comprehensive health scheme. Stewart had made an unsuccessful foray into reviving a programme of national unemployment insurance earlier that year, but had studiously avoided any mention of the dangerous topic of medical insurance. Hence, Cumpston's proposal to divorce health policy from other areas of social security was immediately attractive. As chairman of the NHMRC and Director-General of Health, Cumpston was admirably placed to present himself as both a loyal servant of the government of the day and as the convener of independent advice from all sections of the profession. Representing all sections of the medical profession but dominated by public health administrators, the Council was precisely the type of autonomous expert authority to tackle the almost insuperable tasks of winning the acquiescence of private practitioners to fundamental reform. At the same time, by including the permanent heads of each of the state departments it provided a forum to defuse obstruction by the states.[4]

On Cumpston's initiative, Stewart added a vague proposal for a 'community medical service including hospitalization' to his scheme for social services and the matter was formally referred to the NHMRC for further consideration. By moving swiftly Cumpston had ensured that the planning of health services was not subsumed within a larger social security programme – as had happened with NHI – and detached health policy from the moves already underway for planning postwar reconstruction.

The first of the postwar planning agencies was established by the Menzies government in March 1941. Co-ordinated by the Department of Labour and National Service, the Inter Departmental Committee on Post War Reconstruction directed most of its attention to the effects of demobilization on the labour market and the problems of transition to the postwar economy. The future of health and social services was treated as marginal and left to the departments directly concerned. Commonwealth Department of Health representatives rarely attended meetings and none of the committee's discussion papers concerned health issues. Other initiatives in social security matters implemented during the war years, such as the introduction of child allowances in the 1940 Budget, were the result of inter-vention by ad hoc advisory bodies such as the Finance and Economic Committee attached to the Treasury. This key policy body contained the leading advocates of Keynesian economic management of the war economy and of a more comprehensive co-ordination of social and economic policy for the postwar era. Again, it showed no inclination to interfere in matters peripheral to the immediate problems of mobilization and war finance.[5]

So for the first two years of the war the NHMRC worked independently of other government departments and agencies. There is no evidence of any direct consultation with Stewart or any other member of the government. Cumpston kept firm control over internal discussions, ensuring that he and the other public health officers dominated the Council's reports. Arguing that members were not mere delegates of their individual organizations, he blocked a move by Francis Gaha, now the Tasmanian representative,  to refer any proposals for reform first to the annual meeting of federal and state ministers of health: the council was to publish its scheme as its own, without prior political approval. He then warned John Newman Morris, the BMA representative, not to circulate any of the Council's internal papers to the BMA without prior approval. Only when final recommendations had been agreed by NHMRC members could pub-lic discussion commence. He began the process of drafting by inviting NHMRC members to suggest their views on the main issues in Australian health policy.[6]

The papers submitted by the NHMRC members agreed that any postwar national health scheme must centre on a programme of preventive health, based on a new relationship between private medical practice and state medicine. They also reiterated the pre-occupations of the 1930s, pronatalism, improved nutrition and the national fitness campaign. Cumpston's own memorandum was rather thin, offering few concrete proposals. Although bearing the marks of interwar national hygiene, it also displayed the defensive position into which the Commonwealth Department had been driven. During the 1930s Cumpston had lost his interest in radical schemes for the reorganization of medical services, while Kinnear's rebuff had effectively silenced his brief interest in influencing national health insurance. Instead he had concentrated on the important but less contentious issues of nutrition and national fitness, stressing that 'The vital need of this Commonwealth for increased population has almost lost its appeal by constant repetition, but it is the first question to be faced in any programme of social reform'.[7]

E. Sydney Morris, the New South Wales Director-General of Health, also warned that national survival depended on making the birth rate the central issue of a national health policy. Australia had sunk into a position 'liable to become so static, owing to the refusal of the human units to breed, that if the present trend of the birth rate continues there will be no need for further action. The problem will have solved itself in racial extinction'.[8]

The mechanisms by which this outcome could be achieved were left extremely vague. The NHMRC contributions shared a pessimism about the success of any programme under lay control. Basic to any progress in community health must be full administrative control by experts. All rejected reliance on cash transfers granting recipients discretion in the expenditure of benefits. This negative position was the main thread of unity in almost all the councillors' responses. The hostility of public health officials to national health insurance and cash benefits had been reinforced by the conflicts of 1938–9 and appeared confirmed by the unhappy example of New Zealand. In 1938 the New Zealand Labour government had introduced a national health service based on universal access to medical services with remuneration of doctors on a capitation basis. After a lengthy boycott of the new system by the BMA the government added the option of fee-for-service in 1940. Almost all doctors took this option. The costs of the first year of the new scheme were considerably higher than projected and blame was placed at the door of fee-for-service. As Morris commented in late 1942:

> The present form of payment to the medical profession for services rendered gives a blank cheque to the individual medical practitioner regarding the number of consultations that he considers necessary in the treatment of his patient. When it is remembered that every time he sees a patient he receives a fee of 7s. 6d. or 12s. 6d. if such a consultation occurs on Sundays or at night time, there is a great temptation to exploit the situation.[9]

Two years later the prestigious British journal, the *Lancet*, confirmed this judgement, noting that the wartime shortage of doctors had sheltered the New Zealand scheme from disaster, but expressing scepticism about how long this happy situation could survive in peacetime.[10]

Hence the contents of a more positive health policy – especially its implications for existing private practice – were left vague. Most contributions confined themselves to general exhortations for greater

Commonwealth educational efforts in public health, the promotion of national fitness and nutrition.[11]

However insubstantial these proposals from public health administrators appeared, organized medicine offered even less. Although the BMA representative, Dr John Newman Morris, was present at the meetings which drafted the scheme, his contribution was slight. Cumpston's injunction that NHMRC members approach the problem as individuals rather than as delegates of their home organizations inhibited Newman Morris from more vigorous attempts to elicit the views of the state councils – although the fate of the Federal Council's attempt to negotiate National Health Insurance *in camera* should have provided an ominous warning. Despite canvassing the state branches for proposals, all he could produce was a scheme for a unified health ministry drafted by the South Australian branch in 1935, and a series of vaguely worded resolutions from the Victorian branch calling for improved employment opportunities, education, child endowment, town planning and preventive health, but avoiding any discussion of the finance and organization of curative health services.[12]

The most radical proposals came from Professor Mark L. Mitchell of Adelaide University, the representative of the university medical schools and, more predictably, from Sir Raphael Cilento. Mitchell, who emphasized that he had not consulted his colleagues and was writing in a purely individual capacity, was the first to recognize that the problems facing the nation went well beyond the limited health promotion and educational activities advocated by his colleagues. Starting from a similar assumption of the need to subordinate curative to preventive health, to shift the emphasis of medical services from acute care to public health, he argued this could not be achieved within the existing health system. All health services must be planned nationally, with centralized control to create a state-controlled medical service. He added that the time had come to replace the honorary staff of large public hospitals with permanent salaried staff while shifting the full financial responsibility for hospital services to the state. Mitchell was a biochemist with no medical training, and his call for the abolition of honorary practice was unlikely to win much support amongst his clinical colleagues. He was soon replaced on the NHMRC with a colleague more prepared to defend the universities' dominance of teaching hospital honorary appointments.[13]

Cilento's critique of existing medical practice was more difficult to brush aside. He saw the NHMRC initiative as an opening to extend Queensland's achievements on a national scale, breaking the barriers the state government had erected in the path of his grander visions, ending the impasse of medical reform at state level by shifting the initiative to the Commonwealth. In his characteristically apocalyptic tones he asserted that national survival depended upon a radical reform of medical practice. Medicine could be no more immune from the growing power of the state than any other sphere of society. This heightened state intervention and its

> continually greater invasion of new or neglected fields and also of those so long considered the monopoly of the private practitioner, has gone far to give something more than lip service to the expression that 'prevention is better than cure', but it has demonstrated that there is no difference in essentials between the public and private aspects of medicine. . .
>
> This, however, would mean a change of outlook comparable to that which occurred when the aseptic surgical technique took precedence over the antiseptic. In practice it would imply that the maintenance of health from the beginning, rather than the correction of defects at any stage, must become the deliberate ideal. Obviously this also implies that the State programme of prevention would finally absorb the greater part of medical care, and would thus automatically ensure State control and direction of medical care. . .
>
> Three defects, inter alia, of the present transitional stage [towards full state control] are making themselves apparent – a tendency to the loss of the personal relationship between practitioner and patient; diminishing contact between the private practitioner and the public hospitals with their full-time and part-time paid medical men; and an increase in outpatient work so overwhelming as to encourage 'spot' diagnosis and slipshod treatment. Outpatient departments, indeed, are beginning to suffer those criticisms popularly levelled at lodge practice.
>
> The net consequence is an increasingly rapid trend towards regulated practice and State control.[14]

The Cilento memorandum drew heavily on the Queensland model. The control of hospital services was to be centralized, honorary practice replaced with a salaried sessional system and the private sector heavily regulated. The reorganization of general practice would be even more sweeping. Private practice would be superseded by a salaried service based on group clinics within a centrally planned state medical service. Funding and general policy guidelines would be Commonwealth responsibilities while direct administration would remain in the hands of state and local governments.

The NHMRC delegated the task of drafting its report to a subcommittee of Cumpston, Cilento, Professor Harold Dew (the representative of the Royal Australasian College of Surgeons) and Newman Morris. They met at the offices of the BMA in Sydney in early June 1941 to collate the contributions of the members and to prepare some general recommendations. Cumpston prepared a composite first draft, a rather bland document which provided a lowest common denominator of the NHMRC members' proposals. It commenced with a call for compulsory military service as a public health measure, and its opening sections summarized the national hygienists' case for a more vigorous national policy to advance maternal and child care, tuberculosis control, nutrition and national fitness. This grab bag of policies was given some unity through a reorganization of public health administration, shifting Australia towards a regionalized health system, rather like the model which Cumpston and the Royal Commission on Health had advocated in the 1920s. Turning to the organization of a 'complete medical service', the Cumpston draft remained vague, attacking capitation panel practice, but remaining agnostic on the relative merits of fee-for-service, limited by a schedule of fees, or a fully salaried scheme. However, several of the key elements of the Cilento memorandum were incorporated: group practice and the hierarchical planning of hospital and clinical services were to be at the heart of the reforms.[15]

Despite the heavy representation of organized medicine, the document which emerged from the sub-committee, again drafted by Cumpston, was even closer to the spirit and practical proposals of the Cilento memorandum. In July it was approved with only minor alterations by the 11th Session of the NHMRC. The 'Recommendations of the National Health and Medical Research Council on Reorganization' were sent to Cabinet at the end of the month.

The 'Recommendations' were an articulate expression of the view that the organization of medical services should be subservient to the aims of national policy, with the interests of national efficiency, not redistributional or socialist conceptions of equity at its heart. The document began with a ringing declaration of support for 'the social reconstruction which is even now proceeding and which will be accelerated when the war is over'. Health policy had to embody certain key principles:

> The first, and most important of these is that health is determined by a complex of social conditions; the total aggregate of community health is affected by national economics, by individual poverty, by industrial conditions, by housing, by transport, by agriculture. It is often said that public health is purchasable but individual health cannot be maintained if the individual income is below the minimum essential for personal health.

Consequently, as 'the care of personal health is a social duty and no longer entirely an individual responsibility', commonwealth and state governments must provide sufficient finance to expand the work of the public health departments. Finally, as medical practice fragmented into narrower specialties and became 'more and more divorced from the principles of the prevention of disease, it is important that a proper administrative organization for bringing together all aspects of medical work be devised and incorporated in any system of social reform'.[16]

The agenda for postwar reform would embrace the major objectives of interwar national hygiene. National health insurance, still the most likely alternative approach, was to be removed from serious consideration. Other direct welfare measures, such as the Child Endowment Act recently introduced by the Menzies government, were criticized for providing 'merely for cash payment. Its value could be greatly increased, at no great expense, by a home service of advice to mothers.' The strongest invective in the 'Recommendations' was reserved for the National Health and Pensions Insurance Act, 'not a Health Insurance, but a Sickness Insurance, Act'. Preventive medicine with higher professional standards could not be achieved under a contributory scheme but only by direct services, controlled or coordinated by the state. In place of national health insurance a national salaried medical service should be established to provide all patients with access to hospital and health facilities. An extensive list of other state initiatives in public health included more effective infant and maternal health services and the provision of diagnostic and institutional treatment to isolate diseases such as tuberculosis at an early stage. Finally, control by public health authorities, rather than the actuaries and accountants of the National Insurance Commission, would ensure that every 'medical man should be so conscious of the preventive possibilities of his work....that the whole system of medical practice will become permeated with the ideal of prevention'.[17]

The subordination of 'curative' to 'preventive' medicine, through administrative control by departments of health, marked a return to the heroic projects of the early 1920s. The national medical service was to be based upon a co-ordinated system of hospitals and centrally planned district clinics, combined in a national salaried service. The 'polyclinic' provided the means to organize the distribution of medical services to these ends of positive preventive health as 'teamwork must be extended deliberately and by agreed means from institutional practice to general practice'.[18] Group clinics were to raise the standards of medical practice and provide the basis for bringing greater specialized services to provincial centres while rostering for night and weekend duties would free practitioners to attend refresher courses, enhancing the attractions of practice in smaller centres of population. Salaried medical services were to be established first in remote areas and the public health and preventive work of private practitioners strengthened under more rigorous and centralized state supervision. The scheme was to be financed by 'evenly spread taxation spread over the whole community...by direct taxation and direct administration without the intervention of any third agency', not by contributory national insurance.[19]

The 'Recommendations' were ambiguous on the sensitive issue of the future of private practice within the new national health scheme. Despite protestations that group practice and the salaried service could co-exist with private practice, the supporters of the NHMRC scheme agreed that in the long term both fee-for-service and the lodge practice of the friendly societies must be superseded. They differed on whether this should be a gradual, voluntary displacement and on the size of the financial and professional inducements and penalties that would be needed to reconcile a considerable section of the medical profession to a state service. E. Sydney Morris, a vocal supporter of salaried medicine, argued that the new system should be established gradually as sufficient financial and human resources became available on a district by district basis. Once a district was reorganized, however, this toleration of private practice could not persist, the government must 'nationalize one suburb then go on to another'. Any compromise could only result in a two-class medical service, with private practice for the affluent and salaried clinics staffed by stigmatized 'poor law doctors' and confined to 'the unemployed and the misfits'. He warned, 'You must put sufficient men in there to provide a complete service for the whole of that district and that would mean wiping out the practices of the men already established there if they did not come in'.[20]

If the NHMRC was vague on the manner in which private practice was to be voluntarily superseded it was dangerously evasive on the highly charged question of compensation for the goodwill of practices. Mention was made in the first chapter of the substantial financial burden most general practitioners bore with the purchase of their first practice. The first five or six years of professional life were dominated by the debts incurred in establishing a practice, and any evasion of this question would guarantee massive opposition. As the major tangible asset held by most general practitioners, the value of the practice, surgery and appointments provided the main route to a more comfortable living or secure retirement. The shift to a planned national salaried service implied an end to the sale of practices. While Cilento and the other advocates of salaried practice brushed this off, arguing that an adequate pension would be more than sufficient recompense, others sensed dangers in not settling the issue immediately and decisively, removing a major area of uncertainty. These fears were confirmed as compensation became central to the debate over the British National Health Service.[21]

Because of its radical rejection of private practice, the NHMRC scheme has frequently been seen as one of the high points of the socialist phase of postwar planning, although its greatest intellectual debts were owed to the programme of national hygiene and racial purity advanced by Cilento. This rewriting of the intellectual and political background of the scheme started with Cumpston. In spite of his authorship of the final draft of the 'Recommendations', as opposition to the scheme mounted he attempted to distance himself, objecting strongly when the medical critics of the 'Recommendations' referred to the 'Cumpston' scheme – emphasizing instead that it was the collective product of the NHMRC. In retirement he took this further, suggesting that the proposal for a salaried service had been thrust upon the reluctant NHMRC by the new Labor government. Although he conceded that several members of the Council (presumably Cilento, E.S. Morris and Gaha) were strong supporters of salaried medicine, he claimed that the 'Recommendations' were prepared, not out of conviction, but 'so that the advocates of socialized medicine – of whom there were many at that time, including the Government – might see in practical terms what issues were involved'.[22]

Cumpston's retrospective attempt to dismiss the NHMRC plan as a gesture to a socialist government suffers from serious flaws. First, as chairman of the NHMRC, he convened the small sub-committee which drafted the proposals, maintaining firm control over the direction of its deliberations. Although the report was based on papers prepared by Council members, it was not a mere compilation. Cilento's input was by far the most substantial, and had the advantage of being based on Queensland's solid administrative achievements. At crucial points, however, Cumpston rejected the views of the state representatives. The Commonwealth Department of Health, rather than the states, was placed in direct control of administration:

> This Council sees no insuperable difficulty in complete control by the Commonwealth, even including the transfer of State Health Departments, and in fact recommends as an ultimate objective such control or transfer with all aspects of preventive and curative medicine including hospitals.[23]

This recommendation appears to have been Cumpston's own initiative, and led to a formal statement of dissent from Cilento and Henry Featonby (the Victorian Chief Health Officer). At the time, Cilento, still locked in a fierce personal rivalry with his former mentor, complained that Cumpston had forbidden the separate publication of his original memorandum in an attempt, he alleged, 'to make it apparent that these measures, which were attracting a considerable amount of progressive political thought, had originated with the Commonwealth'. At the time, Cumpston was prepared to make wider claims for himself. When the progressive industrialist Sir Gerald Mussen published a laudatory appraisal of the NHMRC scheme, Cumpston informed him: 'You may not know that I personally wrote that report of the NHMRC'. Furthermore, the 'Recommendations', which first set out the principles of a salaried service, were prepared and presented to a United Australia Party, not a Labor government. By July 1941 the Menzies government was shaky, but it would seem unusual for an opponent of socialized medicine to prepare such a scheme for a conservative government.[24]

The most likely explanation for Cumpston's ambiguous behaviour was that in 1940 and 1941 the push for a radical reshaping of medicine appeared to have acquired irresistible momentum. In their internal discussions both the BMA and the Royal Colleges accepted the inevitability of a major increase in state control and the end of charity-based medical services for the poor. Given this widespread assumption of the inevitability of radical change, Cumpston saw his essential task as to keep planning under departmental (and medical) control. Furthermore, much of the report covered territory familiar to interwar national hygienists. Proposals for the regionalization of hospitals under centralized control, the co-ordination of general practice, specialist and public health services were all commonplaces of medical debate in Australia and overseas, and much of the public argument over the 'Recommendations' was remarkable for the unanimity with which the BMA and the NHMRC accepted common assumptions about the correct direction for health policy. With the important exception of the forms of bureaucratic control within the national medical service, the issues which provided major stumbling blocks were by and large those Cumpston regarded as peripheral – the form of remuneration and compensation for goodwill of practices.

The NHMRC initiative also succeeded in separating health and social security policies, an objective common to national hygienists in public employ as well as the BMA, and particularly significant as the federal government made moves towards a wider programme of social reform. In the same month that the 'Recommendations' were sent to Cabinet, Stewart proposed to his colleagues that the government should bolster the ambivalent popular support for the war effort by launching a comprehensive programme of social security as, 'One reason for the lukewarmness displayed by many persons towards the war is that they feel that the last war, which promised them so much gave them so little. They believe that they are entitled to something better and this Government is the only authority which can give it to them'.[25]

His programme included widows' and orphans' pensions, unemployment insurance, housing and contributory pensions. These measures were justified not merely on welfare grounds but as a politically palatable means of introducing compulsory savings to block inflationary pressures on the war economy by siphoning off excess demand. Insurance-based schemes were doubly attractive as the relatively full employment of the war years would enable the government to place social welfare funds on an actuarially sound basis before the demands of peacetime.[26]

On Stewart's initiative, discussion of the future of social services was placed in the hands of an all-party Joint Parliamentary Committee on Social Security (JPCSS), which met for the first time in July 1941. During its early deliberations, the committee concentrated on the finance and eligibility for a new system of benefits for widows, the sick and disabled and the unemployed.

The precise influence of the committee over the postwar welfare policies of the Labor government has been a matter of some dispute. Shaver has argued that although it was marginalized early by Chifley and the Treasury, the committee's work on the finance of the social security system had a lasting influence, providing a joint party imprimatur to financing welfare expenditures through the tax system. The crisis of war finances and the appeals of nation and community came together when the Curtin government assumed uniform taxation powers in 1942. The JPCSS endorsement of tax finance of welfare expenditures can be seen as part of the same movement, an assumption that the national community should take responsibility for welfare. However much conservatives may have hankered after a return to a system based on individual responsibility, linking welfare entitlements to an individual's past contributions, the main ideological battle of the late 1930s had been settled once and for all.[27]

The work of the JPCSS on health is even more difficult to assess. Although it produced three reports on the future of the health system and was to end its career in a clash with Chifley over negotiations

with the BMA, the content of its health programme relied exclusively on the work of the NHMRC. On 14 August 1941 it requested that
Cumpston provide a complete statement of the costs of the NHMRC
'Recommendations' and began to take evidence from NHMRC
members on the form of a national health service. Cilento presented
his evidence in late July and Cumpston presented his defence of the
NHMRC scheme the following week.[28]

In response to the request, the NHMRC produced a second major
report on the future of the health services. The 'Outline of a Possible
Scheme for a Salaried Medical Service' provided in greater technical
detail the costing of the scheme, proposals for the location of clinics
and the conditions of employment of medical practitioners.[29]

The intervening months had seen the fall of the Menzies and
Fadden governments and the formation of the Curtin Labor government in September 1941. Dependent, like its predecessor, on
minority support and faced with a hostile Senate, Labor showed little
desire to initiate major policy changes while the war crisis worsened.
If anything, the Curtin government displayed even less interest in
health policy than had its predecessors, and was content, for the
moment, to allow the NHMRC to dominate discussion of postwar
health policy.

Hence, the change in political regime left health policy even more
firmly in the hands of the salaried public health officials. Again,
Cumpston played the leading role in drafting and the NHMRC's
second report made no major departure from the lines established in
the 'Recommendations'. The 'Outline' set out the regions for
planning, provided a comprehensive grading and promotional
structure for medical officers and costed a salaried service. The
national medical service was to be based on salaried medical officers
rather than private practitioners and would be 'freely available to all
the people of the Commonwealth' without means testing. The
indecision about the powers of the Commonwealth had now
vanished; the service was to be administered as part of the Commonwealth Department of Health, under the Public Service Act.
The emphasis on the reorganization of health services around the
hospital was continued. A regional hierarchy of medical services was
to extend from the large urban teaching hospitals down to district
and base hospitals. General practitioners were to be employed in 'a
ring of suburban consultation centres for primary consultation and
casualty treatment, and a ring of small hospitals for minor cases
staffed by local men'. [30]

The chance of an immediate public debate on the scheme was lost
in the emergency atmosphere of early 1942. Hopes for an early move

towards a salaried service were dashed by an assurance made by the new Minister for Health, E.J. Holloway, that no major changes would take place until the end of hostilities. In a letter which was to loom large in later wartime conflicts with organized medicine Holloway assured Sidney Sewell, the president of the Royal Australasian College of Physicians (RACP), that:

> In reference to the question of Nationalization of the Medical Services or a complete salaried Medical Service, and the fear that such a scheme may be introduced in the absence of so many medical men abroad, I can only say that no comprehensive scheme could be put into operation with so many men away, even if other organising and/or financial difficulties could be worked out during the war. Hence I can assure you that no complete salaried Service will be inaugurated during the war.[31]

While this fell well short of the absolute prohibition on wartime initiatives which the BMA sought (and later claimed to have obtained), it did rule out Cilento's plea that the basic structures of the national medical service be prepared to welcome returning medical officers. Curtin's assurance of inaction seemed confirmed when Sewell requested that he meet with the BMA and the Royal Colleges to discuss the NHMRC schemes. The Prime Minister refused on the grounds that such senior medical men would be too busy and there was little likelihood of further action until the end of the war.[32]

## Better than Beveridge?: the Joint Parliamentary Committee on Social Security

By the end of 1942 developments in federal politics and the progress of the war made the prospects of implementing a far-reaching reform of medical practice seem brighter.

In December a Constitutional Convention of representatives of each of the state parliaments and the Commonwealth agreed that a power over 'national health in co-operation with the states' should be referred to the federal government. Evatt had assured the convention that it should not be interpreted as more than an aid to federal intervention in areas not already covered by the states; more drastic moves would require the consent of the states. Hence, the new health power would be considerably more limited than that needed for the Commonwealth to institute the NHMRC scheme. Whatever these limitations, this concession of greater central power seemed a first step towards the removal of the obstructions with which the defenders of states' rights had thwarted national health policies in the interwar years. Although the referral soon bogged down in political wrangling and the opportunity was lost, popular sentiment for a major shift in the financial burden and access to health care remained strong. Welcoming the moves for a constitutional change, the Melbourne *Herald* compared the Australian plans favourably with the British government's recently released Report on Social Insurance and Allied Services (the Beveridge Report). This widely acclaimed scheme had promised Britain a greatly extended, but still insurance-based, comprehensive health service after the war. Endorsing the move for stronger federal powers, the *Herald* declared that Australia was set to achieve a non-contributory universal health scheme 'better than Beveridge'.[33]

In early December Cabinet discussed the future shape of a postwar system of social security. For the moment, the government's plans for the health service remained sketchy. Its main energies were invested in developing a comprehensive social security scheme comprising unemployment and sickness benefits and a widows' pension. Watts has argued that the timing of this scheme, just after the transfer of uniform income taxation powers from the states, had more to do with problems of war finance than a sudden surge of humanitarianism. Dropping its former opposition to the regressive effects of contributory insurance, the Labor government planned to fund the benefits through a National Welfare Fund, created by the extension of income taxation to the working class. In this view, the Curtin government's welfare schemes provided a smokescreen to justify taxation measures aimed primarily at soaking up inflationary pressures stemming from consumer demand in the overheated war economy. It is certainly consistent with this view that Chifley's Cabinet submission made only the most general references to a health scheme, but included Cumpston's costing of the NHMRC proposals, comprising a salaried medical service, consultation centres and Commonwealth financial responsibility for hospitals and public health services. Despite this interest in the detailed proposals of the NHMRC, no immediate action was to be taken. The government received a political dividend from promises of future reform, while remaining uncommitted on the details – and any immediate outlay of funds. For the moment, Cumpston and his medical colleagues remained in charge of planning but, more ominously, Chifley included in the package of income support schemes a proposal for pharmaceutical and dental benefits, contradicting the direct service emphasis of the NHMRC's proposals. [34]

Public reaction to the NHMRC reports remained muted until late in 1942. In October Chifley requested that the JPCSS report on health services 'with particular reference to such measures as it might be possible to introduce during the period of the war'. The following month, at the request of the JPCSS, Cumpston prepared a lengthy memorandum surveying those sections of the NHMRC reports which could be implemented immediately.[35]

Cumpston provided the JPCSS with a radical scheme for immediate action. Stressing the obstacles to co-operation from the states and the medical profession, he suggested that the resistance of both parties could be overcome if planning was left under NHMRC control. A joint council could be formed by the Federal Council of the BMA and the NHMRC to supervise the gradual introduction of salaried services. A start could be made in 'remote areas', in which he included the large provincial centres of Townsville, Cairns, Wagga Wagga and Albury. The salaried service would draw on younger prac-titioners recruited on discharge from the armed services and could be planned immediately and implemented in stages as opportunity and resources permitted. Gradual introduction would allow administra-tors to gain experience and convince detractors of its superiority. The foundations of a national hospital system should also be laid in stages. First, a small expert committee should report on the availability of services and the transfer of control. The reorganization of hospitals should commence in more remote areas, gradually extending to provincial centres and country towns, and, finally, to the cities. Planning should begin immediately, although sufficient resources for a full-scale reconstruction would not be available until the end of the war. Again, planning and control were to be dominated by public health administrators and insulated from political interference.[36]

The first cracks in the unanimity of the NHMRC soon appeared. In a harbinger of troubles to come, before the Council's November 1942 meeting Harold Dew, the NHMRC representative of the Royal Australasian College of Surgeons and a member of the original drafting committee, moved to dissociate himself from plans for a salaried service. Dew insisted that the call for a salaried service must be qualified with assurances that there would be full consultation with the medical profession. The advocates of salaried medicine replied with calls for a public campaign of education to sell the scheme to the profession. E.S. Morris argued that drawn-out discus-sions with the Federal Council of the British Medical Association would see the scheme destroyed in prevarication and disagreements over details. He proposed that the direct approach taken by Cilento to the doctors of Queensland – the 'Open Letter' appealing over the heads of BMA leaders – would demonstrate the scale of support for the general principles of the national medical service, obliging the leaders of organized medicine to negotiate seriously:

> I believe that once the policy had been definitely determined and the scheme proposed to the government was clearly visualized, the National Health and Medical Research Council, either collectively or individually, should publish a booklet explaining to the medical profession exactly what it means; otherwise the whole thing would be distorted, you would have criticism based on hearsay evidence, and all sorts of bogies would arise. It is essential to get down to the individual medical man. They should be taken in groups all over the state rather than that the matter should be left to a mouthpiece of the British Medical Association, who may represent in large measure the very highly specialized people who may be in control of that organization. That is the line that we must take if we are to take in a national medical service...After all, it is the rank and file of the medical practitioners rather than the superman in the profession that you have to satisfy.[37]

While Cumpston added his weight to the calls for more decisive action, the NHMRC came under increasing pressure from organized medicine and conservative state governments to withdraw from active planning. Cumpston's memorandum for the JPCSS, setting out those matters which could be implemented immediately, sparked the first public breach with the BMA. Sir Henry Newland protested that Chifley had broken Holloway's promise of no changes to medical practice until after the war, and warned that 'If the feelings and sense of justice of the practising medical profession in Australia are to be outraged, dissolution of what was wrought with high hope is inevitable'. The new atmosphere of hostility was heightened as the supporters of the government scheme denounced this 'sabotage' by the BMA.[38]

A turning point came in November when the NHMRC met in Canberra. To proceed with his plans for unified control of hospitals Cumpston had proposed that the NHMRC should sponsor a national survey of hospitals. A small body would work for two years to prepare for a Commonwealth takeover of the state hospitals, starting with the small outback hospitals and bush nursing centres and gradually extending, in six-monthly stages, to the metropolitan areas. The NHMRC delivered its first major rebuff to its chairman. Cilento later recalled, a 'meeting of medical men' – presumably excluding the supporters of the 'Outline' – gathered at the Hotel Canberra on 22 November, and agreed to remove Cumpston's proposals from the agenda of the formal meeting of the NHMRC that evening. Members objected that the survey (and the implied nationalization of the hospitals) was premature as the constitutional powers of the Commonwealth would remain dubious until after the Constitutional Convention due to meet on 24 November. Secondly, the state representatives pointed to the complexity of the task of taking over the mixture of state-owned, state-subsidized and private hospitals over such a short period. Although the November Council meeting reiterated support for the general principles of the 'Outline', the NHMRC made it clear that it was no longer prepared to take the initiative in postwar planning.[39]

The actions of organized medicine had rendered the NHMRC incapable of representing a corporate and united medical interest. The supporters of a national medical service shifted their hopes to the Joint Parliamentary Committee on Social Security, as it had hitherto relied on Cumpston and the NHMRC plans for guidance on medical planning. In March 1943 the JPCSS established a Medical and Hospital Survey Committee (MHSC) to carry out the task refused by the NHMRC.

Although the idea of a survey committee had originated with Cumpston, its membership and programme owed more to Cilento. The fate of the JPCSS reports was influenced by their old rivalry. In a lengthy note to Claude Barnard, the Labor chairman of the JPCSS, Cilento proposed that it move beyond a mere survey of existing resources and examine the possibilities for forming regions to group hospital and other medical services on the Queensland model. It should direct its attention to the means for achieving 'positive health ...the maintenance of health to prevent the appearance of disease. This has never been done in hospitals, which have been regarded merely as repair shops, or places for patch work jobbing for injured or diseased persons'. Consequently, the MHSC's brief included the examination of the technical problems of a transition to the salaried system proposed by the NHMRC reports as well as a census of the distribution and regional imbalances in medical services. Cumpston no longer saw the MHSC as a means to jog the reluctant NHMRC, but as a threat to the influence of his own department, an instrument of Cilento's ambition to control the direction of health policy. This view won some support within Cabinet. Chifley, who as Treasurer had ministerial responsibility for the JPCSS, had never been enthusiastic about its independence, so Cabinet gave very reluctant consent to the establishment of the survey committee. At the same time he acceded to pressure from Cumpston and Holloway and forced the committee to accept a representative of the Department of Health. Frank McCallum, Cumpston's loyal deputy, was appointed as vice-chairman.[40]

The Survey Committee was headed by Dr Alan Bruce Lilley, the chairman of the New South Wales Hospitals Commission. Lilley had strong connections with the Commonwealth officers: he had been acting director of the Australian Institute of Tropical Medicine from 1927 to 1928 and had then made his reputation as a formidable administrator as general superintendent and chief executive of the Royal Prince Alfred Hospital in Sydney until his appointment to the Hospitals Commission in 1940. Cilento and Arthur Brown, a Victorian country general practitioner, were also appointed; both were well-known supporters of salaried schemes but critical of Cumpston's plans for Commonwealth departmental control of the new service. The remaining members were McCallum (who took little active part, either by preference or exclusion), Agnes Walsh, a nursing matron from Western Australia, and Herbert J. Goodes, who was co-ordinating social security planning in the Treasury. They were to confine themselves to specialized areas. Goodes was to cost hospital benefit schemes, and Walsh was to examine the perennial problem of shortages of trained nurses in the public hospital system.[41]

The MHSC approached its work with enthusiasm. Despite the short time it was given to carry out its survey, it gathered data essential to the success of a salaried service. While Brown surveyed general practice, looking at the feasibility of group clinics, Lilley and Cilento collected hospital statistics and worked to develop viable administrative regions. They examined the location of medical services, the capital works needed to extend the availability of public hospital services and the extent and the possibilities of group practice. Its collection of medical statistics, which was never published, concentrated on measuring spatial disparities of services. As with the two NHMRC reports, social justice was seen as a question of readjusting geographical imbalances in the provision of services.[42]

Goodes and Walsh were marginalized from these central preoccupations. Nursing, while a pressing preoccupation of wartime health services, was not seen as a central policy issue for the national medical service. Equally, the committee saw Goodes' work on benefit schemes as the least pressing of its tasks, although he was the Treasury's nominee, working on the problems which those in control of reconstruction planning defined as its central concerns. While his colleagues continued the NHMRC's work, planning the co-ordination of hospital services and a salaried medical service, Goodes worked on the financial problems of the scheme – questions which the medical planners had largely brushed aside. He warned of the strains which a comprehensive scheme of free public ward care and the end of honorary practice would create for the state public hospitals.[43]

When it reported to the Parliamentary Joint Committee the MHSC largely ignored Goodes' contributions. It merely pointed to the administrative difficulties of establishing a uniform scheme of hospital benefits throughout the Commonwealth. However the grants to the states were calculated – on the basis of current expenditure, the level of patients' fees or on bed occupancy rates – the vast differences between state funding systems, the committee suggested, meant that each system would have inequitable results. It concluded, 'We leave the problem there. We cannot solve that. It is a problem for discussion between the State authorities and the Commonwealth'.[44]

This negative conclusion contrasted sharply with the enthusiasm with which the MHSC tackled an outline for capital expenditure to develop hospitals and integrate them in planning with regional health centres.

The Sixth Interim Report of the JPCSS, covering health legislation and services, was published in July 1943, one month before the federal election. It identified two central problems at the centre of health reform. One was the difficulty faced by the 'middle income group', which was 'ineligible to receive the free treatment provided to the poor by combined charitable and government agencies and by individual doctors and which at the same time is not financially able, as are the rich, to meet the large unexpected increases of expenditure which illness may bring about'. Second, and as a further consequence of the system of private health care, the report attacked the inequitable geographical distribution of medical services, an oversupply in the 'more attractive residential suburbs' and shortages in industrial areas, where accidents and diseases were more common, and in rural districts. National health insurance was again rejected. The future national medical service was to be based on a salaried service with vastly increased powers for the Commonwealth over public health, medical registration and education. Assessing the rival positions taken by the BMA and the NHMRC, the committee recognized that the profession's antagonism to salaried service and departmental control represented a formidable obstacle to reform. However, as the BMA's ideal of fee-for-service 'is open to grave abuse by both patient and doctor, and against this no adequate means of protection has been suggested':

...the ultimate solution will probably be found in a full-time salaried med-ical service with standardized uniform hospital provision, within which complete medical, hospital and public health services will be available to all and will be financed by a tax on incomes for this purpose... Such solution, however, must be regarded as a long-range objective, since, apart from the insuperable obstacles to its introduction at this stage or until after the war, it is opposed, at present, by a large majority of the medical profession whose co-operation is vital to the success of any plan.[45]

The report rejected any sweeping socialization of health services, calling for 'an *evolutionary* and not a *revolutionary* change'. The Com-monwealth government should proceed in gradual stages, winning the agreement of the medical profession. The national medical service should commence with clinics on the group practice model in rural and suburban areas. All local practitioners would be eligible to work on a salaried sessional basis in these group clinics while maintaining their outside private practice. The unspoken assumption was that the financial security and greater technical resources of the salaried group practice would gradually assert its superiority. Outside the wealthiest suburbs private practice would quietly wither.

This had the attraction of avoiding a frontal attack on private practice while preserving the fundamentals of the NHMRC scheme. Instead of merely subsidizing existing personal health care services – the national health insurance approach – the Commonwealth could use its financial strength to assert strategic control over the direction of the health system. Dr A.R. Southwood, the chairman of the South Australian Central Board of Health and a signatory of the NHMRC plans, set out the thinking behind this approach:

I think that attention is far better concentrated on hospitals and public clinics, for the next 7 or 8 years anyway, than on ordinary medical prac-tice. After all, illness of any real seriousness needs the facilities of a clinic or a hospital for investigation and treatment. Domiciliary treatment of illness is generally unsatisfactory to the doctor and to the patient – except in the case of very trivial troubles.

First, deal with hospitals in cities and 'regional areas', and set up outpatients clinics in suburbs, and you will receive a tremendous advance. Ordinary routine medical practice will gradually fit into the picture and will in a few years present no great problem in administration.[46]

At the same time, this represented a major retreat for the advo-cates of public medicine. By postponing even further the implemen-tation of the scheme in the major centres of population, the national medical service could play little part in the reintegration of returned medical officers during the unsettled postwar period. Instead, the advocates of salaried medicine would have the much more difficult task of winning the support of a medical profession back in civilian life and unwilling to face further upheavals after the disruptions of the war years. In spite of its brief from Chifley to propose immediate measures, the committee warned that:

> any action at present to implement any major scheme of medical, hospital or other related health services would seriously jeopardize the success of any comprehensive scheme for adoption at a later stage during the war or immediately following the war. It is beyond doubt that any such action at present would be considered precipitate by the medical profession and would be vigorously opposed.[47]

This problem was compounded by the committee's refusal to recommend the form of remuneration in the new service and its relationship with private practice, questions which the NHMRC reports, for all their lacunae, had attempted to confront. While expressing its preference for salaried service, the committee's Sixth Report set out the relative merits of each of the main alternatives, leaving the profession with a very ambiguous message. This indecision was repeated with salaried services. An assurance that private practice would coexist with the national medical service was accompanied by a warning that means testing and similar restrictions on access to free health care must be discarded. As critics from the BMA quickly pointed out, if services at the new consulting and outpatient clinics were to be free and universal, how could private practice survive? The committee itself recognized it would be in the interests of medical practitioners to 'combine to discourage all but the very poor from taking advantage of the part-time service'.[48]

Both the NHMRC and the JPCSS plans discarded the basis of existing concessional services – the capitation-based friendly society panels and the subsidized fee-for-service systems of repatriation and workers' compensation practice. Their radical attempt to reorganize and centralize control over medical practice took the form of abstract schemes which failed to address the compelling problems faced by most general practitioners, and left them unable to suggest any means to gain the support of the medical profession. Instead, when their discussions turned to the means of implementation, they relied on inducements which would require a massive programme of capital investment. The support of the medical profession was to be won by providing diagnostic facilities and premises that would exceed any available to private practitioners. New regional group clinics with radiography and pathology staff and a centrally planned network of base hospitals were to form the base of a system in which general policy would be decided by the public health officials at state and

Commonwealth levels, and leadership of the profession provided through the research and teaching activities of the great metropolitan public hospitals.

The insistence on centralized control also dampened support for a salaried health scheme from many potential sympathizers within the profession. For example, when the Goulburn railway unions introduced their complete contract medical service (discussed in Chapter 5) the Central Southern Medical Association approached the Commonwealth Department of Health for assistance in obtaining a building permit to construct a clinic suitable for group practice. Cumpston's acerbic comment on such schemes helped to ensure their rejection. While they were 'in line with the present tendency of medical men to combine together in the interest both of themselves and their patients [it] also has this aspect that it is a defensive move, in view of the fears of the profession as to possible Government action; it is, in fact, the alternative which the profession is putting forward as a reply to suggestions of a salaried medical service'.[49]

Erstwhile sympathizers with the NHMRC proposals from within the BMA received short shrift from the supporters of greater state control. Cilento lumped together all the criticism of direct departmental control, including that from the supporters of salaried medicine, as, 'based on the suggestion that practising medical men are to "write their own ticket", the State, the public and the administrative medical services being entirely outside the picture or merely brought in as an afterthought'.[50]

Despite their disagreements about the Commonwealth's powers, Cumpston expressed similar hostility to critics of departmental control. When Arthur Brown, the most articulate defender of a salaried medical service, expressed strong reservations about the centralism of the NHMRC scheme, in particular the implication that doctors would be employed by the Commonwealth under public service conditions, Cumpston responded bitterly to the 'implication that the Commonwealth Department of Health has no recognizable value, notwithstanding all that it has achieved during the thirty-one years of its existence'.[51]

Finally, the emphasis on central control aroused the dangerous antagonism of the Roman Catholic Church. Several months after the Report was tabled J.D. Simmonds, the Coadjutor-Archbishop of Melbourne, launched a direct attack on the scheme, deploring its 'materialistic' viewpoint: 'the mentality of the planners inclines too much towards State regimentation', especially the prospect of Catholic hospitals falling under the control of an 'authority that does not respect the principles for which they were founded'. Simmonds even drew parallels with the heroic resistance of Dutch doctors to incorporation into the Nazi 'Physicians Chamber' several months earlier, warning that 'the medical profession of Australia will be just as strong, and equally successful, in resisting any attempt to impose an Australian brand of National Socialism upon its noble calling'. The *Catholic Worker* employed the same analogy, assailing the nationalization of hospitals as a deliberate attempt to exclude the sick poor from contact with religion. 'Nationalization of the medical profession is one of the worst forms of Fascism. We oppose it with all of our might'. Instead, family wages should be increased to enable workers to afford fees, assisted by untied government subsidies to all hospitals.[52]

## The abandonment of salaried medicine

There are two ways of interpreting the term 'Social Service'. These two ways may be roughly indicated by two familiar commercial terms –

'Cash and Carry', which means pay money but you get no help. Cash over the counter and after that no responsibility, except to see that the customer does not cheat.

'Sales and Service', which means that the transaction is not completed with the original passing of money, but that it is to the interest of the manufacturer to see that the purchaser is helped in his difficulties.

At present, the various activities of the Commonwealth included under the term 'Social Service' are on the 'Cash and Carry' basis – cash only but no service. The term 'Social Service' is a misnomer...

If the system is a mechanical system under which the doctor gets paid for whatever service is rendered on a limited schedule basis, then no social progress is possible. Even under this so many professional and technical questions arise that professional direction is imperative...But it can be said that a sound, wisely devised, and socially valuable system can be built upon the foundations quietly and solidly laid by the Health Department during the last thirty-two years: whereas any attempt to graft such a sensitive plant upon the mechanical money system of the Department of Social Security could only produce either a barren branch or disaster. [53]

Until the end of 1942 the Curtin government had been content to leave health planning in the hands of the NHMRC and the JPCSS. The published plans and public hearings of the parliamentary committee provided the necessary encouragement to morale, and created a bipartisan air to postwar planning, while not committing the government to any definite action. It was only with the approach of the 1943 election, and the changing fortunes of the war, that Canberra began to prepare seriously for the postwar world. These changes brought in a new, more politicized period of medical planning. The locus of planning shifted from the independent, medically dominated NHMRC and the bipartisan parliamentary committee to the Treasury, where the planning of postwar reconstruction was concentrated. The Commonwealth Department of Health became an increasingly marginalized onlooker as health policy lost its separate status and became incidental to wider fiscal and social goals.

The main battles over the future of Australia's health service were waged at a bureaucratic level. The eclipse of the NHMRC, while helped by BMA disquiet at Newman Morris's compliant attitude, owed more to this new assertiveness of the Commonwealth Treasury in health policy. Over the next year Cumpston and the medical planners lost their power base in the NHMRC and the JPCSS was discredited and stripped of its influence. Increasingly dominated by Treasury, Labor's health plans bore little resemblance to the radical proposals of the NHMRC.

In January 1943 Cabinet approved the package of social welfare reforms, including hospital, pharmaceutical and tuberculosis benefits. Drafted by Treasury, these cash benefit programmes made no attempt to alter medical practice directly. The national public health and hospital policies of the NHMRC and JPCSS survived in rhetorical calls for 'socialized salaried medicine' from some ministers, but these objectives were postponed to a hazy and uncertain future. For the moment, planning was to be confined to relieving the costs of medical services for the consumer, with minimal changes in the organization and control of private practice. These foundations of the national medical service were in sharp contrast to the dreams of the national hygienists, a shift to the distributive emphasis that marked Labor's health policies at state level – spreading benefits as widely as possible rather than applying resources to grand projects of state-controlled social engineering. For Chifley and those now in control of policy-making this shift had the additional attraction of enabling a scheme more amenable to cost-control as well as minimizing strains on the limited administrative resources available to the federal government.

After Labor's landslide electoral victory in August 1943, Cabinet pressed for immediate action. Senator James Fraser was appointed as

Minister of Health and was soon showing signs of exasperation at the slowness and indecision of the JPCSS to make recommendations on the benefit programmes which now lay at the centre of the government's health scheme. It was increasingly clear that medical programmes were to be considered as merely one element of a package of welfare measures, all aimed at supplementing the incomes of those most in need. A meeting of the state and Commonwealth ministers of health on 6 and 7 December 1943 agreed to go ahead with a comprehensive national health service. The Commonwealth was to lay down the general standards but finance the system through grants in aid to the states, with schemes of hospital benefits administered on these lines.[54]

Setbacks to constitutional reform put a seal on the abandonment of the national salaried service. When the Constitutional Convention failed to win a voluntary referral of powers from the states, the federal government called a referendum requesting fourteen new Commonwealth powers, covering the areas the convention had approved. Labor confirmed its rejection of the unificationist thrust of the NHMRC scheme by seeking a very unambitious health power, 'in co-operation with the states', with all its new powers expiring five years after the end of the war.[55] Even with these restrictions the fourteen powers referendum failed, its only effect on health policy being to confirm the demise of the radical stage of planning. The ambitious visions of the national hygienists were swept aside as health policy became a minor element within the government's social welfare plans.

The end of the independent role of the Joint Parliamentary Committee was signalled on the day that Cabinet approved the fourteen powers referendum. The committee had convened a meeting with representatives of the BMA, the Defence Medical Services and the NHMRC on 8 and 9 December 1943. Since August, and the NHMRC's first discussion of the JPCSS's Sixth Interim Report, the representatives of the Royal Colleges, Ritchie and Dew, had withdrawn from any meeting which they judged to be 'political', leaving the BMA as the sole voice of organized medicine. Consequently, the NHMRC refused active participation, authorizing Cumpston to attend only as an observer. In an angry outburst, he warned the conference that the government's new course meant an end to the hopes of the last two years:

> the road to uniformity and even to an improvement in the existing position will not be easy. The famous outline presented by our Council is now dead and we must make a new start. That is largely true of the report

of the Social Security Committee. We have submitted a scheme in which the Commonwealth should be the dominating authority, striving for an ideal which we consider desirable, but I cannot any longer contemplate unity of Commonwealth control.[56]

Cabinet's decisions to base the health service on cash transfer payments and to seek a limited constitutional power made the shift to Treasury dominance final. From being the marginal lay representative on the MHSC, Goodes became the principal architect of Commonwealth health policy. One of the group described as the 'off-siders', those policy advisers who entered Chifley's 'official family' from outside the Commonwealth public service, Goodes had been given principal responsibility for social security policy, again emphasizing the government's treatment of health policy merely as a minor part of the larger social security scheme. He brought two major changes to health planning. First of all, control of costs began to dominate official thinking, a concern which meshed with the other preoccupations of the Chifley government. In an important analysis of Labor's economic policies of the 1940s, Robinson has emphasized the pivotal place occupied by the fear of inflation. For monetary radicals on the left, such as Eddie Ward, as much as Chifley and other party leaders, the prime problem of postwar economic management was to avoid the dislocations of unfettered demand, particularly in the building and construction industry. The half-hearted planning initiatives at federal level were largely attempts to continue the rationing and price controls of the war economy into the period of adjustment. Public works expenditure was a prime casualty. Hence, Treasury and the government showed little sympathy for a health scheme which aimed to buy medical support through a massive capital works programme of clinic and hospital building.[57]

In a second major shift in policy-making, the medical profession – within and outside the bureaucracy – lost its privileged position in consultations. As the Treasury's Reconstruction Liaison Officer, Goodes consulted with the state and Commonwealth departments of health, but treated them (and the BMA) with rather more disdain than they had been accustomed to receiving, contrasting the obstructive behaviour of organized medicine in Australia with that of its more conciliatory English colleagues:

> The Australian doctor, on the other hand, seems to feel it incumbent upon him – at least in his Association – to offer comments to the government on the political, social and every other kind of aspect of the medical scheme, for example, the Federal Council recently stated in the *Sydney Morning Herald* to the effect that the approach to the health

scheme in this country was quite wrong, and then proceeded to tell us exactly how it should be done. I might add that no new thought was contained in the statement, and in general it showed a lamentable lack of understanding of the social and economic categories involved.

However, one has little doubt that in due course our local brethren will come down to brass tacks. They have, of course, a lot to offer the authorities, so long as they realize that they are only one element of the scheme.[58]

Paradoxically, this shift meant an abandonment of ambitious schemes to alter the organization and content of medical practice. In contrast to Cilento and the other architects of the NHMRC schemes, Goodes accepted the adequacy of existing services, the goal of state intervention was reduced to improving access while ensuring that vested interests within the system did not reap all the rewards. The advocates of a salaried service were forced to admit that for the present their chance had slipped away. Their energies were now directed to retaining some medical control over the content of benefit policies, to salvage some influence over the future of the health system.

With his well-honed instinct for bureaucratic survival, Cumpston was quick to react to the political turn. In the high tide of optimism about the NHMRC scheme he had informed his Minister that if the national medical service was 'merely paying cheques I was not interested'. Now, faced with the prospect of a cash benefit health scheme administered by the Department of Social Services he reconsidered his opposition, noting that 'while I have the same distaste for any scheme which consists only of paying cash, I feel that you cannot carry this through without the help of the Health Department. I still hope that you may be able to approach these changes with a wider vision than merely paying money'.[59]

This retreat from the priorities of national hygiene was seen most clearly in the case of hospital policy. Administrative co-ordination of hospitals and group clinics provided the basis of the NHMRC and the JPCSS schemes, integrating general practitioners, specialists and public health practice. Instead, the new policy took the form of an income support programme, subsidizing beds. The traditional Labor antagonism to means testing access to public beds was the beginning and end of the scheme. Instead of the cornerstone of a comprehensive national health service, the hospital and pharmaceutical benefits schemes were developed as cash benefit programmes within the larger social security system. The solitary gesture towards a more comprehensive planning of resources was left powerless.

The reluctance of the Joint Parliamentary Committee's medical advisers to produce a workable hospital benefits scheme has already been mentioned. In the committee's Sixth Interim Report the issue had been left unresolved while the planners, led by Lilley and Cilento, proceeded to the more exciting task of planning the integration and regionalization of services. Anxious for a detailed hospital benefits scheme to add to its social security package, the government directed the committee to reconsider the issue and produce a more positive statement. Goodes was given the task of drafting the scheme, which was outlined in the committee's Seventh Interim Report, tabled in February 1944.

Unlike previous schemes of state support for hospitals, grants were not to be used merely as a part of general hospital maintenance funds but as an indirect income subsidy to patients, cushioning the impact of hospital costs on patients to alleviate the economic impact of acute illness. The hospital benefits scheme also accepted the limitations of the divided control imposed by federalism. Avoiding the constitutional and administrative problems of direct Commonwealth control, all payments would be made as tied grants to the states. The scheme embodied the income relief principle which now underlay the Commonwealth's health and welfare programme with a Commonwealth subsidy of 6s. 6d. per daily occupied hospital bed for general medical, surgical and obstetric cases. To ensure that the benefit was received by the individual patients and not absorbed in the state or hospital budgets, a condition of the grant was the abolition of all means testing for public wards. In return, the states would be compensated for the lost revenue while patients in intermediate or private wards would receive a subsidy of 6s. a day, paid to the hospital.

Finally, the subsidy was to be extended to patients in private hospitals. This was included as a partial response to an anticipated postwar shortage of hospital beds, but indicates how far the government was from a thoroughgoing socialization of medical practice. On this basis, Goodes costed the scheme at £4,500,000 per annum, a calculation which estimated that the Commonwealth grant would leave the states a small surplus over their existing revenues from patient contributions to compensate for any decline in private donations for capital works.[60] Under pressure from the Commonwealth government, the JPCSS adopted Goodes' scheme, but its members did not abandon their reluctance about the cash benefit principle. The Report warned that:

We are of opinion that it is useless making grants to patients of moneys for hospital accommodation benefits, free medicine, &c., if there is no provision for patients to utilize these benefits by being able to gain admission to hospital when needed. We feel that the first and most urgent call on any fund should be the making good of all deficiencies in hospital accommodation for sub-acute and chronic diseases. . .[61]

This would be achieved by adopting the Medical and Hospital Survey Committee's proposal to defer the first year's subsidy and establish a trust fund for capital expenditure on hospitals – under the direction of a small committee of experts. Commonwealth control of the approval of hospitals before they could participate in the scheme could also be used as a powerful weapon to raise standards, especially in the private sector.[62]

The remaining months of the Joint Parliamentary Committee were stormy. It continued to act as though it had the responsibility for planning the national medical service, refusing to acknowledge that the initiative had been wrested from its hands by the Treasury. It sealed its fate by proceeding increasingly as though it not only had charge of government policy, but was exempt from many of the normal constraints of a parliamentary committee, attempting to regain the initiative by forging its own agreement with the BMA which the government would have little choice but to accept. The Health Services Conference in December, boycotted by the NHMRC, appointed a joint Medical Planning Committee, including delegates from the JPCSS, the BMA and the MHSC. Its exact status was rather confused. Under normal procedures such a sub-committee required formal parliamentary approval – a step the JPCSS neglected to take. Second, although appointed by the Health Services Conference, the committee reported directly to the JPCSS. These procedural irregularities gave the critics of the Joint Parliamentary Committee their excuse to destroy its influence. Its isolation was confirmed in February 1944 when Sir Frederick Stewart resigned in protest over the dismissal of its secretary, Roy Rowe (who had been originally appointed by Stewart when the committee was first established). In March, in an unprecedented parliamentary row, the Speaker of the House of Representatives attacked the committee for 'irregular and improper' behaviour, in carrying out activities, such as the health services conference, without specific parliamentary sanction. While this attack referred to some of Rowe's personal expense claims, it included the costs of consultations with the BMA.[63]

The Medical Planning Committee reported on 1 March 1944. This interim report was a rather bland document. After surveying the

usual range of public health initiatives it made inconclusive recommendations, suggesting that the Commonwealth fund experimental
group practices, but evaded the key issues of the remuneration and
control of medical practice within a national health service.
Similarly, it prevaricated on which level of government should take
responsibility for a national medical service. Confirming Chifley's
exasperation, after almost three years of discussion the committee
came to the limp conclusion that 'it is quite impossible at the present
time to define clearly the administrative picture of the Commonwealth and state relationships in matters of public health'. The
committee compounded its sins by discussing the report in private
with the Federal Council of the BMA before passing it to the Department of Health and the government. Although Barnard claimed that
the Federal Council had endorsed its proposals, Newland met an
outraged reaction from his state branches and issued a prompt (and
only half-true) denial.[64]

The JPCSS had now offended Chifley and Fraser, Cumpston, the
Treasury, the BMA as well as former supporters from the opposition
benches, such as Stewart, and headed into complete isolation. It
produced an eighth interim report (on a comprehensive health service) in June 1945. This did little more than summarize the findings
of the Medical Planning Committee, which were published as an
appendix. A ninth interim report (on national fitness) followed, but
by now the committee's influence on policy was negligible. The
remaining members reacted bitterly. The ninth report included a
sharp attack on the government's repudiation of its work, claiming
that it had been sabotaged just when agreement with the BMA was
at hand. As we have seen, this was an excessively sanguine view of
the results of the Health Services Conference and the Medical Planning Committee. The BMA had made it clear that no agreement
would be entered into before the end of the war, and any sign of a
shift from this intransigence was met by stern warnings from the state
branches.[65]

The repercussions of this complex and messy affair went well
beyond the isolation of the JPCSS. The bitter bureaucratic warfare
between the Department of Health, the Treasury and the Parliamentary Committee over the control of policy strengthened the BMA's
suspicions of government intentions. This confusion about the ultimate responsibility was just as great within the ranks of the planners.
Cumpston still pressed the case of the NHMRC as the best agent for
achieving agreement with the BMA and the states. For a time the
JPCSS had presented itself as a sufficiently disinterested and biparti-

san body to gain agreement. Meanwhile, the first elements of the national health scheme had been announced by Cabinet with minimal consultation with any of these groups, and as part of a wider package of social welfare reforms drafted by Treasury economists with little reference to the elaborate plans of the NHMRC, the JPCSS and the BMA. In short, the whole exercise of consultative planning had been discarded, leaving a legacy of mutual suspicion and uncertainty about which agencies were responsible for policy and negotiations.

It was becoming increasingly clear, however, that the ultimate scheme would owe little to the optimistic schemes of the national hygienists. As E.S. Meyers, Cilento's successor as Professor of Social and Tropical Medicine at the University of Queensland, lamented, the shift to cash benefits marked the end of the attempt to redirect medical practice from remedial to preventive medicine.[66]

## Towards a national health service?

In June 1944 the Commonwealth government abruptly curtailed the long and inconclusive negotiations between the JPCSS and the BMA. Early in the month the state health ministers agreed in principle to the hospital and tuberculosis benefits schemes and the government prepared to implement its social welfare scheme. With the eclipse of the JPCSS, Cumpston moved to make his own department more central to policy-making and salvage what was possible from the damage. As he noted to Chifley, discussions of the previous two years, since the publication of the NHMRC scheme, had proceeded in a 'disconnected manner…it is now time that these various discussions were brought down to the level of practical talk'. He identified only two issues of principle which must be resolved before any further planning could take place – principles which underlay the protracted sparring between the profession and the planners:

> (1) Is the practising profession, as represented by the BMA, in agreement with the general principle that it is the responsibility of society, through Government, to ensure that every citizen has available the services of the medical profession and of hospitals, the services to be of both general practitioner and specialist standard?
> (2) Assuming the above principle to be accepted…then the form of service and the relationship between the Government as the controlling authority and the doctor as the person rendering the service must now be defined.[67]

Cumpston proposed that the department convene a small conference with BMA representatives to make clear whether the government could expect co-operation or 'obstinate opposition...A
reminder is given that approximately one thousand young medical
graduates without any commitments will become available after the
war, in addition to those subsidized undergraduates who are under
bond to the Government'.[68]

On 29 June 1944 he organized a conference between Fraser,
Chifley, the NHMRC, the Federal Council of the BMA and representatives of the colleges – pointedly excluding the JPCSS. The
weakness of his position was apparent when he warned his minister
that the meeting must remain informal, with no power to make
binding agreements, regardless of the presence of Fraser and Chifley,
as 'In view of the personnel of our Health Council, I might not be
able to prevent a majority in favour of some proposal which might
prove very embarrassing'. The meeting showed how deep the differences in principles had become – and how far the government was
from a coherent vision of its national medical service. While all
rejected capitation fees as the basis of remuneration, the ministers
were equivocal about an alternative, confining themselves to a
statement of principle:

> to make available to every member of the community the best possible
> protective and corrective medical care. The intention of the Government
> is to make such service available to each person without any direct
> liability on the person in respect of individual medical service. Each
> individual will make his contribution through general taxation and not
> through a specific tax for medical services. Payment to the doctor will be
> by direct contract between the Government and the doctor.[69]

However inconclusive its results, this meeting confirmed a new
tone in the style of health planning. There were to be no more
lengthy consultations and joint planning bodies. Instead, the direction of policy was to be decided by the government: the medical
profession and other outside bodies would only be approached to
advise on administrative details. This attempt by the Commonwealth
to seize the initiative entered a new phase of practical action in July
when Cumpston sent a secret memorandum to the senior Commonwealth medical officers in each state warning that the government
had made a definite decision to proceed with planning a medical
service for remote areas. The officers were asked to use the records of
the State Medical Co-ordination Committees to list towns with only
one doctor and to analyse the finances of Civil Emergency Medical

Service practices in their state. He concluded with a strict injunction that no indication was to be made to the BMA that any planning was proceeding.[70]

At the same time, Cumpston and Goodes conducted negotiations with the BMA. To overcome its state branches' suspicion of their Federal Council, the BMA formed a negotiating committee composed of one representative from each state council. Fraser made clear from the start that the committee was to be purely advisory, its powers limited to discussion of the issues of the form of admin-istration and contract under a national medical scheme. These meetings did little to win the Association's confidence. In place of the deferential treatment they had received from the JPCSS, the BMA representatives were given little sense of the direction in which government thinking was moving. The meetings with Cumpston and Goodes were more in the nature of exploratory investigations of the likely BMA reactions to specific policies. Hence, although a full stenographic record was made, only very abbreviated summaries were passed on to the BMA. The result was an increasing uneasiness within the BMA. Its delegates warned that the conferences had become 'entirely for the purpose of getting the attitude of the profession', making the BMA show its own hand, exacerbating its internal divisions and weaknesses while revealing few of the govern-ment's intentions.[71]

This phase of national health planning ended abruptly in August 1945. In a constitutional challenge brought by the Victorian gover-nment on behalf of the BMA, the High Court declared the Pharma-ceutical Benefits Act unconstitutional. The Court held that in the absence of a specific constitutional power to provide or finance health services the Commonwealth could only act through the states. The government's benefit schemes could only proceed by acting in co-operation with the states (as with the hospital benefits scheme) or by the equally difficult route of the constitutional amendment by referendum. The Commonwealth's plans would have to be postponed for several years.[72]

Cumpston had departed in October 1944 on an official visit to Colombo and Karachi, and retired the following June. His replace-ment, the ailing Frank McCallum, never achieved the same authority in dealings with the medical profession. There was a sense in which the chance to introduce the main lines of the medical scheme as part of the general package of social welfare benefits had been lost. Instead of enabling medical officers to return from the armed forces into a restructured medical service, the Commonwealth was unable to take further initiatives until well into 1946.

This chapter has explained the failure of wartime initiatives by the Commonwealth in terms of the weakness of its planning bodies. Left in the hands of the National Health and Medical Research Council and the Joint Committee on Social Security, schemes based on prewar national hygiene dominated the early debate. In the course of only three years debates over the future of health planning moved rapidly from attempts to impose the coherent plans of national hygiene, to a narrower concern with the economic welfare of the family and the individual. The defeat of the ambitious schemes of the NHMRC and JPCSS was not primarily the result of resistance from organized medicine. Instead, the weight of explanation must lie on the intervention of Chifley and the Treasury to include health policy within the social security programme. The failure of these initial efforts at planning resulted from the institutional and political weaknesses of the Commonwealth government. Despite half-hearted and confused opposition from the BMA, the Commonwealth compounded its irresolution over the control of wartime medical administration by postponing action until public support for radical reform had dwindled. It created a series of independent advisory bodies which enjoyed some confidence within the medical profession, then abandoned their work to take unilateral action. Finally, the miscalculation of its constitutional powers and the early abandonment of Cilento's constitutionally stronger solution of administration through the states left its policy in tatters at the end of the war.

It was precisely at this moment of the greatest weakness of the Commonwealth that the British Medical Association regrouped and presented a strong, if negative, front to policy-makers.

# CHAPTER 7

# Paying the Doctor: the BMA Caught Between Salaried Medicine and Fee-for-Service

Medical science, medical practice, has progressed far beyond the stage of the stethoscope, thermometer and bottle of medicine, and it has become a complex and very costly system of diagnosis and treatment. For the proper service of this system, both capital cost and the diversity of skill required demand some pooling of resources and the combination and co-ordination of medical men. Medical science has passed in fact as far beyond the stage at which the isolated individual private practitioner can fully satisfy its requirements as has the science of lighting passed beyond the kerosene lamp stage.

...having reached the stage of the public utility, the medical profession also needs Government help in finance and some form of central control ...I do not believe that this can be brought about by any other method than by some form of nationalization of medicine. I believe that to fit modern medicine properly into modern society you have to attack the very basis of private practice itself – the payment of fees.

*Dr Arthur Brown, 1944*[1]

...the basis of the present-time medical service is the relationship between the patient and the doctor, the doctor–patient relationship, and that is the right of the patient to choose his own doctor, his right to hire or to fire that doctor. If he is dissatisfied with the attention or the skill which he receives, he goes elsewhere, and, if this happens very much to that doctor, he is faced with the alternative of mending his ways or losing his practice. If he wants to sit back and rest on his oars, he will soon find that he is out of the boat, so the competitive system polices itself. But free choice of doctor is impossible to realize in a nationalized service. The family practitioner is turned into the Government official. He obtains promotion not by skill, but by seniority and length of service. He gains no medals by disturbing the routine of the machine and there is no calling in which there is so big a gap between the routine and the best work as in medicine.

...The planners state that the entrance door to medical care is too narrow. Their solution is to pull down the whole structure. Is not the logical and simple solution to widen the door?

*Dr Charles Byrne, 1944* [2]

The burden of explanation of the failure of a national health policy during the 1940s has fallen on the strength and conservatism of the organized medical profession. Its opposition to state intervention in medical practice has seemed so consistent and predictable that most analyses have been content to chronicle the changing tactics of obstruction.

The account presented in this study has stressed the importance of the state. The power of professional medicine was not based upon its autonomy from the intervention by third parties – whether governments or friendly societies – but on a complex set of interdependencies. It is impossible to conceptualize the relationship of medical practice to the state as a zero-sum game, in which advances in the power of one party necessarily mean the weakening of the other. The ambivalence of the medical profession towards state intervention – its support for measures which widened the market for medical services coupled with opposition to any attempt to shift the balance of power within the profession – meant that the initiatives of the NHMRC and the Curtin government did not receive blanket opposition. Instead, the BMA was beset with its own organizational problems, and the difficulties in the way of formulating a coherent alternative proved insuperable.

Theodore Marmor has produced one of the most influential accounts of the politics of medical remuneration. Arguing that 'the political resources of physicians in western industrial countries are so overwhelming that institutional differences among the countries are rendered unimportant in accounting for public policies regulating the payment of physicians', Marmor, in a comparative study of Britain and Sweden, has rejected explanations in terms of local variations in the access of organized medicine to policy-makers, or the degree of corporatism in policy-making, pointing instead to a common conservatism in doctors' attitudes towards attempts to change their mode of remuneration. Accepting that the form and source of payment varies from nation to nation, he leaves the formation of these preferences in a vague realm of 'culture'. More importantly for medical politics, once these initial preferences are formed, doctors cling to them and few governments have been able to achieve major shifts.[3]

We have already seen the tenuous unity of the BMA during the conflict over national health insurance. The complex mixture of fee-for-service and capitation practice in Australia and the marked differences in medical organization and remuneration between states makes Marmor's notions of 'preference' difficult to apply. While fee-for-service commanded the heights of the profession, and consequently the greatest prestige, it remained marginal to most doctors with working class general practices. Far from facing the federal government with a resolute support for fee-for-service in the face of the NHMRC and JPCSS schemes, the federal and state councils of the BMA showed just as much confusion as in 1937–9. Although the supporters of fee-for-service ultimately triumphed, their success was neither smooth nor uncontested.

Organized medicine did not present a monolithic front of hostility towards state intervention. The maintenance of outward signs of professional unity remained a tenet of faith to otherwise warring factions; by and large disagreements were settled in private amongst their peers. To the extent that individuals such as Arthur Brown worked for government bodies they were regarded with suspicion by otherwise sympathetic colleagues. The strength of this professional unity was a testament to the power of the shared mental world of medicine, forged in the rites of passage of medical school, hospital rounds and the struggle of establishing in practice, all of which gave doctors a sense of being a breed apart.

Membership of the BMA remained at relatively high levels throughout the interwar years. The density of membership, and the proportion of registered practitioners belonging to each state branch can be seen in the appendix to this chapter. This ranged from between 75 to 80 per cent in New South Wales and South Australia, and slightly lower in Victoria, to less than half in Tasmania. These proportions undoubtedly understate the strength of the BMA, as the registered included many retired, inactive or interstate doctors. This organizational strength intensified the sense of separateness and intellectual superiority and encouraged hostility towards lay interference in medical matters. Despite its claims to be a scientific and educational body, it was the more strictly 'trade union' activities of the BMA which provided the main draw card for its membership. Its sponsorship of medical defence funds, insurance schemes, fee arbitration services and medical agencies which bought and sold practices, helps to explain the very high concentration of its membership.[4]

The Federal Council of the BMA emerged from the conflict over national health insurance with its veto power over government policy enhanced, but its credibility with its own membership severely weakened. We have seen that one consequence of the struggle over national health insurance was that the initiative on policy questions increasingly passed from the old leadership of Melbourne and Sydney specialists to the hands of men who had entered medical politics during the confrontation with the federal government.[5]

These changes were tempered by the conservative institutional structure of the BMA. Control of BMA policy lay in the hands of its state councils and executives. The state leaderships were self-perpetuating oligarchies, voter turnout in branch elections was low and the rank and file of the profession, the general practitioners, were usually so immersed in the minutiae of practice that the grand issues of medical politics seemed a distant irrelevancy. Although subject to annual election by the minority of active branch members, councillors retained the power to co-opt prominent members who were unsuccessful in winning election. Consequently, despite the overt antagonisms between specialists and general practitioners, even the internal conflicts over national health insurance did little to shake dominance by the higher ranks of specialists in the capital cities. Most members remained inactive, with low participation in branch elections. Disagreements followed a fairly consistent pattern, developing through slow accretions of resentment at what was seen as the high-handed behaviour of those in control of the Association and leading to sudden bursts of rebellion – bitter struggles to repudiate over-conciliatory branch or federal policies. These rank-and-file revolts were rare – although the 1938 national insurance campaign was a clear example. The immediate issue settled (or buried for the moment), the membership would lapse into their characteristic passivity. Even in strong state branches such as Victoria, complaints about the 'apathy' of the members and the lack of attendance at meetings were perennial.[6]

## The Federal Council and professional unity

The most pressing problem facing the profession was to establish a single voice in its negotiations with the government. Since the formation of Australian specialist colleges there had been considerable concern within the BMA at the weakening of its front in negotiations with federal and state governments. Although the Royal Australasian Colleges of Surgeons and Physicians were limited by their articles of association from participation in other than

educational and scientific matters, the threat and opportunities
created by a major reorganization of medical services provided a
temptation to move from this limited role and represent the interests
of their own constituencies. Professor Harold Dew and Harold
Ritchie, the Royal College representatives on the NHMRC, took
part in the planning of the 'Recommendations' and the 'Outline'.
Dew served on the drafting sub-committee with Cilento, Cumpston
and Newman Morris. Under the presidency of Sidney Sewell the
RACP became even more active. In April 1942 he had responded to
Curtin's refusal to discuss the future of the medical service by
appointing committees of three Fellows in each state to examine the
implications of a national medical service on the practice of surgery.
These actions were significant, not for any practical results, but as
evidence that the Colleges were prepared to discuss – or even help
draft – government plans without reference to the BMA, although
the Commonwealth government again showed its lack of interest in
medical planning for the postwar period, failing to exploit the
opportunities created by the internal divisions of its most serious foe.
By the end of the war, when serious planning commenced, the
medical profession had reconstructed a defensive unity, accepting the
BMA as its sole public representative.[7]

Until the Royal Australasian College of Surgeons opens its
archives to researchers the exact circumstances in which this co-
operation was withdrawn will remain unclear. From early 1942 the
Colleges came under increasing attack from the BMA for weakening
the profession in its negotiations with the Commonwealth. In early
1942 the New South Wales branch council called for the representatives of the Royal Colleges on the NHMRC to confine their participation to subjects directly relevant to the professional concerns of
their members, leaving all questions of medical politics to the BMA.
After further pressure from the Federal Council the Colleges ended
their public participation. From mid-1942, whenever a political
question, defined in the most narrow sense, appeared on the
NHMRC agenda, the Royal College representatives withdrew from
the meeting. The state discussion groups also disappeared, although
suspicions persisted that the Colleges were prepared to make their
own settlement with the government. In October 1942 the Victorian
state executive of the BMA discussed rumours of continuing
negotiations between the RACS and the federal government.[8]

After asserting its predominance over rival national organizations,
the Federal Council tightened its control over its own representatives
on consultative and advisory bodies. Although Newman Morris had

played an active part on the drafting sub-committee and initiated amendments calling for close consultation with the profession before making changes in medical practice, he did this on his own initiative. At no stage did he discuss the proposals with the Federal Council or his own state branch of Victoria. This individual freedom of action had been the standard practice since the NHMRC was established. Newman Morris later complained that in six years on the NHMRC the Victorian branch had been the only section of the BMA that had ever conveyed its views to him on any issue.[9]

This attitude changed in July 1941. Before the crucial meeting of the NHMRC which approved the 'Recommendations', Newman Morris came under heavy pressure from the Federal Council to end his direct involvement. Shortly afterwards, the federal president, Sir Henry Newland, reminded Newman Morris that, as a delegate, he possessed no authority even to discuss policy changes without prior approval from the Federal Council. Alluding to the travails of the federal leadership over national health insurance, he instructed the BMA representative merely to convey the views of the Federal Council. Despite Morris's heated rejection of Newland's 'underlying implication that I was disregarding my responsibilities to the BMA', he regretfully informed Cumpston of the Federal Council's decision. The following year Newman Morris was replaced on the NHMRC by the less independently minded W.F. Simmons of New South Wales.[10]

Attempts to assert the predominance of the Federal Council over the state branches met with less success. Scarred by the clash over national health insurance, the state councils, led by New South Wales and Victoria, made it clear that they were not bound by any agreements made by the Federal Council without prior approval by the states. This accentuated the clumsiness of the decision-making machinery of the BMA. The terms and subject matter of negotiations at federal level had to be vetted first by state councils, and any provisional agreement with the Commonwealth referred to the branches for ratification.[11]

State suspicions of the Federal Council were reinforced by rivalries and jealousies between branches. Based in Sydney, the national body relied upon the New South Wales branch for its secretariat. Dr John Hunter held the positions of national and New South Wales general secretary from 1933 to 1949, a situation accepted by the other state branches on grounds of economy but leading to frequent allegations of conflicts of interest. The Victorians were especially sensitive on this point, receiving a legal opinion in 1941 which confirmed that the authority of the federal body was built on shaky foundations.

When the Federal Council attempted to gain a voluntary transfer of the power to enter binding agreements on behalf of the entire medical profession the Victorian branch led the rebuff, declaring that 'its members would accept the Federal Council's decisions only if the Branch had an opportunity to express an opinion regarding them'.[12]

Given these sharp disagreements between the states, federal councillors soon found that the safest response to any initiative from the Commonwealth government was prevarication. Avoidance of clear commitments became a major preoccupation of the Federal Council, an attitude which the Commonwealth government saw as blind obstruction. Even when the Federal Council appeared to have approved a policy, such as the experimental diagnostic clinics proposed by the Medical Planning Committee, adverse reactions from the states led to a quick repudiation, a volte face which confirmed the deceit of the leaders of organized medicine in the eyes of Labor ministers. J. Gordon Hislop, a consulting physician in Perth, long-time BMA councillor and executive officer to the West Australian State Medical Co-ordination Committee, warned the JPCSS:

> If the British Medical Association is asked to devise a scheme, no satisfactory solution of the problem will be arrived at...so long as the profession is allowed to look for a solution, the only result can be the division of the profession into groups; and the longer it is allowed to continue, the more widely separated will become the views of the groups, and the more difficult their co-operation in any scheme.[13]

As if internal fissures were not enough, the BMA entered the war years with its public standing in great disrepute. The repudiation of national health insurance and the stridency of the subsequent public campaign made it an easy task for the Association's critics to paint it as a reactionary organization, bent only on maintaining the privileges of its members. Fellow opponents of national health insurance, such as the trade union movement, were no more charitable, depicting the BMA's position as financial self-interest masquerading as principle. While this demonstrated the continuing hold exercised by the ideal of a medical profession governed by pure altruism rather than sordid commercial calculations – the notion that doctors had no legitimate interests outside the therapeutic needs of their patients – this was of small comfort to the leaders of the profession as they faced the upheavals of war. As the *Medical Journal of Australia* editorialized in November 1941:

> Members of the British Medical Association in Australia have to face the unpleasant fact that, though as individual medical attendants of individual members of the community they are held in high esteem by their

patients and may give advice knowing it will be followed to the letter, as members of 'the BMA' they are supposed to be guilty of unreasoning and unreasonable adherence to a code that seeks its own advantage at the expense of others, of dragooning members of the profession who do not belong to the Association, and of many ill-defined acts of impropriety.[14]

These organizational weaknesses made the task of formulating a national response to government initiatives difficult. The Federal Council's links to its membership were further weakened by the scale of military recruitment and the difficulties of holding meetings in wartime. Even if they could agree on a policy, the problems of obtaining the level of consent needed to avoid a repetition of the embarrassing scenes of 1938 seemed insuperable. Again, this made BMA leaders chary of commitment to postwar plans.

## The Bell–Simmons report

In late 1942 the chairman of the Victorian branch of the BMA reviewed the choices facing the profession. With a Labor government holding power in Canberra, and after the publication of the two reports of the NHMRC, a major change in the conditions of medical practice appeared inevitable. The profession, he argued, must draft its own concrete proposals or risk the imposition of a government plan. He asked his colleagues:

> Did the profession want the whole community or only a portion of it provided for by a nationalized health service, ie, would a portion of the community be required to continue to get its medical needs under a system of private practice?
>
>   If the profession wants a national health service, does it want the doctors in it to be paid by salary or by capitation fee?[15]

Significantly, at this point fee-for-service was not mentioned as a viable option for the majority of the population.

Unwilling to accept a complete salaried service – and the end of private practice for those who could afford it – the BMA found the alternatives of a salaried service confined to the poor or insurance-based panel practice only slightly more attractive. Neither would solve the problem of the middle class patient, excluded from concessional services by the means test, but unable to afford extended treatment.

The first of the BMA's attempts to resolve these dilemmas was a response to the conflict over national health insurance. George Bell and W.F. Simmons prepared a report for the Federal Council on 'A General Medical Service for Australia', in February 1940. Bell was a leading Sydney surgeon prominent in the BMA since the 1920s, while Simmons had been one of the leaders of the New South Wales general practitioners in the struggle against national health insurance. The report was an index of the intellectual poverty of the leaders of Australian organized medicine. Almost every section was copied verbatim from earlier official documents published by the BMA in London. It was dominated by the concerns of the late 1930s – the integration of a wider population into the market for medical care and the perceived threat to the position of the general practitioner posed by both limited incomes and the restrictions of hospital specialization.[16]

The Bell–Simmons report was a manifesto for the general practitioner as the heart of the health system. Calling for a 'complete medical service', the scheme included general practitioner and specialist services centred on the family doctor and 'closely co-ordinated and developed by the application of a planned national health policy'.[17] The system was to be financed through contributory health insurance, with the safeguard of a complete quarantine of medical benefits from other cash benefits such as pensions. The report admitted that private fee-for-service practice could not provide the basis for a national health service. Doctors were to be remunerated on a capitation basis (avoiding the thorny question of the level of remuneration) while existing private practice would be protected by a rigorous income limit of £312 per annum. In contrast to the national health insurance scheme of the Lyons government, all dependants, employed or unemployed, were to be included. In short, the scheme was little more than a more complete version of friendly society panel practice, with greater medical control of the range of services and payments.

Despite a verbal commitment, the Bell–Simmons report confined preventive medicine to a general set of demands for more state expenditure on public health, leaving the existing pattern of private practice undisturbed. Instead, the family doctor was romanticized as the central provider of medical services:

> it is of primary importance that the organization of the health service of the nation should be based upon the family as the normal unit, and on the family doctor as the normal medical attendant and guardian...The first essential for the proper and efficient treatment of individual persons is, therefore, not institutional but personal service, such as can be rendered in their own homes only by a family doctor who has the continuous care of their health.[18]

Hence, specialist services were to be made available only after referral by a general practitioner. This emphasis extended into an attack on the hospitalization of childbirth. The authors argued that:

> There has been in recent years a considerable increase in the number of women seeking to be confined in institutions. This is sometimes seen as an argument in favour of divorcing the general practitioner from midwifery and replacing him by an obstetric specialist. The removal of midwifery from the normal sphere of activities of the general practitioner is likely to damage the interests of the patient and to affect adversely the efficiency of the practitioner. Further, the experience in those urban areas in which the institutionalization of maternity has grown up does not justify its extension. In such areas there has been no corresponding decline in maternal mortality; indeed there is evidence that institutional confinement carries with it a greater danger of infection than domiciliary confinement...All available evidence suggests that the institution is not safer than the home, and in the view of the Association, the remedy for the existing situation lies, not in a more complete separation of the general practitioner from midwifery, but in a full recognition of his position as the person responsible for the continuous care of the mother.[19]

This defence of the general practitioner was extended by a call for the construction of decentralized base hospitals with increased access for general practitioners as: 'The importance to a general practitioner, and to the efficiency of his service to the community, of an association with a hospital is difficult to exaggerate'. The 'abuse of outpatient departments' by those who could afford to use a general practitioner was to be curtailed by stricter controls on admissions.[20]

The Federal Council delayed circulating the report until August, a hesitation vindicated by the overwhelmingly negative reactions of the state branches. The Victorians criticized its reliance on capitation fees as 'essentially an elaboration of the lodge system with the substitution of the Government for the friendly societies', and all branches expressed horror at the attack on the hospitalization of childbirth. A revised version was accepted reluctantly by the Federal Council and remained official policy for the remainder of the war years, but only after the more contentious issues, such as opposition to hospital confinement, had been excluded and a more agnostic approach was adopted towards forms of remuneration.[21]

It was clear that the central principle of a contributory, means tested panel service was unacceptable to large sections of general practitioners. As with national insurance, the lines of a preferable scheme remained as elusive as ever.

## The BMA and a salaried service

Meanwhile, the debate within the medical profession had moved to less familiar terrain. At the beginning of 1940 Mervyn Archdall, the editor of the *Medical Journal of Australia*, challenged his readers to prepare for a radical reshaping of the pattern of medical practice at the end of the war: 'to take stock of themselves, of their objectives, of their ideals and of their very reason for existence'.[22] A special edition of the *Journal* extended this critique to the social conditions which gave rise to ill-health:

> If the social evils of today are the result of slavish adherence to the present economic system (and who will have the temerity to deny that they are?) society will have to readjust its sense of values and by a more equitable redistribution of the burden inherent in the system do away with the evils. If this cannot be done under the present system then the system must be changed.[23]

For the contributors to the *Medical Journal of Australia* debate, postwar reconstruction provided the opportunity to place the remuneration of the medical profession on a more secure basis, to strengthen the position of the general practitioner and restructure the relationship between preventive and curative medicine. The articles and correspondence which followed were marked by a sense of the inevitability of a national medical service and the likelihood that, however strong the reservations of the medical profession, it would be salaried. This common ground was found in advocates of reform stretching from the adherents of racial hygiene and national fitness to advocates of socialism. Much of the sympathy they mustered within the ranks of general practice came not from ideological adherence to socialized medicine, but from a reluctant belief that state control was the lesser of several evils. This view was already common at the time of the conflict over NHI, epitomized in the cry of despair from Thomas Ritchie, a general practitioner from Burra Junction in rural South Australia: 'Under the nationalization of medicine or under the national health insurance scheme we will become mere clerks; but as there is evidently no choice in the matter I prefer that we should at least be under the aegis and protection of a government department'.[24]

For the next two years debate was dominated by calls for a radical reorganization of the finance of medical practice. The administrative and financial details of these schemes were frequently absurdly optimistic or left purposely vague. However, they shared with the NHMRC a conviction that the form of remuneration was to be the key to reforging the relationship between preventive and curative medicine. A drastically reorganized system would develop a strengthened role for the general practitioner and, provided that control remained in medical hands, it could reverse the growing centralization and specialism of medical practice.

One of the first contributions to be published was by Dr Stanley Boyd, a general practitioner from Gnowangerup in the Western Australian wheat belt. Drawing on his early experiences in panel practice in England, Boyd argued that fee-for-service was totally antagonistic to any effective general practitioner-based preventive medicine as:

> Having had to conduct side by side both types of practice has to my dismay and disgust, forced me to become aware that I have a vested interest to the illness of my private patients, while with regard to my 'contract patients' my interest is vested in their health.

The reorganization of medical practice should be dominated by the 'recent trend in discovery towards prophylaxis'. Echoing the eugenism of the population debate, Boyd argued that the radical measures of Nazi Germany, while following mistaken methods, were 'directing patriotic energy towards a high level of physical development and racial efficiency'. Instead of the profession waiting for the 'political dodgery' of yet another lay-designed scheme, its most urgent task must be to assert its position as 'the natural sponsors of racial health' and:

> If we admit that we are not able to influence our race by ordering the choice of mates, there is one way, and one way only, in which we can affect racial health, and that is to secure the general health of all nubile persons; in other words, we must set ourselves to see that every potential parent is brought to reproductive age with tissues uninjured by disease, with their vital capacity and general physique in well-exercised development, and with vital chemistry as perfect as social conditions will permit.[25]

Boyd's combination of eugenism, political authoritarianism and a medically-controlled salaried health service was one of the strongest statements of the national hygienist's faith to come from within the practising profession. The title of a collection of his articles, *Doctor's Conscience or All Illness is Preventable*, summed up his belief that changes in the organization and remuneration of medical practice could achieve a revolution in public health. Writing to Cumpston he said Australia needed a 'social order in which scientific planning can become practical politics'. With three other West Australian doctors, including Gordon Hislop, the BMA branch chairman, he prepared details of a scheme for the Joint Parliamentary Committee, developing his arguments for a new priority to preventive medicine.[26]

If Boyd remained outside the mainstream of medical thought – a marginality underlined by Cilento's enthusiastic preface – equally far-reaching schemes were promoted by more orthodox figures. Arthur Brown was the most eloquent advocate of salaried service from within the medical profession. Born in 1889, the son of a general practitioner in the Victorian country town of Colac, Brown received the education of a typical Western District gentleman. After attending Melbourne Grammar, the Edinburgh Academy and Cambridge University he acquired his clinical training at University College Hospital in London. Graduating in 1914 he served in the British Army, ending the war as a captain in the hospitals of the Australian Army Medical Corps in France. He had specialized in the new techniques of radiology, and on demobilization, Brown, like many ex-AIF medical officers, seemed headed towards a lucrative specialized surgical practice in Melbourne. Instead, in 1919 he returned to Colac and went into general practice with his father. He continued, however, to be an innovator in country medical practice and was an articulate critic of the conservatism of his profession, establishing a pathology laboratory at his father's private hospital and leading a long fight to build the state's first community hospital. This campaign succeeded in 1934 and the new Colac hospital embodied Brown's views of the need to rebuild the links between general practice and hospital work, symbolized by the inclusion of doctors' consulting rooms in the same building as diagnostic services.[27]

Brown grounded his proposals on the changing economic conditions of medical practice: the destruction of the more intimate relationships between patient and doctor and the demise of the family practitioner. He pointed to the growing component of medical incomes derived from insurance companies and the expansion of hospitals from a local and individual service to a centralized state-controlled system with limited access for non-specialists. The increasing intervention of state governments in the location of practitioners and the Commonwealth's attempt to impose national health insurance carried this attack on medical independence to its logical end: full state control. Instead of passively accepting a gradual decay of the conditions of medical practice, the profession had to take the initiative and formulate its own radical plan to meet the demands of the postwar era. The alternative could only be a scheme devised by laymen unsympathetic to the ideals and interests of medicine. Brown drew heavily on the work of Benjamin Moore, a

British medical socialist prominent before the First World War. Moore and the State Medical Service Association in which he was active had argued that only a complete salaried health service could ensure a new and more productive relationship between preventive and curative medicine. It would enable a shift from 'wrong and antiquated lines of tinkering the individual for fees after he has fallen into ill-health', to the organization of 'an army of health and public safety against disease, which shall seek disease at its source and commence to deal with this large problem of eradication in a modern and scientific way'. Only a completely free medical service, paid by salary and armed with plenary powers, could wage this war against disease.[28]

Echoing Moore, Brown saw the financial relationship between doctor and patient as the main barrier to the advance of public health. Preventive and curative medicine could never be united as long as one was paid by a salary and the other by a fee. 'Medical men and women as private traders' were incapable of improving the standard of practice; preventive work was unattractive to the small business mentality of the private practitioner as it contributed little income to a practice. He cited disputes within the BMA over the medical staffing of baby health centres in Victoria. Discussion of more effective management of the centres had been swamped by concern at the unfair commercial advantages which would accrue to any doctor given privileged access to new mothers. A salaried system could solve the financial difficulties of a large section of the profession and enable the development of improved services in rural and industrial areas.[29]

Although Brown accepted that the state, as the embodiment of the public interest, must control the future direction of health services, this influence should not extend to the content of medical practice. A salaried service could only succeed if it was suitably decentralized and protected from political interference with full medical control of administration and professional practice. Although he dismissed the BMA's long-standing opposition to the involvement of third parties – whether the state or friendly societies – in the financial relationship between patient and doctor as 'traditional superstitious rubbish', Brown saw the maintenance of medical independence as crucial to the success of a salaried health scheme. While much BMA opposition stemmed from 'sheer natural conservatism' and a perceived threat to the exalted status of the doctor, he accepted that there was a justified fear of outside meddling in technical questions of medical practice. Any scheme which did not allay this concern was doomed to failure.[30]

This implied strong opposition to the domination of the salaried scheme by full-time public health officials. Brown objected to the state-medicine bias of the NHMRC 'Outline', which proposed higher salaries for administrators and, in particular, administrative control by local government medical officers of health. Public health and preventive medicine, he argued, should be an integral part of the new service, but only as one specialism among many. Any national salaried health service must be decentralized and free from direct departmental control as 'doctors cannot exercise independent judgment and have free action under the scrutiny of a Treasury clerk'. As he told the Joint Parliamentary Committee on Social Security:

> The whole point of my criticism of the report is that it sets out with a blue-print made in an office to impose a system on the country in which every essential system is at present working well. The work is actually being well done by the same men as those who would have to do it under a salaried scheme. If you feel it necessary to change over from the private-fee basis to a salary basis, the less you interfere with the work of the men who have to do it at present the better.[31]

As an active member of the state council of the Victorian branch and its organization sub-committee, Brown tirelessly advocated the need for a fundamental reorganization of medical practice. The profession must propose its own alternative as it was now

> apparent that medical practice as at present existing was in a state of change and that if the profession was to work under a regimented service, it would be better to have one medically controlled rather than departmentally controlled. The profession stood to gain nothing and lose a great deal under an insurance scheme, it would set medical practice back a generation.[32]

By the end of 1942 sympathy for a national medical service embraced a wide cross-section of the profession. South Australia and Queensland had declared themselves broadly in sympathy with the NHMRC approach, although preferring a contributory capitation-based system. In Victoria D.M. Embleton, a prominent and by no means radical longtime councillor, argued that the 'cataclysmic' changes of the war meant that 'nationalization of medicine in some form seemed imminent'. A meeting of general practitioners in Melbourne's eastern suburbs argued that 'the profession must try to steer the Government's chosen scheme into a course which would not be too hard on the general practitioner'. The group practice organization of a salaried service should transfer hospital outpatient work to suburban medical centres; only work beyond the technical capacities of the salaried clinic doctors would be passed on to base hospitals for specialist attention. At the other geographical extreme, a meeting of the three doctors serving the remote Eyre Peninsula in South Australia declared their unanimous support for the full NHMRC scheme.[33]

Convinced of the need for urgent action from within the profession to devise a scheme before one was imposed by less sympathetic hands, the Victorian branch council appointed a sub-committee of John Dale, Arthur Brown and Wilfrid Kent Hughes to draw up a proposal based on 'detailed salaried medical service schemes'.[34] John Dale's support for salaried practice, like that of Brown, came from a mixture of opposition to national health insurance and concern for the integration of public health and private practice. Born in Britain, he worked in Birmingham's public health services before migrating to Australia to become Medical Officer of Health for Perth and then for the City of Melbourne. An active propagandist in the medical press for the single-tax movement, during the depression years he became an outspoken critic of the links between unemployment, poor housing and health conditions. As president of the 'United Electors of Australia (Non-Party)' he had played a leading role in the fight against national health insurance. Kent Hughes was a more anomalous figure. A member of Mebourne's medical establishment, he played little part in drafting the report.[35] In late August the committee's 'Proposals for a Salaried Medical Scheme' followed Brown's ideas closely and were approved by the State Executive and conveyed to the Federal Council. Although it received majority support for a brief period, the scheme was never formally adopted as branch policy. The cumbersome constitutional machinery of the BMA meant that Victoria remained formally bound by a 1935 decision of Convocation, the branch's highest decision-making body, to support a system of capitation-based health insurance, although this was the one option to which the membership had displayed clear aversion. This general assembly of members was extremely difficult to assemble even in peacetime. No attempt could be made in the circumstances of late 1941.[36]

Despite their vigorous critique of the divorce between public health work and curative medicine, the advocates of salaried medicine shared many of the same positions as their more conservative colleagues. Few criticisms were made of the content of medical practice, merely its lack of co-ordination. Similarly, Brown and his colleagues dissented sharply from Cumpston's proposal for the subordination of practitioners to the administrators of the state and federal departments of health. It was left to more radical voices, within and outside the profession, to express more thoroughgoing scepticism about existing arrangements. As Dr W.G. Heaslip of Kensington Park, South Australia, commented sourly:

> It can be said of most of those supporting, as well as those opposing a nationalized service that they are more concerned with the effects on members of the profession than the effects on the national health.[37]

## The BMA and the NHMRC scheme

The salaried schemes produced by the profession developed in parallel, rather than in response to the NHMRC scheme. Where Cilento's proposals had envisaged a radical reorganization of the boundaries of public and private medicine, the schemes promoted by Brown and the Victorian branch centred on the economic and professional problems of general practice – the need for stable sources of remuneration, access to hospital beds and reversal of the threat of specialism. As the debates within public and private medicine proceeded on different assumptions and aims, discussion of the NHMRC scheme from within the medical profession was at first restrained. Although Newland and the Federal Council had moved promptly to constrain the independence of Newman Morris, given the deep divisions within the profession on the question of salaried medicine, for the moment its leaders concentrated on organizational questions, such as asserting the predominance of the Federal Council in negotiations with the federal government.

Even when organized medicine and the federal government appeared to have found common ground – as when the BMA agreed that 'the development of the group scheme in modern medicine is essential in order that the patient may get the advantage of the attention of specialists' – this apparent agreement frequently masked subtle differences of meaning, reinforcing suspicions that the other side was guilty of duplicity. In place of Cilento's vision of a fundamental reorganization of general practice, the BMA proposed an anodyne scheme of 'diagnostic centres', 'a one hundred percent private enterprise arrangement needing no government instrument' to provide general practitioners with access to more sophisticated equipment. Cilento complained: 'the more I discussed the matter with BMA representatives here, the more I found that we were using the same words to express totally different ideas'.[38]

Despite the unenthusiastic response from the branches, the Federal Council remained committed to the general approach of the Bell–Simmons scheme: a means-tested capitation-based service. Hence, it refused even to discuss the Victorian scheme for a salaried service. Arguments from Thomas Price, one of the Queensland branch representatives, for a universal scheme with no income limits also fell on deaf ears. Similarly, the Council rejected the New Zealand model of fee-for-service as incompatible with contributory insurance. The pool from which payments were made to practitioners would be too restricted to cope with the unpredictability and variations in demand in a fee-for-service system. Instead, the national leadership argued for caution in responding to any federal government initiatives, delaying any change until the end of the war, and opposing piecemeal experimentation. As W.G.D. Upjohn, the secretary of the Victorian branch, argued:

> it would be inviting failure of any new plan and would bring into popular disrepute all similar plans, if attempts were made with inadequate equipment and insufficient or not fully efficient medical personnel, to put such a plan bit by bit into practice.[39]

Some BMA leaders simply denied the need for any change. In Victoria, Cecil Colville saw no connection between the argument about remuneration and the reorganization of medical services. His evidence to the Joint Parliamentary Committee on Social Security gave a half-hearted endorsement to a salaried service but qualified this by asserting that 'existing services are in every respect satisfactory and desirable'. Linked to this plea for inaction was a vague call for reform of the social causes of disease and ill-health, poor housing, child health and industrial hygiene, an attempt to appropriate the rhetoric of social medicine to forestall attempts to alter private practice. This approach was found at its most crass when Ronald Grieve, the leader of militant opposition to national health insurance in New South Wales, pointed to the immunization of patients and the use of drug therapies at early stages of disease to suggest that preventive medicine was already the common stock of general practitioners. Money would be better spent giving practitioners greater access to new methods of diagnosis rather than experiments in new forms of public control. Grieve attacked the assumption 'that nationalization being inevitable, men of medicine should begin in a variety of ways to emulate the men of Vichy'.[40]

Grieve's views remained, for the moment, less prominent than those of the supporters of radical change. Even his own state branch had taken on much of the language of social medicine, arguing that 'the problems of tuberculosis tend always to be economic problems' and forming an active 'sociological medicine section' alongside its other specialist sub-groups.[41] In early 1943 a critic of salaried medicine warned the Victorian branch council:

Speak to any member of the profession, other than a member of the Council, about the National Health and Medical Research Council's scheme and you will find that his idea of it is either that 'the scheme is not a bad one', or, 'that it is a very good one'. The idea of the members who favour the scheme is that they are going to be senior medical officers at a high salary.[42]

Whatever their attitudes towards state intervention in medical care, most of the leaders of the profession accepted the inevitability of a national medical service. The universalism of the NHMRC and JPCSS schemes had won considerable sympathy. For many doctors, a national health service, even on salaried lines, could reduce the dominance of 'plutocratic medicine' and restore the central place of the general practitioner – as long as professional control was not abandoned to departmental bureaucrats.

Not surprisingly the supporters of salaried medical services gave guarded approval to the NHMRC 'Outline', objecting mainly to its excessive centralization and control by a government department. Instead, they advocated an independent statutory authority on the model of the State Electricity Commission of Victoria, allowing the medical profession complete control over the conditions of practice. In a private communication to Cumpston, Arthur Brown protested that a successful national medical service must be based on flexible local administration. Curative medicine was not adapted to bureaucratic central office control. In addition, the scheme was seriously flawed and would lose much sympathy by failing to consider the compensation of doctors for the loss of their private practices. The fear of bureaucratism ran through the criticisms of many otherwise sympathetic medical leaders. Jarvis Nye, the founder of the Brisbane Clinic, told a meeting of returned medical officers that while:

> If we feel a conviction that the quality of the service under a salary will fall short of the present standard, we are assuming a poor personnel for a profession which is recruited, generally speaking, from the highest cultural classes of the nation...[However]...to accept a national service without at least the two following safeguards would be utter folly, both from the viewpoint of the profession as well as the common good.
>
> There should be several autonomous group regions in each State. This would give a member the right to leave one area to join another. It would also provide a measure of competition which is so necessary for enthusiasm and efficiency.
>
> Politicians must have no control of the professional aspects of the service; this would include discipline and appointments.[43]

The caution of this welcome was reinforced by the problems of integrating returned medical officers into civilian practice. For both the government and the BMA the future depended on the attitudes of men and women who had proceeded straight from university into the armed services and were accustomed to the security of a salaried service. Acceptance of a national medical service assumed a large degree of medical control of the service, a theme reiterated from August to December as medical practitioners gave evidence to the public hearings of the JPCSS on the NHMRC proposals.[44]

For the moment the Federal Council succeeded in keeping the more acrimonious discussions of the future of medical practice limited to the closed ranks of the profession. Federal Council documents confined themselves to vague generalities about the need for preventive care, divorced from its public health bias to include 'any activity which helps to save or prolong life'. The relationship of the doctor and the state was not broached. Fears that the Commonwealth government would use the disruption of demobilization to introduce a salaried service confirmed the Federal Council in its determination to postpone the planning of a national service.[45]

This period of complacency ended when the government unfolded its wider social security plans in late 1943. The federal and state councils of the BMA prepared for a more open conflict about the future direction of Australia's health services.

## The ascendancy of fee-for-service

The Federal Council had successfully preserved the outward trappings of professional unity by insisting that no serious discussion or planning could be launched until after the war. This attitude provided a lowest common denominator acceptable to all viewpoints within the state branches. During 1942 and 1943 the leaders of organized medicine were too aware of the divisions amongst their members to argue more than the need to postpone action. This negative stance was reinforced when Cabinet moved to announce its social welfare reforms. When the Federal Council continued its desultory negotiations with the federal government and the parliamentary committee, the Victorian and New South Wales branches reinforced this inertia, issuing clear warnings that they would not consider themselves bound by any agreement. Consequently, for the next two years the only real initiatives came at state level, underlining the weaknesses of BMA policy-making processes and confirming government suspicions of the duplicity and obstruction of the medical profession.[46]

Whatever their support amongst a minority of general practitioners, the advocates of salaried service never gained much of a foothold in the national leadership. Their isolation increased as advocates such as Brown increasingly threw in their lot with the federal government. His membership of the Medical and Hospital Survey Committee of the JPCSS – an appointment made without consultation with or approval of the BMA – showed his growing disaffection from his colleagues. Newland and his closest colleagues in the federal leadership remained committed to the residualism of the Bell–Simmons scheme. State health services were to be confined to the most needy sections of the community, those at present attending free outpatients' clinics at the public hospitals. The middle classes were to be encouraged to join contributory voluntary insurance schemes while the working class would remain in friendly societies. In the political climate of 1943 and 1944 these three classes of health care appeared anachronistic and reactionary.

The first move came from the New South Wales branch early in 1943 when it called a Convention – the highest decision-making body of the branch – to decide on a binding policy. Held over two days, with sixty delegates representing all parts of the state, it was a considerable feat of organization in wartime, demonstrating the 'extraordinarily good' branch structure which Victorian observers noted with envy. While it reiterated hostility to national health insurance, the Convention accepted that a radical change was inevitable, approving a list of the conditions under which a national medical service would be acceptable. The New South Wales state executive had recommended that the branch support a capitation-based system, on Bell–Simmons lines. Instead, a motion from the floor of the Convention won overwhelming support for including a much wider  fee-for-service element. The details of this hybrid were not spelled out, but this became the official policy of the New South Wales branch.[47]

The New South Wales Convention revealed the minority  support which the Bell–Simmons and salaried schemes could command within the profession. At the same time, it had revealed a glaring gap between the willingness of the leadership to accept a modest compromise and the members' desire for thoroughgoing change. In March the Federal Council adopted much of this New South Wales scheme as its 'Policy in Respect of a General Medical Service for Australia', but kept some distance from the more unrealistic demands: all references to the finance of the scheme were deleted. The revised scheme still implied a two-class system of health: lodge practice for the working classes and fee-for-service for the affluent.[48]

This set the pattern for the remainder of the war years. The New

South Wales branch, echoed by the Federal Council, expressed opposition towards any government-controlled service but made little effort to produce details on how its alternative scheme would work. The implication, recognized quickly by critics in other states, was that New South Wales wished to continue panel practice for the poor while introducing government subsidized fee-for-service to the middle classes. Far from being a triumph for the opponents of capitation-based NHI and lodge practice, this was seen as yet another set of 'pious resolutions and...pious aspirations', in the abstract a superior medical system but totally lacking in the political means to realize it. Charles Byrne, the most articulate internal critic of the vagueness and defensiveness of the BMA, argued that the NSW Convention had displayed:

> an extraordinary conception as to what would be the reception of a combination of fee-for-service and capitation systems...There were wealthy patients and poor patients. The profession could not expect any Government to hand over to it the good risks, leaving the Government responsible for the poor risks. It was quite inconceivable that a dual system would be acceptable. Health services, too, should be all embracing. The Convention's idea, however, was that they should be strictly limited.[49]

In early 1943 Byrne developed this attack, promoting a universal medical service based on fee-for-service.[50] Despite his fierce criticisms of the NHMRC and other schemes of salaried service, Byrne had long argued that a viable alternative must recognize the political strength of demands for a universal service. Taking up the themes of the JPCSS reports he accepted that neither financial nor geographical barriers to equal access to health could be left to market mechanisms but required intervention from the state. Nor could national health services be restricted to the poorest sections of the community. As he argued at a meeting of the Victorian State Council which rejected the Bell–Simmons approach:

> The scheme submitted would not produce a complete medical service. Unless a patient was sent to a charitable organization he could not receive the treatment that was necessary, nor would the suggested alterations bring about a more equitable distribution of doctors. At the present time Footscray had one doctor to more than 5,000 people, but there was nothing in the proposals which would alter that state of affairs. Neither was there anything in them to co-ordinate medical services or to put welfare services on a proper basis. Social factors had worked into medical practice and their effect could be seen at every turn. The report

contained no criticism of the relationship between the general practitioner and the public hospital. Today, if a general practitioner wants to put a patient into a public hospital, he has to do it per medium of a friend and the friend treats the patient without any knowledge of his social conditions which may have been contributable to his condition...

The time had arrived when medical practice had to be reorganized, and unless the profession realized it and put its house in order, politicians would, and the best that could be hoped for would be a compromise between the doctors and the politicians; the worst was too horrible to contemplate. In England 90% of the profession's patients were members of lodges. If that state of affairs was to be stopped in Australia, the profession would have to produce a decent alternative. The people wanted and were entitled to a good medical service and the ordinary man in the street did not get one.[51]

Byrne's plan was based on a distinctive view of the workings of the medical market. In contrast to the national hygienists, he assumed that patients, advised by their general practitioners, were capable of making a rational choice of appropriate medical responses to their needs. The only barrier to an adequate health service was financial; if the state intervened to underpin the market, other major changes in the organization of practice would be unnecessary. Subsidized fee-for-service would restore the shaky finances and status of general practice without subordinating it to a hierarchical reorganization of the whole hospital and public health system such as that contemplated by Cilento and the NHMRC. At the same time, by abandoning the residualism of earlier BMA schemes Byrne recognized that the paternalist charity of honorary practice and poor law medicine were no longer politically acceptable, nor could the problems of the middle classes be left out of the equation. He also confronted the central administrative problem of fee-for-service: the prevention of abuse and over-servicing by patients and doctors. The price of freedom to control their own practices and the extension of the medical market would be submission to new restrictions.

For the Victorian critics the central issue remained 'the gap between the poor and the rich'. Any scheme which used a poor law government service for the indigent and fee-for-service private practice for those on higher incomes was bound to fail. In March 1943 the Victorian branch attempted to surmount these problems with its own scheme. Drafted by Byrne, it identified the central problems of medical practice with the 'section of the population who are in receipt of only moderate incomes', the lack of services in some rural areas, and the overcrowding of outpatients' departments. The solution to all these problems should be 'within the framework of the existing system'. For the first time the fee-for-service principle was extended to the whole community, financed by a 'Special Government Fund', which would pay a fixed part of each fee.[52]

Byrne told his Victorian Council colleagues that there were only two models of a universal fee-for-service system: the system which had emerged from the profession's boycott of New Zealand Labour's capitation-based national health scheme, and the French health system. In each of these schemes there was no clear tie between contributions and benefits. Given that the numbers of separately remunerated services were unpredictable, fee-for-service would always be vulnerable to the demand for payments exceeding the pool of contributions. Equally, if medical fees remained unregulated, doctors would set their fees independently and recover them from the insurance fund. Lacking a means of controlling either fees or the use of services, both governments had been forced to subsidize medical benefits well beyond the scope of the nominal contribution from taxation. Arguing that no responsible government could follow this route, Byrne suggested that the profession must accept the need for effective mechanisms of cost control. With his own general practice in the Melbourne industrial suburb of Sunshine, Byrne was well acquainted with fee-for-service workers' compensation practice and used this as a loose model. Contributions by insured workers were to form a fixed pool from which payments to doctors were made, with benefits calculated by a joint committee from the BMA and the insurance authority using an agreed schedule of fees:

> The notion was to prevent a situation which had arisen in France resulting from a general raising of medical fees because of the patient's increased capacity to pay. The scheme was not one to enrich doctors and incidentally to bring into existence a political weapon for use against the profession or to destroy the faith of the people in the profession. There was already a germ of justification in the Government's protest against certain practices since the midwifery benefit had been increased to £17/10s. Relationships between the amount paid by the fund and the amount paid by the patient [were] of the utmost importance in a fee-for-service scheme. If this relationship was not preserved, the patient is no better off. The position in New Zealand was too good to last and the alternative was a salaried medical scheme. The only way to prevent fees from rising to the patient's capacity to pay was to have a schedule of fees.[53]

Byrne proposed to strengthen these safeguards by policing the system with salaried medical officers charged with the task of certifying patients' eligibility for benefits. Fees were to be controlled by a

State Adjudication Committee with equal medical and lay representation, and purely medical questions by a State Medical Tribunal with no lay representation.[54]

For the moment, Byrne's scheme won little support outside Victoria. The *Medical Journal of Australia* damned his pamphlet with faint praise. While his approach was idealistic: 'some of his deductions from the evidence would appear at this stage to be impracticable, and few students of the subject are likely to agree with him in toto; the prediction of the ultimate abolition of contract practice and the introduction of restrictions to circumscribe private practice will not find wide acceptance'.[55]

The New South Wales moves had marked the end of serious support for salaried medicine within the BMA. A meeting of Victoria's branch convocation assembled in January 1944 to set out the minimum acceptable provisions of a national health service. The details of the Victorian programme followed Byrne's proposals. The national medical service must preserve 'the existing consultant, general practitioner and hospital services'. However, in contrast to the New South Wales scheme, means testing was rejected. Unequal access to costly services must be redressed with 'some means of bridging the financial gap between a complete medical service and its availability to all...without regard to income'. Support for fee-for-service remained more equivocal than in New South Wales, stressing that 'If a scheme for a National Medical Service on a "fee-for-service" basis is approved by Convocation, it shall be regarded only as one acceptable alternative for any unacceptable scheme proposed by the Government'.[56]

Despite these steps by its two most powerful branches, the BMA was still presenting a far from united front of opposition to the government's plans. When the Commonwealth government swept the JPCSS aside in June 1944 and moved for more decisive action, the Federal Council was again inclined to temporize, continuing negotiations to find common ground. Colville, who was now an advocate of all-out resistance to any government-imposed scheme, reported to the Victorian state council that 'as far as he could see the Federal Council failed to oppose those [government] suggestions as such. In that respect he had to make one exception in the person of Dr H.R. Grieve of New South Wales, to whom he took off his hat'. However, the anti-compromise forces were still a minority on the Federal Council. Grieve received such a hostile reaction to an attempt to reject the entire Commonwealth scheme that he withdrew his motion without risking a vote. Colville added:

The medical members at the conference, so far as he could see, had accepted the Government's intention and had proceeded to discuss how the scheme could be implemented, particularly in regard to the form of remuneration. Further detailed consideration was given to whether the profession generally was opposed to being paid by salary and whether it was likely to seriously abuse a Fee for Service system. Such a discussion to his mind was deplorable, particularly as lay persons were present at the conference.[57]

Despite Colville's denunciation of the weakness of the federal leadership, similar divisions continued to appear at state level. When the Victorian state executive recommended a policy of complete non-cooperation with the government, a bitter argument followed. The supporters of a salaried service, such as Arthur Brown, urged against a policy of 'blind opposition'. The BMA should wait until the government had made its full intentions clear, leaving a wide area open for compromise. Byrne also temporized:

> For once he was in agreement with Dr Brown. It had to be remembered that there was a very large body in the profession who would be willing to serve in a national medical service on their own terms and conditions. He was convinced that the prospects of obtaining unanimity in the Victorian Branch on the policy of outright opposition would be very remote. Convocation had definitely agreed that the profession would accept employment in a national health service on its own terms and conditions.[58]

This debate emphasized the fragility of the victory of the advocates of fee-for-service. As John Dale reminded his colleagues: 'a scheme on the fee for service principle was accepted by the Branch only as the result of a definite fight. There was a great division of opinion and the resolution was passed by only a bare majority.' The state council narrowly rejected Colville's call for non-cooperation with the federal government affirming: 'That the Federal Council be informed that members of the Victorian Branch would be prepared to accept a scheme for a complete medical service, which is available without cost to every member of the community', on condition that it complied with the provisions that had been set out by Convocation.[59]

In private, the BMA's leaders recognized the government's indecision about the best way forward and discounted the threat of any immediate revolutionary changes in medical services. They saw the immediate problem in terms of a war of position, rather than as an attempt at full-scale socialization. Incremental changes in the control of marginal services – such as those in remote areas – could gradually legitimate state control and salaried status, opening the way to a further erosion of private practice. BMA leaders recognized their own political isolation. Just before the national elections of 1943 the Federal Council discussed the wisdom of a public stand. Grieve, a former UAP state member of parliament 'consulted his political friends' and advised that in the current climate any intervention would be counter-productive. 'Politicians might make capital of it and give undue prominence to the question of a medical service'. After Labor's convincing electoral victory, John Hunter wrote to George Anderson, his British counterpart, that the government had no concrete medical policies beyond a vague preference for a salaried service. The failure to obtain referral of constitutional powers from the states had been a major setback in attempts to centralize medical services. Hunter's fears were rather less apocalyptic than those being conveyed to the membership. He declared that:

> Whether the Government, in the event of obtaining these [constitutional] powers, will attempt to force the introduction of a complete salaried service is doubtful in view of the known opposition of the profession to any such proposal. However, there does not seem to be any doubt that more and more medical officers will be employed in the public medical services, and that these medical officers will be used to provide the medical services in the more scattered areas of the country – in effect the beginning of a salaried service.[60]

During the final year of the war the BMA's confusion over the preferred basis for a national medical service heightened. The more hostile and secretive attitude of the Commonwealth government did not help matters. In June 1944 the Federal Council accepted an odd amalgam of the Byrne and Bell–Simmons plans. For the first time fee-for-service was the main plank of medical policy; however, the matter was still far from settled. Fee-for-service was still not seen as the sole basis for a future scheme, but as an ambit claim in future negotiations. The Victorians remained deeply suspicious of the sincerity of the federal leadership, believing Sir Henry Newland would be happy to come to a settlement with the Commonwealth government. At the same time, the New South Wales and other state branches did not share the total horror of the Victorians towards lodge practice. In August 1944 the *Medical Journal of Australia* editorialized in favour of the Kaiser pre-paid capitation scheme in the United States, despite noting the hostility of the American Medical Association.[61]

When a sub-committee of the Federal Council went into detailed negotiations with Cumpston and Goodes in November 1944 they were armed with detailed instructions covering all areas of BMA policy. On the finance of the scheme, the standard protests against action before the end of the war were reiterated. 'A free medical service for all, with control by Government Department and a contract for service between the Government and the doctor' was 'not in the public interest and is not acceptable to the Federal Council'. Instead, the Federal Council was prepared to assist any scheme if action was postponed until one year after the end of the war, provided that 'the scheme should retain the existing doctor–patient relationship' and was free from departmental control. In deference to the continuing disagreements within BMA ranks, no mention was made of the form of remuneration acceptable to the profession. However, when the negotiators met, the BMA representatives interpreted these instructions to include full support for fee-for-service. This met with immediate hostility from the branches – especially from Victorians who complained of BMA negotiators 'appearing as advocates for a scheme which would not be acceptable to many members of the profession'. Even the supporters of fee-for-service agreed that the best stance was to withdraw for the moment, avoid commitment to any definite line of policy, 'sit tight and wait for the next move from the federal government'.[62]

This chapter commenced with Marmor's confident claim that a conservative commitment to existing patterns of remuneration has lain at the heart of medical politics. In the Australian case, in contrast, debate within the BMA was marked by deep divisions over the appropriate form of payment under a national health service. These disagreements were rooted in conflicts over the major shifts in medical practice during the interwar years. The growing power of specialization presented a threat not merely to the incomes but to the professional autonomy of general practitioners. These divisions made unity around any single form of remuneration problematical. While fee-for-service won a victory in 1944, its supporters' hold over the loyalties of doctors remained tenuous, and even the authors of the BMA scheme admitted that its economics were shaky. As the Melbourne barrister, Reginald Sholl, representing the 'public' in an ABC 'Forum of the Air' debate between advocates and critics of salaried medicine, warned:

> If you say your insurance fund would spread the burden over the community, are you not asking to have a national fund contributed by the community, but no control by the State over the expenditure of that national fund but a free-for-all competition by doctors to share in it?[63]

Consequently, it was with some relief that the profession faced its first bouts with the federal government over pharmaceutical and hospital benefits, schemes in which the forms of remuneration or even the direct participation of the medical profession were, for the moment, marginal issues. Conflicts could be fought on general issues of principle, the valid sphere and limits of state intervention; the knotty problems of general practice and specialism, and of rival forms of remuneration could be pushed to one side.

# Appendix

**Table 7.1** BMA Branch Membership

|       | NSW   | Vic.  | Qld   | SA  | WA  | Tas | Total  |
|-------|-------|-------|-------|-----|-----|-----|--------|
| 1920  | 1,200 | 983   | 281   | 266 | 137 | 66  | 2,933  |
| 1925  | 1,423 | 1,260 | 397   | 350 | 180 | 76  | 3,686  |
| 1930  | 1,711 | 1,340 | 475   | 397 | 244 | 80  | 4,247  |
| 1935  | 1,661 | 1,399 | 491   | 359 | 260 | 73  | 4,243  |
| 1940  | 1,857 | 1,467 | 532   | 409 | 300 | 81  | 4,646  |
| 1945  | 2,286 | 1,847 | 627   | 475 | 382 | 127 | 5,744  |
| 1950  | 2,930 | 2,170 | 798   | 579 | 438 | 169 | 7,084  |
| 1955  | 3,804 | 2,770 | 1,134 | 816 | 529 | 236 | 9,289  |
| 1960  | 4,310 | 3,295 | 1,368 | 990 | 745 | 263 | 10,971 |

Source: BMA state branch annual reports, *Medical Journal of Australia*.

**Table 7.2** BMA Membership as Percentage of Registered Medical Practitioners in Each State

|       | NSW  | Vic. | Qld  | SA   | WA   | Tas  |
|-------|------|------|------|------|------|------|
| 1920  | 87.2 | 64.3 | 68.4 | 76.2 | 66.2 | 44.6 |
| 1925  | 74.7 | 72.8 | 70.1 | 80.1 | 69.2 | 48.1 |
| 1930  | 79.5 | 67.8 | 82.0 | 89.2 | 77.7 | 43.5 |
| 1935  | 77.0 | 70.5 | 76.7 | 74.8 | 75.4 | 40.3 |
| 1940  | 73.8 | 62.0 | 84.2 | 77.6 | 80.7 | 31.9 |
| 1945  | 76.2 | 67.2 | 78.1 | 53.8 | n.a. | 40.1 |
| 1950  | 83.8 | 79.0 | 84.2 | 52.1 | 93.4 | 36.3 |
| 1955  | 78.6 | 79.0 | 94.3 | 60.5 | 80.4 | 61.5 |
| 1960  | 73.9 | 79.9 | 94.0 | 58.9 | 90.1 | 77.4 |

Note: For caveats on these statistics, see Table 1.6.

# CHAPTER 8

# Relieving the Patient, Not the Doctor: the Hospital Benefits Act

As the central point of the system of health care and its single most expensive item, the integration of the hospitals into the new health service would be central to its success and cost. Nowhere were the limits that the Chifley government imposed upon its health policies so manifest.

The Commonwealth government was faced with the task of developing policies subtle enough to achieve the major objective of increased equity of access, while general enough to apply to each of the very different state systems without causing financial chaos. Two major options were canvassed during the wartime debates over policy. The NHMRC and JPCSS reports had advocated the direct involvement of the Commonwealth, using control of the public hospitals as the basis for an integrated national health service. This would require a massive injection of central funding to expand bed capacity and construct a centralized, hospital-based medical care system. It could be achieved either directly, by the constitutionally difficult road of a Commonwealth takeover of the state hospital systems, or by grants-in-aid to the states, with strict conditions on their use. The second possibility was to accept the prevailing structure of the health system as given and merely improve access to services, reducing the financial burdens of serious illness. This option of income support was adopted as the basis of the hospital benefits scheme. The bed fees of individual patients within the hospital system were drawn from the National Welfare Fund, while constitutional problems would be avoided by paying tied grants to the states with strict conditions to ensure that the benefits reached the patients and were not swallowed into general hospital revenues.

The most striking feature of the new Commonwealth hospital policy was the extent to which it ignored the advice of the NHMRC and the JPCSS. Both had placed the heaviest stress on capital expenditures and expansion of public hospitals. Instead, the Chifley government concentrated on changing the conditions of access to the existing service, leaving capital and most current expenditures in the hands of the states. The few gestures towards a national hospital advisory committee (one of the projects of the Medical and Hospitals Sub-Committee) disappeared at the first sign of resistance from the states. Cilento had proposed using the carrot of Commonwealth financial grants to lure the states into a unified national policy, while leaving actual control at local level. The federal government adopted half this programme. State action was to be spurred by financial incentives, but the radical reorganization envisaged by Cilento was abandoned in favour of a scheme which went little beyond ending the remnants of charity and relieving the costs of hospitalization.

## Honoraries and equity: the ALP and hospital reform

While the scheme fell squarely within federal Labor's cash benefits approach to social policy, several elements of it drew on longstanding Labor attitudes towards hospital policy. A condition of funding was the abandonment of the means testing of public hospital beds, extending Queensland and Tasmanian attacks on the vestiges of charity and honorary practice to a national level. The honorary system had relied on a sharp distinction between free charity patients and private fee-paying patients. Although under increasing attack and abolished in Queensland, the position of honoraries had been buttressed in its strongholds of Victoria and New South Wales by the construction of new private and intermediate wards during the interwar years. Hence, in these two states in particular, at first sight the abolition of means testing delivered a direct blow at the basis of private hospital practice. This placed heavy pressures on hospital honoraries to follow the Queensland example and demand salaries, heightening BMA anxieties that the scheme was a Trojan horse for a general salaried service. These fears were underscored by the well-known views of powerful administrators such as Cecil McVilly of the Victorian Charities Board. In his evidence to the Joint Parliamentary Committee on Social Security he had urged that:

> Whatever is done should include abandonment of the principle of honorary medical service as the basis for medical care in hospitals because it now imposes unjust obligations on the medical profession, is foreign to

any true conception of social service, does not provide a large section of the sick with adequate attention and disrupts nursing and administrative organization.[1]

McVilly blamed much of the congestion in outpatient clinics on 'the inability of men to attend the clinics strictly in accordance with the prescribed timetable owing to the demands upon their time as private practitioners'.[2]

The strength of this critique and the resonance it won from sections of the medical profession meant that many leaders of the BMA were prepared, however reluctantly, to discard honorary practice as an archaic survival. Cecil Colville, the chairman of the Victorian branch, himself a general practitioner with an honorary appointment at the Alfred Hospital, echoed McVilly's views to the Joint Parliamentary Committee agreeing that 'the honorary system is far from satisfactory and I think its days are numbered'.[3]

In practice, the Chifley government showed little interest in following the full Queensland model. Rather than grasping the opportunity to increase control over hospital administration, the Commonwealth saw the threat to the honorary system as a dangerous obstacle to control of the costs of the hospital scheme. Hospital benefits were to support the incomes of patients, not a lever to re-organize the delivery of health services. Goodes had already rejected McVilly's call for greater administrative control over honoraries, warning that 'If patients are relieved from hospital fees in public beds, doctors may take the opportunity to claim fees where they now give honorary services. In this case a subsidy would "relieve" doctors to some extent rather than patients'.[4]

A scheme confined to benefits alone would also placate the Roman Catholic Church. The Australian Catholic Hospital Association was formed in April 1944 to defend the independence and the religious and charitable aspects of the Catholic hospitals against the 'cold attitude of governments' which threatened to reduce them to 'public utilities' within a national scheme. By merely subsidizing access to existing arrangements – and offering this to the private and church hospitals at the same level as offered to public hospitals – the hospital benefits scheme avoided embroiling the federal government in this sectarian quagmire.[5]

In August 1945, with negotiations with the states well under way, Chifley warned Cabinet of the financial dangers of an end of honorary practice. While he did not reject a salaried hospital staff out of hand he argued that this must be postponed until a more comprehensive plan for a national medical service had been framed. Frank McCallum, the Director-General of Health, underscored these warnings. When the Hospital Benefits Bill was introduced into the House of Representatives in September he urgently requested his senior officer in Brisbane to supply information on Queensland hospital salaries, predicting that the end of the means test would lead to BMA demands for salaries.[6]

Although government ministers such as Fraser and his successor Senator Nick McKenna continued to use the language of 'socialized medicine' and called for a thorough reorganization of medical institutions, there were few signs of this radicalism in the hospital benefits scheme. Little attempt was made to use the Commonwealth's financial leverage to induce any change in the priorities of the state medical services. Far from the opening shot of a campaign for socialized national health, the hospital benefits scheme is best seen as a further step towards ending the charitable status of public hospitals. It was part of a more general Labor commitment to universalism, towards eliminating the taint of pauperism by dismantling restrictive means tests, extending access to the public hospital system to all: 'only one phase of a wider matter [as] the whole trend of opinion today is leaning towards abolition of the means test in all the social services'. As a consequence, the middle classes and more affluent sections of the working classes were to obtain the right to free public ward accommodation. It was assumed, however, that most would use their benefit to pay for intermediate or private beds.[7]

The scheme also recognized and entrenched the split in Australian civilian and ex-service welfare systems. When it came to repatriation services the federal government showed little of its reticence about direct intervention. With clear constitutional powers and backed by the nation's strongest political lobby, the medical services of the Repatriation Commission were greatly expanded with large new hospitals at Heidelberg in Melbourne, Greenslopes in Brisbane, Concord in Sydney, all of a size and standard to become university teaching hospitals. Nor did Canberra hesitate about ending the honorary system. By mid 1949 repatriation hospitals were treating almost 55,000 inpatients and 82,000 outpatients, providing generous conditions and the most modern facilities for ex-servicemen, while most women, except for the small minority who had served overseas in the armed forces, and male civilians, however important or dangerous their war work, were confined to the less generous civilian hospitals.[8]

## The Hospital Benefits Act and the medical profession

The Hospital Benefits Act had a rather subdued reception from the organized medical profession. This relative acceptance stemmed from divisions within the profession and, in particular, the blurred line between the specialties and general practice.

The immediate impact of the scheme would fall on honorary practice in public hospitals. If means testing was ended and patients previously capable of paying entered public wards, the potential incomes of honoraries from private practice would be undermined, creating real pressures towards a salaried or salaried sessional system. The leadership of the BMA saw this as the opening move towards a fully salaried system of medical practice. The Victorian state council warned its members that 'The acceptance of a salary involves a degree of control by the authority which pays the salary, and a consequent loss of freedom which is proportionate roughly to the proportion which the salary bears to the doctor's total income'. This view was strongest in Victoria, where the honorary system was most entrenched, and stricter means testing and a higher proportion of private and intermediate beds in public hospitals led to the greatest relative contribution of fees to any state hospital system. Dr Bernard Zwar, the president of the board of the Royal Melbourne Hospital, asserted that hospital benefits provided by the state 'ignored and undermined the spirit of independence, destroyed family obligations, and interrupted the friendly relationships of friends and neighbours. The scheme would deprive the sick poor of their present priority on the services of public hospitals'.[9]

Many hospital doctors proved less willing to accept this logic. There was a longstanding tension between junior hospital staff, salaried residential medical officers and honoraries over the distribution of workloads due to the inability of hospital administrators to control or effectively roster the services of honoraries. Again, the Queensland model lay behind the thinking of all parties as these problems had provided the basis for the successful, and largely amicable replacement of that state's honorary system in 1938.

These interstate differences bedevilled the BMA's internal discussions. The strong hostility of the New South Wales branch towards any threat to the honorary system was met by an equally impassioned defence of part-time salaried practice from Queensland representatives, who complained that 'much of the New South Wales fear was fear of the unpredictable'. The South Australians had already expressed their opinion that 'in view of the abolition of the means test, on general principles, the honorary system at hospitals must disappear'.[10]

With these serious divisions within and between its branches, the BMA was unable to develop a national response to the Act. Although reiterating the general principle that honorary service could not survive the end of means testing, the Federal Council affirmed that 'in no case would the doctors walk out of the hospitals – whatever happened'. The final responsibility was passed to the state branches.[11]

As the day of implementation approached the hostility of the medical profession in the larger states turned into resigned acceptance. Whereas in late 1945 St Vincent's was the only large Melbourne hospital where honoraries supported salaried sessional payments, by April 1946 a general meeting of the Victorian branch called for adoption of the sessional system. The branch council decided to ignore the views of the members until a full referendum had been held, despite the warning of Charles Byrne that it would have to accept a major change in the remuneration of hospital practice or risk even wider consequences as 'It was obvious a considerable number of those at the Branch meeting favoured a system of socialized medicine and he thought that the Council was going to have difficulty in continuing its past policies'.[12]

The remainder of 1946 saw further major reverses for the more conservative sections of the BMA. By July all states had passed enabling legislation to implement the Hospital Benefits Act and the Commonwealth acquired a constitutional health power in the August referendum. The Victorian branch, recognizing its isolation and the unlikelihood of a successful challenge to the Act, reluctantly instructed its members to comply. Hospital doctors could no longer apply a means test nor charge fees to any patient occupying a public bed. Instead, political opposition to federal hospital policies concentrated on well-worn campaigns for increased private and intermediate beds and using all possible means to 'discourage' patients from the use of public wards.[13]

By the end of 1947 a 'radical change in the views of hospital staff' shifted opinion even further towards acceptance of a sessional payment system. After studying the Queensland system and the scales agreed by the BMA in England, the New South Wales branch recommended that visiting specialists at repatriation hospitals move to a salaried system based on the number of sessions they worked each week. Although this carried no necessary implications for civilian hospitals, it was a significant shift from the branch hitherto most critical of any form of salaried practice.[14]

This tendency was strengthened the following March when a plebiscite of honorary staffs in the Victorian branch found country hospital practitioners almost unanimously in favour of sessional fees. In rural areas medical practice was closely tied to the hospital, with all local general practitioners treating their own patients in hospital beds. As few country towns were able to provide funds for private or intermediate wards in local hospitals, even with the Commonwealth subsidy, practitioners were faced with the prospect that with the end of the means test only bed numbers set limits on free hospital care. In contrast, doctors in metropolitan teaching hospitals remained more evenly divided. In the urban teaching hospitals payment for honorary services mattered little to senior honoraries as their monetary reward came from private patients. Acceptance of a salary could only increase administrative controls over these honoraries, and interfere with time spent on research, teaching or private practice.[15]

These rural/urban divisions and the generational divide within the teaching hospitals added to the BMA's difficulties in reaching a unified view on the question of payment in public hospitals in each state. When these disagreements within the states still adhering to honorary practice were added to the sharp differences between the states, the problems of formulating a national policy became insurmountable. Even at the height of its confrontation with the Commonwealth government over the Pharmaceutical Benefits Act, the Federal Council declared that it had no policy on the honorary system and continued to refer the matter back to the branches.[16]

Ironically, the fears expressed by medical conservatives were mirrored in Cabinet. Far from seeing the Hospital Benefits Scheme as the thin end of a socialist wedge, the government's main concern for the scheme was that a demand for salary or sessional fees by honoraries would swallow the benefit. In the circumstances the pressures for an immediate end to the honorary system, feared by governments and sections of the profession for quite different reasons, failed to eventuate. Dire warnings from senior honoraries of the swamping of the public hospital system under a wave of public ward admissions to the detriment of the poor quickly proved to be groundless.[17] Bed shortages combined with continuing restrictions on new building to block major changes in the pattern of hospital admissions. Many with direct experience of the hospital system now took a less apocalyptic view, pointing out that the scheme was a far from radical measure. In Victoria Cecil Colville noted that:

He had not heard of any member of the profession being seriously affected. Most patients admitted to public hospitals entered through the outpatients departments where means tests still existed. Medical practitioners sending patients to public hospitals usually applied what might be called a private means test. Doctors who were not able to find beds for their patients in private hospitals in the metropolitan area and forced to use public hospitals were protected by Clause 8(2) of the Act – 'The State may permit a public hospital to charge fees in respect of beds in a public ward which are temporarily designated as non-public ward beds'.[18]

## The states and the Hospital Benefits Act

Winning the acquiescence of the BMA had not proved to be a major obstacle, but the Commonwealth faced a more decisive hurdle in achieving agreement with the states. Despite the political costs of rejecting the proffered Commonwealth money, even the Labor-controlled states had severe reservations about entering the scheme. The central issues were financial. In 1948 the Minister for Health, Senator Nick McKenna, reiterated Goodes' warning of five years before: 'After all is said and done, the Hospital Benefits Agreement was designed not to relieve state budgets at all, but merely to lift the burden off the patient'. The states feared, with some justice, that Commonwealth funding would soon prove inadequate to meet popular demand for free hospitalization. With no promise of capital funds to increase the available beds, the states would be left to bear the political opprobrium of overcrowded wards and deteriorating services.[19]

The federal system set major constraints on the Commonwealth's freedom of action. Whatever federal and state Labor's preferences, the scheme had to abide by the constitutional requirement that all states be treated equally, yet recognize the fundamental differences in sources of finance and forms of political control of each of the state hospital systems. During Hanlon's tenure as Minister for Health from 1932 to 1944 Queensland had spent massively on hospital capital works, as had the Ogilvie government in Tasmania. Consequently, both states objected strenuously to any Commonwealth expenditure on capital works which did not compensate for this earlier record. At the opposite extreme, Victoria, with a system governed by nominally independent boards and hospital revenues relying heavily on voluntary donations, feared that the Commonwealth subsidy would destroy private charity without fully compensating the state for the current cost of the public hospital system. The Labor government in

New South Wales also expressed concern that the scheme would destroy its contribution funds, at best leaving the finances of the state's hospitals no better than they were.[20]

Hence, the states responded with quite distinct negotiating positions, hoping to gain concessions – or delay implementation until the full implications could be seen. Many of these complaints were merely for public consumption. In private their reactions were far more favourable, especially when the Commonwealth made clear that the reluctance of individual states to enter the scheme would not prevent implementation in those more co-operative, setting an impossible political barrier to total opposition. McVilly advised Albert Dunstan, the Country Party Premier of Victoria, that although greater Commonwealth involvement was inevitable, the danger of a vast increase in use of public wards could be averted. Even if the Commonwealth grant was fully absorbed in bed subsidies, this could release state funds for other uses. McVilly marked the conversion of his own board from the restrictive attitudes of the past, arguing that:

> Consideration of this important problem, however, should not be restricted to finance and the varying impulses which give rise to voluntary giving. Of greater importance is the effect which a 'charitable' service has on a major portion of the people insufficiently remunerated to meet the cost of medical and hospital care privately without detriment to the general welfare of themselves and their families. I believe that it could be shown overwhelmingly that such a nationally important service based on charity is inimical to [the] Australian outlook, particularly for the employed or employable groups and does much damage to the health of the community because, being unacceptable many remain sick rather than receive such aid or incur the financial burden of care privately.[21]

By March 1946 South Australia and New South Wales were the only states still holding out, partly in the hope of an assurance that, if the BMA withdrew honorary service, the Commonwealth would meet the increased costs. As it became clear that after two months of operation in Victoria little had changed, the recalcitrant states came into line.[22]

During the negotiations with the states the Commonwealth steadily dropped the vestiges of the NHMRC and JPCSS plans. Suggestions that central financial power should be used to ensure redistribution to areas with poor access to hospital beds and set national standards for accreditation of hospitals were abandoned: decisions on the location and services offered by hospitals were to remain completely in state hands. The National Hospital Council was quietly shelved after Victorian objections that financial, organizational and climatic differences between states could only result in 'constant conflict between such a Council and the States'. Left to their own devices, the state hospital authorities continued to cluster beds and hospital services around the great teaching hospitals of the inner cities. The populations of these areas were already in decline, while the new outer-suburban growth of the postwar period were starved of public hospital services and deprived of the integrated clinics which Cilento and his colleagues had envisaged.[23]

Instead, the focus of hospital politics turned to a constant battle between the Commonwealth and the states over the adequacy of the bed subsidy. Within a year the states were complaining of a growing gap between the costs of free public wards and the amount received from Canberra. The published accounts of hospital finances are so inadequate it is impossible to adjudicate the rival claims. What is more important is the extent to which the sweeping plans for an integrated health system disappeared into squabbling over the marginal costs of hospital bed accommodation. Cumpston's worst fears of a national sickness scheme – based purely on relieving the costs of curative services for the ill – rather than a national health service – based on prevention and public health – appeared to have been realized.

As with other areas of health policy, the restriction of Commonwealth involvement to arm's length financial support did not mean the automatic rejection of wider programmes of centralized control and reform. A socialist rhetoric persisted in ministerial statements: the existing compromise was seen as a stepping stone to wider projects. Reforms by Labor state governments, such as Victoria's move to replace the Hospitals and Charities Board with a Hospitals Commission vested with broader powers to plan and initiate hospital construction were premised on an eventual move to complete Commonwealth control. In the meantime, it was the state government which had to cope with the problems of shortages of nurses and beds for chronically ill patients, and it was the improvised, pragmatic solutions to these crises which formed the basis of policy.[24]

For the moment the only element of the NHMRC/JPCSS vision which the Commonwealth attempted to implement was a scheme for decentralized diagnostic services throughout the nation. The BMA had repeatedly declared its support for this alternative to salaried clinics, opening access to advanced medical technology for general practitioners, even in remote areas.

This attempt to revive Cumpston's Commonwealth laboratory network again foundered on state government obstruction. In mid 1946 the new Commonwealth proposals for a chain of diagnostic services were outlined to the state ministers of health. These centres, it was suggested, would eventually provide full medical services, reviving the old objective of group practice. All states except New South Wales agreed to the general principle, and state committees were to be established to advise on the location of diagnostic centres, the remuneration of practitioners and the mechanics of the transfer from private practice.

In February 1947 a conference of Commonwealth and state health officers was held in Canberra to work out administrative details. Despite the open warfare which was raging between the federal government and the BMA over the pharmaceutical benefits scheme, this meeting achieved agreement on many issues. With Labor governments in power in all states but South Australia, approval of the general lines of a national diagnostic service was not surprising. The major barrier remained, however, the question of whether control would be in state or Commonwealth hands. Even the most sympathetic state officials argued that a scheme co-ordinated and funded at the Commonwealth level must devolve administration to the existing state authorities and allow a wide degree of autonomy. Cecil McVilly, still the most powerful health administrator in Australia and not a man to be cowed by the BMA, argued that 'No insuperable difficulties should be encountered in Victoria in setting up the Centres, provided the Commonwealth is prepared to delegate authority to the states and provide the necessary funds'.[25]

The conference of officers had warned that the loose forms of hospital control available in the subsidized hospital systems of Victoria and New South Wales provided an insuperable barrier, as:

> ...a satisfactory medical service was unlikely to develop unless there was complete power to direct a hospital to carry out certain functions. It would be highly undesirable for policy which had been established by the Government to be disputed by any hospital. It was recommended that the Government [although which one was left vague] must have in all States complete authority over each hospital. Control by subsidy is totally inadequate as the Government cannot satisfactorily use a threat of withdrawal of subsidy as a method of control.[26]

At the meeting of state ministers of health which followed, the Commonwealth attempted to meet these conditions, but again ran foul of the different practices of administrative control in each state. Political changes had also left the states less co-operative. In the two months since the officers' conference the Western Australian Labor government had fallen, and the Cain government in Victoria, increasingly frustrated by a hostile upper house, had been defeated in

November after an election campaign in which state issues were submerged by the campaign against bank nationalization.

In late 1948 the Commonwealth still clung to its proposals for diagnostic centres in the face of stronger opposition from the states. The central question was again the extension of direct Commonwealth control within the hospital system. The experience of the Hospital Benefits Scheme had raised fears that the states were to be landed with yet another ambitious project without sufficient funding to be self-sustaining. One solution to these fears was a complete transfer of pathology and diagnostic services to the Commonwealth, leaving the public hospitals in which they were located under state auspices. A national system of pathology laboratories, utilizing the existing Commonwealth Department of Health laboratories by providing training and a career structure for pathologists, could bring modern diagnostic services into the base hospitals of rural and provincial Australia.

The Commonwealth Department of Health announced plans to train laboratory staff by the end of October and to establish pathology laboratories in the base hospitals at Albury, Wangaratta and Ballarat. Each hospital was to have a medical officer (full- or part-time) in charge, a biochemist and assistants. Again, this plan for dual control within public hospitals was vehemently opposed by the Victorian Hospitals and Charities Board. Faced with this obstruction and with the Commonwealth Treasury adamantly resisting the capital expenditure required, this last vestige of the NHMRC vision met a quiet death.[27]


The relative success of the Hospital Benefits Act was directly related to its evasion of the major issues of hospital reform. Planning and location of new hospitals, the relationship between the medical profession and hospital work, and the access of general practitioners to the public hospital system became extraneous to national policy concerns. This did not mean that the benefit programme was without effect. By offering a general subsidy for all beds – public, private and intermediate – it helped to break down what remained of the stigma of charity. At the same time it confirmed the existing pattern of service provision. Instead of the radical decentralization of the NHMRC 'Outline' based on a network of regional and suburban clinics, the policy confirmed the development of a health system based on the centralization of acute care services in the large inner city hospitals. This direction happened by default rather than conscious plan. Unlike the contemporaneous Hill–Burton scheme of federally-financed hospital construction in the United States, the Australian scheme avoided all questions of the future organization and administration of hospital services.[28]

This limited approach avoided open contestation of power and control within the health system. While changes in funding arrangements may have enforced lip-service to the abolition of means testing and the principle of universal access to hospital care, administration of the new policy remained in the hands of the states and the medical profession. It is not surprising that the scheme evoked few of the passions aroused in other areas of Commonwealth health policy. The Australian Hospital Association, established in 1946 at Sir Herbert Schlink's initiative as a national lobby group for the major teaching hospitals, to defend their interests against the encroachments of centralism, never won support outside Melbourne and Sydney. Its Federal Council met rarely and almost collapsed during its first five years for lack of business. The most contentious issues of hospital policy remained at state level – questions such as the creation of a (non-medical) certification and training scheme for hospital administrators and the festering conflict over administrative control of honoraries – with no Commonwealth involvement. It was not until the Whitlam years that a truly national – and bitterly contested – hospital politics began to emerge.[29]

# CHAPTER 9

# A War of Attrition: the Fate of the Pharmaceutical Benefits Scheme

The failure of the pharmaceutical benefits scheme takes us to the heart of the obstacles which frustrated the Chifley government's health reforms. Most accounts of this have (rightly) been overshadowed by the clash between the Chifley government and organized medicine. In the course of a five-year struggle, the BMA successfully fought the federal government through the courts, by organized boycotts and in a fierce press campaign. The bitterness of the conflict destroyed any hope of a national health service based on cooperation between the Commonwealth and the medical profession, leaving a legacy of hostility and suspicion which persists to this day.

The scheme presented in the 1944 Pharmaceutical Benefits Act was relatively simple. Retail pharmacists and dispensaries were to be reimbursed for supplying pharmaceuticals prescribed by medical practitioners. The scheme would be universal with no means test or other restrictive conditions on access. However, not all drugs would be on the free list. An extensive formulary, compiled and regularly revised by a joint committee of medical practitioners and departmental officials, would list the drugs available under the scheme. Doctors were to prescribe drugs on official prescription forms, an administrative practice borrowed from the British scheme which had been in operation since 1911.

While the scheme did not include every drug listed in the British Pharmacopoeia, the formulary would be extensive enough to cover all the pharmaceuticals used regularly in general practice. The immediate inspiration for this restriction came from the Treasury, concerned to prevent the cost-blowout of the New Zealand scheme. The successful wartime controls on drug imports and distribution had been administered by the Medical Equipment Control Committee (MECC) which had issued a regularly revised Australian War Pharmacopoeia with little dissent from the profession. The MECC had not only successfully stockpiled and rationed scarce drug supplies, but had taken positive action to limit the availability of patent medicines and obsolete preparations, a task which the medical profession had been demanding for decades. The formulary was also attractive for macro-economic reasons. As the postwar years were expected to be a period of foreign exchange shortages, the Treasury was determined to maintain as many import controls as possible. Furthermore, in contrast to the ambitious group clinic schemes of medical reorganization proposed by Cilento and the NHMRC, the benefit scheme required no capital works competing for scarce manpower and resources but would place the approval of formulary drugs in departmental hands, providing another instrument to control price levels.[1]

His misgivings about such cash benefit schemes brushed aside, during the planning stages Cumpston attempted to salvage what he could of the project of national hygiene. While the prime aim of the formulary was to control costs, it could be also used to shape the prescribing patterns of general practitioners. From the early 1920s Cumpston had used the department's network of pathology laboratories and the Commonwealth Serum Laboratories to encourage a more scientific, laboratory-based approach to medical practice. Although the full effects of the therapeutic revolution associated with the new sulpha drugs and penicillin had not yet been grasped, it was clear that the old pattern of relying on a handful of effective remedies would no longer suffice for general practice.[2]

There were more directly political reasons behind the Commonwealth's moves for a rapid implementation of its social policies. It was clearly desirable to get as many elements of postwar policy in place as possible before the disruption of demobilization. The hospital and pharmaceutical benefits schemes were attractive as both (it appeared) could be implemented immediately without waiting for the long and cumbersome negotiations with the medical profession. Furthermore, they appealed to politicians familiar with the friendly societies, offering little more than an extension of services already available to lodge members and repatriation beneficiaries; the government would be merely 'doing in a bigger way what the friendly society has been doing'.[3]

Here the resemblance with the hospital scheme ended. Despite initial fears for honorary service, the hospital benefits scheme had not challenged the existing patterns of power within the health system but had exposed the deep divisions between and within the state branches of the BMA. Outright defiance of the scheme would have achieved little but a public airing of these bitter internal disagreements. In contrast, medical practitioners had no financial interests at stake in the pharmaceutical benefits scheme, but considerable concern over the shift in power to the Commonwealth Department of Health. The consent of general practitioners was essential to the success of the scheme, but it offered them little beyond increased paper work and the potential for greater government interference in the manner in which they conducted their practices.

The conflict focused on these wider questions of power. Labor's supporters shared the BMA view that the scheme was a dress rehearsal for a more comprehensive national health service. This fear (or hope) was underscored by clause 16 of the Pharmaceutical Benefits Act, which enabled the government to appoint salaried medical officers in locations where the private profession was unable to offer an adequate service. This had been added at the behest of J.F. Gaha, the former Tasmanian Minister of Health, and it was not unreasonable to see it as another attempt to revive the remote areas salaried service. In these circumstances it is not surprising that the medical profession used its structural position first to attempt to squeeze the maximum concessions from the federal government and then, as the BMA sensed its power, to destroy the scheme altogether. What is more surprising was the ineptness of Labor politicians in the face of this challenge and of the persistent divisions within organized medicine over tactics and strategy.

## Pharmacists and friendly societies

Several options were open to the Commonwealth government other than indirect subsidy of the distribution and use of drugs. The Commonwealth Serum Laboratories had expanded greatly during the war. At Cumpston's initiative CSL became a major producer of penicillin, exporting sera and vaccines throughout the Pacific. These achievements could have formed the basis of an Australian drug industry. While the costs of research and small local markets provided a major barrier to any attempt at self-sufficiency, federal control could have been achieved by nationalizing the distributive network, establishing a network of dispensaries, on the friendly society model, which would later provide the framework for the decentralized group clinics of the NHMRC scheme.[4]

From the start the Commonwealth rejected the nationalization model, abandoning any attempt to base the scheme on an indigenous pharmaceutical industry. The pharmaceutical benefits scheme was to be based on the controlled distribution of imported drugs. The Australian drug industry was small and dominated by the companies associated in Drug Houses of Australia (DHA) and the local branches of a few major British companies involved in fine chemicals and pharmaceuticals, such as Glaxo and ICI. Very little research and development was carried out in Australia, and drug production followed old-fashioned methods, limited to a few patent medicines. The war changed this conservative framework only marginally. Cut off from its established sources of supply and protected from European and American competition, DHA was forced to move into production. The group's primary focus, however, remained as a wholesale distributor of imported drugs, while its productive effort in Australia concentrated on scarce medical equipment such as ampoules, hypodermic needles and forceps. In the area of pharmaceuticals, DHA's major contribution came in the large-scale production of alkaloids derived from plant material. By the end of the war Australia was exporting considerable amounts of the drugs lyoscine and atropine, distilled from native plants, and morphine from poppies. Both were linked closely to the demands of the war effort and offered little potential for expansion after the war. A subsidiary, Drexo Pty Ltd, was established in 1944 to handle this export trade, but did not shift the local industry's reliance on imports. Admitting its lack of success, DHA wound up Drexo in 1950.[5]

Once the decision had been made to base the scheme on subsidies of largely imported drugs, the crucial financial and administrative problems centred on distribution. A decentralized system of dispensing pharmacies was the key to success and required the co-operation of the retail pharmacists. For the moment the views of organized medicine appeared irrelevant: doctors would have no direct administrative part to play.

The first reactions of pharmacists appeared to confirm this view. Negotiations with the Pharmaceutical Services Guild of Australia began in mid 1943 and initially were both brief and amicable, concentrating on the technical question of finding an acceptable form of dispensing fee. Goodes dominated these discussions as the Treasury attempted to obtain a concessional service in return for the increased business pharmacists would obtain. The Federal Council of the Pharmacists Guild was equally determined to increase dispensing fees for its members. At the same time, the pharmacists insisted on a more complete formulary than the limited Australian War Pharmacopoeia and there would clearly be some hard bargaining over the dispensing fee, but neither of these points prevented agreement over the principles of the scheme.[6]

As with private medical practice, retail pharmacy had a long history of conflict with the friendly societies. The centralized dispensaries run by the lodges made medicines available at heavily discounted prices to lodge members. Since the late nineteenth century pharmacists in all states had fought successful battles to contain the growth of the dispensaries. Although the lodge dispensaries offered a cheap and efficient service to their largely working class clientele, legislative restrictions on the dispensaries under state law had limited their services to a few areas of the major population centres. Requiring a large and decentralized network to make the benefits available to the entire population the government had little choice but to turn to the retail pharmacies. Consequently, the initial agreement between the Treasury and the Pharmacists Guild excluded the dispensaries from the scheme.[7]

This rebuff to the friendly societies proved brief. Many dispensaries had close connections with the trade union movement, within the parliamentary Labor Party, more so than the friendly societies themselves. Within a few weeks of the tabling of the Pharmaceutical Benefits Bill the government moved to placate the dispensaries and accept their full participation in the scheme. The exact circumstances of this shift are unclear, but Labor's parliamentary Caucus set up a special committee to examine the scheme, initiating two amendments to the bill during its committee stage. The friendly societies were to be included in the scheme and provisions for dispensing in remote areas were added. The Commonwealth government was now committed to persuading the state governments of New South Wales, Victoria, Tasmania and Western Australia to change their friendly society acts to permit the supply of drugs to non-members and to end restrictions on the number of branches.[8]

This implied a major shift in the control of retail pharmacy. Pharmacy Acts in these four states prohibited companies and corporations from the practice of pharmacy. The end of this restriction could only reopen the threat posed by non-profit traders and the company ownership of chains of pharmacies to the livelihoods of retail pharmacists. In New South Wales, where competition with more highly capitalized chains was already a sore point, the Guild already faced a vociferous campaign against the Act led by a break-away group. Consequently, the Guild repudiated its January agreement, demanding increases in the dispensing fee and profits allowed under the scheme, as well as the imposition of firm restrictions on the friendly society dispensaries. In the face of this threat the Commonwealth government hid behind the limitations of federal powers. Fraser assured the Guild that the trading rights of the dispensaries remained a state matter. If the pharmacists wished to retain existing restrictions they should lobby the state governments.[9]

For the next year the pharmacists waged a public battle. Guild meetings were regaled with warnings that 'your own Business, and that of every other chemist is under direct attack...Let there be no illusions in this matter – YOU ARE TO BE BUTCHERED TO MAKE A SOCIALISTS HOLIDAY!'[10] At the same time, the Friendly Societies Dispensaries and Pharmacists Association pledged its full support for the new scheme.[11]

The federal government quickly found that its concessions to the friendly societies had become an embarrassment. As Frank McCallum, now Cumpston's replacement as Director-General of Health argued, the dispensaries were too centralized to provide an efficient network: 'The strategic distribution of points of supply is a fundamental requirement of an efficient medical service, therefore the Government is more concerned regarding the provision of a large number of small chemists shops rather than a small number of large shops'. The promises to the dispensaries were forgotten and critics from retail pharmacy soon accepted the basic lines of the scheme, despite reservations about the increase of departmental control. The pharmacists had demonstrated that their public threat of non-cooperation was merely a bargaining position. When the Commonwealth made concessions, the pharmacists prepared to enter the scheme.[12]

A more ominous threat came in the warning of the parliamentary draftsman, Sir George Knowles, that the bill lay outside the constitutional powers of the Commonwealth. The only possible authority was the vaguely worded appropriation power (s.81). A challenge was almost certain from the growing force of other opponents. The defeat of the fourteen powers referendum in August, with its federal health power  increased this risk.[13]

## The BMA and the Pharmaceutical Benefits Act

As the refund system meant that doctors would have no direct part to play in the scheme there had seemed little point in involving the

BMA in its planning stages. Furthermore, the experience of existing programmes of free or subsidized pharmaceuticals gave the Commonwealth every reason to expect co-operation. The BMA already worked within two health schemes based on benefits for a limited range of drugs – the repatriation scheme and many friendly society agreements – so the limitation of the new scheme to a formulary did not seem a major step. In the repatriation service the Federal Council had accepted conditions remarkably similar to those now proposed for general practice. Repatriation medical officers used printed prescription forms issued by the Commission, and agreed that 'where possible, only medicines, drugs, serums, etc., contained in the British Pharmacopoeia and the Australian Pharmaceutical Formulary shall be prescribed'.[14] Similarly, lodge doctors on the central north coast of New South Wales had deliberately limited free medicines so that 'The list of drugs to which Friendly Society members were entitled to free of charge was much less than the British Pharmacopoeia. This arrangement had been in effect for many years and was acceptable not only to Friendly Society members but to [doctors'] private club members'.[15]

Consequently, it was not until December 1943, six months after the start of discussions with the pharmacists, that the BMA was presented with the details of the government scheme. It was made clear that this was not for drastic revision, but for advice on the mechanics of administration.

The hostility of the medical profession appears to have come as a surprise to the government and its advisers. The Federal Council of the BMA immediately passed a resolution critical of the limited formulary, while the Victorian branch expressed fears that the scheme would merely increase drug usage by the public. In contrast to the controversies over the introduction of salaried service or the abolition of means testing in public hospitals, it is difficult to find any significant section of medical opinion fully in favour. The New South Wales branch was representative of BMA opinion when it agreed that:

> the Council is of the opinion, in relation to the proposal of the Federal Government to initiate a Pharmaceutical Benefit Scheme, that the sums proposed to be spent by the government on such a scheme, would be spent with greater profit to the community in the construction, equipping and maintenance of pathological and radiological diagnostic centres throughout Australia.[16]

From the Opposition front benches Sir Earle Page echoed this judgement, calling for priority to be given to preventive measures, the construction of hospital beds and the provision of decentralized diagnostic clinics, adding that 'This is starting the national health service programme in reverse gear. The only further backward step would be to give free coffins before free medicine'.[17]

Many erstwhile supporters of a fundamental reform of medical practice saw the scheme as a totally unsound approach to a national health service, attacking the construction of the 'first plank in the edifice of national health on the dubious foundation of free medicine'.[18] Supporters of social medicine saw the scheme, at best, as the embodiment of the more retrograde aspects of lodge practice – an excessive reliance on medication, a refusal to examine the wider social context of disease and ill-health, reinforcing the dominance of curative over preventive approaches. Dr M. McKenna, the medical officer of health in the Melbourne working class suburb of Brunswick, warned that free pharmaceuticals, while beneficial in the case of penicillin and other CSL products, could only increase pressure from patients demanding a 'bottle of medicine' for every ailment. This became a standard theme of the early criticisms of the scheme. Dr S. Fancourt McDonald, of Wickham Terrace in Brisbane, argued 'The "bottle of medicine" attitude towards disease is dying. Why then should ignorant governments seek to give it a reviving injection of money which might well be used in a positive sense?' In South Australia, Dr W. Heaslip blamed the profession for legitimating a misguided priority to pharmaceutical benefits by its failure to embrace preventive medicine:

> For a great many years the sick in mind, as well as the sick in body, have been given infusions rather than instructions, and pills instead of propaganda. The result is a demand for medicine out of a bottle to cure both their ills and their ignorance. We can agree with the principle of not making the individual pay for his medicine, since we have largely ceased to regard illness as a form of divine retribution. But any honest doctor would have advised the Minister for Health that only a small number of drugs are curative; that nearly all the mixtures which are taken have only a psychological effect; and that, while the people want medicine, it is not medicine, in most cases, that they need.[19]

These reservations extended well beyond private practitioners. The Commonwealth Department's senior medical officer in Queensland warned his superiors that 'Sickness is regarded as too serious a problem to be treated with free medicine which could hardly be expected to be compounded from first quality drugs'. Unless strict quality controls were imposed, the scheme could become a dumping ground for the old stockpiles of international drug companies. A.R. Southwood, president of South Australia's Central Board of Health and a signatory of the NHMRC's 'Recommendations', argued in a personal letter to Cumpston that the scheme was a 'very backward step in Public Health', fixing 'still more firmly in the public mind the idea that to keep well the people need ample drugs'. Instead, the money should be spent on hospitals, tuberculosis clinics, 'or indeed any other public health project at all – would give better results in improving community health'.[20]

This breadth of opposition provided a welcome windfall for the more thoroughgoing opponents of state involvement in medical services, establishing the first major bridge between the advocates of salaried service and the supporters of private fee-for-service practice. The national leadership of the BMA was offered the chance of a trial of strength on terrain decidedly to its own advantage, focusing growing fears of a wider move towards salaried medical practice. Consequently, the BMA concentrated its initial opposition on two of the more vaguely worded clauses of the Act. Clause 5 placed the scheme under the control of the Commonwealth Director-General of Health, and was seen as an explicit repudiation of BMA demands for an independent corporation to control the health service. Similarly, although justified in terms of providing medical services in remote areas, clause 16 was seen as the first step towards a national salaried service. The limitations of the formulary could be depicted as symptomatic of the bureaucratic restrictions of state medicine. As the campaign progressed these anti-socialist themes gradually displaced the earlier stress on social medicine.[21]

From the start the conflict was seen as a dress rehearsal for the ensuing struggle over a national health service. Any easy concessions from either side, whatever the immediate attractions, would be taken as weakness. BMA leaders in Victoria and New South Wales remained suspicious of the narrow terms in which the Federal Council expressed its opposition, terms which left the way open to compromise, raising shades of the betrayal of national health insurance. The Victorian council declared the branch ready to defy the Act on its own if necessary. A minority line that the BMA should be more constructive and develop its own alternative was rejected overwhelmingly.[22]

State suspicions of the national leadership were soon realized. In a meeting with officials from the Commonwealth Department of Health and the Treasury, Sir Henry Newland restricted the Federal Council's objections to reservations about the limitations of the formulary. As Cumpston had already given private indications that the government was prepared to soften its attitude, allowing the prescription of drugs from outside the formulary for a small charge, Newland appeared to be opening the way for a compromise. The Victorian federal councillors warned their branch that Newland saw the freedom to prescribe as the only issue. He had expressed indifference over the Commonwealth's increased influence in the scheme: 'Outside the issue of the formulary, some of the members [of the Federal Council] seemed quite lukewarm. They seemed to take up the attitude that it did not matter very much'. With assertions of implacable opposition from New South Wales and Victoria, the Federal Council abandoned hopes of compromise, and negotiations with the federal government remained in deadlock. The BMA now refused to discuss even the membership of the Formulary Committee until all its other objections to the Act were satisfied.[23]

As with the campaign against NHI and the entrenchment of fee-for-service as BMA policy it was assiduous work by activists from outside the national leadership which blocked compromise. Ronald Grieve used his base of support in New South Wales to drive the Federal Council towards irreconcilable opposition and extend its criticisms well beyond the use of a formulary to embrace the manner in which control was to be exercised through the Act, raising the spectre of socialism as the ultimate intention of the scheme. The vague wording of clause 16, the Federal Council suggested, could afford the government powers to introduce a nationalized health service, even though the Act was not drawn up for that purpose. Such a move, the council noted, would be in flagrant breach of Holloway's promise in 1941 that no major changes would be introduced to medical practice for the duration of the war. Second, clause 22 of the Act required that prescriptions could only be issued after a 'personal examination' of the patient. This could cause problems for many doctors, particularly in rural areas where it was not unusual to prescribe over the telephone, especially in cases of chronic illness. The core of the Federal Council's objections came over the form of control that the Act would impose on medical practitioners. Instead of the regulation of infringements being handed over to the Department of Health, allegations of misconduct should be judged by a competent medical tribunal as under Medical Practitioner Acts in the states. Final administrative control should be vested in an independent corporate body with a majority of medical representatives, and direct responsibility to parliament, not to a minister.[24]

These moves towards intransigence within the BMA were assisted by indecision on the government side. From the start the scheme had been afflicted by administrative problems. The Commonwealth Department of Health, with few direct responsibilities for medical services, possessed little expertise in this area. G.G. Jewkes, previously employed in the Repatriation Commission's pharmaceutical benefits scheme and the Directorate of Materials Supply of the Ministry of Munitions, brought his considerable experience as director of the new Pharmaceutical Services Division of the Department of Health. The recruitment of additional staff remained a serious problem, however, as most suitable technical staff were still tied to war postings. Despite constant pressure from Cabinet to complete the scheme, the department was unable to conclude the more technical elements, such as pricing items on the formulary, until the release of officers from military work. The state offices of the Commonwealth Department warned that the administrative problems of processing claims in the vast areas of inland Australia would require a massive increase in staff and resources. Consequently, at a time when the government was claiming the scheme would be functioning on 1 July 1945, Cumpston was warning that 'Under the circumstances, the only prognostication possible is that this department will be ready for the commencement of the Act three months from the day on which the staff report for duty'.[25]

There were some early indications that the Treasury, in the person of Goodes, was prepared to meet the BMA more than half way. In a letter to a Western Australian doctor Goodes defended the use of a formulary as a defence against the 'use of the "gatling gun" or "blunderbuss" prescriptions', of unnecessary flavourings, redundant drugs or overcomplex compounds, and as a means of reducing administrative costs. The inclusion of a particular drug in the formulary would be a result of purely medical, not financial judgement; 'the cost of the benefits will be determined by the drugs put into the Formulary by the Committee – no drug will be excluded merely because of its cost'. To guarantee this, he proposed that 'If the BMA is prepared to set up an advisory council to advise the Government in respect to this and, if necessary, any other health matters, I feel certain that you will get the co-operation of the Department [of Health]'. Cumpston reacted sharply to this offer, stressing that 'It has always been the policy of this Department to set up its own advisory councils and not to accept advisory councils nominated by the British Medical Association'. Nothing more was heard of Goodes' offer.[26]

## Fighting the socialist tiger

Determined to oppose a popular scheme, the BMA faced the prospect of political isolation. In its internal discussions its leaders conceded that public sentiment was overwhelmingly in favour of an extension of state-funded medical and social services. Whatever the private sympathy offered by conservative politicians, few were prepared to court the risks of public opposition. At the same time, the lack of a direct role in the financial workings of the scheme was a double-edged weapon. If doctors had nothing to lose (except for their patients' goodwill) by refusing to co-operate, many were less than wholeheartedly committed to defying the law. The rank and file of the membership showed little interest in the wider issues of policy which animated the leaders of opposition to the scheme but could be mobilized by the threat of outside interference in their practices. It was on this issue of the freedom to prescribe that the Federal Council had taken its initial stand, condemning the scheme for its failure to allow for the 'freedom of the doctor prescribing for each of his patients exactly what medicine he regards as most suitable to restore him to health'.[27] After meeting with general practitioners in Victoria, A.J. Collins reported to his colleagues on the Federal Council that:

> in the difficult task of presenting the Federal Council's attitude, the one trump card was the question of freedom, and this led those who were disposed to find fault with the Federal Council's attitude to change their minds.[28]

The need for a wider base of opposition was underlined as details of the formulary became known. Cecil Colville warned the Victorians that:

> it appeared that it contained almost everything that it would be possible to order for anybody. It also contained two vital things – penicillin and insulin.
>
> The contents of the Formulary had apparently become generally known to a large number of members of the profession and the Federal Council was confronted with the fact that a very considerable number of members throughout Australia was anticipating the greatest difficulty in observing the wishes of the Federal Council. In fact many were inclined to 'wobble'. They were inclined to say, 'We are quite prepared to observe what you ask us to do if you could tell us how to do it'. The problem confronting individual members and of which a great number of them were apparently afraid was that they would be asked to inform patients that it would be necessary for them to pay up to, say £10 for penicillin, when it was possible, by certain actions on the part of their doctor to obtain it for nothing.

Consequently, he added, it was essential that the profession make clear that its opposition was to this particular scheme rather than to free medicine in general.[29]

The tactical initiative remained with the state branches. In October 1945, New South Wales instructed its members to return all official prescription forms and copies of the formulary unopened to the branch office for return to the Commonwealth Department of Health. A notice for display in surgery waiting rooms was distributed to all practitioners to explain their opposition to the scheme. This approach would provide the state branches with a means of checking on the level of compliance, and recognized the fears of some BMA strategists about the dangers of allowing members to examine the formulary too closely, as all conceded that it was an interesting document. After some debate, and recognizing the necessity for a uniform national approach, the Federal Council advised all branches to follow the New South Wales example and refuse all co-operation.[30]

A major paradox underlay the whole campaign against pharmaceutical benefits. Within the government there was a widespread and unrealistic belief that the membership of the BMA, hitherto duped by their leaders, were about to join the scheme. At the same time, BMA leaders were concerned about the narrowness of opposition. Hostility to the scheme within the rank and file of the medical profession centred on its more punitive regulations, rather than the basic principles of free medicine. As long as a frustrated government obliged with ever more draconian regulations, this problem was submerged. But the BMA was faced with a serious problem about its public opposition to free medicine. This dilemma surfaced when several branches opposed the circulation of a pamphlet entitled 'Back to the Bottle' which used the New Zealand experience to attack free medicine. General practitioners objected strongly to the implication that, given the opportunity, they would abuse prescriptions under a free scheme. Furthermore, this total rejection of the scheme flew directly in the face of Newland's frequent declarations of BMA support for the principle of free medicine, while merely rejecting the main features of the existing scheme. More importantly, opposition was animated by the fear that the scheme represented an opening wedge for socialized medicine. This could cause problems with sections of the BMA; over-zealous suggestions that the struggle was only one front in a wider battle, as 'members need have no illusions regarding the voracity of the socialistic tiger', brought a shower of complaints to the *Medical Journal of Australia* from the still numerous supporters of salaried practice. The Victorian branch Medical

Secretary, Dr C.H. Dickson answered fears that the opposition to the scheme was in danger of losing its focus, arguing instead that:

> at the Subdivisional Meetings he had attended, it was apparent that the opposition of the great majority of members was directed only to the opportunity the Act gave to the Government to nationalize the profession, and the question of free medicine in itself seemed to them only a side issue. [Although] There was, he informed Council, almost complete unanimity among members to oppose the legislation.[31]

With these internal divisions, the BMA showed some hesitation about the best means to express its opposition. Despite the scepticism of constitutional lawyers about the legality of the scheme, even the most conservative state governments were reluctant to challenge the Commonwealth's powers. Furthermore, as the scheme did not require the direct participation of doctors, the BMA would have trouble establishing its own legal standing to launch a challenge. By March 1944 this tactical impasse was causing some panic as reports circulated of health department officers using the records of the Medical Equipment Control Committee to prepare for an early commencement. Menzies, the federal Opposition leader, warned that a successful constitutional challenge to the Act could only assist the federal government's referendum to add fourteen new powers – including a limited but sufficient health power – to the Constitution.[32]

The failure of the fourteen powers referendum opened the way for a full legal challenge. The BMA's lack of standing was overcome when the Victorian Attorney-General agreed to act as a relator in a High Court challenge to the validity of the legislation on behalf of the Medical Society of Victoria. This enabled legal proceedings to commence while protecting the state government from direct responsibility for the challenge.[33]

The first Pharmaceutical Benefits Case was heard by the full bench of the High Court in November 1945. Legal argument concentrated on the constitutional powers of the Commonwealth to enact direct benefit schemes in areas not specified under its powers in the Constitution. The Commonwealth grounded its case in a wide reading of section 81, which provides that the federal government's consolidated revenue can 'be appropriated for the purposes of the Commonwealth in the manner and subject to the charges and liabilities imposed by this Constitution'. As Knowles had warned, five justices out of six found that 'the purposes of the Commonwealth' must be read in the light of the powers given to the federal government elsewhere in the Constitution. The Chief Justice, Sir

John Latham, held that the Act did far more than appropriate money, but seriously encroached on state powers over hospitals, public health and pharmacists. The BMA appeared to have won the first round, but its legal advisers warned that the victory could prove pyrrhic. By implication, the judgement also threatened all direct welfare transfers, other than old age and invalid pensions, which were already included in the Commonwealth's constitutional powers. The measures under threat included child endowment and maternity allowances, both introduced by conservative federal governments, and the new unemployment and sickness benefits. Although it was unlikely that any state government would challenge these schemes, their shaky legal status gave the federal government the grounds for another referendum, this time to give the Commonwealth a secure power to initiate social welfare schemes and, most ominously for the BMA, a health power.[34]

As the critics of the BMA legal challenge had feared, success in the High Court opened the way to an entrenched Commonwealth health power. In 1946 a referendum asked voters to give the Commonwealth the power to legislate in a wide range of social welfare issues and to establish health and dental services. Unlike the 1944 referendum, this time there was no mention of co-operation with the states, nor was there to be any time restriction. In the political circumstances, it was impossible for the Opposition parties to call for a 'no' vote, especially as child endowment, one of the few lasting achievements of the first Menzies government, had been invalidated by the Pharmaceutical Benefits Case. At the same time, having abandoned any plans for a national salaried service, Evatt, the Attorney-General, accepted what appeared to be a minor amendment from Menzies. The Newland–Menzies placitum was initiated by Sir Earle Page and Sir Henry Newland to provide a guarantee that a medical service could not be based on 'any form of civil conscription'. As the Commonwealth had abandoned any idea of a salaried medical service without the full consent of the profession, this appeared a painless concession. Aneurin Bevan, the British Labour government's minister for health, had undermined a threatened BMA boycott of the National Health Service with a similarly empty guarantee that the general practitioner service would not be salaried. As in Australia, the British government had long abandoned plans for a salaried service, a possibility which lived on only in BMA propaganda.[35]

Despite this concession, Newland and other BMA leaders took a prominent place in the opposition to the referendum. Their mixed feelings about the placitum were clear from Page's rueful comment:

'It is a good thing to have it so stated though a bad thing if it leads to the referendum being carried'. The BMA itself took no part in the campaign, preferring to avoid such directly political entanglements, but Newland and forty other prominent South Australian doctors circularized all doctors in their state requesting their financial support to the Constitutional Powers Committee, opposing the referendum proposals.[36]

A comfortable victory to the government in the social welfare and health sections of the referendum (despite the failure of industrial relations provisions) led to a new phase in the battle.

The government's second attempt to implement the pharmaceutical benefits scheme started on a conciliatory note. The BMA was now on weaker ground, faced with a government possessing a majority in the Senate and a health power in the Constitution. In April 1947 the new, and more formidable, minister, Nick McKenna, a Tasmanian senator, met with the BMA to discuss the reintroduction of the legislation. Unlike his predecessor, James Fraser, McKenna was close to Chifley and, as a lawyer, had a more sophisticated understanding of his opponents. The surgeon Victor Hurley reported approvingly to the Victorian branch that McKenna was 'a man of intelligence, with whom it was a pleasure to do business'.[37]

Advice from the Commonwealth Department of Health had for some time emphasized the risks of continuing the confrontation with the medical profession over what had always been seen as a minor aspect of the health scheme. As Metcalfe warned McKenna:

> the medical profession is generally hostile to the use of a Formulary and feel that it is likely to be damaging to the development of any National Health Service. This feeling is not limited to men associated with the Federal Council of the BMA, but was widely spread amongst doctors who are likely and willing to join the NHS. As far as I can see the Formulary has few supporters among the medical profession in Australia.
> ...there will be a bitter fight...and I believe that we will not gain anything but we will lose a tremendous amount of goodwill. Doctors are individualists and like to feel they can prescribe in accordance with the needs of the patient. It is true that their prescribing is not always scientific, but it gives them a feeling that they can satisfy the needs of their patients.
> The objectors to whom I talked are not people who oppose a National Health Service in general, but most of them will willingly come into the scheme if offered reasonable terms, but they feel that the insistence on a Formulary will only lead to bitterness.[38]

Whatever his personal qualities, McKenna had inherited an intractable conflict in which neither side was prepared to make the smallest concession. While each could agree, in private, that their differences over the pharmaceutical scheme involved few principles which could not be settled by compromise, for both the clash was seen as the rehearsal for the coming conflict over a medical benefits scheme. Any premature concession would be seen as a confession of weakness.

So the meeting with McKenna achieved nothing. The BMA recited its well-worn objections to the scheme and when McKenna, in a conciliatory gesture, offered to refer these problems to a commit-tee with equal representation from the department and the BMA, the suggestion was ignored. This did not signal a complete end to attempts at compromise. The Victorian branch agreed to accept a limited formulary if doctors were allowed to use their own notepaper for prescriptions – not government forms – and if the Act did not include penalties for doctors who refused to join. In short, the scheme would only be acceptable if pharmaceutical benefits became a matter between the government, patients and the pharmacists. This conciliatory phase did not last long. By the end of May, in the absence of government concessions, the Victorian branch had reaffirmed total opposition to the use of a formulary.[39]

Cabinet met to approve the redrafted scheme in May. Two other options were considered. Again, the New Zealand approach of no formulary was rejected because of the cost problems. The BMA's preference for a limited list of life-saving and expensive drugs received serious consideration. Metcalfe had already suggested that a very limited formulary of the most costly drugs and CSL products would not only still the BMA resistance but enable the short-staffed department to handle the administrative burden. The main consider-ation should be that 'A serious clash with the medical profession at this stage on a matter of this nature will run the risk of ruining the National Health scheme'. However, Cabinet finally rejected the limited scheme as inequitable. These drugs were already freely available to patients in public hospitals, and a limited scheme would merely extend this subsidy to wealthy patients in private hospitals. The formulary was retained, and both sides prepared for the next trial of strength. On 12 June 1947 the Pharmaceutical Benefits Act again received the Governor-General's assent.[40]

While opposition from the BMA was expected, for a time it appeared that the new Act would obtain a more sympathetic reception. Public opinion was still firmly behind the government and the Opposition parties were reluctant to court the unpopularity of siding with the obstructive tactics of the BMA. At the same time the

BMA remained far from united, although it kept the doubts of its members from any public airing. In August 1947, Albert Coates, the Victorian branch president, had warned:

> It only required a certain number of legally super-conscientious members to break down a fairly strong pledged objection. The matter was therefore one which required close organization. In the profession there was a fairly strong block on which the Council could look for support. This was particularly so amongst the older senior members. He was doubtful, however, about some of the younger members. There must be no show of weakness or division within the profession.[41]

Again, the choice of issues for the confrontation embodied a trial of strength over the control of the future of health services. The BMA chose an issue over which the government could not compromise, by refusing to use official forms to prescribe the drugs included in the formulary. This would leave the decision about the entitlement to benefits to the retail pharmacist, undermining the fragile agreement with the Pharmaceutical Guild. More importantly, the failure to use an enforceable formulary would place the system under intolerable cost pressures. Again, the example of the cost explosion of the New Zealand scheme weighed heavily in official thinking. Estimates in early 1947 calculated that the New Zealand scheme, with its unrestricted formulary, was costing 13s.11d. per head of population. A similar outcome in Australia would mean an annual cost of £7 million, compared to government estimates of £2–3 million under the restricted formulary.[42]

It is clear from the behaviour of the Victorian branch that it was the issue of penalties, not opposition to the content of the Act, which remained a live issue amongst doctors. In private, the Victorian leadership conceded that the formulary included over 90 per cent of drugs used in ordinary practice. When the Commonwealth appeared more conciliatory in early 1948 the BMA faced a crisis of support amongst its members. It was this position which gave rise to the most controversial action of the BMA, to direct its members to refuse all co-operation with the Pharmaceutical Benefits Scheme. Reports from council members confirmed that 'There was certainly not the uniformity among the profession that some members of Council imagined there should be'.[43]

By mid 1948 many former strong opponents of the scheme were more hesitant, and meetings with the regional divisions had revealed 'misapprehensions and doubts' so severe that a general meeting to explain branch policy was abandoned as 'it would be calamitous if the meeting developed into a discussion of the rightness of Council policy'. The position was even worse for opponents of the Act in the smaller states. The Tasmanian branch was reported to be 'wavering', while South Australia had actually voted to abandon its opposition to the Act.[44]

At this point the Commonwealth government again came inadvertently to the rescue. On 10 May the government gazetted draconian new penalties to enforce compliance with the Act. Any doctor who prescribed a drug listed in the formulary on other than the official pharmaceutical benefit form was to be subject to a penalty of £50. A response to three years of frustration, this threat undid the progress of the last few months in a single blow. The growing revolt within the state branches of the BMA was quelled. Tasmania and South Australia rejoined Victoria and New South Wales in defiance, and the minority favouring co-operation fell silent as the BMA leadership prepared to resist the new regulations. The depth of this new intransigence became apparent when Arthur Brown, still an advocate of salaried medicine, declared himself prepared to be the first to return his forms unopened to the Director-General of Health with an invitation to prosecute. Meetings of the local associations of the BMA throughout the nation revealed unanimous opposition, a consolidation of BMA ranks further assisted by heavy-handed intervention from the New South Wales government. Clive Evatt, the Minister for Housing, threatened to evict doctors at the Herne Bay Housing Estate from their state-owned housing unless they complied with the direction of the Hospitals Commission to prescribe under the scheme.[45]

In spite of this unity the BMA's leaders realized the precarious foundations of the new militancy. As an immediate and passing response to McKenna's maladroit handling of the penalties issue it could easily fade with the first whiff of compromise from Canberra. Any concessions by the BMA would be taken as a sign of weakness. In the background was the recent example of Britain, where BMA threats of complete non-cooperation with the national health service were outflanked by skilful government concessions to sections of the medical profession. Sooner or later McKenna would also realize that the penalties had been a major tactical error and, like Aneurin Bevan, offer some major concessions: 'then the weaker states will start to wobble'.[46]

Early in July these fears were realized. McKenna offered some significant concessions, allowing a wider discretion in prescribing mixtures of drugs listed in the formulary and permitting doctors to print their names and addresses on the official forms. He refused to withdraw the requirement of official forms and the penalties for refusal to co-operate. Even without the Commonwealth softening its stance, opposition based on hostility to penalties proved frail. By the end of July there were indications that the support for the boycott was wavering again. Brown reported that in his Colac district there was a growing 'uneasiness of conscience among Doctors' at the ethics of denying their patients free benefits. Few objected in principle to using the formulary or government forms; only the threat of penalties aroused real anger. Brown's points were reinforced by other council members, particularly from rural areas, who agreed that many younger doctors would join the scheme if the penalties were abandoned. While the misleading presentation of the government's plans in the branch Newsletter was temporarily shoring up resistance, they warned that unrest in the profession would become an 'avalanche' if no steps were made to propose an alternative scheme to the government. Both South Australia and Tasmania had returned to their earlier calls for compromise: the former proposed a modification of the government form more acceptable to the profession, the Tasmanians moved to use the Commonwealth scheme to treat pensioners, despite the strong disapproval of their interstate colleagues.[47]

At the same time, the Department of Health received letters from groups of otherwise sympathetic doctors urging changes in the Act to win greater compliance. A group of ten Melbourne doctors set out their reasons for boycotting the scheme. While attacking the negative attitude of the BMA, they argued that all administration should be in the hands of the pharmacists, including the decision of which drugs were on the free list. The threat of penalties was denounced as 'an extreme impertinence'. On a more sinister level, a Western Australian general practitioner wrote to McKenna declaring that his desire to co-operate was being frustrated by the fear of ostracism by his colleagues. His plea for protection was answered with the rather unreassuring promise that 'doctors who do co-operate will be given the fullest support of the Government'. Surveys in the eastern states showed that the private doubts of members were not being expressed, as yet, in abandonment of the boycott. In March 1949 only 11 doctors in New South Wales were reported to be using the forms, in Queensland, only 3 doctors, and in Victoria 111.[48]

Again, the more conciliatory attitude of the smaller branches was undone by swift action from Victoria and New South Wales. In 1947 the Federal Council had been enlarged, ending the equal representation of the state branches. While the smaller states retained two representatives, Victoria gained an additional member and New South Wales doubled its share to four. This strengthened the ability of Victoria and New South Wales to take matters into their own hands, making major decisions over legal strategy without consultation. Fearing that Newland was preparing the ground for a compromise, the Victorian and New South Wales members attacked the 'uncontrolled correspondence' between the council secretariat and the Minister. They ensured that the council's hands would remain firmly tied by passing a motion prohibiting all communications with the federal government without prior approval from the branches.[49]

As the BMA increased its propaganda offensive, the government did little to reply. Departmental officials complaining that the sole literature supporting the scheme had been produced by the Communist Party were instructed that the only avenue for answering the distortions of their opponents would be ministerial statements. Replying to the press would only give the opposition the opportunity to reopen debate.[50]

Frustrated and embarrassed at the complete failure of the scheme, and eager to resolve the matter so that serious discussions of a medical benefits scheme could be resolved, the government returned to even harsher penalties to force compliance. A Cabinet meeting in early 1949 confirmed McKenna's reliance on penalties, although he warned that another High Court challenge was likely. At the end of the first week of July an amendment to the Act added clause 7A, requiring that all prescriptions for drugs contained in the formulary be completed on the official form. Although another clause allowed patients to voluntarily refuse to accept benefits under the Act – an attempt to avoid suggestions that the clause was conscripting doctors into the scheme – in practice they would have little choice but to participate.[51]

Another High Court challenge followed, this time initiated by the Federal Council. The second pharmaceutical benefits case was a watershed, the last round in the long battle. As long as the matter was before the courts members could be counted on to carry out instructions, but should the challenge fail, the dominant feeling was doubt 'whether the loyalty of the profession was sufficiently intact to defeat the Government's measure'.[52]

The High Court handed down its judgment in the second week of October. By a majority of four to two it held that the requirement to use a form, backed by penal sanctions, constituted 'civil conscription'. Chief Justice Latham used a very wide construction of 'civil conscription' to argue that:

It is one thing to provide as a condition of giving a pharmaceutical benefit that a prescription shall be written on a particular form, and another thing to provide that a doctor shall write any prescription for medicines which are included within a formulary upon a particular form, whether or not such medicines are to be provided free under the Act.[53]

The Act itself was still valid: the court had only ruled that clause 7A was invalid. Hence, it was far from being a complete victory and the medical profession still needed to come to an agreement with the Commonwealth government. However, McKenna could offer only a limited array of concessions. As he was unwilling to relinquish the cost controls of the formulary and the use of official forms, the only alternatives were to follow BMA demands and restrict the scheme to a few lifesaving drugs or to adhere to the existing formulary in the hope that another Labor electoral victory would force BMA compliance. His final Cabinet submission in October 1949 had an air of bleak resignation. Cabinet postponed its decision on the future of the scheme while both sides turned their attentions to the electoral struggle.[54]

Always political, the struggle against the Act became part of a wider crusade against socialism, especially with the likely victory of a Liberal government. Stern editorials from the Melbourne *Argus* and *Age* declaring that the BMA must now demonstrate its good faith in frequent declarations of its readiness to negotiate an acceptable scheme went unheeded. The rest of the capital city press called for the government to abandon its attempt to coerce the medical profession – in stark contrast to the outrage with which the first pharmaceutical benefits case had been received.[55]

The profession's leaders waited until after the election before discussing compliance to the law while the state committees formed to fight the Act increasingly aligned with opponents of bank nationalization and other conservative groups. In South Australia the BMA joined the public campaign organized by the Bank Employees Association. Grieve later recalled that in the atmosphere of 1947–9 it was:

> unusually easy to make public the fallacies and inequities of government policy. Top level press conferences permitted confidential discussion of developments and the usual inspired press statements from Ministerial headquarters were accordingly either anticipated or neutralized by statements in the news columns, than which there could be no more telling publicity. From the outset, the strategy of attack was applied. The Government policy was believed to be opposed to the interests of the people so that every public statement issued from the headquarters of the profession was designed to force the Government onto the defensive before the people.[56]

This increasingly partisan stance reached its height during the election campaign. The defeat of the Chifley government was seen as the only way to ensure the end to plans for socialized medicine. Again, even in the fevered political climate of 1949 there were major disagreements between the state branches on the correct tactics to adopt or how involved the BMA should become in party politics. The Victorian branch remained aloof, although many of its leaders participated as individuals. In contrast, the New South Wales branch used its fighting funds to help ensure a Liberal–Country Party victory. With Grieve as political strategist the branch organized a radio campaign in which 500 general practitioners participated on the theme 'the family doctor versus the Government'.[57]

Labor's pharmaceutical benefits scheme foundered on the veto power of the BMA. However, this exercise of professional power is only explicable if two further terms are added. The first of these was the institutional rigidity of Australian politics. There seems little doubt that in the political atmosphere of 1944 and 1945 the federal government would have had small difficulty breaking a BMA boycott of a popular scheme. The reluctance of the Opposition parties to publicly associate with the BMA is eloquent evidence. The successful constitutional challenge provided a breathing space in which the BMA could regroup and the conflict was joined in circumstances far less auspicious for reform. These constitutional problems were compounded by a second political failing. The Chifley government – as in the parallel campaign around bank nationalization – proved singularly inept in mobilizing public support, veering between silence in the face of BMA attacks and McKenna's heavy-handed threats of penal sanctions.

Driven more by Treasury's fears of cost over-runs than socialist fervour, the fiscal concerns which structured the scheme were not dispelled by the defeat of Labor, but rose from the dead to bedevil the early plans of the Menzies government. Throughout these conflicts there seems little doubt of the popularity of the scheme; its failure cannot be laid at the feet of any deep reluctance of the Australian people or labour movement to use the state for redistributive transfers. Instead, the explanation must stress the political and institutional barriers faced by the postwar Labor government.

# CHAPTER 10

# The Limits of Reform: the Chifley Government and a National Health Service, 1945–1949

Man has an individual and a collective fear: his fear of sickness and helplessness is for himself and those whom he loves. This applies to all, but presses especially heavily on the man with a small income. He is afraid that sickness will come upon him or his family and that he will not be able to earn if he is ill, or cannot meet the hospital and medical expenses for his wife or children: the fear of want and fear itself are one. This fear lives with him as a daily companion until the moment comes when he, like Job, must cry, 'The thing which I greatly feared is come upon me'.

It is to some degree possible, by thrift, to lay by a small reserve against temporary periods of economic stress, but provision for the crippling debts of illness has not hitherto been possible.

The [Commonwealth Government's] scheme...is designed to remove this fear.

Senator James M. Fraser,<br>Minister for Health and Social Services, 1944[1]

Ignoring the biological fact that to function in response to necessity, and to make some struggle for existence, is the basis of a healthy mental and physical existence, the Federal Government of the day has in mind a policy of social security so all-embracing that much of the value of the struggle for life will be lost, and the joy of saving against an uncertain future will be killed.

Sir Hugh Devine,<br>Royal Australasian College of Surgeons, 1945.[2]

In the closing year of the war the Commonwealth turned its attention to the details of its national medical benefits scheme. This promised to be administratively complicated, especially given the new uncertainty about Commonwealth powers. The 'complete' and 'free' scheme promised by Labor implied control over the form of remuneration – and the regulation of medical incomes. Experience suggested that the BMA was unlikely to acquiesce quietly on either point. The prospect was for a long conflict even more bitter than that over pharmaceutical benefits.

In the event, the Chifley government proved reluctant to take any initiative. Labor continually postponed the largest part of its national health service. The motives were, again, both fiscal and political. In the constrained fiscal climate of the postwar years any delay in new spending programmes was welcomed by the federal Treasury. As Chifley continued to serve as treasurer after he became prime minister this fiscal caution became even more marked. With its origins in wartime anti-inflationary policy, the National Welfare Fund remained a major instrument of macro-economic policy, building up reserves during periods of high employment against future expenditures. In these circumstances, any delay in the implementation of the medical benefits scheme could only be welcomed. These problems were exacerbated by the constitutional barriers to the regulation of fees. As the price controls Labor sought in the 1944 constitutional referendum had been rejected, regulation would require more indirect and cumbersome measures. Finally, there was also the increasingly forlorn hope that a victory over BMA resistance to the pharmaceutical benefits scheme would make the medical profession more co-operative.[3]

## The end of reconstruction

Delay killed the already slim chances of a radical change in medical practice. By the end of the war the popular enthusiasm for sweeping social reform had considerably diminished. The failure of the fourteen powers referendum of 1944 was an important sign that a large part of the Australian electorate – otherwise prepared to vote Labor – was becoming impatient with government controls. The central welfare reforms of the Curtin and Chifley governments were on the statute books and despite the electoral and referendum victories of 1946, little was achieved that did not build on the foundations laid in 1944 and 1945.

At the same time the support for radical change had fragmented. Many former advocates of planning had begun to shift ground. Hermann Black had been one of a group of Sydney University economists who advocated a national minimum wage to the Joint

Parliamentary Committee on Social Security in 1941. Two years later he was warning of the dangers of 'romantic reconstructionism', which he identified with 'a preoccupation with objectives, an underemphasis on conditions of achievement; it is optimistic about economic limits and presumptuous on the questions of social action and the influence of intelligence; it is committed to a naive doctrine of a new harmony of interest in the post-war world'.[4]

This weakening support for social reform was accentuated by another peculiarity of Australia's postwar reconstruction. The call for radical reform during the war owed much to wider notions of citizenship. The shared dangers of invasion threats and sacrifices for the war effort as well as the more direct hazards of military service encouraged the demands for a better postwar social order. Some of the most sweeping calls for the nationalization of health came from serving soldiers – including medical officers.[5]

As after the First World War, the political unity necessary for this expansion of state social provision soon foundered. Major divisions appeared between ex-servicemen and those who had stayed home. In the face of the political bloc organized by the Returned Servicemen's League, the interests of ex-servicemen and their families were treated as quite distinct from the rest of the population, with a parallel system of health services and pensions on far more generous lines than civilians received. Unlike those nations where the welfare state became securely established in the immediate postwar years, in Australia one of the major potential forces for social reform had been successfully placated.[6]

The views of the Roman Catholic Church were also crucial. Not only did the church control a strategic proportion of hospitals, but it claimed the allegiance of a majority of Cabinet members, and Catholics remained Labor's largest single source of electoral strength. The ambivalence of Catholic thinking on the 'socialistic' aspects of postwar planning had already emerged in discussion of hospital policies, encouraging the Commonwealth's arm's length intervention through the hospital benefits scheme. This hostility towards the 'insatiable demands of the "social service state"' strengthened as peacetime anti-communism hardened. On the right, Catholic Action and the 'Movement' accused welfare planners of undermining the family. While attacking the excessive dedication of sections of the medical profession to materialist greed rather than altruistic service, in 1947 the archbishops and bishops endorsed a Catholic Action statement warning of the 'twentieth century menace of State-control and nationalization'.[7]

Amongst other 'natural' allies of the Labor government support remained strong, but there were difficulties in making this effective. In June 1948 the ACTU entered the conflict over pharmaceutical benefits, meeting with representatives of the BMA to hear their reasons for opposition, a discussion which strengthened union support for the government. However, ACTU and state labour council offers to co-ordinate a national publicity campaign against the BMA were rebuffed; McKenna warned that this would be counterproductive. Rather optimistically, in September 1948 he assured Albert Monk, the ACTU secretary, that 'there was ample evidence that individual Doctors would operate the scheme. He specifically asked that no campaign be launched against the BMA. The difficulty was with the Federal Council, but he felt confident that the differences between the Federal Council and the Government would be resolved during the next couple of weeks'. The trade union movement, in its national and state councils, never went beyond a stream of resolutions supporting 'free medicine and hospitalization' and condemning the 'anti-social attitude' of the BMA.[8]

As lay support for radical reform fragmented, many of the vocal medical advocates of nationalization fell silent. While major divisions continued to wrack the medical profession over attitudes towards state intervention, these disagreements were less likely to be aired in the non-medical press, or even in the pages of the *Medical Journal of Australia*, but settled within the closed councils of the BMA. The gap between the outlook of the Commonwealth government and that of the organized medical profession became an abyss. The clumsy tactics of the Commonwealth government, such as the draconian penalties of the pharmaceutical benefits scheme, suggest that McKenna, despite being the most able of the three Labor ministers to hold the health portfolio, had little understanding of his antagonist.

A major problem in assessing Commonwealth intentions in the postwar years is that instead of the neat plans of the National Health and Medical Research Council and the Joint Parliamentary Committee on Social Security, measures tended to be ad hoc, and considerably affected by political and constitutional shifts. Health remained a marginal element of government policy, overshadowed by the massive conflicts over the attempts to regulate and nationalize the private banks and airlines. Second, there was a shift in the politics of the medical profession itself. The lively, if limited, internal debate of the war years was increasingly supplanted by a unified hostility to almost all projects emanating from Canberra, an antipathy shared by many of the former enthusiasts of salaried medicine and group clinics. This disaffection stemmed not so much from an abandonment of the conviction of the link between a salaried national health service and the advancement of preventive social medicine, but from the growing belief that the Chifley government had little interest in establishing a service on these lines.

There were several major causes of the decline in influence of those advocating social medicine. Even those who deplored any connection between the reform of medical practice and left-wing politics, such as Cilento, had used the Soviet Union as an exemplar of the possibilities of a nationalized medical service. The pro-Soviet writings of the medical historian Henry Sigerist in the United States were frequently quoted by Cilento, and for a publicly committed socialist, such as Eric Dark, Soviet achievements were both an inspiration and a model. The Cold War changed this political environment fundamentally. Just as the allegation of 'Prussianism' had helped to destroy social insurance schemes in the United States after the First World War, the identification of socialized medicine with the Soviet menace moved political argument in Australia to a new, low level. As Australia entered the Cold War, some of the more prominent leftist medical publicists even found their livelihoods under threat.[9]

This move to the right posed some problems for the BMA. More overtly political splinter groups won the support of sections of the profession who felt that the BMA was too conciliatory towards the government. In Britain the Medical Policy Association (MPA), an organization with strong links to Douglas social credit and anti-semitism, built up considerable support in the immediate prewar years with a virulent campaign against refugee doctors. The MPA had strong Australian connections. Dr Bryan W. Monahan, one of its founders and an advocate of social credit theories of the 'Jewish money power', was an Australian. By 1946 Monahan appears to have returned to Australia and was active in social credit circles in Sydney and Canberra, publishing warnings about the conspiracy of 'Zionist Jews' who were using social security programmes and free medicine as part of the plot for world domination by the Finance Power. Monahan's pamphlet, *The Problem of the Medical Profession*, published in Liverpool (England) and Melbourne in 1945, provided the most extended attack on the policy of a salaried service, warning that in group clinics 'doctors would have lost their property rights in surgical instruments and places of practice, and with those property rights, control'. His alternative was muddy but appears to have involved some form of state subsidy of private fees. In New South Wales the MPA campaigned 'to preserve freedom of choice for doctors as individuals'. Warning of a Fabian socialist conspiracy and drawing heavily on the British attacks on planning, the MPA warned that state-financed benefit schemes were 'but a step towards the conversion of a hitherto free and self-reliant profession into a cog in the machinery of the Universal Work State'.[10]

The Australian branch of the MPA was a shadowy organization, with a tiny membership. However, there is evidence of wider influence than these minuscule numbers suggest. During the war W.H. Fitchett, the former editor of the *General Practitioner* and leader of the struggle against national health insurance in Victoria, had opened the pages of his journal *Medical Topics* to reprints of attacks on alien doctors from the MPA's violently anti-semitic journal *Medical World*. More importantly, the significance of such right wing splinter groups lay in helping to develop the general air of threat around even the most trivial of government proposals.[11]

The respectability of the anti-communist extreme right at even the highest levels of the BMA was illustrated in an exchange between Eric Butler, campaign director of the anti-semitic League of Rights, and Sir Henry Newland. In 1949 Butler issued a pamphlet attacking the Pharmaceutical Benefits Act as part of a 'totalitarian strategy for completely enslaving the individual', backed by international communism. He linked free medicine to an international 'Beveridge plot', led by Fabians and graduates of the London School of Economics, headed by Lord Rothschild in Britain with Dr H.C. Coombs, the Australian government's pre-eminent economic adviser, as its Australian representative. The pamphlet contained a strident attack on the role of the Federal Council of the BMA, arguing that the so-called Newland placitum – the constitutional guarantee against civil conscription – was merely a subtle attempt to de-fuse opposition to a national health service. These allegations of treachery provoked an indignant response from Newland, who wrote to Butler requesting that he withdraw all insinuations of a covert alliance between the socialists and the Federal Council. Significantly, when Newland complained of the misrepresentation of his negotiations with the Commonwealth government he did not object to Butler's allegations that a Fabian–Zionist conspiracy underlay government policy, confining his protests to the pamphlet's error in suggesting that he too was a dupe (or worse) of the Rothschilds and international socialism. The correspondence ended with Butler evidently unconvinced of the anti-communist credentials of the

Federal Council, despite Newland's avowal that 'I am entirely in agreement with all that you advocate', but accepting a personal donation for the next edition of his diatribe.[12]

In the fevered political atmosphere of the late 1940s, state intervention in medical practice was linked to the failed attempts to nationalize the banks and airlines. Those BMA members who had expressed sympathy for a salaried service were silenced or joined the opponents of nationalized health. Anti-communism provided a framework in which apparently innocuous initiatives from the Commonwealth were seen as part of a more general pattern of the advance of socialism in other fronts.

At the same time, the generation of public health officials who had been the principal architects of the NHMRC scheme was no longer active in public discussion. Cumpston left for Ceylon in October 1944 and retired in late 1945. Earlier that year Cilento finally received a military position with the British occupation forces in Germany, and remained outside Australia until the early 1950s. Others, such as A.R. Southwood in South Australia and E.S. Morris in New South Wales, withdrew from active involvement in the public controversy following the debacle of the NHMRC scheme. Southwood continued to stress the priority of prevention, the need for a 'social outlook in medicine' recognizing the inability of private practice to provide adequate solutions to the 'unprofitable diseases', but his prescriptions for policy did not venture beyond these vague sentiments. While arguing that the preservation of general practice based in group clinics on the English Peckham model should provide the 'pivot' of the health system, he avoided the central political issues of remuneration and control, merely warning that 'precipitate action, based on scanty thought, may be disastrous'.[13]

The new generation of health administrators had less stomach for public controversy or lacked the bureaucratic skills and wider views of the public health movement. This lack of direction was intensified after the early death of Frank McCallum, Cumpston's long-time deputy and successor. The new Director-General, Arthur John Metcalfe, was a career Commonwealth Medical Officer, and possessed a background in quarantine work and administration, with little of the standing both his predecessors had held with the BMA. The prejudice against public health and state medicine, already strong in the wider medical profession and medical education, helped to intensify this crisis of leadership within the state sector. Nowhere was this more apparent than in the NHMRC. The body which produced the most sweeping proposals for the nationalization of health steadily withdrew from public controversy. Its research committees, which had been dominated by public health officials, were placed under more scientific control. The vestiges of Cumpston's goal of national co-ordination faded rapidly.[14]

Finally, with the shift to a peacetime economy the developments in medical technology of the war years were applied to civilian life. The antibiotic revolution brought a new effectiveness to the well-established bio-medical view of therapy. Armed with a new array of drug therapies many of the problems which had lain at the heart of social medicine – such as tuberculosis – were redefined in more conventional terms. Expensive diagnostic and therapeutic technologies had moved beyond the confines of a few of the larger public hospitals. While the cost of these innovations fed demands that the Commonwealth government should extend its financial support for medical research and provide more accessible diagnostic aids, the fundamental positions underlying social medicine were undermined. The stress on the individual aetiology of disease, on dysfunction within a discrete organism, underlay the acceleration of trends towards medical specialization, shifting attention from the social causes of ill-health. While the work of some medical researchers, in particular Macfarlane Burnet at the Walter and Eliza Hall Institute in Melbourne, went against this tide, stressing the complex ecology of disease, this was quite unrelated to social medicine, with its stress on social and economic conditions. Never at the same level of sophistication as their European and American equivalents, the writings of men such as Dark and Brown appeared old-fashioned in the new age of medical science.[15]

Although these developments appeared to justify the priority the government had given to pharmaceutical benefits in its health scheme, the wider aim of a free medical scheme based on a major restructuring of Australian medical practice and health institutions was never formally abandoned. The stated objective of Commonwealth policy continued to be the development of a decentralized co-ordinated hospital and clinic system throughout Australia. McKenna regularly reaffirmed his party's long-term aim of complete nationalization, even if he conceded that the present circumstances were not propitious. The socialization of medicine remained a vague threat, aired at party meetings to reassure the Labor rank and file that the government had not forgotten its objectives. It also served as an injunction to the medical profession to place its own house in order, at the same time sustaining BMA suspicions that even apparently innocuous measures concealed subtle attacks on freedom. Brian

Fitzpatrick's lament that the ALP leaders' stance had become 'social-ism, but not in my time, O Lord', applied as much to health policies as to industry.[16]

In addition to the opposition of the BMA, the Commonwealth's plans were bedevilled by the old problem of its own institutional weakness. The lack of direct administrative experience within the department, given its limited area of authority, meant that many were rightly suspicious about the capacities of a department still based overwhelmingly on the quarantine service to administer and make policy effectively for the increasingly complex hospital system and private practitioners. Despite the injection of much-needed expertise from the Repatriation Department, low Commonwealth pay scales and the increasing antagonism of the medical profession made recruitment of new officers even more difficult. In late 1947 Metcalfe complained to the Minister that 'extreme difficulty has been experienced in recruiting medical officers in this department, both in permanent and temporary capacities'. Earlier that year eight vacancies had been advertised, only seven adequate applications had been received, and of these six were already employed as temporary officers. Subsequent advertisements for temporary officers had received no suitable applicants, while the *Medical Journal of Australia* was now refusing advertising space on the grounds that remuneration was too low. As a result, the department, far from being ready to take over the administration of a national health scheme, was severely embarrassed at its inability to fulfil its minimum obligations to other Commonwealth departments.[17]

## Medical benefits and the BMA

By the late 1940s the BMA had emerged from disarray to become the model of a united pressure group, single-mindedly pursuing the goal of private medicine, subsidized but not controlled by the state. During 1944 and 1945 the advocates of fee-for-service had won a series of crucial battles within the profession while prevarication by the Commonwealth government and its decision to base the national health service on a system of cash benefits isolated the remaining defenders of salaried medicine.

As we have seen, the conflict over pharmaceutical benefits occupied a pivotal place in this shift. The profession, and even the councils of the BMA, remained deeply divided over the desirable form and control of a national health scheme. Pharmaceutical benefits turned the struggle into a conflict over the constitutional powers of the Commonwealth, and its use of penalties against those who refused to comply, rather than the principles and details of the benefit scheme.

Although by the end of the war the BMA in all states had embraced fee-for-service as the central principle for a publicly subsidized health scheme, this was not without reservations. As Charles Byrne had emphasized from the start, cost conscious governments were unlikely to leave fee-setting in the hands of the profession. The victory over salaried service might prove pyrrhic if the price was more intrusive government scrutiny. While all accepted that publicly subsidized fee-for-service could only work with an extensive government regulation of fees and eligibility of services, the use of a schedule would violate the principle that the individual doctor should be able to use his own methods in his own way. Again, the example of the repatriation scheme loomed large in the discussion. Opponents pointed to instances where repatriation local medical officers had been fined for violating departmental regulations. Byrne had accepted this trade-off, arguing that the losses in autonomy were more than compensated by staving off the prospect of a lay-controlled national health service. To others, contract practice, despite its restrictions, still seemed to offer greater freedom.[18]

These differences over the form, and even the principle of fee-for-service made it difficult for federal BMA policy to move beyond vague homilies against government intervention in the sacred doctor–patient relationship. In June 1946, when the federal government requested details of a scheme acceptable to the BMA, the Federal Council's discussions ended inconclusively as the views of the state branches were 'almost entirely different'. The BMA declined to provide the outlines of a scheme as 'it had been decided that the Federal Council did not wish to show the Minister that the Branches held such divergent views'.[19]

A further constraint on the BMA was the reluctant support of conservative politicians. It is difficult to gauge the importance of public opinion on particular issues in framing political agenda in an age when politicians were less mesmerized by the opinion polls. However, the evidence of polls suggests initial massive public support for 'free medicine' – at 76 per cent in 1943 and still as high as 66 per cent in 1947. This went well beyond the margins of Labor's constituency and may explain some of the reticence of senior conservatives in giving the BMA their public support.[20]

The conflict over the second pharmaceutical benefits case was a watershed: by the end of 1949 support had shrunk to 53 per cent.

More significantly, as the battle returned to the courts, 47 per cent of those polled in June 1949 sympathized with the doctors, only 39 per cent with the government.[21] Even with this shift, however keenly they recruited the medical profession to the anti-socialist cause, leading Liberals remained reluctant to accept the economically dubious baggage of fee-for-service. At a private meeting with Sir Sidney Sewell, former President of the Royal Australasian College of Surgeons and an influential figure in the Victorian branch of the BMA, Menzies warned that:

> Fee for service would not and could not be considered by any political party in the Federal Parliament. The impression Senator McKenna gave the profession that he had an open mind on fee-for-service, he, Menzies, regarded as an excess of politeness and nothing more. It was interesting to recall that, when fee-for-service had first been placed before Senator McKenna, he stated that Caucus would not consider it at all and now, in effect, Mr Menzies had stated that the Liberal Party, were it in power at any time, would not consider fee-for-service either. Apparently both parties were so conscious of the disadvantages of the system as a result of the New Zealand experience, that nothing would induce either party in the Federal Parliament to provide a National Medical Service on a fee-for-service basis.
>
> ...Mr Menzies had expressed himself as being particularly anxious to have a British Medical Association Scheme for a salaried medical service and he undertook, if he received such a scheme from the Association, to support it. Mr Menzies hoped that it would be a better scheme than the one which would be evolved by the Labour Party because he wished to use it as political propaganda on behalf of the Liberal Party.[22]

This rejection revived suspicions of Menzies dating from the national health insurance conflicts of the late 1930s, confirming many medical leaders on the need to avoid all political entanglements. However, an influential section, including conservatives such as Cecil Colville, took the warning seriously. Sewell and F. Kingsley Norris, the current branch president, added their voices to the call for a reconsideration of the discarded schemes of the early 1940s. Furthermore, it was far from certain that the Liberal Party would win the next federal election. Although Labor faced an electorate tired with petrol rationing and had suffered from a recent redistribution of electoral boundaries, Gallup polls showed that support for the conservative parties still lagged during the first half of 1949. Sheridan has recently reaffirmed the view that it was mainly the traumatic impact of the coal strike (which ran from late June to mid August) which reversed these fortunes.[23]

The more ambitious advocates of fee-for-service, led by Ronald Grieve in New South Wales, attempted a more positive response to this dilemma. Building on the success of the voluntary contributory hospital funds, they attempted to extend this approach to personal health services. The Medical Benefits Fund was established by the New South Wales Branch of the BMA in 1943, registered as a limited company in 1946, and it opened its doors to subscribers the following year. Modelled on the American Blue Cross insurance funds, the MBF set out to replace the lay control of the friendly societies with medical control. Its articles of association allowed for three classes of membership. Medical members, on subscription of £10, were not entitled to benefits but elected the controlling board of the fund and were eligible to attend annual general meetings. Associate members, nominated by the Hospitals Contributory Fund and the Australian Hospitals Association (dominated by the metropolitan teaching hospitals of Sydney and Melbourne), could attend and vote at council meetings but were unable to participate in the election of councillors. Finally, contributors received medical benefits but were unable to participate in the policy-making of the fund, although five of their number were appointed as consumer representatives to the board.[24]

Backed by £10 contributions from 1,000 New South Wales doctors, the MBF aimed to extend private medical care to a market consisting of the 'steadiest element in the community', those earning between £7 and £12 per week. This was well above the £5 income limit imposed on the friendly society lodges under the New South Wales Common Form of Agreement in the mid-1930s, but despite further capital backing from the New South Wales branch, after two years of active recruiting the Medical Benefits Fund had enrolled only 2,000 members. A committee of the Victorian Branch Council sent to study the MBF dismissed suggestions from Sydney that similar private insurance schemes could provide the basis of a national health service entrenching both fee-for-service and private practice, as 'There was nothing about the Fund that had any reality in fact'. The committee added that it 'could not for a moment believe that any Government would welcome or adopt such a scheme'.[25] The Bankers Health Society, established as an insurance scheme for bank employees in 1939, was only slightly more successful. Based on a pool of contributions from which members' medical fees were refunded, the scheme supported the principles of fee-for-service and individual contracts between the patient and the doctor. In 1945 its coverage was extended to the general public; however, despite sympathy with its general aims, many BMA leaders remained sceptical about the society's ability to provide adequate coverage for those with lower incomes and job security than bank workers. The Victorian branch expressed concern that to remain actuarially sound any scheme based on fee-for-service would have to restrict its benefits severely or rely on very high contributions by members: 'the more unfortunate a person was, the less he would get out of the scheme, and it was open to abuse by unscrupulous doctors who might charge higher fees to members of the society.'[26]

Despite these reservations, refund benefit schemes were increasingly central to BMA health proposals. However, the financial barriers to a national system based on such high levels of contributions set an insuperable obstacle to establishing these insurance schemes as the basis of a truly national health scheme. At the most, the Federal Council recommended that 'it is desirable that any general scheme for the provision of medical benefits to the middle income group should be controlled by the medical profession'.[27]

For those unable to afford private contributions, BMA proposals remained centred on the means-tested panel model of general practice. The Federal Council's agreement with the Commonwealth Repatriation Commission for the treatment of the dependants of deceased service personnel established a list of beneficiaries to be treated by a medical officer in return for an annual fee of 32s. per family unit, or 39s.5d. outside metropolitan areas, and with similar excluded services to lodge practice.[28]

In October 1949 the Federal Council adopted a more comprehensive scheme, entitled A *National Health Service*, based on this model. Three classes of beneficiary were to be established. The 'middle income group' was to join a fee-for-service based refund scheme, on the model of the New South Wales Medical Benefits Fund. 'For the lower income group, the existing system of lodge benefits [would be] extended to provide a more complete service' – retaining the capitation system, despite the outraged opposition of the Victorian branch to this strengthening of the friendly societies. Finally, a general practitioner service for the indigent would be financed through existing state agencies. While this would widen fee-for-service practice, it was very far from the radical shift that Byrne had proposed. Although the option of salaried service had been destroyed, the leaders of organized medicine were still as far as ever from devising a workable scheme based on fee-for-service.[29]

## 'Free and complete?': the fate of the national health service

Commonwealth planning had floundered in the face of the refusal of the BMA to negotiate seriously. The rhetoric of socialized medicine was still employed with enough conviction to alarm the BMA, but with insufficient action to achieve significant changes. The state offices of the Commonwealth Department of Health continued to collect information on the distribution of health services. In Queensland this process actually reached the stage where a committee of state and federal medical officers was established to plan a medical service 'independent of the state governments'. The state branch of the BMA, reflecting on its reverses in past conflicts with state governments, showed resigned acceptance, warning its members that:

> History shows that the progress of evolution is only slightly altered by the exertions of individuals and but poorly influenced by the concerted action of political groups and other organizations. If this philosophy is true it would seem to be somewhat futile for a body of medical men to attempt to arrest a change in medical practice which, generally speaking, is evolving in other parts of the world, and is an expression of the general attitude of the 'people'...It is wise, however, for us to see that this process of evolution starts on the best possible footing.[30]

This acceptance did not extend to a breach in the Federal Council's national boycott of planning committees. Although the Queensland branch continued to be more conciliatory – it actually took the government's medical benefits scheme to task for its stress on 'remedial as against social medicine' and 'lack of adequate disciplinary control of doctors' – solidarity with interstate colleagues blocked any separate agreement. By the end of 1948 the Commonwealth's senior medical officer in Queensland warned his superiors that 'it would appear desirable to proceed slowly at this stage', limiting direct Commonwealth intervention to remote outback areas.[31]

Although the rhetoric of socialized medicine persisted in Labor circles, it is difficult to see much evidence of serious intent. While legislation to set up cash benefits was rapidly passed, even when its constitutional status was admitted to be shaky, schemes for direct medical services remained nebulous and were constantly postponed. This apparent preference for the Treasury-inspired cash benefit approach lost the government whatever goodwill remained amongst its former sympathizers within the profession. Arthur Brown's public opposition to the pharmaceutical benefits scheme has already been mentioned. Others, such as Lance Hewitt, a self-described 'rather rabid supporter of socialized medicine', responded anxiously to rumours that the government's proposals:

> failed to mention the one thing that the profession (as distinct from the Council) will be adamant about in a socialized service, viz. a limited working day. We have 'had' the 24 hour service and we want a five day 40 hour week...
>
> We, the rank and file, have an uneasy suspicion that when all the talks and conferences are over we will be sold up the river into a 24 hour contract service. If this is so then you will really meet the very formidable passive resistance of a hostile profession...I personally would not want anything to do with a service in which any Tom, Dick or Harry could demand my services at night after my day's work was done and report me to the appropriate authority if I did not respond...
>
> Admit this first principle of a limited working day and for the rest, your basic salary plus capitation scheme has an excellent chance of going over in spite of the lack of co-operation you will meet from our elected representatives, who in fact largely represent specialist opinion rather than that of the rank and file.[32]

The failure of the Commonwealth to come up with any coherent new proposals left its opponents able to speculate on the forms socialized medicine would take, guided only by vague – and to some, ominous – assurances from McKenna that a national health service would be 'complete, free and at the highest technical excellence'. While he protested to the Federal Council about selective leaks of its discussions with the government as 'mischievous in its effect whatever may be the intent of those responsible', in the absence of public discussion rumour ruled supreme.[33]

Even when it came to the medical benefits scheme promised in 1944, the Chifley government showed little enthusiasm for rapid action. The first barrier was constitutional. The first pharmaceutical benefits case set a clear obstacle in the path of any national health benefits scheme, and not until 1946 could serious planning recommence. However, the government and its opponents were almost immediately distracted by the renewed battle over pharmaceutical benefits. Both sides accepted that little could be decided on the form of medical benefits until this trial of strength had been settled. The BMA refused to enter serious discussions and McKenna, urged along by the Treasury, was adamant that the costs of the national scheme must remain under strict central control – the very issue at the heart of the pharmaceutical benefits conflict.

The government had a further motive for postponing action. Facing serious balance of payments problems, the Chifley government kept a very tight rein on its own expenditure. Postponement of such a major expenditure item was quietly welcomed by the government's senior economic advisers. These concerns about costs had been underlined by the New Zealand experience, where the cost over-run of both an unlimited pharmaceutical benefits scheme and publicly subsidized fee-for-service were apparent. At the end of 1944 senior health and social services public servants had accompanied the then minister, Senator James Fraser, to New Zealand to examine that country's new health service. The BMA sent John Hunter and C.H. Dickson, its federal and Victorian secretaries, to shadow the official tour. The reaction of both groups to the New Zealand scheme underscored the growing abyss between the federal government and the leaders of organized medicine. The visiting officials were horrified at the cost explosion of publicly-funded universal fee-for-service systems. The example of New Zealand provided ammunition for both sides over the next five years, and its immediate effect was to increase the concerns of the Treasury about cost controls in the national medical scheme.[34]

It was not until late 1948 that McKenna reopened the issue of medical benefits in Cabinet – and with a very different set of proposals to the earlier schemes of salaried service. In what proved to be the dying gasp of Labor's ambitious programme he abandoned compulsion on doctors to join the government service. Salaried practice was relegated to a long-term ideal; the scheme was to grow gradually, with a slow expansion of facilities and the numbers of practitioners employed. McKenna now favoured a modified fee-for-service, with a fixed schedule of fees and co-payment of half the fee by the patient – a scheme bearing a remarkable similarity to that proposed by Byrne five years earlier. The measure of how embittered relations with the BMA had become was McKenna's recognition that there was no chance of active co-operation, even if the health scheme was administered by an autonomous commission – another potential point of compromise which the BMA had shed as the conflict intensified. Instead, McKenna favoured direct administration by a greatly strengthened Commonwealth Department of Health.[35]

Cabinet quickly agreed to the new, heavily compromised scheme. The National Health Service Act, passed in November 1948, set up the legal framework for Labor's health services. It was based on the new constitutional powers of the Commonwealth but left the details to be established later by regulation, after negotiations with the BMA and other interested bodies. If the new Act was intended to enable the federal government to recapture the initiative, this was undermined by the administrative incompetence which had marked the whole course of the conflict. When the Department of Health began to prepare health benefit regulations so many drafting errors and other mistakes were discovered that the exercise had to be postponed until the National Health Service Act was amended. The new Act did not receive assent until October 1949.[36]

Labor's medical benefits scheme had now been reduced to subsidized fee-for-service. Reworked in May 1949 it bowed to BMA opposition by allowing patients to opt out, recognizing 'a person's right to seek medical attention unfettered by regulation', and it remained limited to general practice: the fees of specialists would be regulated only in the unlikely event that they expressed a willingness for this to happen. McKenna's scheme retained a commitment to greater equality of access to services, but few other elements of the wartime plans. Little, however, was conceded in the financial control of the scheme. Doctors would have a direct contract with the Commonwealth Department of Health, providing full records of each service provided and the amount charged, with penalties for breaches of regulations.[37]

As the Chifley government entered its final year in office it reluctantly accepted that the health service must be based on both fee-for-service and co-payment. Although this was a major concession to BMA resistance, the administrative system McKenna proposed did little to endear him to organized medicine. Continuing the Treasury-inspired obsession with cost control, the Commonwealth Department of Health was to obtain a level of control unacceptable to the BMA. Two weeks before the federal election of 1949 the National Health (Medical Expenses) Regulations gazetted fee schedules for 192 items, despite the refusal of the BMA to co-operate. This final attempt to demonstrate that Labor could implement its health scheme did not affect the election result. The Menzies government took power on 8 December.[38]

# PART III

# The Public and
# the Private

# CHAPTER 11

# Private Practice, Publicly Funded: the Page Health Scheme

When the Menzies government took power in December 1949 the way seemed clear for a swift settlement with the BMA. The fragile unity of the medical profession had been sustained by the High Court challenge and then the imminence of federal elections, but its membership was increasingly anxious for a workable scheme of subsidized private practice. The appointment of the veteran Country Party MP, Sir Earle Page, a surgeon and longtime member of the BMA, as Minister for Health seemed to augur well. This period of goodwill on both sides offered the new government an unparalleled chance to achieve a settlement, but only if planning did not again become mired in endless negotiations and another fruitless war of attrition.

The coalition's health policies of 1949 were a confused attempt to extricate the Commonwealth government from the impasse of the previous five years. They were presented as part of a wider project to free the people from the restraints of socialism – relying on individual intitiative and the market rather than the dead hand of bureaucracy – a programme forged by the policy advisers of the Institute of Public Affairs in the blackest days of Australian conservatism.[1]

The new government promised a system based on voluntary insurance, what the Country Party leader and Treasurer Arthur Fadden termed 'the Christian idea of mutual assistance', on similar lines to the BMA's *A National Health Service* of 1949. Pensioners would receive a free, complete service, the friendly societies would be subsidized to provide a means-tested contract system for the working class. Fee-for-service – again subsidized by the federal government, although at a lower rate – would be limited to the middle classes and administered by the medical benefit funds and friendly societies, not the Commonwealth Department of Health. Fadden added the rash and uncosted promise of a massive hospital-building programme. In the areas of public health the new government confined itself to providing free milk for school-age children – a measure applauded by its dairy farming constituency as much as by public health doctors – and a wider tuberculosis benefit scheme, which built on the foundations already laid by Labor.[2]

There were few traces of the preventive and social concerns of the 1940s. Page's approach to health policy was firmly underpinned by an individualistic notion of the causes of ill-health. Gone was the stress on bad living conditions, nutrition and housing which even the more conservative sections of the BMA had accepted as the primary causes of disease. Instead, the discourse of health policy had shifted to the asocial individual:

> Sickness is a vitally personal and individual matter to each sick man, sick woman or sick child. No disease runs an exactly similar course in every person. Its course is determined by the constitution and heredity, previous diseases and condition of other organs. It is obvious, therefore, that human disease cannot be overcome by mass treatment...Successful treatment lies in the cumulative effect of many things – confidence in the doctor, the efficiency of the treatment, the wise and balanced use of various therapeutic measures, exact diagnosis and consideration of the patient's general condition. All these are helped by the retention of the self-respect of the individual and his pride in his independence.[3]

Page presented his 'health plan' as a coherent alternative to the statist schemes of the Chifley years: 'Australia's answer to socialized medicine'. As he explained to the British Commonwealth Medical Congress in Brisbane in 1950, the new National Health Service was to be aimed at a new class created by the advances (and growing expense) of modern medicine, those neither poor nor rich but '"medically indigent". The existence of this new class has created a disposition on the part of governments to attempt to control en masse what is essentially an expert personal matter dealing with the relationships of individuals to one another'.[4]

However, the final form bore little resemblance to the plans Page placed before Cabinet early in 1950. The Page national health service was born, not out of a new sense of co-operation between Government and doctors, but as a continuation of the tense struggle over the control of medical services. It stalled in the face of the same institutional obstacles which had blocked Labor: the antagonism between the friendly societies and the BMA, obstruction by state governments, and the resolute opposition of organized medicine to any direct contract between the doctor and the state.[5]

## The planning of the Page scheme

Page's period as Minister of Health has been seen as marking the final triumph of the BMA. From obstructing Labor's plans for a universal national health scheme, it moved into a position where it virtually dictated government policy.[6]

Certainly, there is much evidence of a major change in the political atmosphere by early 1950. The minority of doctors who had supported Labor's schemes felt the force of official disfavour. Page ordered his officials to prepare a list of Victorian doctors who had participated in the pharmaceutical benefits scheme, and compared it with lists of known communists prepared for the Royal Commission on Communism. At the same time, well-known socialists were arbitrarily removed from sources of income controlled by the Commonwealth. Eric Dark, who earned his living as a repatriation local medical officer in the Blue Mountains, was removed from repatriation lists, and was forced to move to a salaried post in remote western New South Wales.[7]

Within a few weeks of winning power the new Cabinet established a Social Services Sub-committee to supervise the planning of the new health service. Chaired by the Treasurer, Arthur Fadden, it included Senator William H. Spooner, the Liberal Minister for Social Services, Senator Walter Cooper, the Country Party Minister for Repatriation and former member of the Joint Parliamentary Committee on Social Security, as well as Page. The Committee's immediate priority was the extension of child endowment, to fulfil one of the Coalition's major election promises. This expensive programme doubled the numbers of beneficiaries, drained the reserves of the National Welfare Fund and became an excuse to defer other election promises, especially the major hospital construction programme.[8]

Cabinet declared support for the basic principles of a new medical scheme, starting with a pharmaceutical benefits scheme more politically acceptable to the BMA than that of the Chifley government. In practice, Page was given a free hand in negotiations with health interest groups, while Herbert Goodes, now an assistant secretary in the Treasury, took an active part in the discussion of costs.

The cornerstones of the Page health scheme were set in place during the first two years of government. The pharmaceutical benefits scheme commenced in August 1950, the pensioners' medical service in February 1951, and the pensioners' pharmaceutical benefits scheme the following July. Hospital and medical benefits provided more intractable problems. Page's hands were tied by existing agreements between the Commonwealth and the states under the Hospital Benefits Act. Because of resistance from Labor governments in Tasmania, New South Wales and especially Queensland, changes in this area would be a hard and slow process. Equally, attempts to move quickly to implement medical benefits were frustrated by the problems of finding private agencies capable of administering such a complex system, as well as continued obstruction from the BMA.[9]

The principles underlying the Page scheme were clear. The Coalition accepted that the Commonwealth could not withdraw from the finance of health care – a position that had been relatively uncontroversial in abstract principle since the late 1930s. Administration was, however, to depart radically from Labor's reliance on the Commonwealth Department of Health and shift to private organizations. This was far from a 'free market' solution. Page displayed no more interest than the BMA in extending the workings of the market into medical services. Instead, not-for-profit organizations such as the friendly societies and benefit funds were to be the sole providers of health insurance with costs regulated by strict means testing and controls to ensure the fiscal solvency of the funds. The only truly 'free' services were to be available to recipients of Commonwealth pensions; those in the workforce or ineligible for a pension were required to make substantial contributions to the cost of each service and to take out medical insurance with a private fund. As Page explained to Cabinet in January 1950:

> The essence of my proposed attack is to help those who help themselves – to encourage the formation and strengthen the working of voluntary organizations which could handle the problem of administration, thus providing a real nursery of democracy. Incidentally, by subsidizing voluntary effort many of the pitfalls in universal compulsory medical schemes will be avoided and, at the same time, definite control secured over the amount of money to which the Government and the taxpayer are committed.[10]

## Pharmaceutical benefits

Again, a pharmaceutical benefits scheme was the first plank of the health service. The Coalition parties had supported the BMA campaign against Labor's scheme and were pledged to introduce a plan similar to the Federal Council's preferred option, which limited the scheme to 'expensive and life saving drugs'. The main obstacle to swift implementation was no longer organized medicine, but a hostile Senate controlled by the Labor Party, which was threatening to block any legislation which diluted the Chifley–McKenna scheme. Page was able to by-pass this opposition by gazetting regulations using the framework of Labor's proclaimed but ineffectual legislation. Parliament adjourned in late 1950, and by the time it reassembled for the autumn session the scheme was fully operational, making it politically difficult for Labor to use its Senate numbers to disallow the regulations. Ironically, it was precisely this scope for government by regulation which had inspired BMA resistance to the Act under Labor.[11]

The scheme was based on the provision, on doctor's prescription, of a restricted list of 'life saving and expensive' drugs drawn up by a committee including BMA nominees. No charges were to be made for drugs on the free list and the whole population was to be eligible. This limited scheme was to be supplemented by a means tested pensioners' pharmaceutical scheme with a full range of drugs. Both schemes departed from Labor's model in abandoning the forms of financial control that had aroused the ire of the BMA. This meant brushing aside protests from the Department of Health and from Goodes at the Treasury on the lack of effective checks on expenditure and the certainty of cost over-runs. Page overcame Cabinet resistance, arguing that the essential question was to get the scheme up and running.[12]

The scheme faced two initial problems. For at least a year the public hospitals of the Labor states had been implementing the full pharmaceutical benefits scheme for inpatients in private and intermediate as well as public wards. This created a major potential embarrassment for the Government as Page echoed the concerns of general practitioners, private hospitals and pharmacists at the advantages this gave to public hospital patients 'forced', in Page's words, to accept free pharmaceuticals and so creating 'a discrimination between the people, which should not continue'. He faced strong resistance from hospital administrators. Bruce Lilley, the chairman of the New South Wales Hospitals Commission and the prime target of Page's strictures, pointed to the tight controls that the Commission exercised over prescribing in hospitals. At the same time, Goodes in Canberra repeated his warnings that the restriction of the free list to 'life saving and expensive drugs' would create pressures for doctors to prescribe more expensive preparations. These protests were brushed aside and Page sent instructions that in future the Commonwealth would only reimburse the limited list of 'lifesaving drugs' dispensed by registered pharmacists. This last provision was to end the use of salaried medical officers to dispense in many smaller hospitals. Page also placated the pharmacists by easing their worries about their traditional rivals, the friendly society dispensaries, and rejecting Treasury advice for tightly controlled pricing structures. An indignant Treasury official recorded his dissent on the file: 'Minister proposing to circulate against advice of Department proposal to chemists on pricing of drugs in the new lists – to offer to accept the Guild prices whatever the Guild charges'.[13]

Professional compliance with the new scheme was to be won by sacrificing cost controls and the freedom to prescribe a wide range of drugs – although the latter had been at the heart of the BMA campaign against the Pharmaceutical Benefits Acts.

The first three years of the Page pharmaceutical benefits scheme confirmed Treasury suspicions. The original estimates given to Cabinet by Page costed the scheme at £2.5 million in the first year, increasing to £5 million in subsequent years. In practice, by the end of the first full year, 1951–2, the cost had already exceeded the £5 million target and the Treasury estimated that it would continue to increase to over £7 million. Although part of this cost increase is attributable to inflation caused by the Korean War, as Whitwell has recently noted it formed part of a more general explosion of government expenditure during the early Menzies years as the financial controls imposed by the Chifley government were abandoned. Page's original estimates had been accurately criticized by both Metcalfe and Goodes (who had predicted the actual cost over-run from the start), and so changing international circumstances must bear only a marginal share of the blame.[14]

There remained the problem of finding a system of financial controls satisfactory to both Treasury and the BMA – an impossible task, especially after the Department's rearguard attempt to preserve the stricter regulation of a formulary had been defeated. While only a restricted range of expensive drugs was available, doctors were to have the freedom to specify any brand name they wished. Given the inability of the Commonwealth to regulate drug prices, and the large range of prices for basically identical products, this meant that drug manufacturers and wholesalers could set their own prices. Indeed, to the extent that price and quality were confused in the public and medical mind, this encouraged a system of reverse price competition. Manufacturers had an incentive to raise the price of their products above that of their competitors, and rely on advertising and other promotion to the medical profession to obtain sales. The advisory committee which proposed the inclusion of drugs on the benefit list soon complained that 'the whole scheme was getting away from medical control' as 'inclusions in the formulary were manoeuvred entirely by enterprising importers'.[15]

A further problem with the limited scheme was that patient pressure and the wish of doctors to prescribe at low cost established powerful incentives to use and extend the listed drugs, even where a cheaper but unlisted alternative would have been more appropriate. By late 1950 this problem was causing disquiet amongst public health authorities in the states and within the medical profession as shortages of penicillin and other antibiotics became widespread. Less than two months after the commencement of the scheme complaints were flooding in of shortages in aureomycin, and the Commonwealth government was forced to respond to formal complaints from the Queensland government with an admission of the need for greater control on prescribing to 'prevent their indiscriminate use by doctors who are not prepared to act in the best interests of the community'. This legitimate, but often unnecessary, use of expensive drugs – not fraud – was the principal obstacle to cost control. The only solutions lay in widening the scheme with a full-scale formulary or infringing the rights of individual doctors to prescribe as they wished. As both had been ruled out in advance the government was thrown back on moral exhortation.[16]

Consequently, Page was forced to rely on the BMA to restrain the prescribing habits of its members. In May 1951 the *Medical Journal of Australia* published a strongly worded leader attacking 'steam hammer medicine': the indiscriminate prescription of streptomycin, chloromycetin and aureomycin. Admitting that 'the state of affairs is shocking' it attacked the 'ineptitude' of many doctors, and warned that the excessive prescription of antibiotics could have a deleterious effect on public health.[17] These fears were not confined to Australia but occupied a major place in British and American medical journals in 1952 and 1953. Instead of being used as a specific remedy for a limited number of diseases, costly imported drugs such as cortisone, aureomycin and streptomycin were being used as non-specific treatments or prophylactics in 'clean' surgical cases. Several dramatic cases of allergic reactions to antibiotics, and fears of immunologists that new, antibiotic-resistant strains of pathogens would appear if the indiscriminate use of antibiotics continued, coincided with the demand for cost controls to bring stricter regulation. The Antibiotics

Committee of the National Health and Medical Research Council responded with a call for the Commonwealth Department of Health to regulate the use of all antibiotics but penicillin, increasing controls of levels of dosage, providing tests for sensitivity and ending the prophylactic use of these drugs. In early 1952 a list of the conditions and circumstances under which the more expensive antibiotics could be prescribed was published by the Commonwealth Department of Health and then, with BMA co-operation, widely disseminated in the medical press.[18]

Finally, the abandonment of Labor's attempt to enforce the use of a government prescription form increased the opportunities for widespread abuse. By late 1951 the increase in costs above all estimates was causing concern in Treasury and the Department of Health. Measures to increase financial control within the scope of the system were discussed as 'this must be done urgently otherwise the scheme will become destroyed by the vested interests which are being created in it'.[19] In meetings with the pharmaceutical importers and manufacturers in early 1952 Page attacked their 'abuse of trust', complaining that identical drugs were being sold at higher prices under different names and that high pressure sales tactics were being used, exaggerating the efficacy and applicability of the limited number of drugs on the free list.

Although he called for a basic price for all manufactured drugs and a limitation of the more expensive to specific conditions, Page successfully withstood his department's calls for a stricter regulatory structure, leaving matters in the hands of the industry and the BMA. Hence, despite his warnings of the need for 'savage cuts' throughout the economy, in the wake of the Fadden budget which had placed the economy 'almost on the same scale of expenditure as fighting a war', little progress had been made by the end of the year as the worst predictions of an explosion in the costs of the pharmaceutical benefits scheme were exceeded.[20]

## Towards residualism?: the Pensioners' Medical Service and cost control

The second element of the Page scheme was the Pensioners' Medical Service. Limited to those receiving Commonwealth old age and invalid pensions – both of which remained means-tested – this concessional service was reluctantly agreed by the BMA as the price of government abandonment of the friendly societies. It provided an essential condition for a medical benefits scheme based on private insurance. By making the highest risk group a government responsibility and reducing the need for cross-subsidies within the insured population, the private funds could keep their premiums at affordable levels.[21]

The first problem was a question of control. Goodes and Metcalfe had agreed that while policy-making should remain with the Department of Health, it would be simpler to administer the benefits through the Department of Social Services (DSS), which held all pension records. Strenuous objections from the BMA could be expected, but the cost savings would be so substantial, they concluded, that such sectional pressures would 'surely be overruled'. They won a powerful ally in William Dunk, the chairman of the Public Service Board, who estimated that in the first year this transfer would save £25,000 in administrative costs. These arguments persuaded Cabinet, so in October 1950 all administrative responsibilities were given to DSS while Health was confined to a policy function. This decision was taken without Page's participation: the same day Menzies sent formal notification of Cabinet's request for additional administrative staff for the health scheme.[22]

In the subsequent bureaucratic battle Page demonstrated both his own considerable political skills and the effectiveness of the threat of a BMA veto. Warning that a medical profession 'flushed with success' would withdraw all co-operation from the government, he cautioned his colleagues: 'I have known all along that they would not have minded in the least if there was no medical scheme. Only a personal sense of loyalty to me and a loyalty to this Government has got any agreement'. He concluded with a heavy threat that if the decision was not reversed he would take the matter to the party room. Dunk's victory proved short-lived.[23]

The Pensioners' Medical Service (PMS) soon suffered from similar problems of cost over-runs and abuse to those besetting pharmaceutical benefits. Initial estimates that pensioners would average three visits to their doctor each year soon proved over-optimistic, the actual level being closer to five visits. Successful in controlling the PMS and with medical benefits still deadlocked, the BMA pushed its advantage by demanding a fee increase even before the PMS was in operation. This first conflict shows that the BMA could crumble in the face of a determined government. Page accused the Federal Council of a 'breach of faith', and threatened that if it persisted, control would pass into the unsympathetic hands of his Cabinet colleagues and the Treasury, who would happily use it as the occasion for a drastic revision of the scheme. This political manoeuvre was successful. Hunter and Collins (the Federal President) suggested the BMA push had been a misunderstanding, and agreed that all the correspondence be placed in 'the limbo of forgotten things'.[24] However, doctors pressed successfully for an increase in their remuneration in line with rises in the basic wage.

More seriously, department investigations pointed to 'flagrant overvisiting on the part of [some] doctors' as a major component of the cost increases.[25] Reports that 'abuses are rampant in the Pharmaceutical Benefits Scheme and the Pensioners' Medical Service' began to filter through to the Department of Health. In June 1952, after conferring with his state directors, Metcalfe concluded that:

> In general, the impression is that there is widespread laxity among the medical profession in their handling of the Pharmaceutical Benefits Schemes, and that many obtain the utmost they can out of the Pensioners' Medical Service without actually committing fraud.
>
> The statement has been made, and I believe that the senior members of the profession are greatly alarmed on this count, that if ever another government, favourably disposed to the nationalization of the medical profession, comes into power, the medical men themselves will have their own actions used against them as justification for such a measure. At the present time the arrangements under the Pensioners' Medical Service are far too loose – in fact the absence of regulations makes effective control almost impossible.
>
> Under the Pharmaceutical Benefits Act, we are almost powerless to deal with abuses by medical practitioners owing to the removal of penalties by the previous Government. Unless, therefore, action is taken under the Crimes Act to deal with cases of collusion [between doctors and chemists] and other fraudulent practices, I am afraid our efforts to establish medical and pharmaceutical benefits on an efficient and economic basis will be completely frustrated. I also feel that, until some effective action has been taken to deal with these cases, no action should be taken in regard to the demand for increased fees under the Pensioners' Medical Service.[26]

Metcalfe concluded with a stinging attack on the BMA for its reluctance to assist the department in administration, its preference for giving 'lip service to the idea of Disciplinary Committees', while objecting to all specific proposals for regulation of abuses on the grounds that 'it was going to involve certain members of the profession in some difficult decisions'. Self regulation was proving a failure as the BMA showed itself unable to make the move from sectional interest group to an instrument of corporatist regulation.[27]

These pressures for the control of the costs of the scheme were reinforced by national economic problems. With the end of the Korean War boom, Australia faced a major balance of payments crisis and demands by the federal Treasury for cuts in expenditure and for stricter import controls, creating a political climate more favourable to regulation of the medical profession and the drug industry. Instead of the vague understanding between the BMA and the government which had proved so ineffectual, Metcalfe called for a new system of regulation, still based on professionally controlled committees, but with clearer duties and powers including:

> penalties for contravention of the Regulations…[and] provisions designed to limit the income now being derived by some doctors through 'services' to individual pensioners. Power might also be given to refuse payment in particular cases where the Department in association with the Committees, is satisfied that the payments are not justified.[28]

Anxious to avoid offence to the BMA, at least until the medical benefits scheme was in place, Page entertained anodyne schemes of self regulation by committees of pharmacists and doctors in each state who would exercise a 'strong moral influence' on their colleagues. The first offence would be punished with an official warning, the second would result in the publication of the offender's name in the *Commonwealth Gazette*, and a third offence would lead to the suspension of rights to prescribe under the Act for up to twelve months. The accused would be given the right of appeal to the State Supreme Court. Even so, despite the agreement of the Federal Council (under protest), the Victorian branch repudiated any external regulation of the right to prescribe. The National Health Act of 1953 followed this limited model. The Act required the Minister to obtain the *agreement* of the BMA. In contrast, the Act only required *consultation* with the Pharmacy Guild, which had no representation on any of the committees.[29]

The options of government control and regulation of pharmacy and the medical profession having been excluded, the government had no option but to adopt indirect methods, reached only through a long and painful process of trial and error. From the start Goodes had advised that a wider scheme would actually cost little more and be considerably easier to administer, ending the incentive for doctors to prescribe expensive drugs from the free list. At the same time, political pressure grew to expand the scheme from a narrow range of life-saving drugs. New products were added so quickly that from March 1960 the Pharmaceutical Benefit Scheme was finally increased to cover the full range of drugs. A scheme similar to Labor's much reviled PBS had gradually emerged. This was not because the Menzies government had embraced the redistributional aims of

Chifley's programmes, nor had it merely capitulated to demands for an extension of benefits to its own middle class constituency – the 'creeping universalism' which some have perceived in the growth of welfare expenditures in the Menzies era. Instead, by widening the formulary to match the pensioners' scheme and adding a co-payment of 5s. per prescription, the government hoped to bring the costs of the scheme under control.[30]

The costs of the scheme could also be limited if the federal government influenced the prices charged by pharmaceutical manufacturers. Again, the 1950s saw constant complaints about international pharmaceutical companies abusing the system and charging inflated prices. As the scheme became more inclusive the Australian government began to exploit its position as the major purchaser of therapeutic drugs. By the mid 1960s it regularly used its monopsony to dictate prices considerably below those holding in more competitive markets. With the exception of co-payment, each of these cost controls had been implicit in Labor's original scheme, and so the BMA victories of the 1940s had achieved little lasting product.[31]

At the same time the costs of the PMS were contained by more traditional methods. As with the old contract lodge practice, the BMA resented giving a concessional service to any patient who, in the eyes of the medical profession, could afford to pay fees. In November 1955 a more restrictive means test was introduced. Where previously all eligible for pensions had access to free care under the PMS, only those who drew the maximum pension were now included: by the early 1960s over one-quarter of pensioners were excluded from the service.[32]

Page's attempts to deal with two of Labor's projects: extending personal health care to those previously dependent on charity, and the national pharmaceutical scheme, were examples of the 'muddling through' which characterized his health scheme. Unwilling to antagonize the BMA, yet unable to allow costs to remain uncontrolled, the federal government was left with rather blunt instruments with which to shape its health policies.

## Medical benefits

Both the pharmaceutical benefits and pensioner medical service schemes dealt with issues which the BMA regarded as peripheral to the main lines of medical practice. The crucial testing point was to be the formulation of a medical benefits scheme. Labor's hybrid fee-for-service system had been rejected by the medical profession and the new government came to power with a substantial store of goodwill (and considerable trepidation about the alternative) from the BMA. However, Page and his colleagues quickly found that the problems which had defeated Labor had survived the change in political regime. Although negotiations with the BMA commenced within weeks of the election, it was not until August 1953, more than three and a half years and one election later, that Page's medical benefits scheme was implemented.

Drawing on his long experience in medical politics and intimate knowledge of the BMA, Page initially asserted a more active role in policy-making than his Labor predecessors. Again, Page worked within a framework of issues established by the ineffectual legislation of the Chifley government, making extensive use of regulations to overcome parliamentary opposition.

At the same time, his scheme abandoned the universalism of Labor's national health service. Access to benefits was to be tightly means tested and regulation was to be passed into the hands of the provider groups. Voluntary organizations, particularly the friendly societies, were to administer and control expenditure. The BMA would be satisfied as doctors' fees were underwritten by the Commonwealth while the legal fiction of purely private practice would be maintained as patients claimed their benefits as refunds. At no stage would the practitioner enter into a direct contract with the Commonwealth. By subsidizing contributions to private insurance funds and friendly societies the Commonwealth could avoid the thorny problem of directly regulating fees and benefits. Instead, it could use its indirect supervisory powers, in conjunction with the states, to ensure the actuarial soundness of the funds, thus maintaining an adequate ratio between reserves and benefits. In theory, this would set constraints on the level both of benefits and of fees. The costs of the scheme would be both predictable and controlled, even though the payment of fees would remain, as the BMA demanded, a private matter between doctor and patient.

The main intended beneficiaries of the Page scheme were the 'forgotten people' of Menzies' postwar political campaigns, 'the great bulk of the middle income group, those persons receiving between £700 and £1400 per annum, who have three or four dependants'. Pride as well as financial resources kept this group from utilizing medical services. The extension of subsidized medical services to this group would lead to a 'great increase in the demand for medical attention'.[33]

The dominant considerations in government thinking were revealed as these proposals were revised over the next six months. As

Charles Byrne had pointed out in 1943, a publicly subsidized insurance scheme based on fee-for-service and without regulation of doctors' fee schedules would be open to grave abuse. By setting their own fees, doctors would immediately create a pressure for an equivalent rise in benefit. Page's first response to this problem was to turn to the friendly societies to 'assist in the continuance of contract practice'.[34] A Cabinet Sub-Committee consisting of Page, the Treasurer, the Attorney-General and the Minister of Social Services met to consider these proposals. The requirements of solvency imposed on friendly societies by the state registrars, coupled with a requirement that the patient pay at least 10 per cent of all fees were intended to set an indirect but powerful barrier to exploitation of the scheme by unscrupulous doctors. In sharp contrast to the philosophy of Labor's plans, doctors were reassured that 'It is not intended to introduce safeguards to ensure that the benefit flows to the patient and not to the doctor. The integrity of the medical profession will be relied upon'.[35]

To increase Commonwealth control over the direction of expenditure, Page acceded to departmental advice that the subsidy should be on a claims basis – that is, a refund for actual expenditure on approved items of health care, rather than a general subsidy to voluntary societies. This would make the cost of the scheme less predictable – it would rise greatly in years with epidemic illness and fall in relatively healthy years – but would ensure that societies spent their subsidy on health services and not on administrative overheads or additional (unauthorized) benefits.

Despite Page's refusal to sweep capitation practice away in one blow, the Federal Council assented in principle to the new scheme, although with the important reservation that all payments through the NHS should be by fee-for-service. The swift agreement of the BMA came partly from the sense of relief at the end of a long struggle and reluctant acceptance of Page's assurances that the survival of contract practice was merely tactical. He promised the Federal Council that, faced with the competing alternatives of capitation and fee-for-service practice, both patients and doctors would be quickly won to fee-for-service.[36]

The scheme drew heavily on the practices of the American Blue Cross private health funds. Established by the American Hospital Association in the 1930s, by the late 1940s these funds had enrolled a high proportion of the middle classes in hospital and medical insurance. In early 1951 Page took a study trip to the United States, accompanied by T.R. Cox, from the department. Formerly an officer of the Taxation Department, Cox was an actuary who had worked for the National Insurance Commission planning the ill-fated Kinnear scheme of national health insurance. Despite Page's claims, however, the American model did not prove transportable to Australia. Blue Cross had been the model for the BMA-supported Medical Benefits Fund in New South Wales. The MBF had found that, in contrast to the United States, the Australian middle classes seemed reluctant to invest in voluntary health insurance. In Australia, insurance was to take a far more state directed route with different benefit and contribution structures for each major income group. In Page's original conception, the state would subsidize middle class membership of the medical benefits funds, based on fee-for-service, while the working class would be encouraged to stay in an even more restricted friendly society contract service. Only the limited groups of heavily means tested pensioners would qualify for the free medical service of the PMS.[37]

This first version of the Page scheme divided the Australian population (then about 8,000,000) into three groups. Each was to receive a different level of subsidy of their medical costs.

The first and most generously subsidized group was to consist of civilian pensioners. The Commonwealth Department of Health planners estimated that approximately 1,000,000 were receiving old age, invalid, widows' or war pensions or were unemployed. In his original Cabinet submission Page proposed that the pensioner medical scheme provide this group with complete free care. This quickly became a settled part of government policy, with the exclusion of the unemployed.

The second class of benefit included the working class and lower middle class – the 3,000,000, consisting of 600,000 heads of household who earned between £250 and £550 a year, their 1,400,000 dependants and the 1,000,000 widows and single persons who also fell inside this income range. Most members of friendly societies fell into this category. A further 600,000 had retired from the workforce but were excluded from pensions by the means test. Medical services for this group would be provided by an extension of the existing system of lodge practice. Benefits would be subsidized, with a patient contribution of 10 to 20 per cent. As a gesture to appease medical hostility towards lodge practice the friendly societies would be required to establish ancillary benefits to include specialist consultations on a fee-for-service basis. While the friendly societies could establish separate insurance funds, based on the MBF model, for members above the means test Page was insistent that this should not undermine contract services. 'A very definite line must, however, be drawn between the two classes of Societies as there is a great difference in the cost to the Government in the two cases. Strict action along this line would facilitate amicable arrangements with the medical profession.'[38]

Finally, the 'middle classes', those earning in excess of £550 per annum, would receive a lower level of subsidy. Their benefits would be conditional on joining private insurance funds, such as the Medical Benefits Fund, providing medical benefits on a refund, fee-for-service basis. This class numbered around 3,400,000, consisting of 950,000 heads of household, 2,500,000 dependants, and 400,000 single and widowed persons. In short, the scheme was to combine the existing mixed medical system of capitation fee and fee-for-service. More than half of the population would receive its benefits on a basis calculated 'to assist in the continuance of contract practice and to enable an extended cover to be given' with the Commonwealth paying 50 per cent of capitation fees. An outline of the scheme went to Cabinet in late January 1950, with a note from Page assuring his colleagues of the consent of the Federal Council, provided that the income limits were rigorously policed. Page optimistically predicted the scheme would be running within a year.[39]

The dominant picture of the Page scheme has been of a pusillanimous government anticipating the wishes of the BMA on every score. Page proudly recalled his own prominent role as a general practitioner in Grafton in 1904 when he organized the North Eastern Medical Association to defeat and restrict the activities of the friendly societies. In his early meetings with the Federal Council Page stressed his commitment to destroying the remnants of capitation-based lodge practice, arguing that the BMA's own scheme was 'essentially an extension of that plan proposed by me in 1904'. The new scheme did widen fee-for-service practice: continuing the slow extension of excluded services. However, for most of the population, general practitioner services would remain on a capitation basis. There was some justification for the fears expressed within the BMA that Page was reversing the concessions to fee-for-service won with such difficulty from McKenna.[40]

It is clear from these early Cabinet submissions that Page saw the survival of capitation-based lodge practice fees as more than a mere interim measure, despite feeding the BMA with carefully worded hints to the contrary. Both Cabinet colleagues and bureaucratic advisers, including Goodes at the Treasury, saw cost containment as a central objective, warning of the dangers inherent in a subsidized fee-for-service scheme in the absence of rigorous – and politically unacceptable – policing of fees. Page could best achieve these dual objectives: widening the private market for medical services while containing costs, by extending contract practice to those unable at present to pay fees or maintain friendly society subscriptions. By paying 50 per cent of the capitation fees the Commonwealth would make insurance affordable and establish an incentive for wider membership.[41]

Given the similarity of the government scheme to the BMA's *A National Health Service* of 1949, the initial reaction from organized medicine was favourable. Victor Hurley, the President of the Federal Council, commented to Sir Henry Newland:

> It is difficult to reconcile the views of all persons and all states and some of our doctrinaire representatives will have to get down to tin tacks. I know you agree that we have a golden opportunity which we may never get again and if we fail to achieve a satisfactory solution now we deserve anything which may come to us in the future.[42]

Shortly after the election Grieve and Hunter had declared the profession happy with a medical benefits scheme based on subsidy of friendly society practice. BMA representatives made apparent progress, negotiating new agreements with the friendly societies, increasing income limits to realistically enforceable levels and creating new ancillary benefits to cover specialist fees.[43]

Already, however, there were rumblings from general practitioners. When the agreement went to BMA branches it received a hostile reception. While the New South Wales Branch Convention on 24 February welcomed the government's proposals on pensioner and pharmaceutical services, the delegates totally rejected any medical benefits scheme not based on fee-for-service. Page attempted to assuage these concerns with an unsuccessful plea to the large life insurance companies to enter the field to 'refute the suggestion that the effect of the proposals would be to increase the power and influence of the friendly societies'. Speaking from his department's long and unhappy experience of tensions between the Federal Council and the state branches, Metcalfe warned his minister that the Federal Council's agreement was now worthless, and recommended delay until a more acceptable alternative had been constructed. By the middle of 1950 Page's promises of an early start to the health scheme were earning public derision. The *Age* declared that 'after six months, a national health scheme is farther from reality than it was in the hands of the previous Government'.[44]

The core of the problem was administrative. Both the BMA and the government were faced with the absence of an efficient network of organizations to administer a voluntary insurance scheme. Page had no reason to love the friendly societies, but they were the only organizations with the coverage and administrative resources for a private insurance scheme. The societies had weathered the Chifley years remarkably well, given the intrusion of the Commonwealth government into many of their traditional areas, such as unemployment and sickness benefits. Their hospital funds had actually grown under the Hospital Benefits Act, supplementing the basic government benefit to provide their members with intermediate ward treatment. Their rivals, the medical benefit funds sponsored by the BMA, had made little progress. As Charles Byrne commented, 'such organizations were not established to any large extent throughout Australia. The fund which had been in operation in NSW for some three or four years had a very small membership'.[45] Byrne concluded that:

> the Government's proposals would greatly increase the membership of lodges and thereby the power of the lodges would be increased. Although the Conference [of the Federal Council with the Minister] ended with mutual congratulations about its success his personal opinion was that it was the most calamitous conference in which the profession in Australia had ever taken part, and that it had left the profession in the most serious position in which it had ever been.[46]

As the details of the Page scheme were released the BMA expressed increasing dismay at the privileged status won by the friendly societies. Byrne warned the Victorian branch council that despite the minister's assurances of his abhorrence of contract practice, the Page scheme could only work if it relied upon the lodges. The Pharmaceutical Guild added its concern that the medical benefits scheme would 'hand control to the lodges, and could make the friendly society dispensaries powerful enough to crush us'. Mass meetings of pharmacists in Adelaide and Melbourne supported their leaders' view that 'In the Page scheme redeeming features are hard to find'.[47]

Lodge practice, which at present covered 1,700,000 members and their dependants, would swell to 3,570,000 if the Page scheme was accepted. Again, despite Page's promises to enforce the income limit rigorously, there was little chance that he would succeed where BMA pressure had been such a conspicuous failure. The new expanded friendly society contract practice would soon become universal.

Byrne renewed his earlier arguments against such inadequately means-tested schemes: a more palatable scheme could only function if it was open to anyone able to contribute.[48]

Hostility to the friendly societies and the lure of subsidized fee-for-service were even enough to tempt the BMA into modifying its earlier categorical rejection of direct contracts with the department. When Page caused further consternation in BMA ranks by threatening that, if the BMA did not come to a swift agreement the friendly societies would become the sole agents for the pensioner medical service, the Victorians responded by calling for a direct contract between the doctor and the Commonwealth Department of Health, reimbursing practitioners at concessional fee-for-service rates.[49]

## The BMA counter-attack and the end of contract practice

The possibility of shifting friendly society contracts from capitation fees to fee-for-service had been discussed seriously by BMA leaders as early as 1943. The main obstacle was financial. Under a capitation system the pool of contributions was distributed amongst the limited number of doctors on contract. Sudden increases in demand for medical services, such as epidemics, placed no extra strain on the reserves of the societies but were met by longer working hours by lodge doctors. Fee-for-service would add an unknown dimension – as demand for services rose, so would the calls on the pool of funds. Without massive financial reserves or a government subsidy such a scheme would be financially dangerous, as the limited success of the fee-for-service MBF and Bankers Health Society provided ample testimony. Instead of a complete shift to fee-for-service, BMA pressure on the societies followed the well-worn route of widening the list of excluded services, tightening the means test and encouraging supplementary insurance schemes to cover the excluded services.[50]

These calls fell on increasingly sympathetic ears. The uncertainty of the Chifley years, the slow erosion of the coverage of contract services and dismay at the strict means testing of Page's scheme all took a toll on friendly society resistance to fee-for-service. A conference of the Federal Council of the Friendly Societies Association held in Canberra in June 1950 included vigorous denunciations of means testing. The Tasmanian societies, some of which were already experimenting with limited fee-for-service insurance, attacked contract practice as out of 'line with the spirit of the times', reinforcing the old-fashioned image of the societies. In contrast to

BMA fears they saw the Page scheme as reinforcing the second class status of lodge practice: 'I want no door for friendly society patients and another for the private patient'. Fee-for-service was seen as the more desirable alternative; only the barriers of cost and the higher administrative overheads – already crippling the MBF and Bankers Health Society – inhibited the societies from a wholehearted embrace.[51]

The federal government remained a bystander through most of these arguments. Unable to win BMA acquiescence to the capitation-based scheme, Page could only plead with the friendly societies to prepare a supplementary schedule of fee-for-service benefits and hope that the BMA would eventually agree. However, neither side showed much willingness to compromise.[52]

The impasse was broken by the BMA. Led by New South Wales, each BMA state branch gave notice of an end to its Common Form of Agreement with the lodges, terminating contract practice by the end of 1950. The speed of success was directly in proportion to the strength of the friendly societies in each state. In the smaller states, with weaker lodges and a record of greater harmony between the BMA and the societies, the medical profession responded reluctantly and only after heavy pressure from the New South Wales branch and the Federal Council. Once they moved, however, the societies' resistance crumbled swiftly. In South Australia the lodges admitted their inability to police the income limit. Offered the choice of fee-for-service or strict means testing, they reluctantly accepted fee-for-service. Similarly, in Western Australia, another state in which lodge practice had never been very strong, the BMA achieved an even more rapid success. All agreements switched to fee-for-service on 1 January 1951.[53]

With its long history of conflict with the strongest friendly society movement in Australia, Victoria moved far more slowly. The BMA's own membership produced considerable resistance to a peremptory abandonment of capitation fees. Despite chidings from New South Wales for lack of action, in September 1950 the Victorian branch council argued that it would be dangerous to appeal directly to the membership to repudiate lodge agreements without a considerable period of prior education.[54]

For its own protection the profession required fee-for-service, an end to income limits and contracts – including concessional fees – and a refund system so that all payments were confined to doctor and patient without the direct involvement of the government. The branch warned:

Under these conditions, it is quite obvious that the tactics of an Aneurin Bevan would fail. It is also obvious that if the profession wishes to place itself in this invulnerable position the time is now and not when under the Earle Page scheme the lodges will be two or three times as powerful.[55]

Abandoned by the Commonwealth government, and faced with the capitulation of most of their interstate colleagues, the Victorian friendly societies eventually fell into line. The only major area of compromise was BMA agreement to establish a concessional, means-tested service for old-age pensioner members excluded from the strict means test of the Pensioner Medical Service. This would be policed by a Conjoint Committee with equal representation from the societies and the BMA. On 1 September 1951 capitation service ended in Victoria.[56]

## Towards fee-for-service

The first victim of the defeat of the friendly societies was the different classes of benefit. It would now be impossible to administer a system based on two different fee structures, so the means test was abandoned (although retained for the 'free' pensioners' service). The scheme was now to be based on a flat rate of subsidy irrespective of income or the level of contributions to a scheme. Beneficiaries would, in principle at least, all receive the same type of care; pensioners would no longer rely on crowded hospital outpatients' clinics for primary health care, and the working class patient would no longer be subject to the grudging service often associated with the lodge system.[57]

The end of contract practice did not spell a cessation of BMA hostility towards the friendly societies. In the absence of alternative health funds, the Page scheme would still move thousands into the societies, an explosion in membership which could, Charles Byrne warned, 'constitute, if there were a little organization, a huge block of people, which as a pressure group could be compared with the ACTU'. In Queensland and New South Wales this threat was met by the BMA-backed Medical Benefits Fund, which had survived its financial problems of the 1940s by contributions from BMA members. 'Failure to do likewise in Victoria', Byrne added, 'would not only weaken the profession in this State, but would also weaken the all-over Australian position'. In mid 1952 the MBF expanded to Victoria, using the Hospital Benefits Association as its agent.[58]

The private health funds were still far from strong, and they lacked the financial and membership coverage to provide a private sector based insurance scheme. At the same time, many of the friendly societies had found the transition to fee-for-service difficult. There was a danger that the BMA had been too successful in its strike against the friendly societies, weakening the one agency which could administer a privately based insurance system. Smaller societies such as the Rechabites in Victoria lost members as contributions increased, and reported 'confusion' in the administration of funds as none of the established actuarial guidelines was applicable to the unlimited liabilities of fee-for-service. In mid 1953 Page brought two of the leading American proponents of private funds to Australia, William McNay, of the Michigan Hospital Service in Detroit, and E.A. van Steenwyck, of the Associated Hospitals Service of Philadelphia. They painted a gloomy picture. The Australian health funds were financially weak and ill-prepared for a national scheme, there was too much competition, many funds were too small to remain viable, and far too much was spent on management. The societies were unlikely to solve these problems without a strong regulatory structure imposed from without.[59]

The Commonwealth Department of Health responded with far more stringent regulations on registration. The new regime restricted management expenses to no greater than 15 per cent of contributions, despite protests from the friendly societies that 20 to 25 per cent was the lowest possible, and enforced minimum membership requirements of 1,500. The first casualty was the Blue Cross Health and Insurance Society Ltd (formerly the Bankers Health Society), which had evaded Victorian government regulation by registering in the Australian Capital Territory. It was refused registration on the grounds that almost one-half its gross contributions were being eaten up in management expenses. The second regulatory intervention was to restrict competition between funds. The MBF was given a strong warning that it faced cancellation of its registration unless it ceased paying commissions to employers to win members from the other funds.[60]

While the friendly societies represented the major challenge blocking a fully fee-for-service based medical system, the BMA dealt with the smaller salaried and contract services based on occupational groups. The Yallourn Medical and Hospital Society, based on the employees of the State Electricity Commission of Victoria, had long been an object of loathing for sections of the Victorian branch. Private practitioners in Yallourn and Morwell had already successfully resisted attempts to extend the society's services to other than SEC personnel, and in late 1951 the BMA used a salary dispute as the excuse to withdraw all doctors from the society. A conflict between the board and the medical officers employed by the society led to the resignation of all but one salaried doctor. The society retaliated by ordering doctors tenanting its houses to vacate immediately and won the support of the SEC which refused to make other premises available for private practice. Realizing the gravity of the challenge, the society advertised for new salaried staff, offering increases of 50 per cent on existing levels of salary. The conflict ended with the Hospitals and Charities Commission taking over the hospital's finance, opening the way to private and intermediate beds and an end to the universal salaried service which the SEC had offered its employees.[61]

Other foes were too difficult to challenge. The main areas of contract services outside the friendly societies were in the coalfields and repatriation services to dependants of ex-servicemen. Moves from Victorian and New South Wales doctors to shift repatriation contract practice for the dependants and survivors of veterans to a fee-for-service basis were blocked by the other states. Repatriation doctors with large numbers of widows on their lists were happy with the existing arrangements.[62]

In most mining areas a contribution of between 1s. and 1s. 6d., paid directly to the doctor, ensured a complete general practitioner service for the miner and his dependants. All but the most expensive and difficult operations were included, and an extra 3d. contribution per week gave full access to hospital outpatient clinics, with full radiology and pathology services. In some regions even better conditions prevailed: Wollongong had a contract service which, for a weekly contribution of 1s. 3d., included complete medical, ambulance and hospital services, and covered specialists' fees when a patient was referred from the hospital. The unique conditions on the coalfields, and the continuing strength and militancy of the unions, despite their recent setbacks in the 1949 coal strike, led Page to conclude that 'the special case of the mining districts will need to be dealt with in a rather different manner to that in which the general population is treated'. In both New South Wales and Victoria the BMA also decided to avoid any direct challenge to contract services on the coalfields.[63]

These conflicts, however, remained sideshows to the BMA's continuing concerns at weaknesses in the political and legislative foundations of the new scheme. A major BMA concern had been the weakness of the political foundations of the scheme. To avoid certain rejection by the hostile Senate, Page had used the sweeping regulatory provisions of the National Health Act to implement both the pharmaceutical benefit scheme and the pensioner medical service. Despite its long hostility to government by regulation under Labor, the BMA acquiesced, on the understanding that a new consolidated national health act would enshrine the whole system as soon as the Senate changed hands.

The 1951 double dissolution saw Liberal–Country Party domination of both Houses, but no move from the government to carry out this pledge. Fee-for-service, the refund system and the distancing of the profession from state control were all established by regulation, and an incoming Labor administration could easily reverse these conditions by using the same expedient. Hence, there was a strong push by the BMA in mid-1952 to pressure the government to introduce new legislation and to strengthen institutions such as the MBF to make it difficult for a more hostile Commonwealth government to reverse the gains of the previous two years. It was not until the end of the following year that the Page scheme was finally given this legislative base in the National Health Act.[64]

## Hospital benefits

The shift in Commonwealth policy towards the hospitals proved one of the easier elements of the Page plan. It did little more than reorganize the hospital benefits scheme to introduce co-payment – the end of 'free hospitalization' – and reintroduce charitable means-tested public wards for the indigent. Neither provision, as we have seen, represented a major shift from the practices in force under Chifley. Again, like Labor, the new government toyed with direct involvement in capital works expenditure. Fadden had promised in his election speech to use a National Development Fund of £250 million to tackle the estimated shortfall of 70,000 beds.[65]

The hospital benefits scheme represented a major difficulty. The abolition of means testing in public wards had been a major condition of Commonwealth funding, and had seen the weakening of most of the hospital contribution funds. While Page's objectives were clear enough – to reintroduce means testing and encourage voluntary insurance – state control of the hospitals provided a major barrier to a swift change. By 1950 the 8 shillings per day benefit had been so eroded by inflation that all states were clamouring for an increase, arguing that the Commonwealth had destroyed alternative sources of finance by accepting a duty to subsidize access to hospitals. Major figures in public hospital administration, such as Sir Herbert Schlink, immediately approached the new government with pleas for the return of means testing of public hospital beds, as well as a final end to honorary practice.[66]

The first meetings between the Commonwealth and the states in August 1950 ended in an impasse. The Labor governments of Queensland and Tasmania, with their heavy political and financial stakes in free hospitals, strongly resisted the imposition of means tests. Victoria and New South Wales remained more agnostic, requesting increased funding but expressing mistrust of Commonwealth motives.[67]

As with Labor's scheme, the BMA saw this debate as rather tangential to the real needs of the hospital system, complaining that it was a problem of limited current rather than capital expenditure, for example, 'trained nurses have never been so difficult to obtain, even during the war years'. The 8s. subsidy provided under the Act covered only 20 per cent of hospital running costs.[68]

Again, the Menzies government worked within the general structure of the policies inherited from Labor. Advice from within the department even suggested that there was no need to negotiate a new agreement with the states, but that hospital funding, if any continued, could merely be an annual budgetary item. Metcalfe advised Page to make as few public references to the hospital benefits scheme as possible and hope that the problem would just go away.[69]

The growing gap between the level of Commonwealth subsidy and actual costs of beds made this policy of inaction difficult, so Page moved to restructure the benefit. In February 1951 the Commonwealth gave notice that it would terminate the existing hospital benefits agreement and passed a new act. In place of Labor's commitment to universal access and an end to the class divisions of charity wards, two classes of benefit were to be created. Canberra would continue to make an 8s. per diem payment to the states for all patients (12s. for pensioners), but only if access to public beds was means tested. Those ineligible for beds in public wards could receive a further benefit of 4 s., but only if they took out private hospital insurance giving a benefit of at least 6s. a day. Half the ordinary benefit would be paid to these patients in approved hospitals who belonged to registered hospital insurance organizations. This approach would reduce the pressure on public beds while forcing those above the rigorous means test to take out private insurance.

All states but Queensland had agreed to the new arrangements by the end of 1952. The Liberal Party-controlled states (South Australia and Western Australia) expressed strong ideological support for the return to means testing and Tasmania – despite following Queensland in abolishing honorary practice in its hospitals – lacked the financial resources to defy federal policy. The Labor states of New South Wales and Victoria also presented few problems. Neither had shown much enthusiasm for Labor's scheme which, by weakening their strong voluntary and contributory hospital arrangements, had proved a burden on state budgets. Schlink had already privately conveyed the readiness of New South Wales to accept major changes, although warning that 'they would be too frightened to put the question of the means test to their backers'. The Page scheme enabled Labor to pass the odium to the federal government and in early 1953 the New South Wales Labor government reintroduced means testing.[70]

With the strongest tradition of labourist health politics Queensland proved more recalcitrant. The Gair government refused to sign the new agreement, remaining outside the new scheme, and retaining its policy of free beds, at the cost of much of the Commonwealth subsidy. The historians of Queensland Labor have noted that Labor's hospital policies were 'the greatest policy success of the Labor leadership in the 1940s and 1950s' – so entrenched as to remain unassailable when Country–Liberal Party governments took power in 1957. By this stage the Queensland medical profession had experienced two decades of salaried sessional service in state hospitals and there was little pressure for a return to the honorary system, even though Queensland was forced to pay more for its services.[71]

The last remnants of the vision of a new relationship between public health and curative medicine faded. The Page scheme continued the subordination of health policy to problems of cost control, a mixture of budgetary and (decreasingly) medical decisions concerning the scope of schedules of benefits. A pattern soon set in of militant action from the rank and file of the BMA pressing for higher fees. The Federal Council generally responded by calling for restraint, then succumbed to the pressure. In 1955 Page admitted that the government contribution to the scheme had been largely 'mopped up' by increased fees.[72]

Nor was Page's health scheme the coherent alternative to socialized medicine that he liked to present. It was a pragmatic, unplanned set of benefit programmes cobbled together in the face of intense suspicion from the BMA. Although cost control remained central in policy-making, the Coalition government gave up much ground in order to get BMA acquiescence. Unwilling to confront organized medicine, the Commonwealth spent much of the next two decades in a vain attempt to bring the scheme under control, either restricting benefits – at growing political cost – or experimenting with ineffectual advisory committees aimed at introducing self-regulation. Having won such success in the past through blind resistance to initiatives from Canberra, the BMA (from 1962, the Australian Medical Association) was no more prepared to surrender its autonomy to the discipline of corporatism than it had under Labor. 'The aristocrat of all trade unions soon realized what a bonanza had been opened up for its members'.[73]

# CHAPTER 12

# Conclusion

The conflicts of the 1940s and 1950s left Australia with a particularly rigid set of institutions. Despite claims by the federal government and organized medicine that the Page scheme was a victory for free enterprise, it had required a major expansion of state intervention in the market for medical services. Fee-for-service was enshrined as the central principle of medical remuneration, but only at the expense of handsome subsidization by the taxpayer. Pensioners were now guaranteed free personal health care, but specialist services continued to be excluded. Rigid means testing limited access even further – with a more rigorous income test which removed health benefits from many old age pensioners.[1] At the same time the constitutional and political limits to direct control of price levels and planning of medical and hospital services set extraordinary barriers to the management of public expenditures. Hospitals remained the province of the states, with vast differences in financial arrangements, equity of access and regulation. The ambitious schemes for co-ordination of general practitioner, public health and institutional services had come to nothing.

The goals of the new system were never clear, beyond the preservation of medical autonomy from direct state control. For most of the medical opponents of the Chifley government's schemes this seemed sufficient, a perfect compromise between the rigours of the free market and the regulation of a departmentally-controlled scheme. The general practitioners of the 1930s had been caught between the constraints of a limited market for personal medical services and the threat of the expanding hospital sector. One part of this dilemma had now been resolved, at least for the moment, with federal government subsidy of medical incomes. This gave general practitioners a brief respite from economic pressures, but the focus of medical care continued to shift towards the hospitals. Some critics, such as the Royal Newcastle Hospital's medical superintendent, Chris McCaffrey, retained a wider view of the possibilities of state intervention, complaining that 'these schemes are not health policies at all, they are simply a means of making sure that doctors and hospitals get paid'. But this dissent was limited. For most doctors the future seemed certain and simple: widen benefit schedules to incorporate new procedures and services while increasing government expenditure on medical research, new technologies and on hospitals. Major changes to the limited scale of the original Page scheme resulted from advances in medical technology and new drug therapies, without challenging its basic institutional and power structures.[2]

The problems faced by both Labor and Coalition governments revolved around the relationship of the medical profession to the state. The two decades of conservative governments which followed the establishment of the Page scheme established a distinctive pattern of interest group regulation – the 'private government' of the health scheme by an intimate network of health professionals in the Commonwealth Department, private practice and the insurance funds. The BMA (which became the Australian Medical Association in 1962) had won a privileged place, with direct access to policy-making and advisory positions within the Commonwealth Department of Health. Although the profession continued to regard the federal government with considerable suspicion, policy-making developed within a closed and secretive informal network of medically-trained departmental officers and BMA leaders. The major academic study of health policymaking during the 1950s and 1960s suggested that the entrenchment of the profession in advisory committees provided a major barrier to attempts to tighten regulation of the health benefits system.[3]

Consequently, the cost control problems of the early Page scheme were never eliminated. The half-hearted attempts by Liberal–Country Party governments to regulate fees were swiftly pre-empted by the BMA raising its own recommended fee schedules before the Commonwealth could act. In the absence of a federal constitutional power over wages and prices, organized medicine retained the initiative.[4]

In these circumstances the profession and the BMA entered into a period of high membership and rising incomes, in the face of which the discontent of the early 1940s vanished. A 1964 survey of general practitioners found that 91 per cent supported the Pensioners' Medical Scheme, 94 per cent the hospital and medical benefits schemes, while all those surveyed expressed support for the pharmaceutical benefits scheme. At the same time, although the rank and file of general practitioners maintained their 'deeply ingrained sense of loyalty to the Association', suspicion of specialist dominance remained strong, with criticisms of AMA policy as 'too indefinite and mainly devoted to awaiting encroachment on professional freedom before taking action'.[5]

Surveys of general practice in the early 1960s brought out an alarming picture, although one which would have been remarkably familiar to the medical critics of the 1930s and 1940s. In 1964 the Commonwealth Department of Health and the Australian College of General Practitioners jointly sponsored a survey of the standards of general practice, based on an intensive study of a sample of 114 general practitioners. Clifford Jungfer, the author of the important Adelaide Hills study twenty years before, directed the survey. Jungfer found preventive medicine was severely neglected; there was 'little recognition by practitioners of the opportunities available for prevention at the clinical level...most practitioners regarded prevention at all levels as the responsibility of the public health authorities'. Even the better general practitioners focused their attention exclusively on organic disease to the neglect of emotional and environmental problems faced by their patients. The national health service had staved off the threat of specialism by allowing benefits for specialists' services only if patients were referred by their general practitioner. Far from being swallowed up in group practices and clinics, by the mid 1960s around 40 per cent of New South Wales general practitioners were in sole practice. This preservation of general practice occurred, however, at the cost of a remarkable – and often alarming – proportion of 'specialist' work performed by general practitioners.[6]

Sir Theodore Fox, a British visitor who drew heavily on Jungfer's research, reported that while in Britain the health system favoured the patient – at the doctor's expense – in Australia the positions were reversed. Echoing Charles Byrne's warnings of two decades before, he warned that the massive incentives for over-servicing created by subsidized fee-for-service, and the complacency of organized medicine in the face of these abuses, were preparing the ground for radical reform under a future Labor government.[7]

For those outside the safety net things were less comfortable. The inadequacies of voluntary insurance were becoming apparent. Fox noted with alarm that hospitals were using debt collection agencies to extract fees from recalcitrant former patients: 'what happens if they do not [pay] may not be pleasant...The grim thing about voluntary insurance is the penalty is often exacted from people who chance their luck or never had any'. By 1960 the proportion of the population covered by subsidized health insurance had stabilized, with around 72 per cent covered by medical benefit funds and a slightly higher proportion by hospital funds, at varying levels of adequacy. A further 10 per cent received repatriation and pensioner services, leaving a little under 20 per cent of the population without any cover at all, with even greater gaps amongst the young, the unskilled, the unemployed and less educated, and recent immigrants.[8]

The Page scheme relied for administration on the private health funds, organizations which were reshaped (in the case of the friendly societies and hospital funds) or effectively created (the medical benefit funds) by the policy of subsidy. Despite their use of a rhetoric of 'choice' and the 'market', the funds remained creatures of federal policy. With Commonwealth benefits to all but those eligible for the PMS conditional on beneficiaries taking out 'reasonable' levels of private insurance, the private funds had a guaranteed market. This system of 'farmed out' social security had been adopted as the only means of withdrawing the Commonwealth from direct responsibility for the payment of benefits. Despite their shaky beginnings, by the 1960s the five Blue Cross funds, with close links to the AMA, handled 70 per cent of insurance under the National Health Act. The friendly societies were confined to the remaining 30 per cent.[9]

Chapter 11 pointed to the inadequacies of the benefit funds at the outset of the Page scheme. If anything, many of these problems intensified in the 1960s. By 1966 federal ministers of health were receiving regular warnings that the inefficiency of the large funds and the 'risk skimming' drive for quick, government subsidized, profits by some of the newer funds could lead to 'the eventual destruction of the whole Scheme'. The excessive proportion of funds expended on administrative expenses and the impossibility of any accurate measure of over-servicing by doctors provided the political setting for Labor's shift towards compulsory, Commonwealth-administered health insurance. Even fund managers registered concern at the drift within the system, caught between the growing cost of hospital services and medical fees, both completely beyond Commonwealth control, and the public expectation that insurance should provide access to a complete health service.[10]

An essential element in the success of the Page consensus had been Labor's inability to develop a clear alternative. Shell-shocked by the defeat of 1949, and outmanoeuvred by Page when the ALP Senate majority made a final attempt to block his legislative programme, Labor merely defended its existing positions. Hamstrung by the growing sectarian conflict in its own ranks which was to lead to the split of 1955, the party had little time for new thinking. At most the Opposition leaders Evatt and Calwell went into federal elections promising a return to the Chifley health scheme and an end to the requirement of voluntary insurance to obtain Commonwealth subsidies.[11]

Whatever the problems faced by the Page scheme with cost overruns and lack of control, any attempt to develop a more radical model was unlikely to gain much support. By the mid 1960s the demographic structure of medical practitioners was heavily skewed towards those in the age cohort 35 to 50, with a disproportionately small representation of those under 35, a result of the rapid growth in the immediate postwar years. Consequently, attitudes towards state intervention were formed in the conflicts of the 1940s. Labor's policies remained too vague to offer a clear alternative to the failings of the Page scheme, but sufficiently radical to provide the AMA with a convenient threat of 'socialized medicine' to populate the nightmares of its timorous rank and file.[12]

These local fears of state control were strengthened by Australian perceptions of the British health system. From the interwar rejection of national health insurance through to more recent attacks on British socialized medicine the alleged costs and bureaucracy of the British system have provided a major armoury for the struggle against a socialized scheme. In the early 1950s these claims of cost explosions appeared justified, and were certainly accepted by British governments and Treasury. It was not until the Guillebaud Report of 1956 exposed the mythology on which this was based that a more rational debate could develop in Britain. Unfortunately, this failed to influence Australian thinking. Well into the 1980s – when international comparisons made the comparative cheapness of the NHS inescapable – the excessive cost of socialized medicine remained an article of faith. This British influence was reinforced by migration. British surveys of the 'medical brain drain' of the 1950s and early 1960s found that doctors emigrating to Australia, South Africa and Canada were far more likely to give political motives for their departure than those who moved to the United States.[13]

The success of the British NHS did register in ALP thinking, and led in the early 1960s – at a time when the party's fortunes seemed to be improving – to a return to some of the more radical themes of the 1940s. Unlike the earlier period, Labor now had medical expertise within its own ranks. Dr Moss Cass, an activist from the Victorian branch and heart surgeon at the Royal Children's Hospital, produced the most comprehensive set of proposals in a Fabian pamphlet in 1964. Pointing to the deepening problems of general practice, he argued for a salaried service, based in medical centres.[14]

The Cass scheme was a victim of Labor's electoral catastrophe of 1966. Under Whitlam the shift of the party towards electoral prag-matism led to the abandonment of such schemes which had little likelihood of AMA support. In contrast to Cass's albeit rather sketchy attempt to develop a unified health policy, Labor's new approach, identified with the Melbourne economists John Deeble and Richard Scotton, shifted attention squarely back on the issue of access to services, without any radical change in their organization. Breaking with the voluntarism of the Page scheme, Labor's Medibank revived the main themes of the 1940s. Based on national compulsory health insurance, Medibank provided universal coverage in place of the inadequate safety net of subsidized voluntary insurance. Its hospital subsidies, like those of the Chifley government, required the states to end means testing in public wards. Signalling a breach with the AMA's powerful position in policy-making over the previous two decades, the administration of the new scheme was pointedly placed in the hands of the Department of Social Security.[15]

While this marked a return to concerns for social justice, widening access and redistributing resources within the health system, Labor accepted the permanence of the structures set in place during the 1950s. Medibank was based on public subsidy of fee-for-service, although the recipients of federal money were to be made more accountable. While some of the wider goals of health policy struggled on in the Community Health Program this remained small and embattled.[16]

This is not the place for a discussion of the subsequent troubled history of relations between Australian governments and the medical profession. But there have been several regular themes. Government concerns about cost control and managerial efficiency have dominated policy discussions, while the medical profession has been divided between those prepared to accept government funding, but not the regulation of fees and incomes which follows, and those desiring a more fundamental reform of the organization, control and delivery of medical services. The latter, like their predecessors of the 1940s, have most often been left frustrated by the narrow interests of supposedly reformist governments. Public defences of Medicare, the Hawke Labor government's revival of Medibank, have concentrated on the savings it has enabled, through the elimination of unnecessary medical services and the introduction of price competition in general practice, by setting a standard, discounted fee through the system of bulk billing. The economic benefits claimed stem from restrictions on public expenditure rather than from improvements in the health of the population.[17]

Pressures on government expenditure have meant that debates over the appropriate forms of medical remuneration, apparently settled almost four decades ago, are being reopened. Proposals to revive forms of prepaid practice, such as the American model of Health Maintenance Organizations, while motivated by further cost-cutting, open wider questions than mere access to the existing pattern of services. The medical profession is 'Finally being stripped of its small shopkeeper status, medicine is now joining the ranks of modern professions which are distinguished by their technical, not their entrepreneurial autonomy'.[18]

At the same time, as internal divisions within the medical profession deepen, medical politics is moving beyond a concentration on legal regulation and the policing of abuses by individual practitioners to raise questions of consumer information and control.[19] A wider crisis of medical authority has developed, even as its technological capacities reach new heights. But a danger remains that a narrow concern with public expenditure constraint will again subvert these possibilities. As the historian Paul Starr has written, in the context of similar American debates over national health insurance:

> To make national health insurance into an instrument of cost containment – or, to use the voguish term – 'rationing' – threatens its popular appeal. For, however important appeals to efficiency have been, questions of equity have always been the true moral basis of health insurance as a social movement. Today, however, health insurance seems less like a moral cause than an argument about economic management. What once would have been a statement of social equality is now, if carried out, likely to be an effort of financial rationalization.[20]

These current concerns are a long way from the self-confident projects of nationalization in the 1940s. Even if the some of the language of preventive health, professional autonomy and cost control seems remarkably unchanging, the contents of the programmes of modern 'corporate rationalizers' and 'medical monopolists' contrast sharply with the racially inspired schemes of the national hygienists and their opponents. However, the structural problems faced by any national health policy and the options open to policy-makers have remained remarkably constant. Future reform will depend on a recognition of the extent to which these limits have been self-imposed.[21]

# Notes

## Preface

1  R.R. Alford, *Health Care Politics*, Chicago 1975, S. Duckett, 'Structural Interests and Australian Health Policy', *Social Science and Medicine*, xviii, 1984, pp.959–66.

2  E. Willis, *Medical Dominance*, Sydney 1983; T. Pensabene, *The Rise of the Medical Practitioner in Victoria*, Health Research Project Monograph 2, Canberra 1980.

3  L.J. Opit, 'The Cost of Health Care and Health Insurance in Australia: Some Problems Associated with the Fee-For-Service System', *Social Science and Medicine*, xviii, 1984, pp.967–72; M. Scott-Young, 'The Nationalization of Medicine', *Medical Journal of Australia*, Supplement, 18 Aug.1962, pp.21–5; for a more detailed version of the argument presented here see J. Gillespie, 'Medical Markets and Australian Medical Politics, 1920–45', *Labour History*, 54, May 1988.

4  T. Johnson, 'The State and the Professions: the Peculiarities of the British', in A. Giddens and G. McKenzie, *Social Class and the Division of Labour*, Cambridge 1982, p.207; P.M. Strong, 'Sociological Imperialism and the Profession of Medicine: a Critical Analysis of the Thesis of Medical Imperialism', *Social Science and Medicine*, xiii, 1979, pp. 199–215; J. Cornwall, *Hard-Earned Lives*, London 1984, pp.119–23.

5  These underlying unities in health policy have been emphasized in D.M. Fox, *Health Policies, Health Politics: The British and American Experience*, Princeton, New Jersey 1986.

## Chapter 1

1  Royal Commission on National Insurance, 'First Progress Report', *CPP*, 1925, ii, p.1302; Dr H. Lethbridge, Joint Parliamentary Committee on

Social Security (JPCSS), *Minutes of Evidence*, 16 Dec. 1942, p.535, AA CRS AA1969/10/28B; R. Scot Skirving, 'Specialists and General Practitioners: Their Education and Relationship to Each Other', *Medical Journal of Australia*, 9 August 1924, p.139; S. Macintyre, *The Oxford History of Australia, 1901–1942: The Succeeding Age*, Melbourne 1986, p.49.

2  H.M. Moran, *Beyond the Hill Lies China: Scenes from a Medical Life in Australia*, London 1945, p.79.

3  F. McCallum, *Analysis of Australian Legislation Relating to the Registration of Medical Practitioners*, Commonwealth Department of Health Service Publication no. 34, 1927, p.14; E. Willis, *Medical Dominance: The Division of Labour in Australian Health Care*, Sydney 1983, pp.92–200; T. Pensabene, *The Rise of the Medical Practitioner in Victoria*, Canberra 1980, pp.133–46; J. Templeton, *Prince Henry's: The Evolution of a Hospital, 1869–1969*, Melbourne 1969, pp.159–60; M. Lewis and R. MacLeod, 'Medical Politics and the Professionalization of Medicine in New South Wales, 1850–1901', *Journal of Australian Studies*, no.22, 1988, pp.69–82; M. Blakeney, *Australia and the Jewish Refugees, 1933–1948*, Sydney 1985, pp.188–93.

4  C. David Naylor, *Private Practice, Public Payment: Canadian Medicine and the Politics of Health Insurance 1911–1966*, Kingston and Montreal 1966, p.31; P. Starr, *The Social Transformation of American Medicine*, New York 1982, p.126.

5  W.S. Carter, 'Report on University of Melbourne Medical School, 25–31 May 1924', in 'Medical Education in Australia', typescript 1925, pp.163–4, Rockefeller Archives Center, RG 1.1 Series 410 B1; I. Maddox, 'The Doctors', in S. Macintyre, *Ormond College Centenary Essays*, Melbourne 1984, p.127; J.C. Windeyer, 'The Medical School of the University of Sydney', *Medical Journal of Australia*, 25 Oct. 1930, p. 552; JPCSS, Medical and Hospital Services Survey Sub-Committee, *Report*, i, June 1943, pp.10–20; Census, 1921 and 1933.

6  R. Back, JPCSS, *Evidence*, 16 Dec. 1942, p.523; in 1932 one-fifth of Victorian general practitioners held part-time positions as medical officers of health. The BMA published a list of recommended fees for this work, £50 per year for towns of fewer than 5,000 inhabitants with an additional £10 for each further 1,000. Many practitioners, however, earned considerably less than these amounts, contributing to the low esteem in which public health work was held. G.E. Cole, 'The Public Health Responsibilities of the General Practitioner', *Medical Journal of Australia*, 19 March 1932, p.396; BMA (NSW), *Handbook for Qualified Medical Practitioners*, Sydney 1935, pp. 95–6; JPCSS, Medical and Hospital Survey Sub-Committee, *Report*, i, pp. 10–20; H.M.Moran, *Viewless Winds*, London 1939, p.308.

7  W.G.D. Upjohn, JPCSS, *Evidence*, 4 Dec. 1942, p.492.

8  The best account of the friendly society movement in Australia is to be

found in D. Green and L. Cromwell, *Mutual Aid or Welfare State: Australia's Friendly Societies*, Sydney 1984.

9   L. Bruck, *The Sweating of the Medical Profession in Australia by the Friendly Societies in Australia*, Sydney 1896.

10   Willis, *Medical Dominance*, p.77; for a similar opinion see T. Hunter, 'Pressure Groups and the Australian Political Process', *Journal of Commonwealth and Comparative Politics*, xviii, 1980, p.194. As noted above, Green and Cromwell have recently widened our understanding of the importance of the friendly societies in providing medical services. However, they have also overestimated the extent of the defeat of the societies and the degree of BMA strength between the two world wars, *Mutual Aid or Welfare State?*, pp.130–40.

11   Commissioner of Taxation, 'Annual Report' 1936–7, CPP 1937–40, iv, p.1197.

12   D.G. Croll, Royal Commission on National Insurance, *Minutes of Evidence*, 2 Feb. 1924, q.5122. Pensabene, *The Rise of the Medical Practitioner*, chapter 9, Green and Cromwell, *Mutual Aid or Welfare State?*, give accounts which exaggerate the finality of the BMA victory. G. Williams, Royal Commission into the Remuneration of Members of the Medical Profession, *Minutes of Evidence*, 9 Aug. 1938, AA CRS AA 1969/10/2A.

13   BMA (NSW), *Handbook*, p.49; Friendly Societies of Victoria, *Fifty-First Annual Report*, 1929, p.13, D.M.Embleton, 'Symposium on the Hospital Problem', *Medical Journal of Australia*, 20 Sept. 1930, p.389.

14   Royal Commission on National Insurance, *First Progress Report*, p.1297; BMA (Vic.) Council, *Minutes*, 25 June 1947, 'Interview with Dr Wagner, former President Queensland BMA', AA CRS CP 71/10/12; Green and Cromwell, *Mutual Aid or Welfare State?*, p.140; H.J. Goodes, Memo., 10 Jan. 1944, AA CRS A1928/781/3/ pt1.

15   *Medical Journal of Australia*, 28 Jan. 1933, p.105.

16   *Medical Journal of Australia*, 4 July 1931; BMA (Vic.), 'Report of Conference between the members of Council and the Friendly Societies Association (Vic.), Confidential Circular to Secretaries of [Specialist] Sections and Sub-divisions', 1 March 1932; W.H. Best (hon. secretary, Friendly Societies of Australia), JPCSS, *Evidence*, pp.201–2; the much worse plight of Canadian doctors in the prairie provinces during the depression suggests the importance of contract practice in maintaining medical incomes in Australia: Naylor, *Private Practice, Public Payment*, chapter 4.

17   BMA (Vic.) Council, *Minutes*, 26 March 1947.

18   Dr A.E. Brown, 'Interview with Dr McCaffrey, Superintendent, Newcastle General Hospital, 1943', AA CRS CP 71/10/12; BMA (Vic.), *Annual Report*, 1932; W. Hodsdon, (Industrial Officer, Australian Workers' Union, Kalgoorlie), JPCSS, *Evidence*, p. 304; meeting of Minister for Health, Sir Earle Page with Newcastle doctors, 8 July 1950,

NLA Ms 1633/1311; BMA (NSW), *Handbook*, pp.24–7; *Australian Worker*, 1 Sept. 1937; BMA Federal Council, *Minutes*, 10 Feb. 1938, *Medical Journal of Australia*, 5 March 1938.

19   C. Thame, 'Health and the State', unpublished Ph.D. thesis, ANU 1974, p.257; the 1933 Census found 363 herbalists, 136 of whom were in Victoria where they were prominent in many country towns; A.J. and J.J. MacIntyre, *Country Towns of Victoria*, Melbourne 1944, p.130.

20   BMA (NSW), *Handbook*, p.66; BMA (Vic.), *Minutes*, 26 Oct. 1949; T. Lindsay, Royal Commission into the Remuneration of Members of the Medical Profession, *Minutes of Evidence*, 10 Aug. 1938, AA CRS AA1969/10/2A; L.L. Marshall, *The Art of General Practice*, Melbourne 1955, pp. 27–30.

21   Dr Charles Byrne, BMA (Vic.) Council, *Minutes*, 27 Jan. 1943.

22   Willis, *Medical Dominance*; M.S. Larson, *The Rise of Professionalism*, Berkeley 1977; D. Rueschemeyer, 'Professional Autonomy and the Social Construction of Expertise', in R. Dingwall and P. Lewis, *The Sociology of the Professions*, London 1983, p.40.

23   E. Friedson, 'Are Professions Necessary?', in T.L. Haskell, *The Authority of Experts: Studies in History and Theory*, Bloomington, 1984, pp.3–27; Friedson, *Professional Powers. A Study of the Institutionalization of Formal Knowledge*, Chicago, 1986; J.H. Warner, *The Therapeutic Perspective. Medical Practice, Knowledge, and Identity in America, 1820–1885*, Cambridge, Mass. 1986.

24   For an example of this combination of therapeutic advance and political interest in the formation of a specialty see R. Cooter, 'The Meaning of Fractures: Orthopaedics and the Reform of British Hospitals in the Interwar Period', *Medical History*, xxxi, 1987, pp.306–32.

25   M.T. MacEachern, *Report on the Hospital System of the State of Victoria*, Pts I–IV, Melbourne 1926–7; K. Inglis, *Hospital and Community; A History of the Royal Melbourne Hospital*, Melbourne 1958, pp.171–3, 181–2; NSW Joint Committee on Honoraries, Graduands and Patients, 'Report', *NSWPP*, 1940–1, pp.1093–4.

26   'The General Medical Practitioner', *Medical Journal of Australia*, 25 Oct. 1924, p.454.

27   J. Estcourt Hughes, *Henry Simpson Newland: A Biography*, Adelaide 1972 pp.78–80; I.Maddox, 'The Doctors', p.128; M.Hutton Neve, *This Mad Folly! The History of Australia's Women Doctors*, Sydney 1980, pp.110–1; N.Webb, 'Women and the Medical School', in J.A. Young, A.J. Sefton and N. Webb, *Centenary Book of the University of Sydney Faculty of Medicine*, Sydney 1984, pp.226–7.

28   A.M. Mitchell, *The Hospital South of the Yarra: A History of Alfred Hospital Melbourne*, Melbourne 1977, pp.150–1.

29   Sir Louis Barnett, 'President's Address', *Australian and New Zealand Journal of Surgery*, viii, 1938–9, p.13; Sir Henry Newland, 'The College of Surgeons in Australasia', *Medical Journal of Australia*, 25 Oct. 1930,

p.566; Royal Australasian College of Physicians, *Historical Calendar 1938–63*, Sydney 1963, p.iii; J.O. Smith, *The History of the Royal Australasian College of Surgeons from 1920 to 1935*, Melbourne [1971]; Sir Charles Bickerton Blackburn, 'The Growth of Specialization in Australia During 50 Years and its Significance for the Future', *Medical Journal of Australia*, 6 Jan. 1951, p.21; H. Barry, *Orthopaedics in Australia: A History of the Australian Orthopaedic Association*, Sydney 1983; I.A. McDonald, I. Cope and F.M.C. Forster, *Super Ardua: The Royal College of Obstetricians and Gynaecologists in Australia, 1929–79*, Melbourne 1981; Pensabene, *The Rise of the Medical Profession*, pp. 162–3.

30   Blackburn, 'The Growth of Specialization'; BMA (NSW), *Handbook*, p.16–17.

31   BMA (Qld), *Memorandum and Articles of Association with By-Laws and Rules Covering Procedure in Ethical Matters*, Sydney 1928, pp.37–40.

32   J. Barrett, 'Medicine in Australia and Refugees', *Australian Quarterly*, xii, March 1940, pp.14–23; D. Browne, *The Wind and the Book*, Melbourne 1976; 'Obituary: Sir Cecil Colville, 1891–1984', *Medical Journal of Australia*, 9 June 1984, p.731; Estcourt Hughes, *Henry Simpson Newland*, pp.39–41.

33   'The Capacity of a Region to Employ Doctors [Tasmania]', August 1951, AA CRS A1658/611/1/13; R.B.Scotton, 'Medical Manpower in Australia', *Medical Journal of Australia*, 13 May 1967, p. 986.

34   F.L. Davies, 'An Address', *Medical Journal of Australia*, 3 Feb. 1940, p.144; H.D.B. Miller, 'Some Pitfalls to be Avoided if Nationalization of Medicine Comes', *The Hospital Magazine*, February 1944, p. 11.

35   Willis, *Medical Dominance*, chapter 5; Royal Commission on National Insurance, *First Progress Report*, p.1270; Royal Commission on Health, *Minutes of Evidence*, Melbourne 1925, p.682; evidence of Thomas Henry Small, Royal Commission into the Remuneration of Members of the Medical Profession, *Minutes of Evidence*, 31 Aug. 1938, AA CRS AA1969/10/2B.

36   On paybeds in public hospitals, see Mitchell, *The Hospital South of the Yarra*, pp.190–3; E.W. Gault and A. Lucas, *A Century of Compassion: A History of the Austin Hospital*, Melbourne 1982, pp.111–12, 195; BMA (Vic.) Council, *Minutes*, 23 Oct. 1946; A.E. Brown, 'Interview with Dr McCaffrey'; Robert Black (a general practitioner from Petersham, Sydney), JPCSS, *Evidence*, 16 Dec. 1942, q.1319. Frank Honigsbaum has demonstrated the importance of this conflict over access to hospital patients in shaping British health politics, *The Division in British Medicine*, London 1979.

37   W.D.G. Upjohn, JPCSS, *Evidence*, 4 Dec. 1942, q.1237; *Medical Journal of Australia*, 28 Jan. 1933, pp.104–5; Rural Reconstruction Commission, *7th Report: Rural Amenities*, 25 February 1943, p.49.

38   NSW Joint Committee on Honoraries, Graduands and Patients, 'Progress Report', 2 April 1940, *NSWPP*, 1940–1, p.1124.

39 'The Care of the Sick Poor', *Medical Journal of Australia*, 23 March 1918, p.260; T. Lewis Dunn, 'National Health Services', in W.G.K. Duncan, ed., *Social Services in Australia*, Sydney 1939, p.106.

40 H.C. Colville, JPCSS, *Evidence*, 4 Dec. 1942, q.1254.

41 W. Ives and R. Mendelsohn, 'Hospitals and the State: the Thomas Report', *Australian Quarterly*, xii, 1940, pp.49–59.

42 R. Hopkins (Secretary, Hurstville Old Age and Invalid Pensioners' Association) to C.A. Kelley (Minister for Health), 28 June 1941, NSW-SA, 8/1298/H.41/279/74.

43 F. Oswald Barnett, W.O. Burt and F. Heath, *We Must Go On: A Study in Planned Reconstruction and Housing*, Melbourne 1944, p.90.

44 Inglis, *Hospital and Community*, pp.183–90; Mitchell, *The Hospital South of the Yarra*, pp. 151–2; B. Dickey, 'Health and the State in Australia 1788–1977', *Journal of Australian Studies*, no.2, 1977, pp.57–9.

45 Mildura District Hospital to Secretary, Charities Board of Victoria, 7 May 1930, VPRO, VPRS 4523/81/20/106.

46 On Queensland see C.A.C. Leggett, 'The Organization and Development of the Queensland Hospital', unpublished M.A. thesis, University of Queensland, 1974; J. Bell, 'Queensland's Public Hospital System: Some Aspects of Finance and Control', in J. Roe, ed., *Social Policy in Australia: Some Perspectives*, Sydney 1976.

47 'The Metropolitan Hospitals Contribution Fund of New South Wales', *Medical Journal of Australia*, 28 Nov. 1931, pp.695–8; H.R.R. Grieve, 'Hospital Administration in New South Wales', *Australian Quarterly*, vii, 1935, pp.15–24; H. Schlink, *The Hospital Problem of the Metropolitan and Suburban Area of Sydney*, Sydney 1940, p.7.

48 G. Mussen, *Australia's Tomorrow*, Melbourne 1944, pp.98–101; E.J. Tudor (Secretary, Department of Public Health), Royal Commission on Lotteries, 'Minutes of Evidence', *SAPP*, 1936, ii; Schlink, *The Hospital Problem*.

49 BMA (Vic.) Council, *Minutes*, 1 Aug. 1932.

50 BMA (Vic.) Council, *Minutes*, 23 Jan. 1935, 27 March 1935, 22 May 1935, 28 Aug. 1935; L. Gardiner, *Hospitals in Association: A History of the Country and Metropolitan Hospitals Association 1918–1974*, Melbourne 1977, pp.6–7; N. Hicks, 'Cure and Prevention', in A. Curthoys, A.W. Martin and T. Rowse, eds, *Australia from 1939*, Sydney 1987, p.331.

51 JPCSS, *Evidence*, 4 Dec. 1942, q.1240.

## Chapter 2

1 Joint Parliamentary Committee on Social Security (JPCSS), *Evidence*, 5 August 1941.

2 The term 'national hygiene' comes from J. Powles, 'Professional Hygienists and the Health of the Nation', in R. MacLeod, ed., *The Common-*

*wealth of Science: ANZAAS and the Scientific Enterprise in Australia 1888–1988*, Melbourne 1988, pp.292–307; M.Roe, *Nine Australian Progressives*, Brisbane 1984; K. Reiger, *The Disenchantment of the Home*, Melbourne 1985.

3    F.S. Hone, in articles written at each end of the interwar period summed up the novelty of the new preventive medicine, and how little it had penetrated everyday medical education and practice, 'Some Neglected Factors in the Prevention of Disease', *Medical Journal of Australia*, 14 Feb. 1920, and '25 Years of Preventive Medicine in Australia', *Medical Journal of Australia*, 1 July 1939, pp.12–18.

4    There are short biographies of Cumpston and Elkington in Roe, *Nine Australian Progressives* and M. Spencer, *John Howard Lidgett Cumpston 1880–1954*, Tenterfield 1987 and an overview of his career in Milton Lewis' 'Editor's Introduction' to Cumpston's important manuscript, *Health and Disease in Australia: A History*, Canberra 1988; on Hone see *Australian Dictionary of Biography* and Powles, 'Professional Hygienists and the Health of the Nation'.

5    Roe, *Nine Australian Progressives*; H. Sutton, *Lectures in Preventive Medicine*, Sydney 1944, pp.25–7.

6    B. Head and J. Walter, eds, *Intellectual Movements and Australian Society*, Melbourne 1988, p.27; Roe, *Nine Australian Progressives*; M. Lewis, *Managing Madness: Psychiatry and Society in Australia 1788–1980*, Canberra 1988, pp.128–34; on the labile character of eugenics see M. Freeden, 'Eugenics and Progressive Thought: A Study in Political Affinity', *Historical Journal*, xxii, 1979, pp.645–71; G. Jones, *Social Hygiene in Twentieth Century Britain*, Beckenham 1986; C. Bacchi, 'The Nature-Nurture Debate in Australia 1900–1914', *Historical Studies*, xix, 1980–1, p.208; S. Garton, 'Sir Charles MacKellar: Psychology, Eugenics and Child Welfare in New South Wales', *Historical Studies*, xxii, 1986, pp.24–5.

7    Powles, 'Professional Hygienists and the Health of the Nation'; and 'Naturalism and Hygiene: Fascist Affinities in Australian Public Health: 1910 to 1940', unpublished paper, 1987. This need to understand the medical context is stressed forcefully, although from a different perspective, by Margaret Spencer, *John Howard Lidgett Cumpston*, p.154.

8    The concept of medical materialism originates with William James, *The Varieties of Religious Experience*, New York 1902, pp.14–21. Reference to the reduction of forms of religious feeling to pathological causes has been subsequently developed in the sense used here by Robert Jay Lifton, *The Nazi Doctors*, London 1986, pp.482–3. On the affinities between Nazism and aspects of medical thought which rebelled against the narrowness of curative medicine – identified in Germany with the 'socialism' of health insurance – in favour of treating the 'whole organic individual', see M.H. Kater, 'Hitler's Early Doctors: Nazi Physicians in Pre-Depression Germany', *Journal of Modern History*, lix, 1987, pp.25–52.

9   R.W. Cilento, 'White Settlement in the Tropics', in P.D. Phillips and G.L. Wood, *The Peopling of Australia*, Melbourne 1928, pp.230–1.

10  For the clearest statement of the medicalization of tropical settlement see R.W. Cilento, *The White Man in the Tropics*, Commonwealth Department of Health Service Publication (Tropical Division) No.7, 1925.

11  J.M. Winter, *The Great War and the British People*, London 1986, pp.6–7; Winter and M. Teitelbaum, *The Fear of Population Decline*, New York 1985; J. Powles, 'Naturalism and Hygiene'; H. Sutton, Royal Commission on the Constitution, *Minutes of Evidence*, 2 March 1928, q.1222; R.W.Cilento to P. Cilento, 20 April 1934, Fryer Ms 44/21; R.W. Cilento to E. Hanlon, 10 July 1935, QSA, HHA/13.

12  K. Maddox, *Schlink of Prince Alfred*, Sydney 1978, p.141; R.F. Cooper, 'An Australian in Mussolini's Italy, Herbert Michael Moran', *Overland*, 115, August 1989, pp.44–53 discusses the fascist sympathies of another outspoken critic of the traditional organization of medicine; on Cumpston's reservations about a national programme of eugenics, given the limits of existing medical knowledge and administrative practicalities, Royal Commission on Child Endowment, *Minutes of Evidence*, 1929, p.612; H.R. Dew, 'National Health and Medical Research', *Medical Journal of Australia*, 3 April 1937, p.495.

13  H. McQueen, 'The Spanish Influenza Pandemic in Australia, 1918–19', in J. Roe, ed., *Social Policy in Australia*, Sydney 1976, pp.131–47; 'A Federal Ministry of Health', 'Shutting the Stable Door', *Medical Journal of Australia*, 12 Feb. 1921, 19 Nov. 1921. South Australia provided the major exception to this rule. Frank Hone and Albert Southwood both combined clinical practice with the teaching of preventive medicine and public health work, helping to bridge the gap between doctors in private practice and the concerns of public health; N. Hicks, 'Cure and Prevention', in A. Curthoys, A. Martin and T. Rowse, eds., *Australia from 1939*, Sydney 1987, p.333.

14  M. Roe, 'The Establishment of the Australian Department of Health: Its Background and Significance', *Historical Studies*, xvii, 1976–7, pp.176–192; J.H.L. Cumpston, 'The Culture of Human Life', *Australian and New Zealand Journal of Surgery*, xvi, 1945, p.7.

15  Committee Concerning the Causes of Death and Invalidity in the Commonwealth, 'Report on Tuberculosis, 19 Sept. 1916', 'Report on Venereal Diseases, 14 Dec. 1916', *CPP*, 1914–7, v; C.E.W. Bean, *In Your Hands Australians*, Melbourne 1919, p.36.

16  Roe, 'The Establishment of the Australian Department of Health'; McQueen, 'The Spanish Influenza Pandemic in Australia'; Roe, *Nine Australian Progressives*, pp.121–2.

17  G. Davison, 'The City-bred Child and Urban Reform in Melbourne 1900–1940',in P. Williams, ed., *Social Process and the City, Urban Studies Yearbook* no.1, Sydney 1983, p.163; R.W. Cilento, 'The World, My

Oyster', typescript 1972, Fryer Ms 44/4, chapter 3; Australasian Medical Congress, 11th Session, Brisbane 1920; J. Corbin, 'Remarks on Dr Hone's Article on a National Medical Service' *Medical Journal of Australia*, 1 March 1919, p.171.

18   J.H.L. Cumpston, 'The "Nationalization" of Health', *Medical Journal of Australia*, 16 August 1919; 'Quinex' [J.H.L. Cumpston], 'Medical Reform' and 'Medical Practice and Health Reform', n.d., unsourced press cuttings, probably early 1918, NLA Ms 434; see also Cumpston, 'Public Health and the Medical Practitioner', *Medical Journal of Australia*, 27 June 1925.

19   *Medical Journal of Australia*, 4 Sept. 1920, p.223.

20   J.H.L. Cumpston to V. Heiser, 27 June 1919, Rockefeller Archives Center, RF RGS/1.2/81/1147.

21   C. Lawrence, 'Incommunicable Knowledge: Science, Technology and the Clinical Art in Britain, 1850–1914', *Journal of Contemporary History*, xx, 1985, 503–20; H. MacLean, 'The Use and Abuse of Biochemical Methods in Diagnosis', in *Lectures: Melbourne Permanent Committee for Post Graduate Work* , Sydney 1930, p.105.

22   Cumpston to Sir James Barrett, 7 Dec. 1920, AA CRS A1928 443/11; W.A.Sawyer, 'The Sciences Underlying Public Health', *Australasian Medical Congress: First Session, Melbourne 1923* , Sydney 1924, pp.329–32; J.H.L. Cumpston, 'Presidential Address', Sanitary Science and Hygiene Section, Australasian Association for the Advancement of Science, 15th Meeting, Melbourne 1921, pp.4–8.

23   W.C. Sawers, *The Commonwealth Health Laboratories*, Commonwealth Department of Health, Service Publication 27, 1925; K.R. Moore, *Report on a Campaign Against Diphtheria at Bendigo, Victoria, 1923–24*, Commonwealth Department of Health Service Publication 28, 1925.

24   Cumpston to Comptroller General, Department of Trade and Customs, 6 Oct. 1920, AA CRS A1928 443/11.

25   Roe, 'The Establishment of the Australian Department of Health'; J.Gillespie, 'The Rockefeller Foundation, the Hookworm Campaign and a National Health Policy', in R. MacLeod and D. Denoon, ed., *Health and Healing in Tropical Australia*, Townsville 1991. On the priority of tropical research, and the AIF as the model of an organized response to such problems, Bean, *In Your Hands Australians*, pp.82–3; M. Roe, *Nine Australian Progressives*, pp.109–11, 131–6; Cilento, *The White Man in the Tropics*, p.68.

26   BMA (Federal Committee), Resolutions, 30 July 1919, AA CRS A457/H501/5; 'Preventive Medicine and the Medical Profession', 'A Federal Ministry of Health', *Medical Journal of Australia*, 19 April 1919, p.319, 12 Feb. 1921, p.133.

27   'A Civil Medical Service', *Medical Journal of Australia*, 11 Dec. 1920, pp.535–6.

28   Committee Concerning the Causes of Death and Invalidity in the Commonwealth, 'Report on Tuberculosis, 19 Sept. 1916', 'Report on Venereal Diseases, 14 Dec. 1916', *CPP* 1914–7, v, pp.31–2, 125; D.G. Robertson, *Inquiry into the Prevalence of Tuberculosis at Bendigo*, Commonwealth of Australia Quarantine Service Publication 19, 1920, pp.66–7; 'The Maternity Allowances Act', *Medical Journal of Australia*, 5 Aug. 1922, pp.161–2; Cumpston to Comptroller General, Department of Trade and Customs, 22 Jan. 1919, AA CRS A457/I501/Sec.1; Cumpston to Sir Neville Howse (Minister for Health), 25 Feb. 1927, NLA MS 1633/563/1; M.J. Holmes, 'Factors in the Control of Tuberculosis', National Health and Medical Research Council, First Session, Hobart, February 1937, p.5; evidence of John Dale, p.1076, J.H.L. Cumpston, pp.614–5 to Royal Commission on Child Endowment, *Minutes of Evidence*, Canberra 1929.

29   Royal Commission on National Insurance, 'First Progress Report', *CPP*, 1925, ii, p.1276.

30   F. Hone to Cumpston, 14 Nov. 1924, E.K. Bowden to Senator R.V. Wilson, 5 Nov. 1924, AA CRS A1928 195/24; Royal Commission on Health, *Report*, *CPP*, 1926–8, iv, pp.1248–370.

31   C. Thame,'Health and the State', unpublished Ph.D thesis, ANU 1974, p.307.

32   Cilento to Cumpston, 24 July 1928, AA CRS A1928 495/26/pt2; M.J. Holmes, 'Report on the Control of Tuberculosis in Australia', *Report of the Federal Health Council*,1929, pp.19–43; R. Mendelsohn, 'The Introduction of the Commonwealth–State Tuberculosis Scheme 1948–1952', in B.B. Schaffer and D.C. Corbett, *Decisions: Case Studies in Australian Administration*, Melbourne 1965; R. Walker, 'The Struggle Against Pulmonary Tuberculosis in Australia, 1788–1950', *Historical Studies*, xx, 1982–3, pp.460–1.

33   W. Ramsay Smith and J. Dale, Royal Commission on the Constitution, *Minutes of Evidence*, 31 Jan. 1928, qq.1046–7; pp. 707–8.

34   Gillespie, 'The Rockefeller Foundation, the Hookworm Campaign and a National Health Policy'; D.G. Robertson, *The Scope of Industrial Hygiene*, Commonwealth Department of Health Service Publication 20, 1922; R. Gillespie, 'The Limits of Industrial Hygiene: Commonwealth Government Initiatives in Occupational Health, 1921–48', in H. Attwood and G. Kenny, *Reflections on Medical History and Health in Australia: Third National Conference on Medical History and Health in Australia 1986*, Melbourne 1987, pp.101–120; Dame Janet Campbell, 'Report on Maternal and Child Welfare in Australia', *CPP*, 1929–30, p.1523.

35   Cumpston, memo, n.d. [late 1927], AA CRS A1928 443/11.

36   See the Annual Reports of the Repatriation Commission for the growth of its medical services, especially 1934–5, 1935–6 and 1936–7, *CPP*, 1934–7, ii, pp.473–4, 496–7 and 528–30.

37   Royal Commission of Inquiry into Fatalities at Bundaberg, 'Report, CPP, 1926–8, pp.1085–115; 'Report of Visit of Inspection to the Institute by Dr Cilento', 30 July 1928, AA CRS A1928 575/20; Anstey quoted in L.F. Fitzhardinge, *The Little Digger: A Political Biography of William Morris Hughes*, ii, Sydney 1979, p.630.

38   Sutton, *Lectures in Preventive Medicine*, p.ix.

39   S. Alomes, '"Reasonable Men": Middle Class Reform in Australia, 1928–39', unpublished Ph.D. thesis, ANU, 1979; P. Spearritt, 'Sydney's "Slums": Middle Class Reformers and the Labour Response', *Labour History*, 26, 1974, pp.65–81; Davison, 'The City-bred Child and Urban Reform'; Dr R. Mailer, 'The Housing Problem', in J. Dale, ed., *Health Week Official Handbook 1937*, Melbourne 1937, pp.42–3.

40   E. Etheridge, *The Butterfly Caste: A Social History of Pellagra in the South*, Westport Conn. 1972, pp.105–7; Reiger, *The Disenchantment of the Home*, pp.75–6; J. MacNicoll, *The Movement for Family Allowances 1918–45: A Study in Social Policy Development*, London 1980, pp.46–60; C. Webster, 'Healthy or Hungry Thirties?', *History Workshop Journal*, 13, 1982, pp.120–3.

41   G.C.M. M'Gonigle and J. Kirby, *Poverty and Public Health*, London 1936, p.22; for the contrast between the older public health and the new cf. J. Morton, 'The Health of the State' and J. Dale, 'The Application of the Recent Discoveries Concerning Vitamins and Other Accessory Food Factors', *Medical Journal of Australia*, 8 Dec. 1919, pp. 109–10, 2 Sept. 1920, pp.267–8.

42   R.W. Cilento, *Blueprint for the Health of a Nation*, Sydney 1944, p.91.

43   R.W. Cilento, *Nutrition and Numbers: The Livingstone Lectures 1936*, Brisbane 1936, p.63.

44   Cilento, *Nutrition and Numbers*, pp.68–9.

45   On the weakness of interwar social research see S. Alomes, 'Intellectuals as Publicists: 1920s to 1940s', in Head and Walter, eds, *Intellectual Movements and Australian Society*. In 1943 Ryle moved from his clinical chair to become first Regius Professor of Social Medicine at Oxford. On his approach see D. Armstrong, *The Political Anatomy of the Body*, Cambridge 1984, pp.38–41; Ryle, 'Social Medicine: Its Meaning and Scope', *Millbank Memorial Fund Quarterly*, xxii, 1944, p.58 and 'The New Age in Medicine', in *Changing Disciplines: Lectures on the History, Methods and Motives of Social Pathology*, Oxford 1948. For a discussion of the different meanings attributed to 'social medicine' see D. Porter and R. Porter, 'What Was Social Medicine? An Historiographical Essay', *Journal of Historical Sociology*, i, 1988, pp.90–106.

46   M'Gonigle and Kirby, *Poverty and Public Health*; Dark's essays, mainly published in the *Medical Journal of Australia*, were collected in E. Dark, *Medicine and the Social Order*, Sydney 1943; H. Boyd Graham, 'The Incidence of Rheumatic Infection in Victoria', National Health and Medical Research Council, Second Session, Canberra, June 1937,

Appendix II; on the strength of environmental aetiology in tuberculosis after the first world war see F.B. Smith, *The Retreat of Tuberculosis, 1850–1950*, London 1987, pp.168–75.

47   E. Page, *Truant Surgeon*, Sydney 1963, p.373; C. Lloyd, 'The Form and Development of the United Australia Party, 1929–37', unpublished Ph.D. thesis, ANU 1984, p.242.

48   G. Bell (hon. sec., FC BMA) to Earle Page, 4 April 1935, Cabinet Submission – Health no.970, Agendum 1789, 22 May 1936, Bell to Hughes, 7 Sept. 1936, AA CRS A1920/690/1; 'The Medical Research Endowment Act', *Medical Journal of Australia*, 31 July 1937, pp.185–6; C.L. Rubenstein, 'Medical Research Policy Revisited', *Australian Journal of Public Administration*, xxxix, 1980, p.47.

49   J.H.L. Cumpston, 'Inaugural Address', NHMRC, First Session, Hobart, Feb. 1937, pp.12,15.

50   Fitzhardinge, *The Little Digger*, p.630; W.M. Hughes, *Save Our Mothers: Jubilee Memorial Fund*, Canberra 1935; Campbell, 'Report on Maternal and Child Welfare in Australia'; F.W. Clements and M. MacPherson, *The Lady Gowrie Child Centres: The Health Record*, Canberra 1945, pp.6–9; Commonwealth Department of Health, *Summary of Activities, 2 December 1936*, Canberra 1937, p.2.

51   D.H.K. Lee, 'Nutrition', *Australian Quarterly*, December 1936, p.66; F.W. Clements, *A History of Human Nutrition in Australia*, Melbourne 1986, pp.87–112, give an outline of the context in which the committee was established.

52   Cilento to Cumpston, 2 Nov. 1936, AA CRS A1928 726/3/pt2.

53   Second Report of the Advisory Committee on Nutrition, 'Second Report', *CPP*, 1934–6, iii, pp.443–56, and the 'Final Report', *CPP*, 1937–9, iv, pp.253–98; Clements, *A History of Human Nutrition in Australia*, pp.95–6, presents a critique of this early work by a participant.

54   Cumpston, memo., 27 Aug. 1936, AA CRS A1928 726/3 pt2; 'The Commonwealth Report on Nutrition', *Economic News* (Queensland Bureau of Industry), December 1939; press statement by W.M. Hughes, 5 Sept. 1936, AA CRS A1928 726/3/pt1.

55   E. Sydney Morris (Director General of Public Health, NSW), 'Physical Education – An Outline of its Aims, Scope, Methods and Organization', Appendix One, Fifth Session, NHMRC, Canberra, 15 and 16 Nov. 1938.

56   F. Hone, '25 Years of Preventive Medicine in Australia', *Medical Journal of Australia*, 1 July 1939, p.13.

57   C. Jungfer, 'Child Health in a Rural Community: Interim Report of the Adelaide Hills Children's Health Survey', NHMRC, Seventeenth Session, May 1944, Appendix II; 'The Adelaide Hills Investigation', *Medical Journal of Australia*, 28 July 1945, p.118.

# Chapter 3

1   Workers Compensation Commission of New South Wales, *1st Annual Report*, 1926–7, p.12; BMA (NSW), *Handbook for Qualified Medical Practitioners*, Sydney 1935, pp.108–17; BMA (South Australia) Annual Meeting, June 1945, *Medical Journal of Australia*, 11 Aug. 1945, p.192; G.Cass, *Workers' Benefit or Employers' Burden: Workers' Compensation in New South Wales 1880–1926*, Sydney 1983.

2   BMA (Vic.) Executive, *Minutes*, 22 Feb. 1940; 'Notice to Members', 1 March 1940; Council *Minutes*, 28 Feb. 1940, 24 April 1940.

3   K. Welch, 'The Log of the Flying Doctor', typescript 1928, Mitchell Library Ms B669.

4   BMA (SA) Annual Meeting, 25 June 1931, *Medical Journal of Australia*, 17 Oct. 1931, p.495; BMA (Vic.) Council, *Minutes*, 25 Jan. 1932, 24 Feb. 1932; Annual Meeting, 6 Dec. 1934, *Medical Journal of Australia*, 27 Jan. 1934, p.136.

5   G.M.W. Clemons, 'The Changing Face of Medical Practice', *Medical Journal of Australia*, 4 May 1946, p.610.

6   A.E. Brown, 'The Development of Australian Hospitals in the Last 50 Years', *Medical Journal of Australia*, 6 Jan. 1951, pp.40–5; R. van den Hoorn and J. Playford, 'The Adelaide Hospital Row', in D. Jaensch, *The Flinders History of South Australia: Political History*, Adelaide 1986, pp.215–25.

7   Charities Board, *Annual Reports*; on McVilly, see entry in *Australian Dictionary of Biography*; cf. the view that the board's 'independence' was 'little more than window dressing' when it came to relief for the unemployed, in sharp contrast to its hospital subsidies (which occupied 75% of the budget). G.F.R. Spenceley, 'Charity Relief in Melbourne: the Early Years of the 1930s Depression', *Monash Papers in Economic History*, no. 8, 1980.

8   B. Dickey, 'The Labor Government and Medical Services in New South Wales 1910–14', *Historical Studies*, xii, 1967, pp.541–55; W. Ives and R. Mendelsohn, 'Hospitals and the State: the Thomas Report', *Australian Quarterly*, xxii, 1940, p.50.

9   NSW Joint Committee on Honoraries, Graduands and Patients, 'Progress Report', *NSWPP*, 1940–1, p.1124.

10  F.A. Bland, 'Some Problems of Hospital Administration', *Public Administration*, iii, 1941, pp.41–6; J. McCarthy, 'The Making of a Cabinet: the Right in New South Wales 1932–39', in C. Hazlehurst, *Australian Conservatism*, Canberra 1979, pp.158–60; G. Sherington, *A Century of Caring: the Royal North Shore Hospital 1888–1988*, Sydney 1988, pp.74–5.

11  R. Markey, 'The ALP and a National Social Policy', in R. Kennedy, *Australian Welfare History*, Melbourne 1982, p.109; V. Burgmann, *In*

Our Time: Socialism and the Rise of Labor, Sydney 1985, pp.112,160; B. Dickey, 'Health and the State in Australia, 1788–1977', Journal of Australian Studies, no.2, 1977, p.58; J.R. Robertson, 'The Foundations of State Socialism in Western Australia: 1911–1916', Historical Studies, x, 1962, p.322.

12   W.G. Rimmer, Portrait of a Hospital: The Royal Hobart Hospital, Hobart 1981, pp.205–6, 210, 218–19.

13   See the editorial statements representing the views of the Federal Committee of the BMA: 'The Care of the Sick Poor', 'Hospitals and the Medical Profession', 'Hospital Administration', 'Medical Registration', Medical Journal of Australia, 23 March 1918, 27 July 1918, 10 Aug. 1918.

14   'The Tasmanian Muddle', Medical Journal of Australia, 18 Aug. 1920; Rimmer, Portrait of a Hospital, pp.223–32.

15   C. Craig, Launceston General Hospital: First Hundred Years 1863–1963, Launceston 1963, p.40; Rimmer, Portrait of a Hospital, p. 259; Medical Journal of Australia, 25 Oct. 1924.

16   Rimmer, Portrait of a Hospital, pp.274–8.

17   J.F. Gaha, 'Report on a Survey of Hospital Administration in the United Kingdom, Continent of Europe, the United States of America and South America', Tas. PP, cviii, 1935, no.26, p.14.

18   Rimmer, Portrait of a Hospital, p.279; A.G. Ogilvie, 'State Medical Services in Tasmania', Australian Quarterly, x, September 1938, p.64.

19   On Ogilvie see R. Davis, Eighty Years' Labor: The ALP in Tasmania, 1903–1983, Hobart 1983, pp.31–7; BMA (Federal Council), Minutes, 19–20 Aug. 1937, Medical Journal of Australia, 18 Sept. 1937, pp.492–3, 'Report of Visit of General Secretary to Tasmania, 1937', 12 Oct. 1937.

20   A.G. Ogilvie, 'State Medical Services in Tasmania', pp. 57–67; 'Government Medical Services in Tasmanian Country Centres', Medical Journal of Australia, 14 Dec. 1940, pp.642–3; Australian Worker, 30 June 1937; Ogilvie, 'Co-ordination of Health Services: An Outline of the Government's Proposals', in The Royal Hobart Hospital and the Health Policy of the Labor Government, Hobart 1939, pp.21–30.

21   Dr J.F. Gaha, Joint Parliamentary Committee on Social Security, Evidence, 8 Aug. 1941, p.155.

22   Clemons, 'The Changing Face of Medical Practice', p.610.

23   P.K. Jordan, 'Health and Social Welfare', in D.J. Murphy, R.B. Joyce and C.A. Hughes, Labor in Power: The Labor Party and Governments in Queensland 1915–57, Brisbane 1980, pp.312–6; J. Bell, 'Queensland's Public Hospital System: Some Aspects of Finance and Control', in J. Roe, ed., Social Policy in Australia, Some Perspectives 1901–1975, Sydney 1976, p.287; Courier, 13 Jan. 1919; correspondence in QSA, A/31606.

24   R. Markey, The Making of the Labor Party in New South Wales, 1880 to 1900, Sydney 1988, p.262.

25   J. Stopford, The Hospitals Act of 1923, Brisbane 1923, p.6.

26   Australian Labor Party (Queensland Branch) 'Mothers of Queensland: Your Duty is Clear!', Brisbane 1926; E.G. Theodore, Labour's Humane

*Practical Policy*, Brisbane 1926; W. Forgan Smith, 'Labor's Policy Speech, April 17 1935', Brisbane 1935.

27   Elkington, quoted in J.H. Waite to Wickcliffe Rose, 7 October 1917, Rockefeller Archives Center, RF RGS1.2/53/785.

28   J. Huxham (Minister for Public Instruction), 'Report on the Hospitals of the Dominion of New Zealand to W. McCormack, Home Secretary', 20 May 1920; J. Stopford, *The Hospital Act of 1923: Reply to Critics*, Brisbane 1926; T. Cochrane, *Blockade: the Queensland Loans Affair*, Brisbane 1989, pp.131–2; R.H. Robinson, *A Short History of the Failure of the Voluntary Hospital System and the Development of the District Hospital System*, Brisbane 1953, pp.3–7.

29   Hospital boards came under the Act voluntarily, in return for the bait of state funding. The changes in the administration of 'declared' hospitals could be 'subtle' where there was no challenge to the existing groups which dominated boards: D. Carment and F. Killion, *The Story of Rockhampton Hospital and those other institutions administered by the Rockhampton Hospital Board 1868–1980*, Rockhampton 1980, pp.9–15; cf. the complaints about the Labor-dominated Townsville Hospital Board's pressure on honoraries to appoint a Labor sympathizer, A. Baldwin to Elkington, 30 January 1925, AA (NSW) CRS SP1061/1/337.

30   C.E. Chuter, Memo, 18 July 1932, QSA A/27286.

31   BMA (Queensland), 'Deputation to Government', 17 June 1929, QSA A/31611; Chuter, Memo, 7 Jan. 1931, QSA A/31612.

32   On Chuter's career see *Who's Who in Australia 1938*, R. Patrick, *A History of Health and Medicine in Queensland 1824–1960*, Brisbane 1987, p.103, D. Tucker, 'Charles Edward Chuter: an Architect of Local Government in Queensland', *Queensland Geographical Journal*, 4th series, 1988.

33   Royal Commission into Public Hospitals, 'Report', *QPP*, 1930, i, pp.645–726; Chuter to J.S. Collings (State Organizer, Queensland ALP), 6 March 1931, John Oxley Library Ms OM CM/1/4.

34   E.G. Parry to L. McDonald (Secretary ALP Central Executive), Oxley Ms OM CM/1/4.

35   R.W. Cilento, 'Health and Healing', typescript, [n.d., late 1930s], pp. 8–9.

36   Thomas Price (BMA Queensland Branch President), 'An Address', *Medical Journal of Australia*, 2 Jan. 1937.

37   R. Fitzgerald and H.Thornton, *Labor in Queensland from the 1880s to 1988*, Brisbane 1989, pp.111–13.

38   C.E. Chuter to E.M.Hanlon, 18 Oct. 1933, Beresford Jones (secretary, Home Hill District Hospital) to Hanlon, 27 Aug. 1935, Bundaberg Hospital Board, *Circular*, 10 March 1936, QSA A/31619.

39   Cilento to Phyllis Cilento, 6 March 1933, Fryer Library Ms 44/21; Cilento to Cumpston 8 Aug. 1933; Patrick, *A History of Health and Medicine in Queensland*, pp.99–103.

40   *Medical Journal of Australia*, 13 April 1940.

41    Quoted in Price, 'An Address', p.11.

42    Cilento, 'Preliminary Report on the Re-organization of the Home Department to Provide for the Separate Existence or Co-existence of a Ministry of Health', 10 Dec. 1934, QSA A/3780; Memo: 'Re-organization of the Department', 15 July 1935, QSA HHA/11.

43    Ministry of Health (United Kingdom) Consultative Council on Medical and Allied Services (Dawson Committee) Interim Report on the Future Provision of Medical and Allied Services, London, 1920; D. Armstrong, The Political Anatomy of the Body, Cambridge 1984, chapter 4; 'A Civil Medical Service', Medical Journal of Australia, 11 Dec. 1920, pp.535–6.

44    On group practice in the United States, S.J. Reiser, Medicine and the Reign of Technology, Cambridge 1978, pp.146–50; A.J. Viseltear, 'C.–E.A. Winslow and his Era and His Contribution to Medical Care', in C.E. Rosenberg, Healing and History, New York 1979, pp. 218–19; Medical Journal of Australia, 10 May 1924, pp.472–3; on Australian pilgrims to the Mayo Clinic see L.J.J. Nye, 'Notes on a Visit to America', Medical Journal of Australia, 15 Nov. 1924, p.520; Maddox, Schlink of Prince Alfred, p.101; James Elliot, 'The Complete Surgeon', Australian and New Zealand Journal of Surgery, vii, 1937–8, pp.179–8.

45    For a summary of these British developments see J. Lewis and B. Brookes, 'The Peckham Health Centre, "PEP", and the Concept of General Practice During the 1930s and 1940s', Medical History, xxvii, 1983, pp.151–61; and J. Lewis, Whatever Happened to Community Medicine?, Brighton 1986, pp.18–19.

46    Nye, born in Rockhampton in 1891, graduated from Sydney in 1914 and served as a medical officer in the AIF and the RAMC before entering private practice in Brisbane. 'Obituary: Leslie John Jarvis Nye, 1891 to 1976', Medical Journal of Australia, 16 Oct. 1976, p.623. L.J. Jarvis Nye, Group Practice, Sydney n.d, pp.8–11; 'Group Practice', Medical Journal of Australia, 21 Jan. 1939, pp.107–12; Price, 'An Address', p.3.

47    Quotations from J. Bostock and L.J. Jarvis Nye, Whither Away? A Study of Race Psychology and of Factors Leading to Australia's National Decline, 2nd edition, Sydney 1936, pp.1, 75, 79; R.W. Cilento, 'Nutrition and Numbers', pp.68–9. In Cilento's case this included a flirtation with extremist politics, viz. his letter to his wife 'tonight, my darling, I listened to Eric Campbell addressing the New Guard, and realised how infinitely better I could do it myself! He is an organizer but no leader and vanity will end him in nothingness within 6 months, je vous jure'. R.W. Cilento to P. Cilento, 18 Feb. 1932, Fryer Ms 44/21. Unlike Cilento, Nye later became an outspoken critic of the White Australia Policy: Nye, 'The Challenge Ahead', E.S. Meyers Memorial Lecture, Brisbane 1959.

48    R.W. Cilento to L.J. Jarvis Nye, 15 March 1943, QSA HHA/12.

49    D. Gordon, 'The Social, Political and Economic Background to the Genesis of the Faculty of Medicine', and F. Fisher, 'The Role of Sir

Raphael Cilento in the Founding and Development of the Faculty of Medicine', both in R.L. Doherty, ed., *A Medical School for Queensland*, Brisbane 1986, pp.10–15, 16–24.

50   Cilento to E.M. Hanlon, 29 July 1936, QSA HHA/11; 'Statement to the Thomas Committee (NSW)', 7 Dec. 1939, QSA HHA/12.

51   Cilento to Hanlon, 10 July 1935, QSA HHA/11.

52   Cilento, 'The World, My Oyster', typescript 1972, Fryer Ms 44/4.

53   *Report on the Muscle Re-education Clinic, Townsville (Sister E. Kenny) and its Work by R.W. Cilento*, July 1934. Patrick, *A History of Health and Medicine in Queensland*, pp.106–8; Chuter, 'Statement', 16 Jan. 1936, 'Notes on Kenny Clinic' [1936], Oxley Mss OM 65–17/3/1/6, OM 65–17/2/5; Cilento, Memo., [1935], QSA HHA/J1.

54   Chuter, 'Statement', 16 Jan. 1936, 'Notes on Kenny Clinic' [1936]; Cilento, Memo., [1935]; *Courier-Mail*, 23 Nov. 1935. There was a basis for Chuter's allegations of secret talks with the BMA. At the time when Cilento was conducting his first discussions with Chuter about moving from the Commonwealth service to Queensland, Cumpston had authorized him to accept an invitation to attend BMA hospital policy committee meetings with a 'watching brief': Cumpston to Cilento, 25 July 1933, AA CRS A1928 122/2.

55   R.H. Robinson, *For My Country: A Functional and Historical Outline of Local Government in Queensland*, Brisbane 1957, p.194.

56   Although all drafting instructions came from Chuter this does not mean that they necessarily represented his own views, QSA A/6617; Chuter to Hanlon, 19 Oct. 1936, QSA A/31762. This directly contradicts the views of Cilento's apologists who have tried to shift the responsibility for the centralization of the Queensland system on to Chuter's shoulders, cf. F. Fisher, 'Raphael West Cilento, Medical Administrator, Legislator and Visionary 1893–1945', unpublished MA thesis, University of Queensland 1984, pp.115–17.

57   Cilento, 'Brisbane Hospital – Reorganization of Staffing', 6 Dec. 1937, QSA A/27289.

58   Cilento, 'An Open Letter to Medical Men', broadsheet, 1937.

59   Brisbane and South Coast Hospitals Board, Medical Organization Committee, *Minutes*, 4 Aug. 1937.

60   Cilento, 'Preliminary Report on the Reorganization of the Home Department to Provide for the Separate Existence or Co-existence of a Ministry of Health', 10 Dec. 1934, QSA A/3780; BMA (Queensland), 'Policy for a General Medical Service', 1935.

61   *Medical Journal of Australia*, 3 Jan. 1942.

62   Patrick, *A History of Health and Medicine in Queensland*, pp.104–6.

63   BMA (Federal Council), 'Report of Visit of General Secretary to Queensland', 5 Aug. 1937.

64   NSW Joint Committee on Honoraries, Graduands and Patients, *Minutes of Evidence*, NSWPP 1940–1, i, q.487.

65   The Thomas Report in New South Wales was heavily influenced by
     many of the innovations in Queensland, especially in medical education
     (the sixth clinical year), the integration of general practitioner and
     specialist services and the professionalization of hospital administration:
     Joint Committee on the Appointment of Honorary Doctors and Gradu-
     ands for Hospitals, 'Report', *NSWPP*, 1940, pp.1093, 1098–9, 1106,
     1124, 1129. [R.W.Cilento?], 'For Ministers' Information', 1 May 1941,
     Oxley Ms, OM 64–30/Box 76.
66   Queensland People's Party, Political Education Committee, *Hospitals in
     Queensland*, Brisbane 1945.
67   H. Moran, *Viewless Winds: Being the Recollections and Digressions of an
     Australian Surgeon*, London 1939, pp.312–13.

# Chapter 4

1   J. Corbin, 'Remarks on Dr Hone's Article on a National Medical Ser-
    vice', *Medical Journal of Australia*, 1 March 1919, p.171.
2   E.R. Walker, 'National Insurance', in W.G.K. Duncan, *Social Services in
    Australia*, Sydney 1939; on interwar liberalism see T. Rowse, *Australian
    Liberalism and National Character*, Malmsbury, Vic.1978, pp.77–125; R.
    Watts, *The Foundations of the National Welfare State*, Sydney 1987,
    chapter 1. Watts has given an extended account of the 'strange death of
    national insurance' in 'The Light on the Hill: the Origins of the Aus-
    tralian Welfare State 1935–45', unpublished Ph.D. thesis, Melbourne
    University 1983, chapter 3.
3   R.G. Casey, *The Commonwealth Pensions System*, Adelaide 1935; 'Re-
    port of Investigations Abroad by Sir Frederick Stewart, Parliamentary
    Under-Secretary for Employment, 4 April 1935, *CPP*, 1934–5, iii,
    pp.1577–93.
4   'National Health Insurance', *Medical Journal of Australia*, 2 Aug. 1924,
    p.119; BMA (SA), General branch meeting, *Minutes*, 25 Aug. 1924,
    *Medical Journal of Australia*, 11 Oct. 1924; BMA (Queensland),
    'Memorandum: National (Medical) Insurance', *Medical Journal of
    Australia*, 31 May 1924, pp.548–50.
5   'The Panel Doctor', *Medical Journal of Australia*, 15.Nov. 1924, p.531;
    F.S. Hone, 'Medical Report Regarding National Health', *Medical Journal
    of Australia*, 29 Aug. 1925, pp.249–50; S.Argyle, 'Association of the
    Medical Profession with Preventive Medicine', *Medical Journal of
    Australia*, 19 Dec. 1925, pp.611–15.
6   Royal Commission on National Insurance, *Reports*, CPP, 1925, 1926–8.
    The circumstances in which this Royal Commission was established are
    a little obscure. Most commentators have echoed Denning's contem-
    porary judgement of Bruce's weakness for royal commissions as a tactic
    for postponing decision-making: suggesting that the government had

little intention of acting on its findings. W. Denning quoted in S. Macintyre, *Winners and Losers*, Sydney 1985, pp.63–5.

7   BMA (Federal Council) 'Report on National Insurance', 7 Sept. 1935, BMA (Federal Council) 24 Aug. 1936; report of meeting of BMA (Qld) branch, 8 April 1937, *Medical Journal of Australia*, 1 Jan. 1939.

8   L. Dey, 'National Health Insurance', *Medical Journal of Australia*, 10 April 1937.

9   Colin Clark, 'Bacon and Eggs for Breakfast', *Australian Quarterly*, ix, December 1937, p.24.

10  Watts, *The Foundations of the National Welfare State*, chapter 1. In 1935 Cabinet sent Stewart on a study tour to examine overseas experience. Report of Investigations Abroad by Sir Frederick Stewart, 4 Dec. 1935, *CPP*, 1934–7, iii, pp.1577–93; and pamphlets by R.G. Casey, *Australia's Vital Drift*, The Commonwealth Pensions System, Adelaide 1935.

11  F. Honigsbaum, *The Division in British Medicine*, London 1979, p.242.

12  W.J. Hudson, *Casey*, Melbourne 1986, p.104; P.R. Hart, 'J.A. Lyons: A Political Biography', unpublished Ph.D. thesis, ANU 1967, pp.253–5, 307–8; BMA (NSW) Annual Meeting, *Minutes*, 18 March 1937; Sir Walter Kinnear, 'Report on Health and Pensions Insurance', CPP, 1937, v, pp. 2217–38; N. Whiteside, 'Private Agencies for Public Purposes: Some New Perspectives on Policy Making in Health Insurance Between the Wars', *Journal of Social Policy*, xii, 1983, pp.165–94.

13  Cumpston to Senator J. Fraser, 16 Dec. 1943, AA CRS A1928 690/39/pt4.

14  C. Clark, 'Bacon and Eggs for Breakfast', pp.24, 32; Clark's views were somewhat exaggerated. One major departure from British practice has already been indicated, and the new scheme would also pool the surplus funds of the societies, another measure the British administrators had opposed. However, their general unwillingness to make concessions to local conditions became even more apparent in the mutual incomprehension experienced by both sides when they visited New Zealand, where the Labour government was introducing a comprehensive non-contributory social security system: E. Hanson, *The Politics of Social Security: the 1938 Act and Some Later Developments*, Auckland 1980, pp.47–8.

15  BMA (Federal Council) *Minutes*, 19–20 Aug. 1937, *Medical Journal of Australia*, 18 Sept. 1937, pp.492–3; BMA (NSW), Annual Meeting, *Minutes*, 1 Oct. 1937.

16  *Medical Journal of Australia*, 16 April 1938, p.719; 14 May 1938, pp.859–61; 28 May 1938, pp.943–4.

17  *Sydney Morning Herald*, 9 May 1938; Rural Reconstruction Commission, 7th Report: Rural Amenities, 25 Feb. 1943, p.48.

18  *Sydney Morning Herald*, 10 Dec. 1938. [T. Price], 'Some Aspects of the Effect of National Health Insurance on Medical Practice in Australia',

BMA (Queensland), June 1938; C. Byrne, 'How the Proposed Capitation Fee Will Affect the Profession', *The General Practitioner*, 15 June 1938.

19 *Medical Journal of Australia*, 18 June 1938, p.1075; Hunter to Casey, 21 May 1938, printed as appendix to National Insurance Commission, 'Statement Prepared by the Commissioners for Submission as Evidence by the Chairman to the Royal Commission on the Remuneration of Medical Practitioners', August 1938, p.32.

20 A. Cox (Medical Secretary, BMA London) to R.H.Todd, (Secretary, Federal Committee), 20 Nov. 1930; statement, J.H.B. Walsh (Secretary, BMA Tasmania) 12 May 1932; G.C. Anderson (Medical Secretary, BMA London), to C.H.E. Lawes (hon.sec. Federal Council), 8 June 1934; 'The Organization of the Profession in Australia', BMA (NSW) Medical Politics Committee, Minutes, 28 Sept. 1937.

21 Hunter to Anderson, 16 Feb. 1938; correspondence held at BMA House, London.

22 Anderson to Hunter, 7 March 1938.

23 BMA (NSW) Council, *Minutes*, 4 Jan. 1938, 1 March 1938.

24 A. McGrath, 'The History of Medical Organization in Australia', unpublished Ph.D.thesis, University of Sydney 1974, p.450; D. Whitington, *The House Will Divide*, Melbourne 1969, pp.62–7.

25 BMA (Federal Council), 'Health Insurance and the Health of the People', National Health and Medical Research Council, Fourth Session, Brisbane, 24 and 25 May 1938. Recent accounts of the problems of National Health Insurance in Britain between the wars have shown that these fears were not groundless. The combination of Treasury control and friendly society administration led to a very restricted service: N. Whiteside, 'Private Agencies for Public Purposes', pp. 165–94; J. Harris, 'Did British Workers Want the Welfare State? G.D.H. Cole's Survey of 1942', in J. Winter, ed., *The Working Class in Modern British History*, Cambridge 1983, pp. 203–7.

26 'National Health Insurance', *Medical Journal of Australia*, 14 May 1938; 'Questions and Answers on National Health Insurance', *The General Practitioner*, 15 May 1938.

27 Charles Maier has termed these the strategies of the hedgehog and the fox: C. Maier, '"Fictitious bonds. . .of wealth and law": On the theory and practice of interest representation', in *In Search of Stability: Explorations in Historical Political Economy*, Cambridge 1987, pp.252–3.

28 The Country Party critics included H.L. Anthony, B. Corser, Arthur Fadden and Senator W. Cooper, *Commonwealth Parliamentary Debates*, 156, 26 May 1938, pp.1464–5, 27 May 1938, pp.1513–15, 1 June 1938, pp.1698–701, 23 June 1938, p.2370; *Sydney Morning Herald*, 28 May, 1, 4, 8, 16, 21, 22, 29 June 1938.

29  *Sydney Morning Herald*, 8 June 1938.
30  W. Fitchett, 'The History of an Eventful Month', *The General Practitioner*, 15 June 1938, p.47.
31  National Insurance Commission, 'Statement Prepared by the Commissioners for Submission as Evidence'.
32  BMA (NSW) Extraordinary General Meeting, *Minutes*, 5 May 1937, Council, *Minutes*, 12 May, 7 June 1937; H. Radi, P.Spearritt and E. Hinton, *Biographical Register of the New South Wales Parliament, 1901–70*, Canberra 1979, p.119.
33  Price, 'Some Aspects of the Effect of National Health Insurance'; L.S. Abrahams, evidence, Royal Commission into the Remuneration of Members of the Medical Profession, 29 Aug. 1938, AA CRS AA1969/10/2A.
34  BMA (NSW) Annual Meeting, *Minutes*, 30 March 1939, *Medical Journal of Australia*, 15 April 1939.
35  'A Monroe Doctrine for the Medical Profession', *National Insurance Newsletter*, September 1938.
36  W. Fitchett, 'The History', p.47; BMA (Queensland) Annual Meeting, 9 Dec. 1938, *Medical Journal of Australia*, 7 Jan. 1939; BMA (Tas.), Annual Meeting, 4 April 1939, *Medical Journal of Australia*, 27 May 1939, p.808.
37  *Sydney Morning Herald*, 7 May 1938; W. Fitchett, 'The History', p.42; on Fitchett's role see R. Watts, 'The Light on the Hill', p.166; 'Is There a Need for a General Practitioners' Association?', *The General Practitioner*, 15 June 1938, p. 52, 15 Nov. 1938, p.252.
38  *The General Practitioner*, 15 June 1939; 'Collective Opposition to Bureaucratic Control of Medical Practice', *The General Practitioner*, 15 Aug. 1938, pp.169–70.
39  'Audax', 'Friendly Society Control of National Health Insurance', *The General Practitioner*, 15 June 1939; Watts, 'The Light on the Hill', pp. 194–6; 'The General Practitioner', *The People Demand Repeal of the National Health Insurance Act*, Melbourne 1938; *The General Practitioner*, 15 July 1938; 'K.F', *National Health Insurance? A Short Summary of Some Important Provisions of the National Health and Pensions Insurance Act 1938 and the Method of Obtaining its Repeal*, Electoral Campaign, Non-Party Political, NSW Division, 1938.
40  Transcripts of the evidence were published in the *Medical Journal of Australia*, but most of the evidence on incomes was heard in camera.
41  *Report of Conference of the National Insurance Commission with Representatives of Bodies Interested in the Formation of Approved Societies*, Canberra, 11 and 12 July 1938, pp.3,16; *Sydney Morning Herald*, 19 July 1938; C.Byrne, 'Faults in the Medical Provisions of the National Health and Pensions Insurance Act', *The General Practitioner*, 15 Nov., 1938, pp.250–1.

42    Editorial: 'Gagged, Bound and Delivered', *The General Practitioner*, 16 June 1939.

43    *Sydney Morning Herald*, 10 Nov. 1938, 10 Dec. 1938.

44    BMA (NSW) Council, *Minutes*, 2 May 1939, 6 June 1939; 'Health Insurance and Medical Services Proposals of the Commonwealth government', *Medical Journal of Australia*, 8 April 1939, pp.558–9.

45    Compare the British and European experience of successful compromise: D. Ashford, *The Formation of the Welfare States*, London 1986, p.144.

46    *Commonwealth Parliamentary Debates*, 155, 24 May 1938, p.1329.

47    ACTU press release, 'ACTU Secretary Exposes Weakness of Federal Govt's National Insurance and Shows How Labor Can Help People', 19 Aug. 1938, ABL T14/44/4.

48    F. Castles, *The Working Class and Welfare*, Wellington and Sydney 1985, pp.93–4; P. Beilharz, 'The Labourist Tradition and the Reforming Imagination', in R.Kennedy, ed., *Australian Welfare: Historical Sociology*, Melbourne 1989, pp.138–40; G. Cass, *Workers' Benefit or Employers' Burden: Workers' Compensation in New South Wales 1880–1926*, Sydney 1983. The labour movement view may have been based on a fiscal illusion 'that "public funds" were provided by the taxation of the rich and that pensions and other benefits represented a redistribution to the very poor from the rich'. However, this point needs considerably more proof than its advocates have offered: particularly on the incidence of combined federal and state taxation and 'private' (e.g. workers' compensation) as well as public welfare expenditures in the interwar years: N.G. Butlin, A. Barnard and J.J. Pincus, *Government and Capitalism*, Sydney 1982, p.160.

49    J.H. O'Neill to C. Crofts, 17 Aug. 1936, ABL N21/65; *Trades Hall Council Bulletin*, no.5, 1937, ABL N5/810; Melbourne *Herald*, 14 August 1937; see also Queensland Trades and Labour Council, *Minutes*, 18 May 1938; T. Wright, *A Real Social Insurance Plan*, Sydney, Communist Party of Australia, June 1937, pp.13–14; H.E. B[oote], 'The National Insurance Swindle', *The Worker*, 23 June 1937. Wright's proposals were accepted as policy by the NSW Trade Union Congress in April 1938, ABL N21/60; W.H. MacKenzie and M. Hale, *National Insurance: A Burning Question: Lyons Government and the Experts, Another Barefaced Swindle*, State Unemployed and Relief Workers Council of New South Wales, 1937, p.4; *Catholic Worker*, March 1939; L.F. Crisp, *Ben Chifley*, London 1960, p.190.

50    Victorian Trades Hall Council, *Circulars to Affiliated Unions*, 28 Oct. 1938, 6.Dec. 1938; Queensland Trades and Labour Council, *Minutes*, 6 July and 10 Aug. 1938; J.Hagan, *The History of the ACTU*, Melbourne, 1981, pp.173–4.

51    Melbourne *Herald*, 4 Aug. 1938; ACTU, Emergency Committee, *Minutes*, 7 Sept. 1938, ABL ACTU N21/19; *Labour Call*, 4 Aug. 1938; *Sydney Morning Herald*, 26 April 1938, 13 July 1938; 'ACTU Secretary

Exposes Weaknesses of Federal Govt's National Insurance', ABL T14/44/4.

52   *Sydney Morning Herald*, 10 May, 10 Nov. 1938.

53   For the assertions of a financial conspiracy, see F. Green, *Servant of the House*, Melbourne 1969, p.114; G.W. Turnowetsky, 'The 1938 National Health Insurance and Pensions Legislation: Another View on Why It Failed', *Latrobe Sociology Papers*, No. 66, n.d. [1984]; cf. P. Hart, 'The Piper and the Tune', in C.Hazelhurst, ed., *Australian Conservatism: Essays in Twentieth Century Political History*, Canberra 1979, pp.136–9; *Sydney Morning Herald*, 20 June 1938.

54   R.C. Wilson to S.L. Officer, 27 Oct. 1938, Officer to Wilson, 1 Nov. 1938, ABL E256/469; *Sydney Morning Herald*, 10 May 1938.

55   Graziers' Association of NSW, Circular to Members, 19 Aug. 1938, ABL E256/469; H. Adkins (secretary, Pastoralists Association of Western Australia) to the secretary, Graziers Federal Council, 6 Aug. 1938. For examples of pastoralists' hostility to NHI see Graziers' Association Dunedoo branch, *Minutes*, 12 Nov. 1938; Rylstone branch, *Minutes*, 26 Nov. 1938, ABL E256/469. *The Worker*, 31 Aug. 1938, 1 Oct. 1938.

56   On the end of the national insurance scheme see Watts, 'The Foundations', pp.21–4.

57   *Sydney Morning Herald*, 25, 29 July 1939; Watts, 'The Foundations', pp.19–24; W.J. Hudson, *Casey*, pp.105–6; P.R.Hart, 'J.A. Lyons', pp.253–5, 307–8.

58   J.P. Major, 'An Address', *Medical Journal of Australia*, 14 Jan. 1939, pp.48–52.

59   D.R.W. Cowan, 'Gagged', *Medical Topics*, 1 May 1939.

60   F. Hone, '25 Years of Preventive Medicine', *Medical Journal of Australia*, 1 July 1939, p.17.

# Chapter 5

1   S.R. Burston, memo, 28 March 1928, AA CRS A1928 1181/48/8.

2   A. Walker, *Middle East and Far East, Australia in the War of 1939–1945*, Series 5, Medical, Canberra 1953, pp.42–4; BMA (Vic.) Council, *Minutes*, 11 Dec. 1940; Central Medical Co-ordination Committee (CMCC), *7th Report*, 26 Aug. 1940; *19th Report*, 22 July 1942. CMCC reports and minutes are in AA CRS CP94/1/bundle 23.

3   J. Newman Morris, 'Emergency Organization of the Medical Profession', *Medical Journal of Australia*, 21 Oct. 1939, pp.622–4; Walker, *Middle East and Far East*, pp.22, 8–9, 14–16; S.R.Burston, 'Co-ordination of Medical Services in War', *Medical Journal of Australia*, 9 July 1949, pp. 37–41.

4   CMCC, *Minutes*, 7 Sept. 1938, 8 Sept. 1938, 3 March 1939, J.H.L. Cumpston, 'Statement made to Commonwealth and State Ministers of Health', CMCC, *15th Report*, 22 Feb. 1942.

5   CMCC, *18th Report*, 6 June 1942; NHMRC, *Report of 7th Session*, 1–2

Nov. 1939, p.19; *Medical Journal of Australia*, CMCC, 'Report of Proceedings', 4 July 1939.

6    CMCC, *10th Report*, 25 July 1941.

7    H.N. Featonby (Chief Health Officer, Victoria), 'The General Organization of the Profession in a National Emergency', 20 July 1939. *Medical Journal of Australia*, 14 Oct. 1939, pp.586–7; BMA (NSW) Council, 'Co-ordination of Medical Services: Supply and Organization of Medical Personnel in Australia in the War Emergency', 11 Nov. 1940. This unwillingness to interfere in military control was confirmed, rather reluctantly, by Cabinet, 'The Services and the Civilian Practitioner', n.d., J. Curtin to J.M. Fraser, 15 Sept. 1944, J.M. Fraser to J. Curtin, 20 Sept. 1944, AA CRS A1928/1181/48/5.

8    Prof. Keith Inglis to President, BMA (NSW) 12 May 1941, BMA (NSW) branch records.

9    E.S. Morris, Memo to C.J. Watt (Under-secretary for Health), 22 May 1942, NSWSA 6/4491.

10    Committee on the Hospitalization and Treatment of Civilian War Casualties, *Minutes*, 16 Jan. 1942.

11    CMCC, *8th Report*, 8 Jan. 1941; on Victoria, VPRO 4523/R1/103/1005; Western Australia, Emergency Medical Services, Emergency Hospital Organization, *Admission and Discharge of Casualties*, Perth 1939; on Queensland see below.

12    JPCSS, *Minutes of Evidence*, 4 Dec. 1942, p. 489–90.

13    BMA (Vic.) Council, *Minutes*, 24 Jan. 1940, 27 Jan. 1943, 26 May 1943.

14    A.G. Butler, *The Australian Army Medical Services in the War of 1914–18*, iii, Canberra 1943, pp.738–9.

15    BMA (Vic.) Council, *Minutes*, 28 Aug. 1940, 25 Sept. 1940.

16    F. Kingsley Norris, 'Scheme for the Protection of Professional Incomes', BMA (Vic.) *Circular*, 30 Oct. 1939.

17    BMA (Vic.), Annual Meeting, 6 Dec. 1939; Council, *Minutes*, 24 Jan. 1940; Executive *Minutes*, 11 Dec. 1939; Council *Minutes*, 13 Dec. 1939; *Medical Journal of Australia*, 22 Dec. 1945, p.477.

18    A. Walker, *The Island Campaigns: Australia in the War of 1939–1945*, Series 5, *Medical*, Canberra 1957, p.252.

19    BMA(NSW) Medico-Political Committee, *Quarterly Report*, 5 Oct. 1943; Sir Gerald Mussen, *Australia's Tomorrow*, Melbourne 1944, p.111; BMA (NSW) Medico-Political Committee, *Quarterly Report*, 28 March 1944.

20    BMA (NSW), 'The Extension of Contract Medical Services', [October or November 1942].

21    Letter, *Medical Journal of Australia*, 18 Nov. 1944, p.554; BMA (NSW), 'The Organization of the Medical Profession in Australia in the War Emergency', BMA (Vic.) Council, *Minutes*, 10 Dec. 1941.

22    BMA (Vic.) Executive, *Minutes*, 13 May 1942.

23   BMA (Vic.) Council, *Minutes*, 26 Aug. 1942; BMA (NSW) Executive and Finance Committee, *Quarterly Report*, 24 March 1942.

24   Queensland, Department of Health and Home Affairs, *Report upon the Establishment and Operations of the Several Organizations for the Civil Defence of Queensland*, 1 Feb. 1941, pp.2, 9–10;  *Courier Mail*, 28 Feb. 1941; Committee of Investigation Regarding the Adequacy of Medical and Hospital Services in the City of Brisbane in the Event of Hostile Attack, *Report*, 20 Aug. 1941, QSA HHA/15; Memo. R.W. Cilento to E.M. Hanlon, 20 May 1941, QSA HHA/15.

25   BMA (Vic.) Council, *Minutes*, 13 Dec. 1944, 28 Feb. 1945. AA (Queensland) J367 55/6/3, memos. 24 April 1942, 15 May 1942, 6 July 1942; CMCC, *Minutes*, 6 June 1944.

26   *Medical Journal of Australia*, 21 Oct. 1939, p.623; A. Walker, *Middle East and Far East*, pp.58–9, 45.

27   CMCC, *14th Report*, 30 Jan. 1942.

28   Cumpston, memo, 24 April 1942, AA (Brisbane) CRS J367 55–6–3; CMCC, *15th Report*, 22 Feb. 1942, letter, Newland to Chairman, CMCC, 27 Feb. 1942, Special Meeting, 8 March 1942.

29   BMA (Vic.) Council, *Minutes*, 22 April 1942.

30   Cumpston, memo, 24 April 1942; CMCC, Progress Report on EMS, 6 June 1942; CMCC, *Minutes*, 24 Aug. 1945, AA CRS A2700XM vol. 28.

31   CMCC, *19th Report*, 22 July 1942; Report by Director General of Health to CMCC, 30 Sept. 1942; *Minutes*, 5 Dec. 1942; on the British EMS, which was based on the hospitals, see R. Titmuss, *Problems of Social Policy*, London 1950, p.473, and C. Webster, *The Health Services Since the War: Vol.1: Problems of Health Care, the National Health Service Before 1957*, London 1987, pp.22–3.

32   BMA (Vic.) Executive, *Minutes*, 13 May 1942.

33   CMCC, *Minutes*, 8 June 1943.

# Chapter 6

1   B. Dickey, *No Charity There: A Short History of Social Welfare in Australia*, Melbourne 1980, p.179 and p.180; views which stress the socialist content of Labor's schemes 'on the British model' include T. Hunter, 'Planning National Health Policy in Australia 1941–45', *Public Administration*, xliv, 1966, pp.315–32, 'Pressure Groups and the Australian Political Process: the Case of the Australian Medical Association', *Journal of Commonwealth and Comparative Politics*, xviii, 1980, pp.190–205; M. Scott-Young, 'The Nationalization of Medicine', *Medical Journal of Australia*, Supplement, 18 Aug. 1962, pp.21–5; A. McGrath, 'The Controversy over the Nationalization of Medicine,

1941–49', *Journal of the Royal Australian Historical Society*, lxxiv, 1989, pp.348–50.

2   T. Rowse, *Australian Liberalism and National Character*, Malmsbury 1978; R. Watts, *The Foundations of the National Welfare State*, Sydney 1987; C. Johnson, *The Labor Legacy*, Sydney 1989; W.J.Waters, 'Labor, Socialism and the Second World War', *Labour History*, 16, 1969, p.14.

3   C.E.W. Bean, *War Aims of a Plain Australian*, Sydney 1943, p.20.

4   Cumpston to Cilento, 27 Nov. 1940, AA CRS A1928 690/39; 'A Social Securities Programme', Cabinet Agendum 693, 1 July 1941, AA CRS A 2697, vol.1; Cumpston, *The Health of the People*, Canberra 1978, p.86.

5   Interdepartmental Committee on Reconstruction, *Minutes*, 14 March 1941; Department of Labour and National Service, 'Notes for Discussion: Social Security and Population Policy', 23 Oct. 1941, 'Women's Part in Reconstruction', 15 Oct. 1941, AA CRS A571/41/771; Watts, *The Foundations*, pp.27–34; R. Maddock and J. Penny, 'Economists at War: the Financial and Economic Committee, 1939–1949', *Australian Economic History Review*, xxiii, 1983, pp.354–66.

6   Cumpston to Newman Morris, 16 July 1941, AA CRS A1928 690/39; Cumpston to R.W Cilento, Professor H. Dew, 27 Nov. 1940, AA CRS A1928/690/39.

7   Cumpston, memo for Joint Parliamentary Committee on Social Security (JPCSS), 17 Nov. 1942, AA CRS A571/43/715.

8   E. Sydney Morris, 'The Future Outlook of Public Health', 20 March 1941, AA CRS A1928/690/39.

9   E.S. Morris, JPCSS, *Evidence*, 15 Dec. 1942, p. 509.

10   'The Example of New Zealand', *Lancet*, 2 Dec. 1944, p.723.

11   For the strength of the fear of population decline in internal NHMRC discussions see E. Sydney Morris (Director General of Public Health, NSW) to Cumpston, 20 March 1941, AA CRS A1928/690/39.

12   Cumpston to R.W. Cilento, 27 Nov. 1940; H. Dew (Royal Australasian College of Surgeons), 'Nutrition and National Fitness', 26 Feb. 1941; E. Sydney Morris, 'The Future Outlook of Public Health'; J. Newman Morris to Cumpston, 13 May 1941; AA CRS A1928/690/39; BMA (Vic.) Council, *Minutes*, 30 April 1941.

13   M.L. Mitchell, 'Report on Improvements in Public Health Administration', 17 April 1941, AA CRS A1928/690/39.

14   R.W. Cilento, 'The Future of Medical Care', 8 May 1941, AA CRS A1928/690/39.

15   Cumpston to Newman Morris, Cilento and Dew, 5 June 1941, AA CRS A1928/690/39.

16   'Recommendations of the National Health and Medical Research Council on Reorganization', sections 1–6. The report was published in full in the *Medical Journal of Australia*, 16 Aug. 1941.

17   'Recommendations', sections 5, 32 and 30.

18  Cilento, *Blueprint for the Health of a Nation*, Sydney 1944, p.57.
19  'Recommendations', sections 31, 32 and 38.
20  E.S. Morris, JPCSS, *Evidence*, 18 Dec. 1942, q. 1290.
21  JPCSS, *Evidence*, q.1290; *British Medical Journal*, 15 Dec. 1945, p.834; J. Pater, *The Making of the National Health Service*, London 1981, p.66.
22  Cumpston to Sidney V. Sewell, 11 May 1942, A1928/690/39/pt3; Cumpston, *The Health of the People*, pp.89–91; these claims have been repeated by A. McGrath, 'The History of Medical Organization in Australia', unpublished Ph.D. thesis, University of Sydney 1974, pp.473–4 and 'The Controversy over the Nationalization of Medicine', pp.348–50.
23  NHMRC, 'Recommendations', section 18.
24  Featonby and Southwood (South Australia) also joined with Cilento in dissenting from section 13, which opened the possibility of the Commonwealth appointing district health officers, while Gaha and Cilento opposed Newman Morris's amendment to section 30(4), requiring full consultation with the medical profession. As chairman, Cumpston refused publication of these dissents, only allowing them to be recorded in pencil in the confidential record of discussions; Cilento to Hanlon, 31 July 1941, QSA HHA/1; Cumpston to Mussen, 2 Jan. 1945, AA CRS A1928/690/39/pt6. Mussen's views may be found in *Australia's Tomorrow*, Melbourne 1944, pp.96–7.
25  'A Social Security Programme', Cabinet Agendum 693, 1 July 1941, AA CRS A2697 vol.1.
26  S.J. Butlin and C.B. Schedvin, *War Economy, 1942–1945*, Canberra 1977, p.337; cf. R. Maddock, who gives a more complex view of the introduction of uniform taxation, playing down the importance of war finance and emphasizing Labor's longer-term social and economic objectives, 'Unification of Income Taxes in Australia', *Australian Journal of Politics and History*, xxviii, 1982, pp.354–66.
27  Watts, *The Foundations*, pp.62–7; S. Shaver, 'Design for a Welfare State: The Joint Parliamentary Committee on Social Security', *Historical Studies*, xxii, 1987, pp.411–31.
28  Cumpston to members NHMRC, 22 Aug. 1941, AA CRS A1928 690/39/sect.1; JPCSS, *Evidence*, 28 July 1941, 5 August 1941.
29  This second report was published in full in the *Medical Journal of Australia*, 20 Dec. 1941.
30  'Outline', part III.
31  Holloway to Sewell, 23 Jan. 1942, AA CRS A1928 690/39 Sect.3.
32  Curtin to Sewell, 23 April 1942, AA CRS A1928 690/39 Sect.3.
33  Constitutional Convention, Canberra 24 Nov. to 2 Dec. 1942, pp.177–8. *Age*, 9 Dec. 1942; Sydney *Sun*, 3 Dec. 1942; Melbourne *Herald*, 14 Dec. 1942.
34  Watts, *The Foundations*, pp.88–103. 'Estimated Cost of Social Services

in Australia', 24 Dec. 1942, Agendum 414. This recommendation for the JPCSS to proceed was confirmed by the full Cabinet 13 Jan. 1943, AA CRS A2700/XM/Vol C5.

35  JPCSS, 'Sixth Interim Report', 1 July 1943, CPP, 1940–3, ii, p.819; R. Rowe (secretary, JPCSS) to Cumpston, 11 Nov. 1942.

36  Cumpston, 'Memorandum for Parliamentary Committee on Social Security', 17 Nov. 1942, AA CRS A571 43/715.

37  Dew to Cumpston, 19 Nov. 1942, AA CRS A1928/690/39/pt3; E.S. Morris, JPCSS, *Evidence*, q.1289.

38  Newland to Cumpston, 17 Nov. 1942, 20 Nov. 1942; Harold Dew to Cumpston, 19 Nov. 1942, AA CRS A1928/690/39/pt3.

39  *Smith's Weekly*, 5 Dec. 1942. The source of the account of the withdrawal of the College representatives from the NHMRC discussions is Cilento in a letter to H.C.Barnard, the chairman of the JPCSS, 26 Jan.1943, AA CRS CP 71/12/Bundle 1.

40  Cilento to Barnard, Barnard to Curtin, 5 Feb. 1943, AA CRS A571/43/715; Holloway to Curtin, 18 Feb. 1943, Curtin to Holloway, 2 March 1943, AA CRS A461/K347/1/2.

41  Barnard to Curtin, 5 Feb. 1943, A571/43/715.

42  MHSC, Interim Report, 30 April 1943 (unpublished), AA CRS CP71/11/IV 1–2; Goodes, formerly the West Australian Government Statistician, had assisted the WA branch of the BMA to prepare its case for the royal commission on the remuneration of doctors in 1938; see McGrath,'History of Medical Organization', p.462.

43  Note, 30 April 1943, AA CRS A571/43/715.

44  JPCSS, 'Sixth Interim Report,' p.873.

45  JPCSS, 'Sixth Interim Report', section 143. Again, the New Zealand example heavily influenced the committee's rejection of fee-for-service. A meeting between the committee and A.O. von Keisenberg, the secretary of the New Zealand Department of Health in February 1943, had brought out the grave fiscal and administrative problems of publicly subsidized fee-for-service. 'Report of Conference on Social Security, including Health Services', Canberra, 10 Feb. 1943, AA CRS CP71/9.

46  A.R. Southwood to Goodes, 19 July 1944, AA CRS A571 44/2395/pt1.

47  JPCSS, 'Sixth Interim Report', p.835.

48  JPCSS, 'Sixth Interim Report' section 130.

49  Cumpston, 'Memo', 22 May 1944, AA CRS A1928/690/39/sect. 5.

50  Cilento to H.C. Barnard, 26 Jan. 1943, AA CRS CP71/12/1.

51  *Medical Journal of Australia*, 31 Oct. 1942; Cumpston to Brown, 8 Dec. 1942, AA CRS A1928/690/30/pt3.

52  'Liberties Threatened on Home Front: Archbishop Simmonds Warns Against Tyrannical State Control', [1943]; Australian National Secretariat of Catholic Action, *Pattern for Peace: Statement on Reconstruction Presented to the Federal Government on Behalf of the Catholic Community*, Melbourne 1943; *Catholic Worker*, November 1943.

53   J.H.L. Cumpston to Senator J. Fraser, 16 Dec. 1943, AA CRS A1928 690/39/pt4.

54   'National Welfare: Pharmaceutical Benefits', 7 December 1943, Cabinet Agendum 572, AA CRS A2700; Resolution 2, Conference of Ministers of Health, Canberra, 6 and 7 Dec. 1943, AA CRS A461/L347/1/2. These decisions were ratified by the Premiers' Conference the following month.

55   P. Hasluck, *The Government and the People, 1942–1945*, Canberra 1970, pp.530–6, H.V. Evatt, *Post War Reconstruction: Temporary Alteration of the Constitution*, Canberra 1944, p.36.

56   JPCSS, Conference on Health Services, Canberra, 8 and 9 Dec. 1943, *Transcript of Proceedings*, p.37, AA CRS AA1969/10/26/D.

57   'Canberra Research Group', 'Commonwealth Policy Co-ordination', *Public Administration*, xiv, 1955, p.198; L.F. Crisp, *Ben Chifley*, London 1960, pp.189, 257–8; M.L. Robinson, 'Economists and Politicians: the Influence of Economic Ideas Upon Labor Politicians and Governments', 1931 to 1949, Ph.D. thesis, ANU, 1986, pp.242–3, 274.

58   Goodes to F.J. Huelin (Under-secretary for Public Health, Western Australia), 9 Feb. 1944, AA CRS A571/43/715.

59   Cumpston to Fraser, 15 Dec. 1943, AA CRS A1928/690/39/4.

60   Goodes to Huelin, 29 July 1944, AA CRS A571 44/2395 /pt1.

61   JPCSS, 'Seventh Interim Report', 15 Feb. 1944, CPP, 1943–5, ii, p.922.

62   JPCSS, 'Seventh Interim Report', p.917.

63   The unusual end to the committee's independent work is set out in *Commonwealth Parliamentary Debates*, vol. 178, 29 March 1944, pp. 2206–24.

64   The Report was published in full in the *Medical Journal of Australia*, 9 Sept. 1944; Barnard to Cumpston, 1 March 1944, AA CRS A1928/690/39/Pt5; Medical Planning Committee, *Minutes*, 27 Jan. 1944, AA CRS CP71/11/1.

65   JPCSS, 'Eighth Interim Report', 27 June, 1945, 'Ninth Interim Report', 29 July 1946, CPP, 1945–6, iii, pp.1197, 1321; Cumpston to Barnard, 6 March 1944, Newland to Cumpston, 9 March 1944, AA CRS A1928/ 690/39/pt5.

66   E.S. Meyers, 'Widen Preventive Medical Service', *Courier-Mail*, 27 Aug. 1945.

67   Cumpston, 'Notes for Mr Chifley', 21 June 1944, AA CRS A1928/690/ 39/sect.5.

68   Cumpston, 'Notes for Mr Chifley'.

69   'Memo of Meeting', Cumpston to Commonwealth medical officers, 11 July 1944, AA CRS A1928/690/39/pt5.

70   Cumpston to senior medical officers, 12 July 1944, AA CRS A1928 690/39/pt5.

71   Memo, 21 June 1944, AA CRS A1928 690/39/sect.5, BMA (Vic.) Council, *Minutes*, 22 Nov. 1944.

72   P.D. Phillips, 'Federalism and the Provision of Social Services', in J. Roe, ed., *Social Policy in Australia: Some Perspectives, 1901–1975*, Stanmore 1976, pp.257–61.

## Chapter 7

1   'Should Medical Services be Nationalized?', *The Nation's Forum of the Air*, Australian Broadcasting Commission, 15 Nov. 1944.

2   'Should Medical Services be Nationalized?'

3   T.R. Marmor and D. Thomas, 'Doctors, Politics and Pay Disputes: "Pressure Group Politics" Revisited', in T.R. Marmor, *Political Analysis and Health Care*, Cambridge 1983, p.123.

4   BMA, *Business Activities in Australia*, Melbourne 1935.

5   W.H. Fitchett, 'Chaos, Disloyalty and Revolution in the BMA?', *The General Practitioner*, 15 Jan. 1939, pp.326–7; R.D. Robin, 'The British Medical Association in Queensland: Origins and Development to 1945', BA (hons) thesis, University of Queensland 1966, pp.148–51.

6   B.M. Sutherland, 'An Address', *Medical Journal of Australia*, 28 Jan. 1933, pp.103–4; H. Grieve, (JPCSS), *Evidence*, q.1374.

7   Sewell to Curtin, 8 April 1942; Curtin to Sewell, 23 April 1942; Sewell to Curtin, 4 May 1942; Cumpston to Sewell, 11 May 1942, AA CRS A1928/690/39/pt3.

8   BMA (NSW) Council, *Minutes*, 6 Jan. 1942; Sir Alan Newton (RACS) to Fraser, 22 June 1944, AA CRS A1928 690/39 pt5; BMA (Vic.) Executive, *Minutes*, 18 Oct. 1942.

9   BMA (Vic.) Council, *Minutes*, 28 April 1943.

10   Sir Henry Newland to BMA (WA) Council, [July or August 1946]; J. Newman Morris to H. Newland, 17 July 1941, Mortlock Library MS, PRG 288/53; J. Newman Morris to Cumpston, 14 July 1941, AA CRS A1928/690/39.

11   BMA (Vic.) Council, *Minutes*, 28 April, 4 May 1943.

12   BMA (Federal Council), *Minutes*, 23–6 Aug. 1943, 1–2 Feb. 1944, *Medical Journal of Australia*, 1943, p.274; BMA (Vic.) Council, *Minutes*, 28 April 1943.

13   JPCSS, *Evidence*, 10 May 1943.

14   *Medical Journal of Australia*, 22 Nov. 1941.

15   BMA(Vic.) Executive, *Minutes*, 22 Oct. 1942.

16   BMA, *A General Medical Service for the Nation*, London 1938.

17   'A General Medical Service for Australia', para. 6.

18   'A General Medical Service for Australia', para.12; this paragraph was copied from BMA, *A General Medical Service for the Nation*, p.10.

19   'A General Medical Service for Australia', para. 37, copied from BMA, *A General Medical Service for the Nation*, pp.25–6.

20   'A General Medical Service for Australia', para. 45.

21   C. Byrne, *Proposal for the Future of Medical Practice: an Analysis of Proposed Schemes for a National Health Service and an Outline of a Scheme to Provide a Complete Medical Service for the Whole Population*, Melbourne 1943, p.13.

22   'The Medical Profession and the Future', *Medical Journal of Australia*, 3 Feb. 1940, p. 164.

23   *Medical Journal of Australia*, 9 Aug. 1941, p.143.

24   *Medical Journal of Australia*, 25 June 1938, p.1110.

25   'The Future of Medical Practice', read at a meeting of the Western Australian branch of the BMA, 19 July 1939, *Medical Journal of Australia*, 13 April 1940; Boyd gave a more extended account of his proposed salaried service in *Doctor's Conscience or All Illness is Preventable*, Sydney 1944, published with a foreword by Sir Raphael Cilento.

26   J. Gordon Hislop, Stanley Boyd, A.N. Jacobs and J.H. Young, 'The Future of Medical Practice', 28 March 1943, copy at QSA HHA/12; Boyd to Cumpston, 27 Aug. 1941, AA CRS A1928 576/5 section 1.

27   'Obituary: Arthur Edward Brown', *Medical Journal of Australia*, 25 Sept. 1976, p.507.

28   B. Moore, *The Dawn of the Health Age*, London 1911, pp.5–6.

29   A.E. Brown, *The Doctor and Tomorrow*, Sydney 1946, pp.64,78–9.

30   'A Plea for the Reorganization of the Medical Profession', read at a meeting of the Victorian branch of the BMA, 5 June 1940, *Medical Journal of Australia*, 31 Aug. 1940; Robert Black, JPCSS, *Evidence*, 16 Dec. 1942, q.1319.

31   JPCSS, *Evidence*, p.473.

32   BMA (Vic.) Council, *Minutes*, 28 May 1941.

33   *Medical Journal of Australia*, 1 Nov. 1941; meeting of Eastern suburbs sub-division, BMA (Vic.), December 1941, *Medical Journal of Australia*, 7 Mar. 1942; 'Notes of Meeting at Tumby Bay of Medical Practitioners on the Eyre Peninsula, 28 Dec. 1942', AA CRS A1928/690/39/pt3.

34   BMA (Vic.) Executive, *Minutes*, 28 Oct. 1942; JPCSS, *Evidence*, 4 Dec. 1942.

35   See entry for Dale in *Australian Dictionary of Biography*; *The General Practitioner*, 'The People Demand Repeal of the National Health Insurance Act', Melbourne 1938, pp.6–7; J. Dale, 'Social Aspects of Medicine', *Medical Journal of Australia*, 9 Aug. 1941, p.135. Kent Hughes, an old and sick man, died in December. He was the father of the conservative politician, Sir Wilfrid Kent Hughes: F. Howard, *Kent Hughes*, Melbourne 1972, p.111.

36   BMA (Vic.) Council, *Minutes*, 23 July 1941; BMA (Vic.) Branch Council, 'Proposals for a Salaried Medical Service', 7 Dec. 1941.

37   W.G. Heaslip, 'National Health', *Medical Journal of Australia*, 6 July 1946, p.10.

38   Sir Henry Newland, JPCSS, *Evidence*, 30 Nov. 1942, p.464–5, q.1254;

BMA (NSW), Annual Meeting of Delegates of Affiliated Local Associations, 1 Oct. 1943; BMA (Federal Council), 'Policy in Respect to a General Medical Service for Australia', 15 April 1943; Cilento to Cumpston, 8 May 1941, AA CRS A1928/690/39.

39   JPCSS, *Evidence*, qq 1237–8.

40   JPCSS, *Evidence*, Colville q.1254, Grieve, q.1368; H.R.R. Grieve, letter, *Medical Journal of Australia*, 15 Nov. 1941; see also G.C. Willcocks, 'Preventive Medicine: A Point of View', *Medical Journal of Australia*, 6 May 1944, p.407.

41   *Highways to Health: Talks by the BMA Spokesman*, Sydney 1941, p.66. This was a series of weekly talks prepared by the BMA (NSW) Department of Medical Sociology and Research and broadcast by the ABC.

42   Dr Roseby, BMA (Vic.) Council, *Minutes*, 24 Feb. 1943.

43   A. Brown to Cumpston, 31 Aug. 1941, AA CRS 1928/690/39/pt1; A.E. Brown, 'The Dangers of a National Salaried Medical Service', *Medical Journal of Australia*, 17 Jan. 1942; L.J.J. Nye, 'Suggested Draft for Distribution to Returned Medical Officers' Association', 15 March 1943, QSA HHA/12.

44   'Medical Practitioner', 'National Health and Medical Services', *Australian Quarterly*, xvii, March 1945, pp.14–27; BMA (Vic.) Council, *Minutes*, 23 Aug. 1944; JPCSS, *Evidence*, 18 Dec. 1942, q.1383; *Age*, 9 Dec. 1942.

45   Willcocks, 'Preventive Medicine', p.407.

46   BMA (Vic.) Council, *Minutes*, 24 Nov. 1943.

47   BMA (NSW), Resolutions of Convocation, 16 Feb. 1943.

48   BMA (Federal Council), Minutes, 15–17 March 1943, *Medical Journal of Australia*, 24 April, pp. 373–8; 22 May, p.477; 19 June 1943, p.569; BMA (NSW), 'Report on Schemes for Medical Services', 29 July 1943; Special Medical Political Meeting, 17 Aug. 1943.

49   BMA (Vic.) Council, *Minutes*, 24 Feb. 1943.

50   The most extended version of his scheme was published in 1943: C. Byrne, *Proposal for the Future of Medical Practice*.

51   BMA (Vic.) Council, *Minutes*, 27 Jan. 1943.

52   E.M. Ettelson, BMA (Vic.) Council, *Minutes*, 11 Mar. 1943; BMA (Vic.) Organization Committee, 'A Report on Suggested Improvements to the Present State of Medical Practice', 12 Jan. 1943; BMA (Vic.) Council, 'A Further Report on Suggested Improvements to the Present State of Medical Practice', 11 March 1943.

53   BMA (Vic.) Special Council Meeting, 22 and 23 Dec. 1943, *Minutes*.

54   BMA (Vic.) Special Council Meeting, 22 and 23 Dec. 1943, *Minutes*.

55   *Medical Journal of Australia*, 14 Aug. 1943, p.130.

56   BMA (Vic.), Resolutions of Convocation, 28 and 29 Jan. 1944.

57   BMA (Vic.) Council, *Minutes*, 26 July 1944.

58   BMA (Vic.) Council, *Minutes*, 26 July 1944.

59   BMA (Vic.) Council, *Minutes*, 26 July 1944.

60   George Bell to Newland, 30 June 1943, Mortlock Library Ms PRG 288/
     53; J. Hunter to G. Anderson, 15 Oct. 1943, BMA (London).
61   'The Story of a Complete Medical Service', *Medical Journal of Australia*,
     11 Aug. 1944; BMA (Vic.) Council, *Minutes*, 28 June 1944.
62   BMA (Vic.) Council, *Minutes*, 25 Oct., 8 Nov. 1944.
63   'Should Medical Services be Nationalized?', *The Nation's Forum of the
     Air*, 15 Nov. 1944.

## Chapter 8

1    JPCSS, *Minutes of Evidence*, 4 Dec. 1942, p.493.
2.   JPCSS, *Evidence*, p.495.
3    JPCSS, *Evidence*, p.497.
4    Undated marginal note, McVilly to Goodes, 30 April 1943, AA CRS
     A571/43/715.
5    T. McGuire (Bishop of Goulburn), 'Statement of the Australian Catho-
     lic Hospitals Association [to the JPCSS]', n.d. [1944], AA CRS CP71/8.
6    'Commonwealth Hospital Benefits Scheme – Honorary Medical Staff',
     Cabinet Agendum 906, 25 Aug. 1945; F. McCallum to P. Mitchell, 19
     Sept. 1945, AA CRS A1928/690/39/sect. 7.
7    'Notes on conference with the BMA on the Pharmaceutical Benefits
     Act and the Hospital Benefits Act', 16 Oct. 1945, AA CRS A1928/
     781/3/sect. 2.
8    Repatriation Commission, 'Annual Report', 1948–9, pp.4–5; Special
     Advisory Committee on Medical Services of the Repatriation Commis-
     sion, Report, *CPP*, 1950–1, ii.
9    BMA (Vic), *Newsletter*, no.9, 23 May 1946; *Age*, 31 Aug. 1944.
10   BMA (Federal Council), *Minutes*, 15–18 Oct. 1945, *Medical Journal of
     Australia*, 8 Dec. 1945, p. 410; BMA (South Australia) Annual Meet-
     ing, *Minutes*, 28 June 1945, *Medical Journal of Australia*, 11 Aug. 1945, p.
     192.
11   'Notes on Conference with the BMA on the Pharmaceutical Benefits
     Act and the Hospital Benefits Act', 16 Oct. 1945, AA CRS A1928/
     781/3/sect. 2.
12   BMA (Vic.) Council, *Minutes*, 24 April 1946.
13   BMA (Vic.) Council, *Minutes*, 28 Aug. 1946; 25 Sept. 1946.
14   BMA (Vic.) Council, *Minutes*, 26 Nov. 1947; BMA (NSW), Com-
     mittee on Payment of Specialists in Repatriation Hospitals, *Report*, 27
     Nov. 1947.
15   BMA (Vic.) Council, *Minutes*, 24 March 1948.
16   BMA (Vic.) Council, *Minutes*, 23 Feb. 1949.
17   'Commonwealth Hospital Benefits Scheme – Honorary Medical Staff',
     J.B. Chifley, 25 Aug. 1945, AA CRS A432 45/878. The Melbourne
     *Herald* provided some of the most strident warnings of imminent
     disaster, e.g. 26 July 1945, 14 Sept. 1945.

18   BMA (Vic.) Council *Minutes*, 30 Jan. 1946.
19   Senator McKenna at Conference of Health Ministers, 30 June 1948, NLA Ms 1633/1367.
20   Hanlon to F.A. Cooper, 26 Jan. 1944, QSA A/31741; *Age*, 27 July 1944, Melbourne *Herald*, 14 Sept. 1945; C.A. Kelly, 'Statement for Cabinet', 18 Aug. 1944, NSWSA 9/3040.2.
21   McVilly to W.L. Rowe, sec. Dept of Health, Vic., 17 Aug. 1944, VPRO 4523/R1/102/1001.
22   C.A. Kelly, 'Statement for Cabinet', 11 March 1946, NSWSA 9/3042.
23   C.B. McVilly to Minister of Health, 25 Sept. 1944, VPRO 4523/R1/ 111/1071; S. Duckett, 'Assuring Hospital Standards: the Introduction of Hospital Accreditation in Australia', *Australian Journal of Public Administration*, xiii, 1983, pp.385–7; *Annual Reports* of Hospitals and Charities Commission of Victoria and Hospitals Commission of NSW.
24   These moves were part of a long and eventually successful campaign by McVilly to increase his supervisory powers: *Age*, 22 Aug. 1947.
25   C.L. McVilly, 'National Health Service', 15 May 1947, memo to Victorian Minister for Health (W.H. Barry), VPRO 4523/R1/250/2188.
26   C.L. McVilly, 'National Health Service'.
27   Metcalfe to McVilly, 19 July 1948; McVilly to McKenna 6 Sept. 1948, VPRO 4523/R1/250/2188
28   Both schemes shared a relatively easy run when other health schemes of their respective governments were destroyed by medical and political opposition, partly because neither challenged the existing power structures: E. Berkowitz and K. McQuaid, *Creating the Welfare State: the Political Economy of Twentieth Century Reform*, New York 1980, pp.130–1; J.E. Rohrer, 'The Political Development of the Hill-Burton Program', *Journal of Health Policy, Politics and Law*, xii, 1987, pp.137–43.
29   M. Dickenson and C. Mason, *Hospitals and Politics: the Australian Hospital Association, 1946–86*, Canberra 1986, pp.1–11; Duckett, 'Assuring Hospital Standards', pp.387–8; S.Sax, *A Strife of Interests*, Sydney 1984, pp.118–22.

# Chapter 9

1   J.J. Dedman, 'The Labor Government in the Second World War: Part 2', *Labour History*, 22, 1972, p.49.
2   T. Hunter, 'Pharmaceutical Benefits Legislation, 1944–50', *Economic Record*, xli, 1965, pp.412–25.
3   *Commonwealth Parliamentary Debates*, 178, 31 March 1944, pp.2441, 2446. G. Haines, *The Grains and Threepenn'orths of Pharmacy: Pharmacy in New South Wales, 1788–1976*, Kilmore 1976, pp.245–6.
4   A.S. Walker, *The Island Campaigns: Australia In the War of 1939–1945, Series 5 (Medical)*, Canberra 1957, pp.260–6.
5   Drug Houses of Australia, 'To Our Shareholders', [Sydney 1938]; and

[Descriptive Brochure], March 1945, pp.15, 17–20, 37, 54–7; J.F.T. Grimwade, *A Short History of Drug Houses of Australia Limited to 1968*, Melbourne 1974, pp.26–7, 41.

6   Cumpston to A.W. McGibbony, 4 May 1943, AA CRS A1928 781/4; C.B. McGibbon, 'Medicine for All the People: Proposed Pharmaceutical Benefits Scheme', *The Hospital Magazine*, February 1944. McGibbon was the Chief Pharmacist at the Royal Melbourne Hospital.

7   'Report of Conference between the Treasurer and Representatives of the Guild, Canberra 21 Jan. 1944', AA CRS A1928 781/3/pt1; Haines, *The Grains and Threepenn'orths*, pp.238–9.

8   Caucus meeting, 24 Feb. 1944, P. Weller, ed., *Caucus Minutes 1901–1949*, iii, Melbourne 1975, p.328; *Commonwealth Parliamentary Debates*, 1 March 1944, pp.675–6.

9   A.W. McGibbony (FPSG) to Fraser, 28 April 1944; 'Memorandum to the Treasurer, J.B. Chifley, by the Federated Pharmaceutical Services Guild of Australia and the Pharmaceutical Association of Australia', [May 1944]; Fraser to McGibbony, 15 May 1944, AA CRS A1928 781/3/pt1.

10   Circular signed by 7 members of the NSW branch, Pharmaceutical Guild, 12 June 1945.

11   H.F. Wansley (president, FSDPA) to Fraser, 21 June 1945, AA CRS A1928/781/3/pt1.

12   McCallum to Chifley, 29 Aug. 1945, AA CRS A461 Q347/1/8/pt1.

13   Knowles to Cumpston, 7 Feb. 1944, AA CRS A1928/626/11.

14   Repatriation Commission, 'Dispensing for Ex-Soldiers', 1 July 1938; 'A Medical Service for Dependants of Deceased Service Personnel', *Medical Journal of Australia*, 29 Dec. 1945, p. 510.

15   Report of discussions between Central Northern Medical Association and BMA State Council regarding friendly society contract practice at Newcastle, BMA (NSW) Council, *Minutes*, 3 Aug. 1948.

16   BMA (NSW) Council, *Minutes*, 11 Jan. 1944.

17   Press statement, 30 March 1944, NLA Ms 1633/568/5.

18   'Medical Practitioner', 'National Health and Medical Services', *Australian Quarterly*, xvii, March 1945, pp.14–27; J.J. Cahill, who moved the motion condemning the scheme at the Victorian branch of the BMA, was, and remained, a strong supporter of a salaried service: BMA (Vic.) Council, *Minutes*, 15 March 1944.

19   Melbourne *Herald*, 29 Feb. 1944; S. Fancourt McDonald, letter, *Courier Mail*, 16 Feb. 1944; W.G. Heaslip, 'National Health', *Medical Journal of Australia*, 6 July 1946, p.11.

20   SCMO (Queensland) to Cumpston, 2 Feb. 1944, CRS J367 55/8/1; A.R. Southwood to Cumpston, 17 Jan. 1944, AA CRS A1928 781/4.

21   Special Council Meeting with invited representatives of Local Associations, 11 Jan. 1944; BMA (Vic.) Special Council Meeting, *Minutes*, 22–23 Dec. 1943. Clause 16 (moved as a government amendment in

the Senate) provided that: 'The Minister may, on behalf of the Commonwealth, enter into an agreement (on such terms as to remuneration, allowances and otherwise as he thinks fit) with any medical practitioner providing that the services of the medical practitioner shall be available without charge to members of the public for the purpose of furnishing prescriptions and orders for the purpose of the Act'.

22   BMA (Vic), Special Meeting of Council, *Minutes*, 10 and 24 May 1944.

23   BMA (Vic.) Council, *Minutes*, 6 July 1944; Colville to Newland, 27 Sept. 1945.

24   BMA (Vic.) Council, *Minutes*, 6 July 1944.

25   J. Fraser to Cumpston, 16 Dec. 1943, AA CRS A1928 781/3/pt1; Senior Commonwealth Medical Officer (Queensland) to Cumpston, 14 Feb. 1944, AA (Brisbane) CRS J367 55/8/1; Cumpston to Goodes, 30 April 1945, AA CRS A1928 781/3/pt1.

26   Goodes to Dr Aberdeen, 17 Aug. 1944, Cumpston to Goodes, 21 Aug. 1944, AA CRS A1928 781/3/pt1.

27   'Statement by Representatives of the Medical Profession to the Minister of Health', Canberra, 8 Dec.1943, AA CRS A1928/781/3/pt1.

28   BMA (Federal Council), *Minutes*, 12–15 March 1945, *Medical Journal of Australia*, 21 April 1945.

29   BMA (Vic.) Council, *Minutes*, 28 Feb. 1945.

30   BMA (Federal Council), *Minutes*, 15–17 Oct. 1945, *Medical Journal of Australia*, 8 Dec. 1945.

31   BMA (Vic.) Council, *Medico-Political Newsletter*, no.8, 1 Feb. 1945; BMA (Vic.) Council, *Minutes*, 10 May 1945.

32   BMA (Vic.) Council, *Minutes*, 22 March 1944.

33   The most recent account of the case is in B. Galligan, *The Politics of the High Court*, Brisbane 1987, pp.150–5.

34   Meeting of Full Cabinet , 20 Nov. 1944, Cabinet Agendum 1005, AA CRS A2700.

35   Newland to Page, 6 April 1946, Menzies to Newland, 10 April 1946, Mortlock Library Ms PRG 288/53; C. Webster, *The Health Services since the War, Vol.1: Problems of Health Care, the National Health Services Before 1957*, London 1987, p.116.

36   Page to Newland, 10 April 1946; form letter, Newland to 'Dear doctor', 30 Aug. 1946, Mortlock Library Ms PRG 288/53; the full text of the powers added by the amendment, which became section 51 (xxiiiA) of the Constitution,  read: 'the provision of maternity allowances, widows pensions, child endowment, unemployment, pharmaceutical, sickness and hospital benefits, medical and dental services (but not so as to authorize any form of civil conscription), benefits to students and family allowances'.

37   'Pharmaceutical Benefits Act 1947', Cabinet Agendum 1005C, 19 Sept. 1947, AA CRS A1658/813/1/1/pt1; BMA (Vic.) Council, *Minutes*, 23 April 1947.

38   Metcalfe to McKenna, 22 Sept. 1947, AA CRS A1658 813/1/1/pt1.

39  BMA (Vic.) Council, *Minutes*, 23 April 1947; 28 May 1947.

40  Metcalfe to McKenna, 22 Sept. 1947, AA CRS A1658/813/1/1 pt1; Cabinet Agenda 1005B, 27 May 1947, 1005C, 19 Sept. 1947, AA CRS A2700.

41  BMA (Vic.) Council, *Minutes*, 27 Aug. 1947.

42  'Report on Conference with Senator McKenna', 21 April 1947, BMA (Vic.) Council, *Minutes*, 23 April 1947.

43  BMA (Vic.) Council, *Minutes*, 23 June 1948, 28 April 1948.

44  BMA (Vic.) Council, *Minutes*, 22 April 1948.

45  BMA (Vic.) Council, *Minutes*, 26 May 1948; BMA (NSW) Council, *Minutes*, 7 Sept. 1948.

46  BMA (Vic.) Council, *Minutes*, 23 June 1948.

47  Within the leadership this opposition remained a small minority. A motion by Brown that the scheme be supported if penalties were dropped was lost 5 to 22, and another compromise scheme was lost more narrowly. BMA (Vic.) Council, *Minutes*, 28 July 1948; BMA (NSW) Medico-Political Committee, *Minutes*, 5 Oct. 1948; 11 Jan. 1949.

48  [10 doctors] to McKenna, 18 June 1948, H.H. Field-Martell to McKenna, 21 May 1948, see also A. Hamilton Dobbin to McKenna, 21 June 1948, T.S. Campbell to McKenna, 23 June 1948, R. Cilento to Chifley, 21 March 1949. Cilento, the son of Sir Raphael, conveyed his father's support. AA CRS A1658 811/1/1; BMA (Vic.) Executive, *Minutes*, 17 May 1949; BMA (NSW) Medical Political Committee, *Minutes*, 29 March 1949.

49  BMA (NSW) Council, *Minutes*, 2 Feb., 1947; Conference, 3 July 1948, AA CRS A2700/XM vol.21; BMA (Vic.) Executive, *Minutes*, 22 July 1948, Council, *Minutes*, 28 July 1948.

50  G.A. Murray, SCMO Perth, to Metcalfe, 20 Oct. 1948, Metcalfe to Murray 16 June 1948, AA CRS A1658 811/1/1; Communist Party of Australia, *Who is Robbing You of Free Medicine?*, Sydney 1948.

51  Cabinet Agenda 1005G, 1005H, 22 Feb., 1 March 1949, AA CRS A2700.

52  Cabinet Agenda, 20 July 1949, AA CRS A2700.

53  BMA v. The Commonwealth and others, 79 *Commonwealth Law Reports* 1949, p.247; B. Galligan, *Politics of the High Court*, pp.155-7.

54  Cabinet Agendum 1005J, 24 Oct. 1949, AA CRS A2700.

55  *Argus*, 8 Oct. 1949, *Age*, 8 and 10 Oct. 1949.

56  A. Finger, letter, *Medical Journal of Australia*, 9 July 1949, p.68; H.R.R. Grieve, 'The Fight against the Socialization of Medicine in Australia', *British Commonwealth Medical Conference*, Brisbane, 23 May 1950.

57  Grieve, 'The Fight'.

## Chapter 10

1  *The Health Policy of the Australian Government*, Canberra [1944].

2  *Age*, 10 March 1945.

3  G. Whitwell, *The Treasury Line*, Sydney 1986, pp.90–4; B. MacFarlane, 'Australian Postwar Economic Policy', in A. Curthoys and J. Merritt, eds, *Australia's First Cold War: Vol.1 Society, Communism and Culture*, Sydney 1984, pp.29–45.

4  H.D. Black, 'Second Thoughts on Reconstruction', *Public Administration*, iv, 1943, p.349.

5  Gunner G.G. Burgoyne, 'Doctors without Bills? A Serving Soldier's Views on the Nationalization of Medicine', *The Hospital Magazine*, June 1944, reprinted from *Salt: the Army Education Journal*; talks advocating the nationalization of health were sponsored by the Army Education Service, *Medical Journal of Australia*, 10 Oct. 1942, p.351.

6  J. Roe, 'Chivalry and Social Policy in the Antipodes', *Historical Studies*, xxii, 1987, pp.395–410; L. Wheeler, 'War, Women and Welfare', in R. Kennedy, *Australian Welfare*, Melbourne 1989, pp.172–196.

7  Australian National Secretariat of Catholic Action, *Pattern for Peace: Statement on Reconstruction Presented to the Federal Government on Behalf of the Catholic Community*, Melbourne 1943; *Catholic Action in Australia: Official Statement of the Archbishops and Bishops of Australia*, Melbourne 1947; G. Henderson, *Mr Santamaria and the Bishops*, Sydney 1982, pp.29–45.

8  ACTU Emergency Committee, *Minutes*, 12 June, 18 Sept. 1948, Interstate Executive, *Minutes*, 5 July 1948, 28 March 1949; Victorian Trades Hall Council, *Minutes*, 15 July 1948, 26 May 1949; letter, *Argus*, 2 April 1949, ABL N21/26.

9  R.L. Numbers, *Almost Persuaded: American Physicians and Compulsory Health Insurance, 1912–1920*, Baltimore 1978; Reginald Ellery, a prominent fellow-travelling psychiatrist, was denied reappointment at Melbourne's Alfred Hospital after the publication of his overly left-wing monograph *Psychiatric Aspects of Modern Warfare*, Melbourne 1945; Ellery, *The Cow Jumped Over the Moon*, Melbourne 1956, p.222; BMA (Federal Council), *The Socialized Medicine Bedside Book*, [Sydney 1949?].

10  B.W. Monahan, *An Introduction to Social Credit*, Sydney 1947; 'B.W.M', *The Problem of the Medical Profession*, Liverpool and Melbourne 1945, pp.14, 24–5, 29; *Medical Politics in Australia*, Memorandum No. 1 of the Medical Policy Association (NSW), [1946].

11  On the MPA in Britain see F. Honigsbaum, *The Division in British Medicine*, London 1979, pp.274–83.

12  Newland to E. Butler, 16 June 1949, Mortlock Library Ms PRG 288/53.

13  A.R. Southwood, 'Health in Modern Society: Some Thoughts on Medical Planning', *Public Administration*, v, 1945, pp.283–8.

14  On Metcalfe's career see *Health*, September 1960, pp.67–8.

15  F.M. Burnet, *Biological Aspects of Infectious Diseases*, Cambridge 1940. Burnet later recalled the 'almost overnight' shift of interest among 'the "bright boys", the medical scientists ambitious for fame or challenged by intellectual opportunity', from bacteriological research to molecular biology as the sulphonamides and penicillin broke the back of the

problems which had inspired medical scientists of the previous two generations. Burnet, *Changing Patterns*, Melbourne 1970, p.60.

16   Quoted in T. Sheridan, *Division of Labour: Industrial Relations in the Chifley Years, 1945–1949*, Melbourne 1989, p.36; W.J. Waters, 'Labor, Socialism and World War II', *Labour History*, 16, 1969, pp.14–19.

17   A.J. Metcalfe to N. McKenna, 25 Nov. 1947, AA CRS A1658 611/1/3.

18   BMA (Vic.) Special meeting, *Minutes*, 4 Nov. 1948.

19   BMA (Vic.) Council, *Minutes*, 26 June 1946.

20   R. Smith and M. Wearing, 'Do Australians Want the Welfare State?', *Politics*, xxii, 1987, pp.60–1.

21   Smith and Wearing, 'Do Australians Want the Welfare State?', p.61.

22   BMA (Vic.) Council, *Minutes*, 28 Jan. 1948.

23   BMA (Vic.) Council, *Minutes*, 28 Jan. 1948; Sheridan, *Division of Labour*, pp.311–2.

24   'Notes on Medical Benefits Scheme by Mr R.A. Miller, Director, Metropolitan Hospitals Contribution Fund', BMA (NSW) Council, *Minutes*, 5 Oct. 1943.

25   'Notes on Medical Benefits Scheme'; 'Report to Victorian Branch Council re meeting with Representatives of the NSW MBF', 17 Nov. 1949; for a similar judgement from rural New South Wales see BMA (NSW) Medico-Political Committee, *Report*, 16 June 1947.

26   BMA (Vic.) Council, *Minutes*, 25 July 1945.

27   BMA (Federal Council), *Minutes*, 15 to 18 Oct. 1945, *Medical Journal of Australia*, 8 Dec. 1945, p.407.

28   'A Medical Service for Dependants of Deceased Service Personnel', *Medical Journal of Australia*, 29 Dec. 1945, p.510–1.

29   BMA (Federal Council), *A National Health Service*, Melbourne, October 1949; BMA (Vic.) Council, *Minutes*, 24 Aug. 1949.

30   'Minutes of preliminary meeting of committee appointed to report in connection with the establishment of the National Medical Service', 12 July 1946, AA (Brisbane) CRS BP605/85/9/1; Memo to Dr Metcalfe, 28 Feb. 1947, AA (Brisbane) CRS BP605/85/1/1/pt1; BMA (Queensland), *Official Newsletter*, no.67, 1 Dec. 1948.

31   BMA (Queensland), Confidential Notice to Members, 16 Nov. 1948; P. Mitchell to Metcalfe, 24 Dec. 1948, AA (Brisbane) CRS BP605/85/1/1/pt1.

32   L. Hewitt to McKenna, 11 Aug. 1947, AA CRS A1658 611/1/3.

33   McKenna to L. Hewitt, 14 Aug. 1947, AA CRS A1658 611/1/3.

34   Cumpston to A.J. Metcalfe, 3 Oct. 1944, AA CRS A1928 690/39/pt6. See the hostile reports on the New Zealand scheme, T. D'Alton (Australian High Commissioner in Wellington) to Makin (A/Minister for External Affairs) 2 June 1945, AA CRS A1928/690/39/pt7; [Colin Clark] in *Economic News*, xv, Aug–Sept. 1946, pp.8–9.

35   Cabinet Minute by McKenna, 'National Health Service', Sept. or Oct. 1948, agendum no 1519, Cabinet decision, 5 Oct. 1948, AA CRS A2700.

36   The National Health Service Amendment Act 1949 altered s.6, which had rigidly and literally limited payment of benefits for services listed in the schedules to the Act, making impossible the negotiations inevitable in any workable scheme. Other minor changes allowed practitioners fined or suspended from the scheme to appeal to the Supreme Court (s.22) and increased the powers of advisory committees (s.16).

37   N. McKenna, 'Medical Benefits Scheme', Cabinet decision, 12 May 1949, AA CRS A2700 vol.37, Agendum 1519C.

38   Statutory Rule no. 92 was gazetted 25 November 1949 but no date was set for the commencement of the scheme.

## Chapter 11

1   J.R. Hay, 'The IPA and Social Policy in World War II', *Historical Studies*, xx, 1982–3, pp.198–216; P. Aimer, 'Menzies and the Birth of the Liberal Party', in C. Hazlehurst, *Australian Conservatism*, Canberra 1979, pp.213–37.

2   Liberal and Country Party leaders' policy speeches, December 1949, NLA Ms 1633/1323/100.

3   Page, 'A New Conception of a National Health Scheme for Australia', Address to the British Commonwealth Medical Congress, 23 May 1950, AA CRS AA165/669/1/15.

4   Page, 'A New Conception'.

5   Page, *What Price Medical Care?*, Philadelphia and New York, 1960, p.17.

6   T. Hunter, 'Planning National Health Policy in Australia, 1941–5', *Public Administration* (UK), xliv, 1966, pp.324–5.

7   'Doctors who were named during the recent Commission on Communism in Victoria known to have used the Commonwealth prescription forms', n.d., NLA Ms 1633/1441/4: 'Eric Dark: Obituary', *New Doctor*, 45, 1987, pp.2–3.

8   T.H. Kewley, *Social Security in Australia, 1900–1972*, Sydney 1973, pp. 200–7; Conference of Health Ministers, *Report*, 15 Aug. 1950, NLA Ms 1633/1399.

9   Conference of Health Ministers, *Report*.

10   Cabinet Submission, Agendum 16, 9 Jan. 1950, AA CRS A1658/669/1/1.

11   Metcalfe to Page, AA CRS A1658/669/1/1; there was some doubt at the time as to how serious Labor was about threatening the scheme, Melbourne *Herald*, 15 Sept. 1950.

12   Goodes, 'Note on Cabinet Agendum 124, Pharmaceutical Benefits', 2 June 1950, AA CRS A571/50/596.

13   Hospitals Commission of NSW, *Circular* 700, 4 Sept. 1950, [Page], 'Supply of Pharmaceuticals by Public Hospitals at the Expense of the Commonwealth', [November 1950], NLA Ms 1633/1270/2; Notes on Meeting between Page, Lilley, Metcalfe, Jewkes and Goodes, 8 Nov.

1950, NLA Ms 1633/1300; note for file, 20 April 1950, AA CRS A571 50/596.

14  G. Whitwell, *The Treasury Line*, Sydney 1986, pp.96–7.

15  'Report on Pharmaceutical Benefit Scheme', [May 1950], NLA Ms 1633/1346; BMA (Vic.) Council, *Minutes*, 28 March 1951.

16  Goodes, 'Comments on Cabinet Agendum 124, Pharmaceutical Benefits', 26 June 1950, A571 50/596.

17  E.M. Hanlon to Menzies, 1 Nov. 1950, Menzies to Hanlon, 16 Nov. 1950, AA CRS A571 50/596; 'Walnuts and Steamhammers', *Medical Journal of Australia*, 19 May 1951, pp.731–2.

18  NHMRC Report, 8 Feb. 1952, NLA Ms 1633/1300; James C. Whorton, '"Antibiotic Abandon": the Resurgence of Therapeutic Rationalism', in J. Parascandola, ed., *The History of Antibiotics: A Symposium*, Madison, Wis. 1980, pp.126–31.

19  Memo, Metcalfe to G.G. Jewkes (Director of Pharmaceutical Services), 21 Jan. 1952, AA CRS 1658 813/1/1/ s.1. 'Notes of Meeting between Sir Earle Page and Drug Manufacturers', 17 March 1952, Metcalfe to Page, 27 March 1952, NLA Ms 1633/1300.

20  Goodes to Metcalfe, 10 Dec. 1951, AA CRS A571 50/596.

21  Page, *What Price Medical Care?*, pp.107–8.

22  'Notes of Officers' Conference', 7 Aug. 1950, AA CRS A571/50/59; W. Dunk, 'Medical Benefits for Pensioners', [Oct. 1950], NLA Ms 1633/1325; Page to Menzies 17 Oct 1950, Menzies to Page, 19 Oct. 1950, A.S. Brown to Menzies, 19 Oct. 1950, AA CRS A462 702/1/2.

23  Page, 'Notes for Cabinet', Oct. 1950, NLA Ms 1633/1325.

24  Hunter to Page, 6 Jan. 1951, Page to Hunter, 8 March 1951, Page to Collins, 8 March 1951, NLA Ms 1633/1325.

25  Memo, 21 March 1952, AA CRS A1658 813/1/1/ pt1.

26  A.J. Metcalfe to Page, 3 June 1952, AA CRS A1658 813/1/1 s.1.

27  Metcalfe to Page, 3 June 1952.

28  Metcalfe to Page, 3 June 1952.

29  Cabinet Minute, 31 March 1952, AA CRS A1658/813/1/1 pt1; BMA (Vic.) Council, *Minutes*, 30 April 1952; G.Haines, *The Grains and Threepenn'orths of Pharmacy: Pharmacy in New South Wales, 1788–1976*, Kilmore 1976, p.253.

30  Goodes, 'Notes for Cabinet, Agendum 124: Pharmaceutical Benefits', 26 June 1950, A571 50/596; D.A. Cameron, 'National Health Bill 1959', *Health*, March 1960, pp.3–4; T. Hunter, 'Some Thoughts on the Pharmaceutical Benefits Scheme', *Australian Journal of Social Issues*, i, 1963, pp.32–42; R.E. Goodin and J. LeGrand, 'Creeping Universalism in the Australian Welfare State', in Goodin and Le Grand, *Not Only the Poor: the Middle Classes and the Welfare State*, London 1987, pp.108–26.

31  Industries Assistance Commission, *Report on Pharmaceutical Products*, 4 April 1986, p.28.

32  Kewley, *Social Security in Australia*, p.369.

33   'The Capacity of a Region [Tasmania] to Employ Doctors', August 1951, AA CRS A1658 611/1/13.
34   Cabinet Agendum, 24 Jan. 1950, AA CRS A1658 669/1/1.
35   'Medical Benefits', 8 Feb. 1950, AA CRS A1658 669/1/1.
36   Page to Hurley, 18 Jan. 1950, Hurley to Page, 18 Jan. 1950, 'Notes of Meeting with the Federal Council, BMA', 23 Feb. 1950, NLA Ms 1633/1371.
37   Page, *What Price Medical Care?*, pp.76–7.
38   Page, 'Notes of Talk to Federal Executive of Friendly Societies of Australia', 20 Jan. 1950, AA CRS A1658 666/3/4/1.
39   Cabinet Submission 16, 9 Jan. 1950, 'National Health Services – Cabinet Agendum 24 Jan. 1950', AA CRS A1658 669/1/1.
40   Page, 'Notes for Talk to Federal Council, BMA', 23 Feb. 1950, NLA Ms 1633/1371.
41   Page, 'Notes for Talk'.
42   V. Hurley to Sir H. Newland, 12 Jan. 1950, Mortlock Library Ms PRG 288/53.
43   BMA (Vic.) Executive, *Minutes*, 12 Dec. 1949.
44   Meeting of Sir Earle Page with BMA (Vic.) Branch Council, 28 April 1950; 'Note of Discussions with Mr F.F. Innes, Board Member of AMP', 20 and 21 March 1950, AA CRS A1658 669/1/1/pt1; BMA (NSW), Convention of Local Associations, *Minutes*, 24 Feb. 1950; Metcalfe to Page, 14 March 1950, NLA Ms 1633/1340; *Age*, 11 May, 28 June 1950, Melbourne *Herald*, 27 June 1950.
45   A.J. Eade (General Secretary, Manchester Unity), *The Friendly Society Movement and its Future in Australia*, Sydney 1948; BMA (Vic.) Council, *Minutes*, 22 Feb. 1950.
46   BMA (Vic.) Council, *Minutes*, 25 Jan. 1950.
47   E. Scott to A. Townley, 16 Feb. 1950, AA CRS A571 50/599; 'An Answer to Earle Page', *Australasian Journal of Pharmacy*, 30 June 1950.
48   C. Byrne, 'The Earle Page Scheme Must Fail', BMA (Vic.) Organization Committee, 9 May 1950; 'Lodge Practice under Sir Earle Page's Scheme', BMA (Vic.) Executive, *Minutes*, 6 Feb. 1950.
49   BMA (Federal Council), 'Report of Conference with Sir Earle Page', 30 July 1950; BMA (Vic.) Council, Resolution, 14 Aug. 1950.
50   BMA (NSW) Medico-Political Committee, *Minutes*, 21 Dec. 1943.
51   Friendly Societies Association, *Report of Federal Conference*, 26 June 1950, La Trobe Library Ms 10242.
52   Memo, 3 April 1950 AA CRS A1658 666/3/4–6.
53   BMA (Federal Council) Resolutions, 27 May 1950; Friendly Societies Association, Federal Council, *Minutes*, 26 and 27 June 1950; *Medical Journal of Australia*, 12 Aug. 1950, p.270.
54   BMA (Vic.) Council, *Minutes*, 27 Sept. 1950.
55   BMA (Vic.) Council, *Minutes*, 17 Oct. 1950, Circular to Members, 3 Nov. 1950.

56  BMA (Vic.) Council, *Minutes*, 24 Jan. 1951, 21 Feb. 1951, *Circular*, 20 Aug. 1951.
57  'National Health Service: Medical Benefits', Cabinet Agendum 16B, 14 March 1950, AA CRS A1658 669/1/1/pt1.
58  BMA (Vic.) Council, *Minutes*, 26 March 1952; Organization Sub-committee, *Minutes*, 22 April 1952; C. Byrne, 'Medical Benefit Funds', BMA (Vic.) Executive, *Minutes*, 9 Feb. 1953.
59  Independent Order of Rechabites, Victoria, *Annual Reports*, 1951–4; McNay and Van Steenwyck , 'Report to Sir Earle Page', 1 June 1953, AA CRS A462/702/1/2.
60  A.J. Eade to Metcalfe, 28 May 1953, AA CRS A1658 666/3/4; press statement, 21 July 1953, Metcalfe to Acting Prime Minister, 10 Aug. 1953, AA CRS A462 702/1/6; Metcalfe to Grieve (Chairman, MBF), 24 Dec. 1953, circular to all registered medical benefit organizations, 14 Jan. 1954, AA CRS A1658 666/1/7.
61  BMA (Vic.) Council, *Minutes*, 29 Aug. 1945, 23 July 1947; Organization Sub-Committee, *Minutes*, 14 Aug. 1951; Council, *Minutes*, 1 Sept. 1951.
62  BMA (Federal Council), *Minutes*, 10–12 Sept. 1951.
63  'Conditions of Contract Practice in Mining Districts', [Jan. 1950], D. McInnes (Secretary, Wollongong District Hospital) to Page, 29 March 1950, Page to McInnes, 31 March 1950, NLA Ms 1633/1371; BMA (Vic.) Organization Sub-Committee, *Minutes*, 14 Aug. 1951, 22 Aug. 1951.
64  BMA (Vic.) Council, *Minutes*, 23 July 1952.
65  Liberal and Country Party policy speeches, December 1949.
66  H. Schlink to Page, 8 Aug. 1950, NLA Ms 1633/1424.
67  Conference, State Health Ministers, 15 Aug. 1950, NLA Ms 1633/1399.
68  Hurley to Page, 14 Aug. 1950, NLA Ms 1633/1340; 'Notes of meeting with representatives of the BMA', 3 March 1953, VPRO R1/263/2254.
69  [A.J. Metcalfe], 'Statement of the Present Position between the States and Commonwealth Regarding Hospital Benefits', 13 Aug. 1951, AA CRS A1658/200/3/7/s.1.
70  H. Schlink to Page, 8 Aug. 1950, NLA Ms 1633/1424; 'Notes of Meeting with Representatives of the BMA', 3 March 1953, VPRO R1/263/ 2254.
71  R. Fitzgerald and H. Thornton, *Labor in Queensland*, Brisbane 1989, pp.116–17.
72  Sydney *Sun*, 1 July 1955, *Sydney Morning Herald*, 2 July 1955.
73  *Courier-Mail*, 2 June 1955.

# Conclusion

1  T. Kewley, *Social Security in Australia: 1900–72*, Sydney 1973, pp. 369–70.

2   L. Butler, ed., *Chris McCaffrey: A Great Administrator, A Memorial Recollection by his Colleagues*, Newcastle 1985, p.19.

3   J.W. Bjoerkman, 'Who Governs the Health Sector: Comparative European and American Experiences with Representation, Participation and Decentralization', *Comparative Politics*, xvii, 1984–5, p.418; T. Hunter, 'The Politics of National Health', Ph.D. thesis, ANU 1969, p.266.

4   *Sydney Sun*, 1 July 1955, *Sydney Morning Herald*, 2 July 1955; S. Sax, *A Strife of Interests*, Sydney 1984, pp.92–5.

5   C. Jungfer, *General Practice in Australia: A Report on a Survey*, Australian College of General Practitioners, 1964.

6   Jungfer, *General Practice in Australia*; R.B. Scotton, 'Medical Manpower in Australia', *Medical Journal of Australia*, 13 May 1967, p.986; N.A. Andersen, 'An Assessment of the Structure of General Practice in New South Wales: Report of a Survey', *Medical Journal of Australia Supplement*, 30 Nov. 1968, pp.155–9.

7   T. Fox, 'The Antipodes: Private Practice Publicly Supported', *Lancet*, 63, 20 April 1963, pp.875–9; 27 April 1963, pp.933–9

8   Fox, 'The Antipodes'; 'Increasing Demand for Hospital and Medical Insurance', *Health*, December 1960, p.125; the major research of Deeble and Scotton at the Institute of Applied Economic Research at the University of Melbourne in the late 1960s established these levels, esp. J.S. Deeble and R. Scotton, *Health Care Under Voluntary Insurance – Report of a Survey*, Melbourne 1968, Scotton, 'Voluntary Health Insurance in Australia', *Australian Economic Review*, vii, 1968, pp.37–44, Scotton, 'Membership of Voluntary Health Insurance', *Economic Record*, xlv, 1969, pp.69–83, A. Adams, A. Chancellor and C. Kerr, 'Medical Care in Western Sydney: A Report on the Utilization of Health Services by a Defined Population', *Medical Journal of Australia*, 6 March 1971, pp.507–16.

9   Hunter, 'Politics of National Health', p.233.

10  Scotton, *Medical Care in Australia: an Economic Diagnosis*, Melbourne 1974, p.167; J.S. Deeble, 'Unscrambling the Omelet: Public and Private Health Care in Australia', in G. McLachlan and A. Maynard, *The Public/Private Mix for Health*, London 1982, pp.425–65; Commonwealth Health Insurance Council, 10th Meeting, *Minutes*, 14–16 Dec. 1966, AA CRS A1658 666/1/1; W.A. Carson, 'The Australian Health Scheme', *Australian Quarterly*, xxxix, 1967, pp.41–9.

11  A.A. Calwell, 'Policy Speech at the Royale Ballroom, Melbourne, 16 Nov. 1961', quoted in B.J. Kelleher, 'Friendly Societies in the Australian Economy', *Australian Quarterly*, xxxiv, 1962, p.60.

12  Andersen, 'An Assessment', p.155.

13  C. Webster, *The Health Services Since the War*, vol.1, London 1988, pp.204–11; B. Abel-Smith and R.M. Titmuss, *The Cost of the National Health Service in England and Wales*, Cambridge 1956; B. Abel-Smith and K. Glass, *British Doctors at Home and Abroad*, Occasional Papers on Social Administration, no.8, Welwyn 1964, p.57.

14   M.H. Cass, *A National Health Scheme for Labour*, Victorian Fabian Pamphlet 9, Melbourne 1964.

15   G. Whitlam, 'The Alternative National Health Programme', *Medical Journal of Australia, Supplement*, 10 Aug. 1968, pp.15–22; Sax, *A Strife of Interests*, ch.4, has presented the most comprehensive account of the Whitlam years, cf. T. Moynihan and P. Beilharz, 'Medibank: Monument or Mausoleum of the Whitlam Government?', *Thesis 11*, no.7, 1983, pp.151–8, D. Mackay, 'On Medibank' and Beilharz and Moynihan, 'Rejoinder', *Thesis 11*, no.8, 1984, pp.116–23, R. Mathews, *Health Wars*, Melbourne 1989.

16   N. Milio, 'The Political Anatomy of Community Health Policy in Australia 1972–1982', *Politics*, xix, 1984, pp.18–33

17   S. Duckett, 'Structural Interests and Australian Health Policy', *Social Science and Medicine*, xviii, 1984, pp.959–66; J. Richardson, 'Does Bulk Billing Cause Abuse of Medicare?', *Community Health Studies*, xi, 1987, pp.98–107. For a polemical account of this shift in health economics see D.M. Fox, *Economists and Health Care: from Reform to Relativism*, New York 1979.

18   Commonwealth Department of Health, *Health Maintenance Organizations: A Development Program under Medicare*, Canberra 1986; E. Friedson, 'Viewpoint: Sociology and Medicine: a Polemic', *Sociology of Health and Illness*, v, 1983, p.209.

19   'Report of the Task Force to Review the Structure, Function and Constitution of the Australian Medical Association', *Medical Journal of Australia*, 6 April 1987; D. Mackay, 'Politics of Reaction: the Australian Medical Association as a Pressure Group', in H. Gardner, *The Politics of Health*, Melbourne 1989, pp.277–302; T. Hunter, 'Medical Politics: Decline in the Hegemony of the Australian Medical Association', *Social Science and Medicine*, viii, 1984, pp.973–80.

20   P. Starr, 'Transformation in Defeat: The Changing Objectives of National Health Insurance, 1915–1980', *American Journal of Public Health*, lxxii, 1982, p.86.

21   S. Duckett, 'Structural Interests and Australian Health Policy'.

# Bibliography

## Parliamentary Publications and Official Reports

### Commonwealth

Campbell, Dame Janet, 'Report on Maternal and Child Welfare in Australia', CPP, 1929–31, ii

Cilento, R.W., *The White Man in the Tropics*, Commonwealth Department of Health Service Publication (Tropical Division) No.7, 1925.

Commissioner of Taxation, 'Annual Report', 1936–7, CPP, 1937–40, iv

Committee Concerning the Causes of Death and Invalidity in the Commonwealth, 'Report on Tuberculosis, 19 Sept. 1916', 'Report on Venereal Diseases, 14 Dec. 1916', CPP, 1914–17, v

Commonwealth Department of Health, *Health Maintenance Organizations: A Development Program under Medicare*, Canberra 1986

Department of Health, *Summary of Activities, 2 December 1936*, Canberra 1937

Federal Health Council, *Reports of Sessions*

Industries Assistance Commission, *Report on Pharmaceutical Products*, 4 April 1986

Joint Parliamentary Committee on Social Security, *Sixth Interim Report*, 1 July, 1943, CPP, 1940–43, ii

Joint Parliamentary Committee on Social Security, *Seventh Interim Report*, 15 Feb. 1944, CPP, 1943–5, ii

Joint Parliamentary Committee on Social Security, *Eighth Interim Report*, 27 June, 1945, CPP, 1945–6, iii

Joint Parliamentary Committee on Social Security , *Minutes of Evidence*

Kinnear, Sir Walter, 'Report on Health and Pensions Insurance', CPP, 1937, v

McCallum, F. *Analysis of Australian Legislation Relating to the Registration of Medical Practitioners*, Commonwealth Department of Health Service Publication no. 34, 1927

Moore, K.R., *Report on a Campaign Against Diphtheria at Bendigo, Victoria, 1923–24*, Commonwealth Department of Health Service Publication 28, 1925

National Health and Medical Research Council, *Reports of Sessions*

National Insurance Commission, *Report of Conference with Representatives of Bodies Interested in the Formation of Approved Societies*, Canberra, 11 and 12 July 1938

Repatriation Commission, *Annual Reports*

Repatriation Commission, *Dispensing for Ex-Soldiers*, 1 July 1938

'Report of Investigations Abroad by Sir Frederick Stewart, Parliamentary Under-Secretary for Employment, 4 April 1935', CPP, 1934–5, iii

Robertson, D.G., *Inquiry into the Prevalence of Tuberculosis at Bendigo*, Commonwealth of Australia Quarantine Service Publication 19, 1920

Royal Commission of Inquiry into Fatalities at Bundaberg, 'Report', CPP, 1926–8, iv

Royal Commission on Child Endowment, *Minutes of Evidence*, Canberra 1929

Royal Commission on Health, *Minutes of Evidence*, Melbourne 1925

Royal Commission on Health, *Report*, CPP, 1926–8, iv

Royal Commission on National Insurance, 'First Progress Report', CPP, 1925, ii

Royal Commission on National Insurance, 'Progress and Final Reports', CPP, 1926–8, iv

Royal Commission on the Constitution, *Minutes of Evidence*, Melbourne 1928

Rural Reconstruction Commission, *7th Report: Rural Amenities*, Canberra 1943

Sawers, W.C., *The Commonwealth Health Laboratories*, Commonwealth Department of Health, Service Publication 27, 1925

## New South Wales

Workers Compensation Commission, *Annual Reports*

Hospitals Commission, *Annual Reports*

Joint Committee on Honoraries, Graduands and Patients, 'Minutes of Evidence and Reports', NSWPP, 1940–1, i

## Queensland

Cilento, R.W., *Report on the Muscle Re-education Clinic, Townsville (Sister E. Kenny) and its Work*, Brisbane, July 1934

Department of Health and Home Affairs, *Report upon the Establishment and Operations of the Several Organizations for the Civil Defence of Queensland*, Brisbane, 1 Feb. 1941

Royal Commission into Public Hospitals, 'Report', QPP, 1930,i

## South Australia

Royal Commission on Lotteries, 'Minutes of Evidence', *Parliamentary Papers*, 1936, ii

## Tasmania

Gaha, J.F., 'Report on a Survey of Hospital Administration in the United

Kingdom, Continent of Europe, the United States of America and South America', *Tas.PP*, 1935

*The Royal Hobart Hospital and the Health Policy of the Labor Government*, Hobart 1939

## Victoria

Charities Board, *Annual Reports*

Hospitals and Charities Commission, *Annual Reports*

'Summary of Recommendations from the Report by Dr Malcolm T. Mac-Eachern on the Hospital System of the State of Victoria', *VPP*, 1926, ii

## Western Australia

Emergency Medical Services, Emergency Hospital Organization, *Admission and Discharge of Casualties*, Perth 1939

## United Kingdom

Ministry of Health, Consultative Council on Medical and Allied Services (Dawson Committee), *Interim Report on the Future Provision of Medical and Allied Services*, London, 1920

# Periodicals

*Australasian Journal of Pharmacy*
*Australian and New Zealand Journal of Surgery*
*Australian Worker*
British Medical Association (Victorian Branch), *Medico-Political Newsletter*
*Catholic Worker*
*Economic News* (Queensland Bureau of Industry)
*The General Practitioner*
*Health* (Commonwealth Department of Health)
*The Hospital Magazine*
*Knox's Medical Directories*
*Labour Call*
*Medical Journal of Australia*
*Medical Topics*
*National Insurance Newsletter*
*Smith's Weekly*
*Victorian Trades Hall Council Bulletin*
*The Worker*

# Unpublished

Alomes, S. ' "Reasonable Men": Middle Class Reform in Australia, 1928–39,' Ph.D. thesis, ANU 1979

Carter, W.S. 'Report on University of Melbourne Medical School, 25–31

May 1924', in *Medical Education in Australia*, typescript 1925, RAC RG 1.1 series 410 B1

Cilento, R.W. 'The World, My Oyster', typescript 1974, Fryer Library Ms. 44/4.

Fisher, F. 'Raphael West Cilento, Medical Administrator, Legislator and Visionary 1893–1945', MA thesis, University of Queensland 1984

Hart, P.R. 'J.A.Lyons: A Political Biography', Ph.D. thesis, ANU 1967

Hunter, T. 'The Politics of National Health', Ph.D. thesis, ANU 1969

Leggett, C.A.C. 'The Organization and Development of the Queensland Hospital,' M.A. thesis, University of Queensland 1974

Lloyd, C. 'The Form and Development of the United Australia Party, 1929–37', Ph.D. thesis, ANU 1984

McGrath, A. 'The History of Medical Organization in Australia', Ph.D. thesis, University of Sydney 1974

Powles, J. 'Naturalism and Hygiene: Fascist Affinities in Australian Public Health: 1910 to 1940', unpublished paper, 1987

Robin, R.D. 'The British Medical Association in Queensland: Origins and Development to 1945', BA (hons) thesis, University of Queensland 1966

Robinson, M.L. 'Economists and Politicians: the Influence of Economic Ideas Upon Labor Politicians and Governments, 1931 to 1949,' Ph.D. thesis, ANU 1986

Thame, C. 'Health and the State', Ph.D. thesis, ANU 1974

Watts, R. 'The Light on the Hill: the Origins of the Australian Welfare State 1935–45', Ph.D. thesis, University of Melbourne 1983

Welch, K. 'The Log of the Flying Doctor', typescript, 1928, Mitchell Library Ms. B669

## Books and Articles

Abel-Smith, B. and Glass, K. *British Doctors at Home and Abroad*, Occasional Papers on Social Administration, no.8, Welwyn 1964

Abel-Smith, B. and Titmuss, R.M. *The Cost of the National Health Service in England and Wales*, Cambridge 1956

Alford, R.R. *Health Care Politics: Ideological and Interest Group Barriers to Reform*, Chicago 1975

Armstrong, D. *The Political Anatomy of the Body*, Cambridge 1984,

Ashford, D. *The Formation of the Welfare States*, London 1986

Australasian Association for the Advancement of Science, *Proceedings of 15th Meeting*, Melbourne 1921

Australasian Medical Congress, *Transactions*, 11th Session, 1920, Brisbane 1920

Australasian Medical Congress, *Transactions*, 1st Session, 1923, Sydney 1924

Australian Broadcasting Commission, 'Should Medical Services be Nationalized?', *The Nation's Forum of the Air*, 15 Nov. 1944

Australian Labor Party (Queensland Branch), *Mothers of Queensland: Your Duty is Clear!*, Brisbane 1926

Australian National Secretariat of Catholic Action, *Pattern for Peace: Statement on Reconstruction Presented to the Federal Government on Behalf of the Catholic Community*, Melbourne 1943

Australian National Secretariat of Catholic Action, *Catholic Action in Australia: Official Statement of the Archbishops and Bishops of Australia*, Melbourne 1947

Bacchi, C. 'The Nature-Nurture Debate in Australia 1900–1914', *Historical Studies*, xix, 1980–1

Barnett, F.O., Burt, W.O. and Heath, F. *We Must Go On: A Study in Planned Reconstruction and Housing*, Melbourne 1944

Barrett, J. 'Medicine in Australia and Refugees', *Australian Quarterly*, March 1940

Bean, C.E.W. *In Your Hands Australians*, Melbourne 1919

Bean, C.E.W. *War Aims of a Plain Australian*, Sydney 1943

Beilharz, P. 'The Labourist Tradition and the Reforming Imagination', in R.Kennedy, ed., *Australian Welfare: Historical Sociology*, Melbourne 1989

Beilharz, P. and Moynihan, P. 'Rejoinder', *Thesis 11*, no.8, 1984

Bell, J. 'Queensland's Public Hospital System: Some Aspects of Finance and Control', in Roe, J., ed., *Social Policy in Australia: Some Perspectives*, Sydney 1976

Berkowitz, E. and McQuaid, K. *Creating the Welfare State: the Political Economy of Twentieth Century Reform*, New York 1980

Black, H.D. 'Second Thoughts on Reconstruction', *Public Administration*, iv, 1943

Blakeney, M. *Australia and the Jewish Refugees, 1933–1948*, Sydney 1985

Bland, F.A. 'Some Problems of Hospital Administration', *Public Administration*, iii, 1941

BMA, *A General Medical Service for the Nation*, London 1938

BMA, *Business Activities in Australia*, Melbourne 1935

BMA (Federal Council), *A National Health Service*, Melbourne, Oct. 1949

BMA (Federal Council), *The Socialized Medicine Bedside Book*, [Sydney 1949?]

BMA (NSW), *Handbook for Qualified Medical Practitioners*, Sydney 1935

BMA (NSW), *Highways to Health: Talks by the BMA Spokesman*, Sydney 1941

BMA (Qld), *Memorandum and Articles of Association with By-Laws and Rules Covering Procedure in Ethical Matters*, Sydney 1928

Bostock, J. and Nye, L.J.J. *Whither Away? A Study of Race Psychology and of Factors Leading to Australia's National Decline*, 2nd edition, Sydney 1936

Boyd, S. *Doctor's Conscience or All Illness is Preventable*, Sydney 1944

Brown, A.E. *The Doctor and Tomorrow*, Sydney 1946

Browne, D. *The Wind and the Book*, Melbourne 1976

Bruck, L. *The Sweating of the Medical Profession in Australia by the Friendly Societies in Australia*, Sydney 1896

Burgmann, V. *In Our Time: Socialism and the Rise of Labor*, Sydney 1985

Burnet, F.M. *Biological Aspects of Infectious Diseases*, Cambridge 1940

Burnet, F.M. *Changing Patterns*, Melbourne 1970

Butler, A.G. *The Australian Army Medical Services in the War of 1914–18*, iii, Canberra 1943

Butler, E. *The Real Policy Behind 'Free' Medicine*, n.d.

Butler, L. ed. *Chris McCaffrey: A Great Administrator, A Memorial Recollection by his Colleagues*, Newcastle 1985

Butlin, N.G., Barnard, A. and Pincus, J.J. *Government and Capitalism*, Sydney 1982

Butlin, S.J. and Schedvin, C.B. *War Economy, 1942–1945, Australia in the War of 1939–1945, Series 4, Civil*, Canberra 1977

Byrne, C. *Proposal for the Future of Medical Practice: an Analysis of Proposed Schemes for a National Health Service and an Outline of a Scheme to Provide a Complete Medical Service for the Whole Population*, Melbourne 1943

Canberra Research Group, 'Commonwealth Policy Co-ordination', *Public Administration*, xiv, 1955

Carment D. and Killion, F. *The Story of Rockhampton Hospital and those other institutions administered by the Rockhampton Hospital Board 1868–1980*, Rockhampton 1980

Carson, W.A. 'The Australian Health Scheme', *Australian Quarterly*, xxxix, 1967

Casey, R.G. *Australia's Vital Drift*, Adelaide 1935

Casey, R.G. *The Commonwealth Pensions System*, Adelaide 1935

Cass, G. *Workers' Benefit or Employers' Burden: Workers' Compensation in New South Wales 1880–1926*, Sydney 1983

Cass, M.H. *A National Health Scheme for Labour*, Victorian Fabian Pamphlet 9, Melbourne 1964

Castles, F. *The Working Class and Welfare*, Wellington and Sydney 1985

Cilento, R.W. 'White Settlement in the Tropics', in Phillips, P.D. and Wood, G.L. *The Peopling of Australia*, Melbourne 1928

Cilento, R.W. *Blueprint for the Health of a Nation*, Sydney 1944

Cilento, R.W. *Nutrition and Numbers: The Livingstone Lectures 1936*, Brisbane 1936

Clark, C. 'Bacon and Eggs for Breakfast', *Australian Quarterly*, ix, Dec. 1937

Clements, F.W. and MacPherson, M. *The Lady Gowrie Child Centres: The Health Record*, Canberra 1945

Clements, F.W. *A History of Human Nutrition in Australia*, Melbourne 1986

Cochrane, T. *Blockade: the Queensland Loans Affair*, Brisbane 1989

Communist Party of Australia, *Who is Robbing You of Free Medicine?*, Sydney 1948

Cooper, R.P. 'An Australian in Mussolini's Italy, Herbert Michael Moran', *Overland*, 115, 1989

Cooter, R. 'The Meaning of Fractures: Orthopaedics and the Reform of British Hospitals in the Interwar Period', *Medical History*, xxxi, 1987

Cornwall, J, *Hard-Earned Lives*, London 1984

Craig, C. *Launceston General Hospital: First Hundred Years 1863–1963*, Launceston 1963

Crisp, L.F. *Ben Chifley*, London 1960

Cumpston, J.H.L. *The Health of the People*, Canberra 1978

Curthoys, A. and Merritt, J. ed., *Australia's First Cold War: Vol.1 Society, Communism and Culture*, Sydney 1984

Dale, J. ed. *Health Week Official Handbook 1937*, Melbourne 1937

Dark, E. *Medicine and the Social Order*, Sydney 1943

Davis, R. *Eighty Years' Labor: The ALP in Tasmania, 1903–1983*, Hobart 1983

Davison, G. 'The City-bred Child and Urban Reform in Melbourne 1900–1940', in Williams, P. ed., *Social Process and the City*, Sydney 1983

Dedman, J.J. 'The Labor Government in the Second World War: Part 2', *Labour History*, 22, 1972

Deeble, J.S. and Scotton, R. *Health Care Under Voluntary Insurance – Report of a Survey*, Melbourne 1968

Dickenson, M. and Mason, C. *Hospitals and Politics: the Australian Hospital Association, 1946–86*, Canberra 1986

Dickey, B. *No Charity There: A Short History of Social Welfare in Australia*, Melbourne 1980

Dickey, B. 'Health and the State in Australia 1788–1977', *Journal of Australian Studies*, no.2, Nov. 1977

Dickey, B. 'The Labor Government and Medical Services in New South Wales 1910–14', *Historical Studies*, xii, 1967

Doherty, R.L. ed., *A Medical School for Queensland*, Brisbane 1986

Duckett, S. 'Assuring Hospital Standards: the Introduction of Hospital Accreditation in Australia', *Journal of Public Administration*, xiii, 1983

Duckett, S. 'Structural Interests and Australian Health Policy', *Social Science and Medicine*, xviii, 1984

Duncan, W.G.K. *Social Services in Australia*, Sydney 1939

Eade, A.J. *The Friendly Society Movement and its Future in Australia*, Sydney 1948

Ellery, R. *Psychiatric Aspects of Modern Warfare*, Melbourne 1945

Ellery, R. *The Cow Jumped Over the Moon*, Melbourne 1956

Estcourt Hughes, J. *Henry Simpson Newland: A Biography*, Adelaide 1972

Etheridge, E. *The Butterfly Caste: A Social History of Pellagra in the South*, Westport, Conn. 1972

Evans R. *Strained Mercy: the Economics of Canadian Health Care*, Toronto 1984

Evatt, H.V. *Post War Reconstruction: Temporary Alteration of the Constitution*, Canberra 1944

'The Example of New Zealand', *Lancet*, 2 Dec. 1944

Fitzgerald, R. and Thornton, H. *Labor in Queensland from the 1880s to 1988*, Brisbane 1989

Fitzhardinge, L.F. *The Little Digger: A Political Biography of William Morris Hughes*, ii, Sydney 1979

Forgan Smith, W. *Labor's Policy Speech, April 17 1935*, Brisbane 1935

Fox, D.M. *Economists and Health Care: From Reform to Relativism*, New York 1979

Fox, D.M. *Health Policies, Health Politics: the British and American Experience*, Princeton, N.J. 1986

Fox, T. 'The Antipodes: Private Practice Publicly Supported', *Lancet*, 63, 20 April 1963, 27 April 1963

Fraser, J.M. *The Health Policy of the Australian Government*, Canberra, [1944]

Freeden, M. 'Eugenics and Progressive Thought: A Study in Political Affinity', *Historical Journal*, xxii, 1979

Friedson, E. *Professional Powers. A Study of the Institutionalization of Formal Knowledge*, Chicago, 1986

Friedson, E. 'Are Professions Necessary?', in T.L. Haskell, *The Authority of Experts: Studies in History and Theory*, Bloomington, 1984

Friedson, E. 'Viewpoint: Sociology and Medicine: a Polemic', *Sociology of Health and Illness*, v, 1983

Friendly Societies Association, *Report of Federal Conference*, 26 June 1950

Friendly Societies of Victoria, *Annual Reports*

Galligan, B. *The Politics of the High Court*, Brisbane 1987

Gardiner, L. *Hospitals in Association: A History of the Country and Metropolitan Hospitals Association 1918–1974*, Melbourne 1977

Garton, S. 'Sir Charles MacKellar: Psychology, Eugenics and Child Welfare in New South Wales', *Historical Studies*, xxii, 1986

Gault, E.W. and Lucas, A. *A Century of Compassion: A History of the Austin Hospital*, Melbourne 1982

'The General Practitioner', *The People Demand Repeal of the National Health Insurance Act*, Melbourne 1938

Gillespie, J. 'Medical Markets and Australian Medical Politics, 1920–45', *Labour History*, 54, 1988

Gillespie, J., 'The Rockefeller Foundation, the Hookworm Campaign and a National Health Policy', in MacLeod, R. and Denoon, D. eds, *Health and Healing in Tropical Australia*, Townsville 1991

Gillespie, R. 'The Limits of Industrial Hygiene: Commonwealth Government Initiatives in Occupational Health, 1921–48', in Attwood, H. and Kenny, G. *Reflections on Medical History and Health in Australia: Third National Conference on Medical History and Health in Australia 1986*, Melbourne 1987

Goodin, R. and Le Grand, J. *Not Only the Poor: the Middle Classes and the Welfare State*, London 1987

Green, D. and Cromwell, L. *Mutual Aid or Welfare State: Australia's Friendly Societies*, Sydney 1984

Green, F. *Servant of the House*, Melbourne 1969

Grieve, H.R.R. 'The Fight against the Socialization of Medicine in Australia', *British Commonwealth Medical Conference*, Brisbane, 1950

Grieve, H.R.R. 'Hospital Administration in New South Wales', *Australian Quarterly*, vii, 1935

Grimwade, J.F.T. *A Short History of Drug Houses of Australia Limited to 1968*, Melbourne 1974

Hagan, J. *The History of the ACTU*, Melbourne, 1981

Haines, G. *The Grains and Threepenn'orths of Pharmacy: Pharmacy in New South Wales, 1788–1976*, Kilmore 1976

Hanson, E. *The Politics of Social Security: the 1938 Act and Some Later Developments*, Auckland 1980

Harris, J. 'Did British Workers Want the Welfare State? G.D.H. Cole's Survey of 1942', in Winter, J. ed., *The Working Class in Modern British History*, Cambridge 1983

Hasluck, P. *The Government and the People, 1942–1945, Australia in the War of 1939–1945*, Series 4, Civil, Canberra 1970

Hay, J.R. 'The IPA and Social Policy in World War II', *Historical Studies*, xx, 1982–3

Hazlehurst, C. *Australian Conservatism: Essays in Twentieth Century Political History*, Canberra, 1979.

Head, B. and Walter, J. eds, *Intellectual Movements and Australian Society*, Melbourne 1988

Henderson, G. *Mr Santamaria and the Bishops*, Sydney 1982

Hicks, C. Stanton, 'Medical Studies: A Plea for Readjustment of Values', *Adelaide Medical Students Society Review*, July 1928

Hicks, N. 'Cure and Prevention', in Curthoys, A., Martin, A.W. and Rowse, T. eds, *Australia from 1939*, Sydney 1987

Hollingsworth, J. Rogers *A Political Economy of Medicine: Great Britain and the United States*, Baltimore 1986

Honigsbaum, F. *The Division in British Medicine*, London 1979

Hoorn, R. van den and Playford, J. 'The Adelaide Hospital Row', in Jaensch, D. *The Flinders History of South Australia: Political History*, Adelaide 1986

Howard, F. *Kent Hughes*, Melbourne, 1972

Hudson, W.J. *Casey*, Melbourne 1986

Hughes, W.M. *Save Our Mothers: Jubilee Memorial Fund*, Canberra 1935

Hunter, T. 'Pharmaceutical Benefits Legislation, 1944–50', *Economic Record*, xli, 1965

Hunter, T. 'Planning National Health Policy in Australia, 1941–5', *Public Administration*, xliv, 1966

Hunter, T. 'Pressure Groups and the Australian Political Process: the Case of the Australian Medical Association', *Journal of Commonwealth and Comparative Politics*, xviii, 1980

Hunter, T. 'Some Thoughts on the Pharmaceutical Benefits Scheme', *Australian Journal of Social Issues*, i, 1963

Hunter, T. 'Medical Politics: Decline in the Hegemony of the Australian Medical Association', *Social Science and Medicine*, viii, 1984

Hurley, J.V. *Sir Victor Hurley: Surgeon, Soldier and Administrator*, Hawthorn 1989.

Hutton Neve, M. *This Mad Folly! The History of Australia's Women Doctors*, Sydney 1980

Independent Order of Rechabites, Victoria, *Annual Reports*

Inglis, K. *Hospital and Community; A History of the Royal Melbourne Hospital*, Melbourne 1958

Ives, W. and Mendelsohn, R. 'Hospitals and the State: the Thomas Report', *Australian Quarterly*, xii, 1940

James, W. *The Varieties of Religious Experience*, New York 1902

Johnson, C. *The Labor Legacy*, Sydney 1989

Johnson, T. 'The State and the Professions: the Peculiarities of the British', in Giddens, A. and McKenzie, G. *Social Class and the Division of Labour*, Cambridge 1982

Jones, G. *Social Hygiene in Twentieth Century Britain*, Beckenham 1986

Jungfer, C. *General Practice in Australia: A Report on a Survey*, Australian College of General Practitioners 1964

K.F. *National Health Insurance? A Short Summary of Some Important Provisions of the National Health and Pensions Insurance Act 1938 and the Method of Obtaining its Repeal*, Electoral Campaign, Non-Party Political, NSW Division, 1938

Kater, M.H. 'Hitler's Early Doctors: Nazi Physicians in Pre-Depression Germany', *Journal of Modern History*, lix, 1987

Kelleher, B.J. 'Friendly Societies in the Australian Economy', *Australian Quarterly*, xxxiv, 1962

Kewley, T.H. *Social Security in Australia, 1900–1972*, Sydney 1973

Klein, R. *The Politics of the National Health Service*, London 1983

Larson, M.S. *The Rise of Professionalism*, Berkeley, 1977

Lawrence, C. 'Incommunicable Knowledge: Science, Technology and the Clinical Art in Britain, 1850–1914', *Journal of Contemporary History*, xx, 1985

Lee, D.H.K. 'Nutrition', *Australian Quarterly*, viii, 1936

Lewis, J. and Brookes, B. 'The Peckham Health Centre, "PEP", and the Concept of General Practice During the 1930s and 1940s', *Medical History*, xxvii, 1983.

Lewis, J. *Whatever Happened to Community Medicine?*, Brighton 1986, 1988

Lewis, M. *Managing Madness: Psychiatry and Society in Australia 1788–1980*, Canberra 1988

Lewis, M. and MacLeod, R. 'Medical Politics and the Professionalization of Medicine in New South Wales, 1850–1901', *Journal of Australian Studies*, no.22, 1988

Lifton, R. J. *The Nazi Doctors*, London 1986

M'Gonigle, G.C.M. and Kirby, J. *Poverty and Public Health*, London 1936

MacIntyre, A.J. and J.J. *Country Towns of Victoria*, Melbourne 1944

Macintyre, S. *The Oxford History of Australia, 1901–1942: The Succeeding Age*, Melbourne 1986

Macintyre, S. *Winners and Losers*, Sydney 1985

Mackay, D. 'On Medibank', *Thesis 11*, no.8, 1984

Mackay, D. 'Politics of Reaction: the Australian Medical Association as a Pressure Group', in Gardner, H. *The Politics of Health*, Melbourne 1989

MacKenzie, W.H. and Hale, M. *National Insurance: A Burning Question: Lyons Government and the Experts, Another Barefaced Swindle*, State Unemployed and Relief Workers Council of New South Wales 1937

MacLean, H. 'The Use and Abuse of Biochemical Methods in Diagnosis', in *Lectures: Melbourne Permanent Committee for Post Graduate Work*, Sydney 1930

MacNicoll, J. *The Movement for Family Allowances 1918–45: A Study in Social Policy Development*, London 1980

Maddock, R. 'Unification of Income Taxes in Australia', *Australian Journal of Politics and History*, xxviii, 1982

Maddock, R. and Penny, J. 'Economists at War: the Financial and Economic Committee, 1939–1949', *Australian Economic History Review*, xxiii, 1983

Maddox, I. 'The Doctors', in Macintyre. S. *Ormond College Centenary Essays*, Melbourne 1984

Maddox, K. *Schlink of Prince Alfred*, Sydney 1978

Maier, C. '"Fictitious bonds...of wealth and law". On the theory and practice of interest representation', in *In Search of Stability: Explorations in Historical Political Economy*, Cambridge 1987

March, J.G. and Olsen, J, 'The New Institutionalism: Organizational Factors in Political Life', *American Political Science Review*, lxxviii, 1984.

Markey, R. 'The ALP and a National Social Policy', in Kennedy, R. *Australian Welfare History*, Melbourne 1982

Markey, R. *The Making of the Labor Party in New South Wales, 1880 to 1900*, Sydney 1988

Marmor, T.R. *Political Analysis and Health Care*, Cambridge 1983

Marshall, L.L. *The Art of General Practice*, Melbourne 1955

Mathews, R. *Health Wars*, Melbourne 1989

McDonald, I.A., Cope I. and Forster, F.M.C. *Super Ardua: The Royal College of Obstetricians and Gynaecologists in Australia, 1929–79*, Melbourne 1981

McGrath, A. 'The Controversy over the Nationalization of Medicine, 1941–49', *Journal of the Royal Australian Historical Society*, lxxiv, 1989

McLachlan, G. and Maynard, A. *The Public/Private Mix for Health: the Relevance and Effects of Change*, London 1982

McQueen, H. 'The Spanish Influenza Pandemic in Australia, 1918–19', in Roe, J. ed., *Social Policy in Australia*, Sydney 1976

'Medical Politics in Australia', Memorandum No. 1 of the Medical Policy Association (NSW), [1946]

Medical Practitioner, 'National Health and Medical Services', *Australian Quarterly*, xvii, 1945

Mendelsohn, R. 'The Introduction of the Commonwealth-State Tuberculosis Scheme 1948–1952', in Schaffer, B.B. and Corbett, D.C. *Decisions: Case Studies in Australian Administration*, Melbourne 1965

Milio, N. 'The Political Anatomy of Community Health Policy in Australia 1972–82', *Politics*, xix, 1984

Mitchell, A.M. *The Hospital South of the Yarra: A History of Alfred Hospital Melbourne*, Melbourne 1977

Monahan, B.W. *An Introduction to Social Credit*, Sydney 1947

Monahan, B.W. ['B.W.M.'] *The Problem of the Medical Profession*, Liverpool and Melbourne 1945

Moore, B. *The Dawn of the Health Age*, London 1911

Moran, H.M. *Beyond the Hill Lies China: Scenes from a Medical Life in Australia*, London 1945

Moran, H.M. *Viewless Winds: Being the Recollections and Digressions of an Australian Surgeon*, London 1939

Moynihan, T. and Beilharz, P., 'Medibank: Monument or Mausoleum of the Whitlam Government?', *Thesis 11*, no.7, 1983

Murphy, D.J., Joyce, R.B. and Hughes, C.A. eds *Labor in Power: The Labor Party and Governments in Queensland 1915–57*, Brisbane 1980

Mussen, G. *Australia's Tomorrow*, Melbourne 1944

Naylor, C.D. *Private Practice, Public Payment: Canadian Medicine and the Politics of Health Insurance 1911–1966*, Kingston and Montreal, 1986

Numbers, R. *Almost Persuaded: American Physicians and Compulsory Health Insurance 1912–1920*, Baltimore 1978

Nye, L.J.J. *The Challenge Ahead*, E.S. Meyers Memorial Lecture, Brisbane 1959

Nye, L.J.J. *Group Practice*, Sydney n.d. [194?]

Ogilvie, A.G. 'State Medical Services in Tasmania', *Australian Quarterly*, x, September 1938

Opit, L.J. 'The Cost of Health Care and Health Insurance in Australia: Some Problems Associated with the Fee-For-Service System', *Social Science and Medicine*, xviii, 1984

Page, E. 'A New Concept of a National Health Scheme for Australia', *British Commonwealth Medical Congress*, 23 May 1950

Page, E. *Truant Surgeon*, Sydney 1963

Page, E. *What Price Medical Care?*, Philadelphia and New York, 1960

Pater, J. *The Making of the National Health Service*, London 1981

Patrick, R. *A History of Health and Medicine in Queensland 1824–1960*, Brisbane 1987

Pensabene, T. *The Rise of the Medical Practitioner in Victoria*, Health Research Project Monograph 2, Canberra 1980

Porter, D. and Porter, R. 'What Was Social Medicine? An Historiographical Essay', *Journal of Historical Sociology*, i, 1988

Powles, J. 'Professional Hygienists and the Health of the Nation', in MacLeod, R. ed., *The Commonwealth of Science: ANZAAS and the Scientific Enterprise in Australia 1888–1988*, Melbourne 1988

Queensland People's Party, Political Education Committee, *Hospitals in Queensland*, Brisbane 1945

Radi, H., Spearritt, P. and Hinton, E. *Biographical Register of the New South Wales Parliament, 1901–70*, Canberra 1979

Reiger, K. *The Disenchantment of the Home*, Melbourne 1985

Reiser, S.J. *Medicine and the Reign of Technology*, Cambridge 1978

Richardson, J. 'Does Bulk Billing Cause Abuse of Medicare?', *Community Health Studies*, xi, 1987

Rimmer, W.G. *Portrait of a Hospital: The Royal Hobart Hospital*, Hobart 1981

Robertson, J.R. 'The Foundations of State Socialism in Western Australia: 1911–1916', *Historical Studies*, x, 1962

Robinson, R.H. *A Short History of the Failure of the Voluntary Hospital System and the Development of the District Hospital System*, Brisbane 1953

Robinson, R.H. *For My Country: A Functional and Historical Outline of Local Government in Queensland*, Brisbane 1957

Roe, J. 'Chivalry and Social Policy in the Antipodes', *Historical Studies*, xxii, 1987–8

Roe, J. ed. *Social Policy in Australia: Some Perspectives, 1901–75*, Stanmore 1976

Roe, M. 'The Establishment of the Australian Department of Health: Its Background and Significance', *Historical Studies*, xvii, 1976–7

Roe, M. *Nine Australian Progressives*, Brisbane 1984

Rohrer, J.E. 'The Political Development of the Hill-Burton Program', *Journal of Health Policy, Politics and Law*, xii, 1987

Rowse, T. *Australian Liberalism and National Character*, Malmsbury, Vic. 1978

Royal Australasian College of Physicians, *Historical Calendar 1938–63*, Sydney 1963

Rubenstein, C.L. 'Medical Research Policy Revisited', *Australian Journal of Public Administration*, xxxix, 1980

Rueschemeyer, D. 'Professional Autonomy and the Social Construction of Expertise', in Dingwall R. and Lewis, P. *The Sociology of the Professions*, London 1983

Ryle, J. 'Social Medicine: Its Meaning and Scope', *Millbank Memorial Fund Quarterly*, xxii, 1944

Ryle, J. 'The New Age in Medicine', in *Changing Disciplines: Lectures on the History, Methods and Motives of Social Pathology*, Oxford 1948

Sax, S. *A Strife of Interests*, Sydney 1984

Schlink, H. *The Hospital Problem of the Metropolitan and Suburban Area of Sydney*, Sydney 1940

Scotton, R.B. *Medical Care in Australia: an Economic Diagnosis*, Melbourne 1974

Scotton, R.B. 'Membership of Voluntary Health Insurance', *Economic Record*, xlv, 1969

Scotton, R.B. 'Voluntary Health Insurance in Australia', *Australian Economic Review*, vii, 1968

Shaver, S. 'Design for a Welfare State: The Joint Parliamentary Committee on Social Security', *Historical Studies*, xxii, 1987–8

Sheridan, T. *Division of Labour: Industrial Relations in the Chifley Years, 1945–1949*, Melbourne 1989

Sherington, G. *A Century of Caring: the Royal North Shore Hospital 1888–1988*, Sydney 1988

Smith, F.B. *The Retreat of Tuberculosis, 1850–1950*, London 1987

Smith, J.O. *The History of the Royal Australasian College of Surgeons from 1920 to 1935*, Melbourne [1971].

Smith, R. and Wearing, M. 'Do Australians Want the Welfare State?', *Politics*, xxii, 1987

Southwood, A.R. 'Health in Modern Society: Some Thoughts on Medical Planning', *Public Administration*, v, 1945

Spearritt, P. 'Sydney's "Slums": Middle Class Reformers and the Labour Response', *Labour History*, 26, 1974

Spenceley, G.F.R. 'Charity Relief in Melbourne: the Early Years of the 1930s Depression', *Monash Papers in Economic History*, no. 8, 1980

Spencer, M. *John Howard Lidgett Cumpston 1880–1954*, Tenterfield 1987

Starr, P. 'Transformation in Defeat: The Changing Objectives of National Health Insurance, 1915–80', *American Journal of Public Health*, lxxii, 1982

Starr, P. *The Social Transformation of American Medicine*, New York 1982

Stopford, J. *The Hospitals Act of 1923*, Brisbane 1923

Stopford, J. *The Hospitals Act of 1923: Reply to Critics*, Brisbane 1926

Strong, P.M. 'Sociological Imperialism and the Profession of Medicine: a Critical Analysis of the Thesis of Medical Imperialism', *Social Science and Medicine*, xiii, 1979.

Sutton, H. *Lectures in Preventive Medicine*, Sydney 1944

Templeton, J. *Prince Henry's: The Evolution of a Hospital, 1869–1969*, Melbourne 1969

Theodore, E.G. *Labour's Humane Practical Policy*, Brisbane 1926

Titmuss, R. *Problems of Social Policy*, London 1950

Tucker, D. 'Charles Edward Chuter: an Architect of Local Government in Queensland', *Queensland Geographical Journal*, 4th series, 1988

Turner, B.S. *Medical Power and Social Knowledge*, London 1987

Turnowetsky, G.W. 'The 1938 National Health Insurance and Pensions Legislation: Another View on Why It Failed', *La Trobe Sociology Papers*, no. 66, n.d [1984]

Viseltear, A.J. 'C.-E.A.Winslow and his Era and His Contribution to Medical Care', in Rosenberg, C.E. *Healing and History*, New York 1979

Viseltear, A.J. 'Compulsory Health Insurance and the Definition of Public Health', in Numbers, R.L. *Compulsory Health Insurance: the Continuing American Debate*, Westport, Conn. 1982

Walker, A. *Middle East and Far East, Australia in the War of 1939–1945*, Series 5, Medical, Canberra 1953

Walker, A. *The Island Campaigns: Australia in the War of 1939–1945*, Series 5, Medical, Canberra 1957

Walker, R. 'The Struggle Against Pulmonary Tuberculosis in Australia, 1788–1950', *Historical Studies*, xx, 1982–3

Warner, J.H. *The Therapeutic Perspective. Medical Practice, Knowledge, and Identity in America, 1820–1885*, Cambridge, Mass. 1986

Waters, W.J. 'Labor, Socialism and the Second World War', *Labour History*, 16, 1969

Watts, R. *The Foundations of the National Welfare State*, Sydney 1987

Webb, N. 'Women and the Medical School', in Young, J.A., Sefton, A.J. and Webb, N. *Centenary Book of the University of Sydney Faculty of Medicine*, Sydney 1984

Webster, C. 'Healthy or Hungry Thirties?', *History Workshop*, 13, 1982

Webster, C. *The Health Services Since the War: Vol.1: Problems of Health Care, the National Health Service Before 1957*, London 1987

Weller, P. ed., *Caucus Minutes 1901–1949*, iii, Melbourne 1975

Wheeler, L. 'War, Women and Welfare', in Kennedy, R. *Australian Welfare*, Melbourne 1989

Whiteside, N. 'Private Agencies for Public Purposes: Some New Perspectives on Policy Making in Health Insurance Between the Wars', *Journal of Social Policy*, xii, 1983

Whitington, D. *The House Will Divide*, Melbourne 1969

Whitwell, G. *The Treasury Line*, Sydney 1986

Whorton, J.C. '"Antibiotic Abandon": the Resurgence of Therapeutic Rationalism', in Parascandola, J. ed., *The History of Antibiotics: A Symposium*, Madison, Wis. 1980

Willis, E. *Medical Dominance: The Division of Labour in Australian Health Care*, Sydney 1983

Winter, J.M. and Teitelbaum, M. *The Fear of Population Decline*, New York 1985

Winter, J.M. *The Great War and the British People*, London 1986

Woodruff, P. *Two Million South Australians*, Kent Town, SA 1984

Wright, T. *A Real Social Insurance Plan*, Sydney (Communist Party of Australia) June 1937

# INDEX

Aboriginal people, 54, 75
abortion, 76, 99
access and equality (health services), 3–4, 61, 62, 64–5, 67, 69–70, 73–4, 76–7, 81, 82–3, 131, 143, 150–1,158–60, 163, 196, 197, 199, 202–3, 208, 277, 280, 285; *see also* class
acute care services, 207
administration and finance (hospitals), 57–86, 205–8
administration (public health), 31–56; Department of Health, 241; Page health scheme, 261
admissions policies (hospitals), *see* access and equality; means-tested services
*Age*, 230, 269
age pension, 91, 92, 98, 223, 260, 267; *see also* pensioners; pharmaceutical benefits scheme; Pensioners' Medical Service
Alfred Hospital, 19
alien doctors, 128, 237, 238
alkaloids, 212
allowances and benefits, 43, 45; *see also* cash benefits; friendly societies; insurance; pensions; social security
American Hospital Association, 266–7
anaesthesia, 19, 99
Anderson, G. C., 96
Anstey, Frank, 48
Anthony, H. L., 98, 99
antibiotics, 240, 259–60
anti-semitism, 238, 239
Archdall, Mervyn, 176; *see also Medical Journal of Australia*
*Argus*, 230
army, *see* Australian Army Medical Corps; military medical services
atropine, 212
Australasian Association of Physicians, 19
Australasian Medical Congress (1920), 38, 39, 41
*Australian and New Zealand Journal of Surgery*, 19
Australian Army Medical Corps, 116, 126
Australian Catholic Hospital Association, 198
Australian Coal and Shale Employees

Federation, 122; *see also* miners
Australian Council of Trade Unions (ACTU), 106, 108, 236
Australian Hookworm Campaign, 41, 46
Australian Hospitals Association, 208, 244
Australian Institute of Anatomy, 53
Australian Institute of Tropical Medicine, 41–2, 48, 149
Australian Labor Party (ALP), 97, 284–5; hospital benefits, 204; hospital reform, 197–9; national health insurance, 97, 98, 106; national health service, 234, 240–3, 246, 248; pharmaceutical benefits, 211, 213, 231; *see also* Chifley government; Curtin government; Labor governments; labour movement; trade unions; Whitlam government
Australian Medical Association (AMA), 279, 281, 283, 284, 285; *see also* British Medical Association
Australian Natives Association, 12–13
Australian Pharmaceutical Formulary, 215
Australian War Pharmacopoeia, 210, 213
Australian Workers Union (AWU), 68, 69, 71, 104, 107, 109–10

baby bonus, 22
bacteriology, 49, 50
Bank Employees Association, 230
bank nationalization, 230, 231, 236
Bankers Health Society, 244–5, 271, 272, 274
Bathurst industrial health schemes, 122
Bean, C. E. W., 37, 131
bed subsidies, 158–60, 196–9, 204, 205, 207, 276–8
Bell, Dr George, 93, 100, 173–4
Bell–Simmons report and scheme, 173–6, 183, 186–8, 192
benefits and allowances, 43; constitutional powers, 223; postwar planning, 149, 155–6; *see also* friendly societies; insurance; names of allowances, benefits and pensions; pensions; social security
Beveridge Report, 145
birthrate, 133, 134; *see also* population policy
Black, Hermann, 234–5